Gita for Work and Life

The *Bhagavad Gita* is a philosophical and spiritual poem about truth, duty, good actions and the purpose of life. This book collates the wisdom it offers and applies it to contemporary life and work offering lessons on how to foster excellence and fulfilment in today's competitive world.

The corporate world and the contemporary society focus on winning, performing and developing a competitive edge. *Gita for Work and Life* offers readers a deeper philosophical understanding of the interconnectedness of all beings, the importance of self-reflection and improvement, purpose, duty, morality, equanimity and peace. These guiding principles provided by Krishna to Arjuna in the *Bhagavad Gita* are meant to rekindle the dormant human spirit and inspire the reader to elevate their understanding of the mind and soul and how these relate to their work. The book explores themes such as depression management, realised action, knowing oneself, work and fulfilment, balance and discipline, material and spiritual knowledge and *raja yoga* among others.

A unique work, this will be a valuable resource for corporate leaders, middle and senior managers, and those interested in leadership, management and organisational studies. Leadership practitioners will also benefit from the accessible and practical lessons this book has to offer.

Rama Prosad Banerjee is a prolific academician, philanthropist, edupreneur and thought leader. He is a pioneer in establishing the study of ethics and values in management academia. Over the course of three and a half decades, he has gathered a wealth of experience as an international educationist, teaching at some of the most prestigious institutions in the world. His work focuses on using ancient Vedic texts to learn more about stress management, leadership and economics. He is the Chairman and Director of EIILM-Kolkata, one of India's leading business schools and Founder of EIILM-Kolkata Centre for Leadership and Ethics (EKCLE).

Gita for Work and Life

Rama Prosad Banerjee

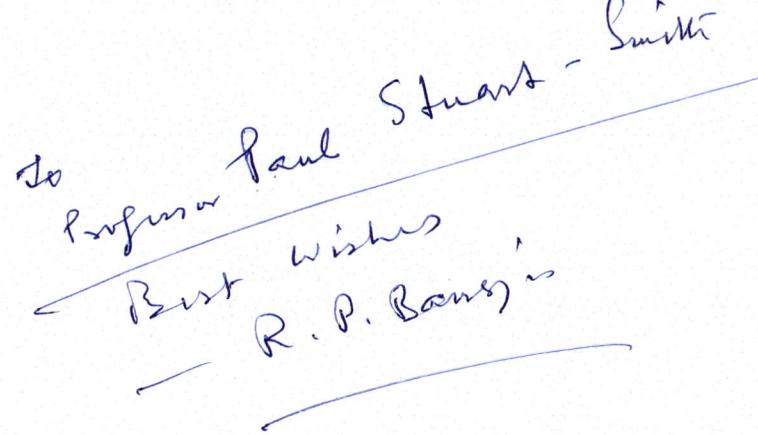

LONDON AND NEW YORK

Designed cover image: Getty Images
First published 2026
by Routledge
4 Park Square, Milton Park, Abingdon, Oxon OX14 4RN

and by Routledge
605 Third Avenue, New York, NY 10158

Routledge is an imprint of the Taylor & Francis Group, an informa business

© 2026 Rama Prosad Banerjee

The right of Rama Prosad Banerjee to be identified as author of this work has been asserted in accordance with sections 77 and 78 of the Copyright, Designs and Patents Act 1988.

All rights reserved. No part of this book may be reprinted or reproduced or utilised in any form or by any electronic, mechanical, or other means, now known or hereafter invented, including photocopying and recording, or in any information storage or retrieval system, without permission in writing from the publishers.

Trademark notice: Product or corporate names may be trademarks or registered trademarks, and are used only for identification and explanation without intent to infringe.

Disclaimer: The transliterations and translations of verses from *The Bhagavad Gita* and other sources in this book are the author's. They may deviate from standard conventions of transliteration and translation.

British Library Cataloguing-in-Publication Data
A catalogue record for this book is available from the British Library

Library of Congress Cataloging-in-Publication Data
A catalog record has been requested for this book

ISBN: 978-1-041-09104-2 (hbk)
ISBN: 978-1-041-09106-6 (pbk)
ISBN: 978-1-003-64851-2 (ebk)

DOI: 10.4324/9781003648512

Typeset in Sabon LT Pro
by HBK Digital

Dedicated to the cause of human actions and human urge to make and live a good life based on the spirit of *daivi guna* (divine attributes) culminating in harmony, poise, victory and prosperity

Contents

Preface ix
A Note on the Bhagavad Gita xxvii
Acknowledgements xxxiii
Introduction xxxv

1 Depression Management 1
2 The Awakened Spirit 15
3 Eternal Truth in Realized Action 33
4 The Atman 52
5 Work for Fulfilment and Liberation 72
6 Art of Knowledge-driven Work 87
7 Divine Wisdom for a Better Life 101
8 The Corporate Sadhu 122
9 Discovering Inner Reality: Look Within 140
10 Material and Spiritual Knowledge 162
11 The Absolute Revealed 179
12 Raaj Yoga – The King of all Yogas 200
13 God Revealed 218
14 Man Sees God 236

15 Consecration through Devotion	255
16 Divine Personality	275
17 Divine Attributes	295
18 Moksha: The Liberation	316
19 Achieve Fortune, Victory and Liberation	335

Afterword: Message of the Bhagavad Gita — 357
Bibliography — 359
Glossary — 360

Preface

The *Bhagavad Gita* is the song of God for human emergence. It is present in the form of a conversation between Arjuna, the great warrior-performer, and Lord Krishna. Krishna is the embodied presence of God on Earth in human form. The purpose of God's appearance on Earth in human abode is multiple. The generic reason for God's descent on Earth is usually mentioned as to protect the noble and good-hearted, and to bring an end to the influence and atrocities of unholy forces. The basic objective of righteousness is to get established in the world. The *Bhagavad Gita* has a profound context where the atrocities of unruly and unholy forces were finally crushed by the righteous spirit in the war of Kurukshetra. In the field of war in Kurukshetra, the forces of the king of vices and the righteous warriors faced each other. It was in this context that the war of the Mahabharata was on, and the *Bhagavad Gita* began to unfold. The material fact about the *Bhagavad Gita* is as follows:

In the *Bhagavad Gita,* the personalities who have spoken are:

a) Dhritarashtra: The blind king. During the war of the Mahabharata, the power of the kingdom was transferred to the prince Duryadhana, who was the real leader and the initiator of all mischief against the Pandavas. The crime committed by Duryadhana was supported and strengthened by the warriors of prominence. These criminal warriors had the art and the science of war. These criminal warriors were not only powerful due to their backgrounds but also engaged in direct criminal activities. Among them, Karna was the most prominent. He was competent in many kinds of warfare and was the closest support and strength behind the criminal king, Duryadhana.

In the context of the war of the Mahabharata, blind father king Dhritarashtra was not only blind in vision but also blind in his emotions for his son Duryadhana. He was always eager to see that his son Duryadhana won the war.

The *Bhagavad Gita* started with the first question asked by the blind King Dhritarashtra :

Dharmakshetrae Kurukshetrae samaveta yuyutsabah.
Mamakah Pandavah cha eva kim aukurbatah Sanjayah. (G.1-1)
The blind king Dhritarashtra had asked his personal assistant, Sanjay, referring the field of work as the place of righteousness in a geographical location Kurukshetra, what was going on between the forces of his Sons and the enemy force of Pandavas.

Dhritarashtra, the blind king, asked Sanjay, his close and reliable aide and chariot driver, what was happening on the holy battlefield of Kurukshetra where the Pandavas and their sons had assembled for war. Though not physically present at the war, Sanjay was able to narrate the events from the palace. However, Sanjay was an ardent devotee of Lord Krishna. He was gifted by God the power of distant vision and hearing. Sanjay had been blessed with the power and capacity of seeing any incident in clear perspective and hearing in detail from a distance. This was how Sanjay could narrate all to the blind king Dhritarashtra.

b) Sanjay has spoken from the beginning until the end of the deliberations in the *Bhagavad Gita*. Whatever had happened on the battlefield at the Kurukshetra, the blind king was eager to know. Apart from reporting to the blind king the scenario or whatabout of the war, Sanjay was sharing with the king all the material facts of importance and the scenario of conversations between Lord Krishna and Arjuna. Sanjay had a strong role in the entire *Bhagavad Gita* in terms of documenting records. Also, many verses have Sanjay in the major role as the reporter. This will be evident from the distribution of verses in the *Bhagavad Gita*. This is as follows.:

Total number of verses in the *Gita*:	700
Verses involving Dhritarashtra:	001
Verses of Sanjay:	041
Verses of Arjuna:	084
Verses by Lord Sri Krishna:	574

Sanjay ubacha, or 'Sanjay speaks', is evident in 41 verses of the *Bhagavad Gita*.

c) Arjuna has spoken evidently in 84 verses. Arjuna had fallen into the grip of the usual pattern of life. Some of the verses where Arjuna have spoken include the severe depression that Arjuna had his own solution and stands as a major forerunner in the act of establishing righteous ways of human living.

The first verse where Arjuna speaks is:
Senoyoh ubhayo madhyae ratham sthapaya mae iha Achyutah. (G.1-21)
Arjuna urged Lord Krishna to place his chariot between the two warring forces so that he could get a feel of the fighters on both sides of the war.

It was a proposed instruction to the person driving the war-chariot of Arjuna. He wanted to witness the arrangements of the army on both the sides of the war. So, in the context of the war of Mahabharata at Kurukshetra, it was an order placed by human on the incarnation of God on Earth. Highlights of such arrangements was mentioned by Sanjay to Dhritarashtra.

Drishta tu Pandava anikam budyam Duryadhanam tatha
Acharyam upa samgamya rajah bachana brabit. (G.1/2)
By seeing the relatives of each other standing across the war zones as enemies, Sanjay narrated that the Son of King Duryadhana had approached the great warrior Dronacharya about the war strategy of the Pandavas.

Sanjay narrated to the king that he could see by the side of the Pandavas a lot of warrior people, as by the side of Duryadhana. He highlighted the presence of the master Dronacharya on the side of Duryadhana also.
Sanjay provided a real-time visual commentary of the war to the blind King Dhritarashtra, narrating everything happening on the battlefield. The Lord gifted Sanjay with the power of distant video and audio to describe the war's proceedings. Arjuna's first utterance was an urge to physically understand the actual scenario of the war. But eventually, Arjuna got infected by the usual worldly emotions. He saw on the other side close relatives, teachers and the people with whom at one point in time or for a long duration he had emotional bonding. All these combined infused in the mind of Arjuna the spirit of the human senses of favouring the relations with concern. This input in mind had caused Arjuna a huge amount of mental setback. He became depressed. His body and mind had lost focus and started trembling; he could not even stand, and his weapons fell from his hand.
Depressed Arjuna had lost his power of body and mind. He said to Lord Krishna that waging war against the teacher, grandfather, and relatives is a social crime and causes great sin. Therefore, he was against doing the same. Also, imagining the consequences for societies and humanity, the kind of horror the war was likely to create amounted to causing sinful acts of profundity. With these and other similar arguments in him, Arjuna became unable to stand up and fight in the war. This is why, having totally lost his mental strength and power, Arjuna began with many marginal and petty arguments. However, as Lord Krishna started telling him the *Gita*, Arjuna gradually woke up and regained his senses and strength.

Kutah tva kashmalam idam vishamae samay upasthitam.
Anaryam Ausvargam Aukirtikaram Arjunah. (G.2/2)

Sri Bhagavan said, 'Arjuna, how has this infatuation overtaken you at this critical hour? It is shunned by noble souls; neither will it lead to heaven nor bring fame to you.

Overwhelmed by deep depression and dejection, Arjuna approached Lord Krishna, seeking to become his disciple. Krishna began by advising him, saying, 'Arjuna, why have you, a person chosen by the Lord himself to fight the war of righteousness against unholy and evil forces in human society, given such prominence to a smallness of emotion?' Lord Krishna had wondered how a great mind like that of Arjuna could be affected by the negative attitudes and approaches of life when Arjuna was the chosen force on the side of the divine intent. Thus, with the questioning by Lord Krishna, Arjuna could get back to the realm of thoughts and works that really have the standing of being on a cause of the Earth system and the future of mankind. The warrior class of which Arjuna is a major character in is not supposed to break away from the cause, even if it is dreadful and not tuned to the spirit of a good warrior.

Kleivyam masma gamah Partha na etad tvaei upapadyatae.
Kshudram hridayah dourbalam tyaktva uttishtha Parantapah.   (G.2/3)
Yield not to unmanliness, Arjuna, this does not become you. Shaking of this has faint-heartedness, stand up, Arjuna, you are a person with strength of mind.

Lord Krishna had urged Arjuna to undertake a major role in the act of the war of Kurukshetra. He was taken up and accepted as the major force on the side of the divine intent to wage war. Situational sequence shows that Arjuna had received the best training from the human teachers and the Gods embodied in different functional forms. Thus, he had the privilege to have receiving a special variety of the most powerful and winning weapon directly from Lord Shiva. Similarly, he had received weapons from Indra and other forms of the Gods. Arjuna was not only having a mandate or a promise, but he was destined to have the blessings of the Gods while in the act of the war. In the field of war or in the process of war, Arjuna was endowed with the privilege of having the mental force of having God on the path of performing the duty towards God on Earth.

Sanjay continues speaking:
Evam uktva Hrishikesham gudakesham parantapah.
Na yotshaeh iti Govidnam uktva tushnim babhubah ihah.   (G.2/9)
O King, having thus spoken to Sri Krishna, Arjuna again said to him, 'I will not fight and became silent.'

Sanjay started narrating the entire episode to the blind king in detail. The entire *Bhagavad Gita,* as the background scenario of the war of Kurukshetra, was not only being narrated by Sanjay with his own description, but also with the exact conveying of the facts, utterances, and the mood of the personalities involved. Thus, Sanjay was also a chosen person of God, narrating, reproducing and projecting the scenario through descriptions for the benefit of people on Earth. Sanjay had documented the war of the Mahabharata, in general and that of the words of Lord Krishna, in particular. This incident was crucial, not only for shaping history but also for establishing a just society and human rights on Earth. Upholding an ethical spirit and actions requires righteous and just individuals. Simultaneously, the drive for human transformation in the world must be maintained with the right perspective, facilitating the emergence of humans as divine beings.

Lord Krishna started advising Arjuna on the spirit of righteous principles. He was eager to see that Arjuna undertakes the destined role of the crusader of the principles of righteousness and the spirit of righteous life. The arguments put across by Arjuna were social in nature. Social and temporal arguments, which the lives lived at that point in time had an unusual sequence of things from the perspective of the elements of the society. Krishna's interventions in the matters of Arjuna in the context of the war are a suggestive voice for the world.

Aushochayan anvashocham tam prajna badam cha bhasasae.
Gatasun agatasun cha na anushochanti panditah. (G.2/11)
Arjuna, you grieve over those who should not be grieved for and yet speak like the wise men. Wise men do not sorrow over the dead or the living.

The matters of lament by Arjuna were arguably confined within the domain of material and Earthly spirit. It was thus a kind of sentiment suited to the ordinary minds without having any destined objective in life. Since Arjuna had a destined objective in life, he was expected to remain strong in mind.

Karpanya doshah aupahata svabhavah.
Prichhayami tvam dharma sam mudha chetah.
Yat shreyoh syat nischintam bruhi tat mae.
Shishyte aham shadhi mam tvam Prapannam. (G.2/7)
With me being very smitten by the vice of faint-heartedness and my mind puzzled with regard to duty, I beseech you, tell me, what should be my role, which is decidedly good? I am your disciple, pray instruct me, who has taken in you.

Lord Krishna suggested that Arjuna set aside all those points of usual social concern. Lord Krishna has suggested that the objective of life of a personality like Arjuna is to strive to attain a steady mind with the spirit of perfection and dedication, with the mind detached from the desires of the world in the sense that is the life's mandate destined by God in the perspective of God.

Sthita prajnasya ka bhasha samadhih tasya keshabha
Sthitadhih kim prabhashet kim aasitah brajeet kim. (G.2/54)
Arjuna said, 'Krishna, what are the characteristics of a God-realized soul, stable of mind and established in *samadhi* or perfect tranquillity of mind? How does the man of a stable mind speak? How does he sit? How does he walk?' Lord said, 'Arjuna, when one thoroughly casts all cravings of the mind and is satisfied in the self through the joy of the self, then he is called stable of mind.'

The Lord's initial advice to Arjuna infused a spirit of divinity within his inner core. Arjuna learned the concept of *Sthita Prajna* in the context of human actions in the world. This focused incident profoundly instilled the spirit of divinity in Arjuna's personality. His honest nature and ardent dedication inspired him to pursue spiritual attainment and fulfillment, leading to a deep concern for the divine spirit. At that point, Arjuna was genuinely curious to understand the true meaning and condition of being Sthita Prajna.

Prajahati yada kaman sarban Partho manogatan
Atmani eva aatmana tushtvah sthitaprajnagah tat uchyatae. (G.2/55)
The person who is indifferent to worldly gains and is always satisfied with the condition of life as a gift of God and doesn't have any desire, greed or negative emotions in mind is a person of wisdom.

Sthita Prajna is the condition of a personality which talks about remaining at the same or similar condition when confronted with the direct or the apparent opposites in life. This is a state of the mind and also the condition of consciousness of the person. Whenever the person is confronted with situations opposing in nature, either physical or virtual, the mind of this person remains unmoved. This situation depends on many factors. One of these factors is the urge of the vital force of her or his life that makes its own wishful demand on the life lived. The vital force of a personality makes the person attain the forces of life to build and run the activities of life in a manner that makes it so smooth and happening as that of the people with winning profiles in the context of the world. It is thus the ultimate condition of attainment of a life where the thoughts, works and habits of life converge to a single point of attainment and positions. The issue is that of the attitude and behaviour of the person from an external sense, and that of the character of the person in the long-term sense of the term.

Thus, Krishna holds the hand of Arjuna and takes him ahead of his time and context to his own destiny of winning the war of the Mahabharata and at the same time, re-establishing the truth and purpose of life in the context of the flow of life and that the matter is oriented to life in particular. Arjuna is not just a contextual warrior or a hero of an incident. Rather he is the human face of the forces of human society that is faced with odds and evils in the pathway of its own journey. This was in the process of making an initiative towards facing challenges in establishing a cause of Divine but got infected with the usual worldly sentiments.

Principles of Work and Life

Lord Krishna, throughout the *Bhagavad Gita,* guides the entire thought process towards conquering evil and establishing a harmonious human society. This poise makes social life conducive to actions centred on divine principles and policies, ultimately blessing people's thoughts and deeds. These principles are best explained in the following elaborations, drawing from the divine teachings Lord Krishna imparted to all of humanity through Arjuna, representing the emerging human society.

दशात्मक कर्म चरितम् पुर्ण प्रज्ञायाम निवेदितम्
[*Dasatmaka Karma Charitam Purna Prajnayam Nibeditam*]
Ten fundamental principles of the Actions in Life

1. सदा प्रसन्नम कर्मम् (*Sada Prasannam Karmam*):
   Work with love and a smile in real terms. The work that you are endowed with in your life is a blessing of the cosmic spirit. Have a pure and positive orientation to your life.
2. कार्यम् विश्व चेतन सन्निवेशितम् (*Karyam Visva Chetana Sannibeshitam*):
   Work of yours is continuously contributing to the emergence and rolling forward the spirit of the cosmic system. Your work is thereby an elemental support to the cosmic consciousness. You are serving the cosmic spirit.
3. निवेदितम फलम् कर्माणि सम्पादितम् (*Nibeditam Phalam Karmani Sampaditam*):
   Dedicate your work to the spirit of the entire cosmic system. Do your work in the best possible manner. Do not be a seeker of the result.
4. कर्मम् कर्मानन्देन कृतम् (*Karmam Karmanandena Kritam*):
   The joy of doing is drawn from the domain of the work itself. You will have the work done with the spirit of perfection.
5. कर्माणि परिवेशितम प्रतिरूप फलम् (*Karmani Paribeshitam Pratirupa Phalam*):

Like cause – like effect. Never indulge in an action with a known or understood evil element inbuilt. Do good and honest work – reap in goodness. Bad work returns evil.

6. **कर्म-प्रज्ञान् विश्व कल्यान सदा आहम्** (*Karma Prajnanam Visva Kalyana Aahritam*):
Work begets the wisdom for the growth, sustenance and wellbeing of the entire world. Good thoughts beget good actions. Cultivate good and honest thoughts always. Your work serves the universe.

7. **आहतम् निवेदित कर्मम दिव्य कृपायम** (*Aahritam Nivedita Karmam Divya Kripayam*):
Work has the divine grace infused in. Any challenge in the work can be met with your graceful work and habits in life.

8. **सदा हृदयम् धारणम शिव-सनातनम शुद्ध-निर्मल कर्मम आवेशितम्** (*Sada Hridayam Dharanam Shiva Sanatanam Shuddha-Nirmala Karmam Aabeshitam*):
While into the thoughts about action or action proper, be tuned to the spirit of the divine in mind and hearts.

9. **कर्मात्मक विशेष भक्ति-प्रज्ञा सञ्चारम** (*Karmatmakam Bishesha Bhakti Prajna Sancharam*):
Work in which you are absorbed contributes to your spiritual realisation in terms of divine wisdom, devotion and the blessed span of life.

10. **दिव्य कर्म सदानन्द मानस सम्पादितम स्व-मोक्षार्थम् जगत् हित कल्प सदा प्रसारम** (*Divyo Karma Sadananda Manasa Sampaditam Sva-Mokshartham Jagat Hitah Kalpa Sada Prasaram*):
Work dedicated to God offers the blissful context of life. This is the ultimate attainment through dedicated work – *nishkama karma*.

The character:

Lord Krishna has identified attributes of the right character for making a good life in the world. The character is comprised of good qualities. The classifications made by Lord Krishna are as follows:

1. *Sattwa guna*: Meaning the rightful qualities of a character.
2. *Rajah guna*: Meaning the vibrant and dynamic, energetic character.
3. *Tamah guna*: Meaning the character with attributes that make a person deluged in certain negative thoughts, emotions, words, and actions.

These three characters' attributes blend to form a personality. The dominant attribute then shapes the individual's life path. Sattwa guna encompasses qualities like tolerance, cooperation, honesty, integrity, truthfulness, delight in others' victories, being delightful to the world, emotional containment, the power of positive thought, the ability to offer good to the world, sacrifice, non-selfishness in attitude, behaviour, and character, and prioritizing others' well-being before one's own. Sattwa guna elaborates upon the good habits and good characters in life. It attempts to talk about the perennial attributes that would make a person like a divine in a human abode. A sattwa personality at the outset looks at the world with a positive view. A sattwa personality is always positive about others. She or he tries to identify the good elements in others first, before getting into any critical analysis of the other people in the world. A sattwa guna is honest in thoughts, honest in behaviour, honest in actions of life. A sattwa guna person is a person who is always helping others. An element of sacrifice is always present in the personality of sattwa guna. The sattwa guna person is always on the pathway of truthfulness and therefore even if the person finds a disaster or a problem faced in life, even then the person withstands the situation, faces the situation, takes up the situation as a challenge, but tries to stick to the attributes of truthfulness and the attributes of fairness. The sattwa guna person is always fair in all transactions in the situations of work and thoughts of the world. The sattwa guna person is always a person with hands extended to help others. Even if the help is not sought, the person will extend the hand of cooperation to the other person.

Rajah guna makes a person dynamic and energetic. 'Rajah' is derived from 'raja', meaning king; hence, rajah guna is kingly in habit. This kingly nature manifests in its power of action, work ethic, and the energy applied to tasks and worldly transactions. It represents the internal energy a person can draw upon to accomplish things in the world. The rajah guna person is not that careful about maintaining truthfulness, maintaining honesty, maintaining the skills of cooperation and is not really into the attribute of sacrifice. However, the rajah guna person offers dynamism, strength and the power of the body and mind together. It does not care for fairness in all situations. However, it cares for the strength and power of the world. A rajah guna person is a person good at putting in energy for assigned work in the world. A rajah guna person cultivates energy, strength and power. While cultivating the energy, strength and power towards making life dynamic, the rajah guna person may become a problem for the world. An example of a rajah guna person is there in the Mahabharata. Duryadhana's personality exemplified rajah guna: he was powerful and energetic, capable of taking on challenges with prompt, courageous, and enigmatic action. However, he never aligned himself with truth, honesty, or integrity, refusing to sacrifice his personal, selfish gains or calculations for attainment. Duryadhana, a king, derived his powers from his father, the blind king Dhritarashtra. At the beginning of the Mahabharata war, he compelled Dhritarashtra to transfer the state's authority and kingly power to him. He had certain ultimate wrong and devil desires in mind to kill the good forces of Pandavas and capture the entire nation to control the nation to enjoy the control and power over the entire nation and not to share any bit of that with other claimants who are the Pandavas. Therefore, he did not hesitate at all to create evil towards others. The rajah guna person like him is a person with lots of energy, dynamism and the strength and power of body and mind together to drive things through, but the direction of driving this through may be disastrous, as it was disastrous in the case of Duryadhana.

Tamah guna is characterized by delusion and indolence. A person dominated by tamah guna is often sleepy, disinclined to work, and unwilling to expend energy or do good for anyone. Even if they harbour ill will towards others, they lack the courage or power to act on those negative thoughts. Such individuals fabricate things in their minds and are consistently oriented towards negativity. The first thought that comes to a tamah guna person is always negative, and they cultivate this negativity throughout their life. This constant negative cultivation can lead to situations where they might be forced into rigorous or unpleasant interactions. The tamah guna person does not have the authority and power to do the rigour of doing many things together. A tamah guna person who contributes to the addictions, the selfish attractions, the negatives of our individual content, always considering things from the perspective of selfish gain, but is never energetic enough to do things to fulfill the wishes and promises of life. A tamah guna person is considered the darkness and is out of ignorance in life. A tamah guna person is considered full of ignorance, and that ignorance is about others in the world and the world always.

The ideal personality

Lord Sri Krishna has advised Arjuna to be an ideal in personality. The make of an ideal personality is neither sattwa alone nor *rajas* alone nor even *tamas*. The ideal personality is a mix of many of these or all of these. The profile of an ideal personality, as Lord Krishna has depicted in the *Bhagavad Gita* and through a series of advice and counselling to Arjuna, is a mix of the three characters. In this mix, the dominant, as he has advised Arjuna to become, is sattwa. Dominant sattwa is the attribute of sattwa that should be the leading and characteristic feature of the person. However, the person with truthfulness, honesty, cooperation, simplicity, goodness to others, integrity, fairness and always in a mood and mind of sacrifice, giving. This cannot withstand the person and lead the person towards success in a competitive life. In the competition of life and the race of our movements in the world, the person should be careful about being energetic, dynamic and with a powerful body, mind and also a synthesis through synchronization between the body and the mind.

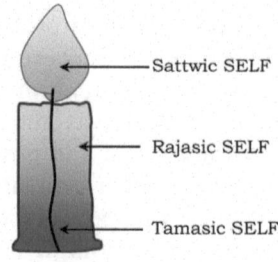

Source: Author

Individual Personality

The example of a candle is a befitting example to prove the point, as Lord Krishna has suggested. A candle is considered important because it can be used to create a flame of light. A flame of light and a flame of power is what the candle has at its best output in its life. The candle can give an ideal flame or the best possible flame in a particular mix of three things that it is comprised of. A candle is comprised of the wax around the wick with the objective of creating a flame, which is not visible unless lighted for. Now ignited candle is a full candle. It now has three distinct components visible. The first component is the wax around, the inside is the thread or wick, and the output is the flame. Now, what does the candle contribute to the world? If we consider the contribution of a candle to the world, we find that the candle gives light, or we may call it an illumination of life. Life's illumination is possible when a candle has the right mix of wax and wick. If we assume varying proportions of wick and wax, we can identify the ideal condition for the physical candle before it's lit. Our goal is to achieve the best flame from a candle. To meet this objective, let's consider three different scenarios.

Situation 1: The candle is made in such a way that the thread inside is very thin, silky, and the wax around is very thick.
Situation number 2: The candle is made in such a way that the thread inside is very thick, it's got a very wide diameter, and the wax around is very thinly coated wax.
Situation number 3: The candle is made as such that the wax around the thread inside has a proportion wherein wax is sufficient and the thread inside is sufficiently made with an understanding and with an estimation that it can glow properly.

Out of these three situations, our experience will tell that in situation number 1, the candle cannot give the flame because the wick or the thread inside is very thin. In situation number 2, it cannot really give the flame because the thread inside is too thick, and the wax around melts immediately, and the wax cannot hold the flame for even a reasonable time. Situation number 3, the candle burns and yields to the flame. This flame is the best possible flame from the composition of the candle. The assessment of these three examples and situations says that a balanced position between the wick inside and the wax around is what can contribute to the best flame and best illumination out of one candle. The metaphor used in this example of a candle is that sattwa is the final outcome, which is the flame given by the candle. The wax around is rajas, it burns and melts and therefore, it is the power and the energy which takes the candle forward to offer the illumination in life of the candle and thus the candle creates a situation wherein the candle has the illumination in the proper sense of the term and this illumination which the candle offers requires a balance between the wax and the thread inside. While the illumination is the sattwa component of the life of the candle, the wax around it is the rajas or the power and energy that holds the candle and makes it burn and provide and give illumination for a longer period of time. The thread inside is the tamas component of the life of a candle. The thread is larger in proportion and holds the candle from having a good illumination. A very thin presence of the thread inside cannot hold the candle forward, towards giving illumination. Therefore, a proper proportion between the wax and the thread inside is essential to make the candle burn to give proper illumination. Considering human life, a person has much to contribute to the world, and this requires the right mix of character attributes. Elements of rajas, such as the power of mind and body and the strength of vital energy, are essential to create dynamism in a person's thoughts, habits, and activities. This dynamism contributes to igniting the 'flame of life', enabling an individual to offer their best to the world. However, certain elements of tamas are also necessary for life. Some connection and association with the world—some endorsement of its things, thoughts, and emotions—are needed to sustain life. A certain amount of rest and sleep, as well as pauses in thought, are also vital parts of life. This life is an ideal life that contributes the best of a personality in the world, and finally, this is a combination of sattwa with a thin presence of tamas and rajas within the personality to make it dominant sattwa in the world of work and life. Rajas is the next in importance, and could be in the range of 20 to 25 per cent of the personality and tamas is the least important and present in a refined manner in the personality in the range of five to ten per cent, maximum. This personality type is the best on Earth. Wherever they work, whatever their function or profile, and whatever their objectives or aims in life, they are a winner and a successful person. They are also good and friendly to the world.

The recommended things in life to make this ideal personality are to address the negative emotions directly. Certain negative factors of life are classified by Lord Krishna in the *Bhagavad Gita* and in other scriptures as collectively *Shara Ripu*: Shara is six, Ripu is enemy, meaning six enemies to a good life. Among this certain are very disturbing and major. Lord Krishna has talked about the management of these major disturbing attributes of life. The disturbing attributes include, among others, anger, depression, jealousy, and envy. When it comes to anger, Lord Krishna has talked about the consequences of anger in life. Anger creates delusions in life, and the moment the thoughts and consciousness are covered by the wrong emotions and covered by the factors of anger, it acts as a kind of barrier to your memories in life. Memory has been mentioned as *Smriti*. Smriti loss is a loss of connection with the entire functional activities of the mind. When Smriti, or memory, is lost, a person's condition deteriorates into a loss of inner intellect. Losing intellect is akin to losing almost everything in life, as intellect drives the personality to make things happen and participate in the world's work.

Without memory and intellect, an individual ceases to be a thinking personality. Their creative functions are hampered or lost, and their ability for rational identification and understanding of worldly matters becomes disturbed or vanishes. The person becomes inert, save for a focused element of anger, which further causes them to lose their rational estimation and internal analytic power. This analytic power originates from the core of the brain and the integrated functioning of the brain, heart, and entire biological system. Now, when the functioning of mental analytics and the power of the vital are withdrawn or disconnected from that, the person loses the capacity to proceed normally in life. This person is now a skewed personality, skewed with the factors of anger at the centre of it. So much time, energy, mind and attention given to the factors of anger are because the person has an addiction to the desired condition, and the anger is because of deviation from the desired conditions of life. Anger is generated out of the desired conditions and a very strong or rigid specification about certain things in life. The desired conditions are driven by the elemental desire which is present within the personality. The desire drives the person towards developing anger or deviations from or getting away from the absolute structural position of the desire. Now, this is destructive to the person. When the person loses memory, when the person loses the intellect, when the person loses the power of thinking, when the person loses the power of creativity, when the person loses the power of rational analysis and when the person loses the power of understanding the situation with a calmness of the mind, the person leads the life towards a destructive end.

Lord Krishna is suggesting to Arjuna that he needs to become *Nirmalaha*. Nirmalaha means simple and pure. What is Nirmalaha? Nirmalaha is apart from any kind of desire in life, a desireless life. But Krishna has suggested that Arjuna do constant work, but not to have a hankering or a seeking or a desire for the results as life expects from it. A nirmalaha mind is a simple mind.

A simple mind can be pure, known as a *Vishuddha Manaha*. Vishuddha manaha, or the nirmalaha mind, is a state where the mind is free from the pull or push of momentary worldly desires and well-being. The Vedas clearly describe this while advising Nachiketa on eternal truth. The Lord of *dharma* told him that there are two categories of actions one can undertake in life.

One category of action is *Shreya* and the other category of action is *Preya*. Shreya is a category of life into action which is electable. Electable in the sense that you select and elect for your life certain attributes which would make life a sustainable one and contribute to the human system and the global system together. This Shreya is also the elevating parameter and factor for your life from the present condition of whatever that you are contained in to a desired condition which is truthful, which is oriented to an ideal personality as Lord Krishna has mentioned as a dominant sattwa guni or a person with divine attributes in life. On the other hand, Preya is something that is desirable, and Preya is something which is temporary; it gives temporary happiness, temporary joy in life, but that could prove in a period of time destructive to life. Anger is one of the elements of Preya. The person who is dissolved in the functions of anger actually becomes blind to the world. The person does not see the rationales of other elements and other factors in life besides the element of anger.

The element of anger is not only destructive but also suicidal for the person and those who are around him/her. Lord Krishna advises Arjuna not to harbour anger, not even towards his enemies. Instead, he urges Arjuna to wage war and perform his duty for the world, fulfilling his objective to contribute his nurtured illumination for the world's betterment. By doing so, Arjuna will find his life elevated, leading him toward victory.

The personality that Lord Krishna finally recommends is a personality of *Samatwaha*, equal in all situations. The samatwaha personality is one who is equal in the conditions of happiness, conditions of sorrow if any in life, conditions of problems, conditions of prospects in life. He has mentioned that *samaha lustwasmo kanchanaha*, meaning the positives of life and negatives of life, are applauded by millions or thousands, and also criticism by many is taken equally, and the person remains indifferent to that. This has been coined by Patanjali in clear terms with four different emotions for life. These four different emotions are *Maitreyi, Karuna, Mudita* and *Upeksha*. Maitreyi is friendly to everybody, even those who are thinking evil or trying to do evil to you. It suggests that you be friendly to all, but you are required to be determined in your objective to become a winning personality in the world. Do not be a party to any conflicting things; however, be dedicated to the cause of your life. If you are dedicated to the cause of your life, you have accepted the elements of winning for your life. Therefore, Maitreyi plays a very important role in the factors of victory in life. Friendliness to everybody should be cultivated by the person who is the leader of a society, leader of an organization, leader of certain functions, leader of certain activities and who believes in the individual leadership of herself or himself firmly. The person should have friendliness to herself or himself as well. This means the person should not belittle his or her own personality to sacrifice in any way. However, the person would sacrifice things of possession, things of endowment with others, to make the world better, to help others in the world.

Karuna is the next element, which is known as compassion. It requires that you be compassionate to everybody in the world. More for those who require compassion to be offered from yourself, and that compassion that you are required to offer is for everybody in the world, and it includes those who cannot make and drive life forward in the right sense of the term. So you be compassionate to those who are defeated in life, compassionate to those who have lost things in life, compassionate to those who deserve handholding, compassionate to those who are weaker in proportion to others in the life, compassionate to those you are required to become, who are fighting to establish their own self in the world for a good life and good survival.

Mudita is taking delight in others' success. You take delight in the success of others, that is known as Mudita. Success of others means when you have seen that in the rest of life, in the competition of life, somebody has not been able to succeed and the other person who has been able to succeed. If you are unable to succeed and the other person has succeeded, then also should be happy and should be positive to the person. But then you try to be successful in the next round of life, in the next race of life towards other ways in life. Success does not come only in a linear pattern. Success is a spherical thing. It may come from any direction of the sphere. The global system is spherical. Lord Krishna is mentioning that you maintain those attributes of goodness and the attributes of divinity in life and you will find you have succeeded in winning the race of life. Your race of life is not a momentary thing, it's a long-drawn thing. So look at the canvas of life from that long-term perspective. If someone looks at the canvas of life from a long-term perspective, the person is definitely going to be a person winning and a winner in the life. A person who is a winner in life is someone who can handhold others to become winners in their own ways.

There are occasions when you need to cultivate other attributes also. Upeksha is such that, Upeksha is being indifferent to certain situations. Now when do you become indifferent? You become indifferent to situations where you are personally involved. So Lord Krishna has suggested Arjuna that you need to have a *nirupeksha* condition, meaning neutral condition in life, with respect to the inflicts and responses from around in the world. Who says whatever to you and for you, do not pay heed to that, that much way. You need to pay heed to those parameters which are normal and which are recommended for a good life. But don't get into those parameters which are further or apart from those normal conditions of life. And therefore, the normal conditions of life deserve and require that

- Maitreyi,
- Karuna,
- Mudita and
- Upeksha

are cultivated in life in the right sense of the term. Anger is thus maintained and managed in life if life maintains these four emotions properly. Lord Krishna has suggested Arjuna to become

Samaha, Dukha, Sukha, Swastwaha,

when facing unhappiness or sorrow, one should not be swayed. Darkness is temporary, like night, and even in its most rigid condition, light is just ahead. One can overcome and escape darkness by cultivating mental strength to find illumination and maintain a balanced personality. Such a balanced personality conquers anger, preventing it from derailing life, clouding intellect, and diminishing one's standing as a good, balanced individual.

Depression, particularly affecting youth, is another disturbing element in our highly competitive world of winners and losers. Most people are not consistent winners; a winner may be momentary or short-lived. A mind solely desiring constant victory gets disheartened by fluctuating situations. Depression arises when individuals are consumed by the normal emotions of winning and losing, and by mental attachments to the world.

This is what afflicted Arjuna. Lord Krishna initially remarked on Arjuna's smallness of mind. When Arjuna's chariot was positioned between the Pandava and Kaurava armies, he suddenly saw his grandfather, teacher, guru, and other revered elders on the opposing side. He realized victory would necessitate their defeat or death, and he feared incurring sin. This situation plunged Arjuna into deep depression; he became unable to stand, hold his weapons, or even speak, trembling and sweating on the chariot floor. His only focus was Lord Krishna's presence, and he lost all desire to fight. This extreme depression incapacitated Arjuna, the formidable and highly regarded warrior and devotee, stripping him of his power and ability to perform even basic tasks, let alone creative ones.

Lord Krishna addressed Arjuna's temporary emotions by explaining the doctrine of *karma* good actions yield rewards, and bad actions bring consequences. He argued that the Kauravas, though relations, were siding with crime and were thus criminals themselves. Anyone supporting crime, visibly or actively, is complicit. Therefore, Krishna asserted that these individuals were already spiritually 'dead' due to their criminal and unfair actions, forfeiting their right to ultimate victory. He urged Arjuna to be honest, fair, and uphold his ideal personality, fulfilling his righteous duty as a warrior to establish truth and fairness by removing evil forces.

Lord Krishna's approach to depression management has two components: conceptual and functional/practical. Conceptually, he advised Arjuna to recognize that he is not merely his physical body. He prompted Arjuna to ask, 'Who am I?' and to know his true self (*atmano viddhi*). Krishna explained that one is not merely the mind, body, intellect, or visible personality, but a part of the eternal, supreme being—an embodiment of the divine. As the Vedas state, '*tat tvam asi*', meaning one possesses the *atman* in the core of their heart. This atman is the supreme, subtle, and invisible personality, whose realization brings true self-identification.

Thus, Krishna taught Arjuna to transcend material attachments and selfish delusions, to be truthful, honest, caring, and compassionate, yet remain focused on duty. He emphasized Arjuna's duty as a warrior to fight for righteousness, even if it meant defeating or killing evildoers, for the long-term survival and sustainability of the world. Lord Krishna urged Arjuna to rise above his smallness, pettiness, and meanness, and fulfill his responsibility righteously to achieve victory. Be truthful and know for certain that Lord is within yourself and the fact that Lord is within yourself, realize that this is the ultimate truth of your being and the moment you understand this ultimate truth of being, in whatever function a personality is into, in whatever kind of work, variety of work the personality is into, whatever kind of situation you are confronted with and you can be a winner and you can have a victory in life provided you maintain those righteous principles in life, the sattwa guna in life and the kind of combination of ideal personality that Lord

Krishna has suggested to make a personality of that kind and to be a personality of that kind. The moment you become a personality of that kind, you become a winner in life, and Lord Krishna suggests you become a winner but in a righteous manner. The ends and means are very important. It is not only important to reach the end but it is also important to maintain the means to reach the end. You maintain the honest, pure and righteous means to win the ends which are destined for you to win and Lord Krishna suggests that this is the durable and this is the long-term sustainable way of becoming victorious in life, living a good life and attaining the freedom from all the restrictions of bad emotions and negatives and ignorance in life. This is a delightful and this is an illumined life and obviously this life is going to lead to happiness forever.

Lord Krishna described the conceptual component of depression to Arjuna as being rooted in the constraints of worldly conditions and the understanding of worldly relationships. He advised Arjuna to be indifferent to external circumstances and to recognize God in the form of atman residing within himself. The moment one realizes this supreme truth within, it gets unleashed through thoughts, which are then translated into actions.

For that, he has mentioned *dhyana yoga*. Dhyana yoga is a practice wherein a person does a meditative practice day in and day out. This person is known as a yogi, though in normal work and life. The yogi does not have to spend a long period of life, but needs to do a meditative practice.

In the meditative practice, Lord Krishna has suggested doing pranayama. The pranayama is a process of breath and mind control through a specific position. In the context of the modern way of living, the Pranayama can be performed in the following manner:

1) Sitting on a chair with the feet parallel to each other placed on the floor and when the person is in the realm of this process, she/he sits erect without leaning in back and the entire backbone is straight now.
2) Now the yogi would begin alternate nostril breathing, and in this process of alternate nostrils breathing. While doing this, the yogi shall make an emotional initiative towards drawing all good elements that are prevalent in the atmosphere within herself/himself.
3) Lord Krishna suggested to Arjuna a unique procedure: while sitting erect with feet parallel and eyes closed, inhale air through one nostril, visualizing and believing that one is drawing in the goodness that pervades the entire cosmic system. This is for those who choose to see the universe as full of goodness, rather than as comprised solely of negative or wrong elements, as others might perceive it.
4) However, if someone thinks that the universe and the cosmic system are full of dirt and negatives and ignorance prevails, the person is now caught by the ignorance of the situation and that ignorance is something which is going to blur and hide the objectives of life and make life constrained by the conditions around.

5) Now, if the negative person has to come out of that she/he has to think of the positives which are prevailing upon. So, when the yogi is drawing in the air inside in the position of that, meditative position, she/he is thinking that only drawing the goodness and goodness of the divine which is around. The air, the water, light which are there, are endowments of the Divine. The moment the yogi finds the divine endowments are around in a form and inhaling the divine endowment and divine presence throughout.

Atmano Viddhi, meaning 'know yourself'. The moment you identify your personality as being drawn from and merged with the divine, you become a perennial winner in the world. Instead of causing problems, you'll be able to handle situations where others face defeat or ignorance, uplifting everyone towards goodness, illumined fairness, and righteous conditions. Therefore, righteousness isn't just established in one individual's life, but also within the society and the world at large. This transforms civilization into a new state where humankind is elevated to an elemental divine humanity.

A Note on the *Bhagavad Gita*

'Tat Tvam Ausi' or 'You in Me'

The *Bhagavad Gita* is the song of God for human salvation. It was sung in the form of utterances by Lord Sri Krishna to Arjuna in the context of the Mahabharata war, held at Kurukshetra. The purpose of the *Bhagavad Gita* was to elevate Arjuna from a condition of a depressed mind to an emergence of thoughts, towards doing things which are rightful and which were destined for him to do for the world.

The depression which Arjuna was deluged in was because of certain perceptions based on worldly relations and thoughts. Lord Sri Krishna suggested that Arjuna not be influenced by those thoughts in a way that would distract him from his normal duties, actions, and the rightful pathways for achieving success in life. Therefore, it is relevant to every human person, everywhere on Earth, irrespective of any creed, colour, religion, national identity and any social or emotional categories. The *Bhagavad Gita* is a source of universality. It talks about the remedies to human problems and evils, and at the same time, offers the rightful pathways, the path which is actually for not only winning the wars of life, but also making life superior and great in the context of things presently happening and having happened in the world. The *Bhagavad Gita* addresses human emotions and offers remedies for overcoming the evils or impositions inflicted by wrongdoers on the mind and soul, enabling individuals to rise and act in their own best interest.

The *Bhagavad Gita*, therefore, applies to the lives of human beings towards living life in any particular manner and at the same time, for anyone involved or engaged in any different kinds of actions and interactions in the world. It is true to the spirit of children, early youth, youth, middle-aged individuals, and people in upper age limits, making it beneficial for any category of person and any gender identity. The *Bhagavad Gita* offers a life which is based on the spirit of goodness. The spirit of goodness is based on certain attributes, which are usually known as daivi guna or divine attributes. Divine attributes are something which elevate a person from a normal, ordinary being to a person who possesses godly elements but lives a life of a mortal person. Therefore, *Gita* is a principle-centric source of knowledge and thoughts for action, that pivots around the divine principles or divine attributes towards making those thoughts a transformative one on a continuous basis. The *Gita* has elaborated things with the aim of complete realization of the supreme spirit, called God-realization. In this particular context, Arjuna had attained God-realization in two ways. One is Arjuna's attaining the spirit of God through a gradual learning process, and the other is attaining things based on the contextual items and elements in life. Therefore, the *Bhagavad Gita* not only teaches how to live a good life but also teaches how to make a life really transform into a life of divinity with a realization of the Supreme, the God within. Lord Krishna takes Arjuna through the process of learning. At the outset, he says that this life is not just an end in itself. The end of the physical body is not the end of life, and that's contained in the *shankha yoga*. Shankha yoga discusses the ultimate, eternal identity of a person who nonetheless lives an empirical life. This empirical life offers options and possibilities: one can choose to live purely empirically, or simultaneously embrace the eternal and divine.

Lord Krishna had offered this knowledge of the ultimate identity, and it is such that the supreme soul is residing within the human soul in the human heart, and it is *ajaha, nitya, sashwataha, puranaha, nahanyate, hanyomane, sharire*. This spirit is omnipotent, omnipresent, omniscient, and cannot be reduced or destroyed in any way. Lord Krishna has mentioned that the divine Supreme resides in the life of any person, within the cave of the heart in the form of an invisible, minutest small element, atman and at the same time, having identities of multiplications through residing within different lives. Lord Krishna says that this atman is eternal and cannot be destroyed in any way through any means. Anybody who understands and realizes the spirit of this Supreme attains the realization and with this realization the person is now in a position to proceed towards the superior identity and thereby understands that the entire cosmic system is one and the individual is just a part of the cosmic system and is the same in spirit and nature.

The eternal identity of the person is such that all good qualities of the divine entity are present in everyone. Therefore, it is the volition of the person through which the person may or may not maintain goodness throughout life. So, it is the wish and the thought that determines the course of work for the person, which is delivered and done by people. The quality of work would attract the quality of results. So, it is the work which creates the doctrine of life. If you do good work, you'll reap its rewards at the right time. Conversely, if you do bad work, you'll also face its consequences at the appropriate moment. Therefore, your work determines the course of your life's actions. And therefore, *Gita* suggests that when you do the work, personal attractions, selfish gains are always there in the primary focus and motive of the person doing the work. Krishna suggests that Arjuna do nishkama karma. Nishkama karma is something where you don't have any desire. So, it is known as desireless work, where you devote your mind and energy fully to the work, and therefore, the work will be more perfect than in other situations. With this perfection, the work now delivers the best out of the situation and is possible for any individual at any time. Nishkama karma contributes optimally to personal life, society, nations, and the global system. This is precisely why Lord Krishna advised Arjuna to embrace this path—the eternal living, the eternal way—and to act in a manner that fosters personal excellence and perfection. The perfection thus takes the person forward to do better work in the next round. So, nishkama karma is dedicated work which is always good for the collective system, society, organizations, and ultimately talks about the goodness of the person and society, ultimately contributing to a good civilization. Lord Krishna suggests that the person, in order to become a person of action in the category of nishkama karma, the person has to have the wisdom, and the wisdom is a God realization, that one can attain through different processes of meditation for which the *jnana vijnana yoga,* dhyana yoga, raja yoga, *sanyasa yoga* and all the processes are there. All the processes through which the person has to pass will create a mind which is strong enough to think of God and do things from the perspective and in a way that the noble expectations are fulfilled and are taken care of. As a person gradually develops realization, they'll understand that the world isn't just for extracting things and benefits, but also for contributing to it. At this point, they'll start to consider: 'What can I give back to the world, having received so much from it?' The example of a candle is given, like, there are three different varieties of gunas or attributes, sattwa, rajas, and tamas, and the sattwa guna is the essential contribution that you can make to the world. It is the person's ability to contribute to the growth and maintenance of human civilization, and therefore to do this, one needs to have a candle giving the flame, the light, to make this happen. In order to make this happen, what one has to do is to have the candle in the right sense of the term, and to have a proportion which is the right proportion among the thread inside, the wax around, and the kind of flame that an individual expects out of it. So this is a learning process, and in this process, you attain the goal through meditation. Lord Krishna had suggested that Arjuna have this meditation in the right sense of the term. This meditation involves invoking God externally, inviting God into your presence. Gradually, you then invite God within yourself, a process of identifying God internally through that initial external invocation. So, God within and God without now meet each other in the context of the aspiring person. The person is now elevated and has got a combination of attributes, the major of which is the sattwa guna, the rightful characteristics and perspective, the person is truthful, and is eager to maintain cooperation, to do the sacrifice. The person is in any different fields, all these are there for the elevation of the supreme realization in the context of the Earth system. The person serves as a favorable element and agent for transforming the Earth system toward humanity's next desired goal. Lord Krishna classifies these as daivi guna, or divine attributes. These divine attributes, when present in the workplace, make it happier, stronger, and more united. The people united, people on one cause, people in a unilinear path, will make the system work further, better and vibrantly. Victory requires a consistent and devoted orientation to the core principle of the work. This is possible through the support of any means from any end in empirical terms. However, perennial victory in life and works demands a transformation in the personality. Sattwa or truth-oriented person usually garners the flavour and strength of illumination which not only helps the person to transform herself or himself but contribute to the process of transformation of the world in the right sense of the term. The flame of sattwa offers a goodness and penetrating position in the society and organizations. However, the dynamism of rajas supporting the flame of sattwa creates a unique mix of personality which is ethical, moral on one hand, and strongly dynamic and teleological on the other. The *Bhagavad Gita* offers a suggestion of a personality in a corporate leader with a mix of strengths of rajas and the illumination of sattwa. This is poised to bring in victory, sustainability and universality in all respects in the context of human works and life. So what one needs to do, he/she needs to have a focused dealing, focused transactions and focused interactions with people on Earth and if someone can do this, the person adds value to the global system and in this way, the human being can rise to the level of victory and can go beyond the level of victory and the person will have power of strength of mind, power of strength of the vitals, power of strength of the energy which the person has cultivated and garnered within.

विजय विधान (Victory Visualised)

[*Vijay Vidhan*]

1ˢᵗ Understanding:	You are alone, one and single (अहम् एकम्) [ahom ekam].
2ⁿᵈ Understanding:	You and God – The Supreme are connected directly (तत् त्वम् असि) [*Tat tvam ausi*].
3ʳᵈ Understanding:	God is present within the cave of your heart as 'atman' or self (हृत् कन्दरम् अधिष्ठितम्) [*hrit kandaram adhishthitam*].
4ᵗʰ Understanding:	Atman is the form of Paramatma or supreme self (आत्मात् परमात्मानुम्) [*atmat paramatmanum*].
5ᵗʰ Understanding:	Through spiritual practice one can have god realization (तत् साधन सिद्धम्) [*tat sadhana siddham*].
6ᵗʰ Understanding:	Path of Wisdom, Path of Work, Path of Devotion and Path of Consecration are different ways of god realization (नाना पथ योगम्) [*nana patha yogam*].
7ᵗʰ Understanding:	Nishkama karma or selfless work or work without any desire leads to the realization of god (निष्काम कर्मत् ब्रह्म प्राप्तम्) [*nishkama karmat brahma praptam*].
8ᵗʰ Understanding:	Selfless love for and total Consecration to god is the ultimate call by Lord Krishna to the world of humans through Arjuna (प्रेमभक्ति भगवत् योगम्) [*prema bhakti bhagavat yogam*].

The Bhagavad Gita is not only the source of elementary knowledge but the eternal source to have God-realization in life and to make work of life winning with poise and peace and live a life of godly harmony, freedom, strength, victory, equality, and peace in the world.

Acknowledgements

This work, *Gita for Work and Life*, draws deeply from the wisdom, guidance, and exhortations of Lord Krishna as expressed in the *Bhagavad Gita*, in the form it has been made available to human society. The intent behind this endeavour has been to explore the practical applications of the Gita's teachings in the realms of work and life, particularly within the context of post-modern human society. It is a humble attempt to contribute toward building a more evolved and harmonious society by fostering Godly individuals through actions rooted in divine qualities, and by nurturing human character in alignment with such ideals.

The author expresses profound gratitude to the collective knowledge of human civilization, and in particular, to the analytical interpretations of the *Bhagavad Gita* undertaken by scholars and seekers over time.

This work would not have reached completion without the steadfast support of several individuals. I am especially grateful to Mr. Shanti Gopal Hazra for his tireless assistance, Mrs. Nilima Rani Hazra and Prof. Manjistha De for their valuable contributions, and my wife, Mrs. Sipra Banerjee, for her unwavering encouragement.

My heartfelt thanks go to my son, Dr. Debajyoti Banerjee; my daughter-in-law, Dr. Dimple Banerjee; and my grandson, Master Divyodeep Banerjee, for the emotional support they extended throughout this journey.

I am deeply indebted to the thousands of students with whom I have had the privilege of interacting over the years, whether in classrooms, seminars, or informal discussions. Their thoughts, reflections, and queries have enriched and shaped this work in meaningful ways.

I also convey my sincere appreciation to Ms. Shoma Choudhury of Routledge, Taylor & Francis Group, India, and her dedicated team for their meticulous involvement in the publication process and for remaining in constant coordination with me and my collaborators.

I extend heartfelt thanks to all current and future readers. Your engagement with this work is both valued and deeply encouraging.

With reverence, I offer my salutations to the wisemen of the world at large, and especially to the Vedic sages of India, whose spiritual legacy continues to inspire.

Finally, my gratitude extends to all who are already associated with this endeavour, as well as those who will connect with it in the future. I hope that, through their journey of work and life, readers may find meaning in and adopt at least a part of the insights offered in this work.

Thanks,
Prof. (Dr.) Rama Prosad Banerjee
New York, USA, July 10, 2025

Introduction

Song of God on Earth, urging the human emergence through noble values to foster peace, poise and victory in Life on Earth

Forward to Creation

Since the creation of the universe, the spell of emotions expressed by individuals in human society has been somewhat non-fulfilling. The entire creation has been shaped by the spirit of the microcosm, and most of the time tends to overlook the dimensions of the whole. The individual makes the synchronised rhythm that penetrates through the boundary of consciousness. Human sense was destined to take into account the perennial essence of the gross cosmic creation with priority. Left to their own devices, an individual calls upon their psyche to intensely focus on its essence. This process delves into the depths of understanding, giving priority and dominance to the wealth of human potential. Therefore, the individual must address the factors of their personal mind and become engrossed in the psyche, which ultimately marks the progress of this unfoldment. The urge of God thus gets overshadowed by the urge of the individual in a way that the dominance of the concern for self comes as the highlight of life. The significance of collective concern thus gets a second seat to the selfish concern of his life.

Human priority for the small and petty concerns of life has made individuals forget about the concerns of the self and gradually position the same to the perspective of human society in its bid to discover the factors of growth and poise. Society is thus fragmented to the extent of its microcosm and minuscule, and pushes it to the realms of the unit that appears and works as particles in the movement or things to suit the factors of growth and poise.

The smallness, meanness, and pettiness in human consciousness enhance the scope for the broad and vast to connect with the particles of life and make it grow in a fashion and pattern that God wants to happen. The concern thus comes down to the condition of mind and the position of the human spirit. Thus, God has to appear in empirical identity to contain the spirit of human consciousness in the design of things.

Aatma vai idam ekam augrae aasit
Tat byakuratah bahushyam tat etat. (Composed by the Author)
The creation began with the Supermen having taken up the form of atman and maintaining non-duality, infinite existence. He wished to become many in many forms in a randomness and thus the multitude of creation occurred.

The revelation of God, the Supreme, in the beginning was such that he had taken up the form and position of the Supreme in the living context. He took up the cudgels for the creation and thought to be present in the human context. At the outset, on the point of creation God had a wish within to take up a very nice form, the human, which was in a flow of the creation and maintain the existence as a human in order to experience the eventualities of the life of a human being.

While making the creation, God had designed a context of independence and autonomy for human being to take a call on the flow of life and experience the resultant effect through a relationship of the causal effect as mentioned in the 'doctrine of karma (karma yoga)' by Lord Sri Krishna. Therefore, God's interference into the dynamism of life is not present, however, the destiny of a person as of now, as it has happened before, and it is expected to happen in the future, is created by the person through her/his thoughts and actions in life.

Om visva devah aapyaantu tat Brahma Sanatanam.
(Composed by the Author)
Oh, the Lord, Supreme, I pray unto you to get revealed as the Lord of the Universe and eternity in a form which would be understood by those having your grace.

The human urge has now reached the realm where the factors of life have created an eternal call to the Divine to make happen the factors in a way that reaches the conscious spirits of the divine. In this world of the human being, the scope of things thus penetrates down to the innermost of the individual consciousness. When the urge reaches the ocean of the divine spirit, it creates a passage into the pathways of the stream of life, thus allowing the call to reach the Supreme. Without this urge and call, the Divine remains aloof from the world's context. The human spirit thus takes the strength of the divine spirit through the pathways of the human journey. God has made the pathways of human journey with the options of multiple possibilities. It is thus the possibility that the objective of God in this creation gets the divine onset and gets with the transactional principle as policy by God on Earth for the created.

When the divine spirit finds a cause in the creation, the urge to make the cause satisfied may demand a direct intervention of God in the affairs of the creation. Human society thus makes the right inroads into the factors of the creation, where the departures from the divine intent need to be addressed properly. Whenever an individual soul grasps the wide dimensions of the divine cause, it smooths their journey and allows them to sink into that cause. At times, this cause might evoke concern for human lives and society, but at other points, it proves to be, and remains, independent and perhaps even indifferent.

The factors of human consciousness in the way of life, thus, may get their fulfilment with the endowment from the Divine in an optimum condition that again meets the urges of human consciousness and that of the Divine. God on Earth in the form of Lord Krishna makes the announcement that the purpose of God on Earth has its fulfilling dimension through the meeting of the cause. As Lord Krishna declares,

> *Paritranayao sadhunam binashayah cha dushkritam*
> *Dharma samsthapanarthaio cha sambhabami yugae* (G. 4/8)
> For the protection of the virtuous and for the act of dominating or removing the ill-doers or ill-forces from the world, for establishing the righteousness in the world, on a firm footing, I manifest myself from age to age.

The primary cause is the protection of the good souls on Earth from the perils and onslaughts of the worldly demonic elements; the Divine prefers to be present in the human abode on Earth. The primary purpose of this is to protect those affected by evil spells, sometimes achieved through the annihilation of evil forces via divine intervention. Thus, the divine's initial objective and concern are fulfilled in this manner. Human urge may or may not be present here in this case as a direct causative factor towards the divine presence and the participation as a crusade in the way of lives lived.

In another scenario, God has different perspectives of being present on Earth as decided by himself. The humans living across personal earthly emotions want to pull every good effect of this creation to selfish fulfilment. Thus, human existence gets constrained by the notions of individual life and forgets the dimensions larger than the selfish domain. Priority of ego-satisfaction and causative factors towards that becomes the dominant trend, and thus, the human potential of becoming broader in perspective and focus on all other aspects of life gets denied. This has attained such a high, in fact, an infinite proportion that God is required to pull up the human consciousness to the level and identity of these godly values and attributes in life. This would elevate lives beyond their usual boundaries and dimensions. It creates a state where life's factors are immersed in thoughts of God, allowing noble attributes to permeate the very core of a person's consciousness. This, in turn, would compel divine consciousness to focus on creation, fostering its inherent goodness. Individual life thus would remember the wider cause of reaching out to the individual with another identity. It is the urge that reminds us of the equality and unity inbuilt in the spirit, quality and unity not only for a short phase of human life but also in the eternal sense of the term as a matter of continuity of conscious living. God appears now as an intimately known person. He takes the role of a true friend in the flow of lives. In some cases, he takes up the role of a child, a mother or a father in the context of the world. Thus, the barriers of a fragmented sense of separation get disclosed in the spirit of God, and the basic urge of transcendence comes forward as the fact of life on Earth.

Divine Purpose

The purpose of God's descent on Earth is also to be understood in an intrinsic way. Devotion stands as the instrument behind this as well. *Bhagavatam* narrates the course of the God in a way that is quite different. The sage Narada's experience in life is worth mentioning as it supports and positions a wider perspective of divine emergence. Sage Narada explains the context in a way where devotion of the spiritual aspirant makes the way to have God-realization in the right sense of the term.

> *Dhyatah charanah ambujam*
> *Bhava nirjitah suryah chetasa*
> *Oukokantoa aushruh kalak aukshah*
> *Hridi aasin mae sada Harih*   (Bhagavatam 1/6/16)
>
> I concreate upon your lotus feet in a devoted mind with full of my consciousness and heart poured in. I make this prayer to you to relieve your creation from the assaults and dominance of the unruly demonic forces.

Satchit Ananda charanah kamalah Chintan dhyanam nimajjitam. Narada had the vision of the Lord in the depth of his meditation on the spirit of the Lord. The onset of realization of the Supreme gave him the sense of being in touch with the Lord in a way that created a sense of being deluged in the spirit of the Divine. Narada was absorbed in the thoughts of God. When his heart became full with the spirit of the Divine, the watering eyes of the sage couldn't even have the vision of the world as such. He realised that the mind needed to be in a state of being free from its attachments to the world of knowledge and the world of spirituality. When the crisis of the soul finally allows, the total view of the divine truth unfolds. The devotee finds now having achieved the view of the same in the way it is, thus the heart deluged in the depth of the spirit of the Divine in the context of the world.

> *Premah autibharah nirbhinnah pulakangae*
> *iti nirurittah Ananda samplabae linoh*
> *Na apashyam ubhayam munae.*   (Bhagavatam 1/6/17)
>
> Whenever I concentrate upon your holy presence on Earth, I find that my heart and mind get deluged in the honey of your love for the creation in

general, and the devotees in particular. Mind and consciousness with full oneness surrendered to you, oh God.

Whenever this occurs in life on Earth, it integrates deeply with the spirit of God through a realization that touches the very essence of the divine here. The devotee is now manifest in a stream of experiences that contribute to the realization of the Supreme. A condition that is needed to fulfil the love for God. Love for God thus makes it a point that offer a clear pathway to reach out to the spirit of God in the domain of the passage of time. Time eternal now unfolds in its own way to make open the minds to reopen and connect that to the spirit to get the trance of the divine spirit in its own contact. It is not a dream but focussed reality. It's the reality that transcends the barriers of time and other constraints. It was the flow of the spirit of bliss touching aspects of life altogether. This has the power of penetration into the dimensions of eternal spirit in its own profoundness with the spirit of God contained within the self; the senses of the devotee now rise above the limits of consciousness with the vision of God in a context of the world that used to have the spirit vibrant in life in the context of the world of the divine spirit in the world.

Rupam bhagavatah yat tvam
Manah kantak suchah aupaham.
Aupashyam sahasa uttatchae
Vaiklabatha duhmanah iva.   (Bhagavatam 1/6/18)
On my intense urge, I found a conscious response From within myself. I was driven to the vision of the form, It was God himself present in his divine abode before My conscious senses drawn inward did the sweet name chanting Sweeter than honey, the full presence of his eternal abode Engrossed in the whatabouts of the senses and the awareness. Saw his form of the illumined object is the cosmic attire. It was the infinite sky and the endless sea of nectar together Making his feet drenched in the flow of the divine spirit within. The blessed vision thus offers the flow of nectar honey within.

With the vision of the Supreme, the mind of Narada was overwhelmed with joy at the cosmic connection. Narada had felt the continuity in the flow of time to embrace him further. A deep prayer had captured the mind and the consciousness of Narada. On the fate of having visualized the golden presence of yours in spirit and the formless form, you come onto the factors of life, and as such, the barriers of the factors of the world got diffused in the flow of the spirit of the divine. The divine presence as such makes the mind and heart of Narada full with the urge of the divine consciousness in a way that makes him remember throughout the essence of the spirit of God in the inner core of his heart. Now he urges the Divine for the blessings and the presence in the way one understands as being present physically in the context of the world.

> *Sukrit yat darshinam rupam*
> *Etat kamayah tae aunagna.*
> *Mat kamah sonaki sadhuh*
> *Sarvam munchati hrit chayanah.* (Bhagavatam 1/6/22)
>
> I pray upon the good spirit of yours in the creation. I call upon your conscious presence on Earth in abode, whatever be thy intent to get done by the soul of the Supreme. Be it in a way undertaken the form of humans in the world. Let all be deluged in the flow of the causes of Earth in the domain thy presence thus makes this soul get deluged in the love for him. Your solemn presence let the focus of the spirit spread in the light That illumines the minds of humans in the cosmic design of yours.

Narada's intrinsic urge was a call to envision the Divine within the flow of his consciousness on Earth. The Divine's human presence would inspire living beings to focus on a destined journey along the pathways of time's unfolding events. This urge is conveyed through the spirit of devotees, encompassing millions and billions of human souls whose cries for fulfillment aspire to the Lord's presence among good souls. Thus, the Supreme, in the context of His fullness, decides to descend and embody himself on Earth. Heartful cry, intense but silent, makes the divine mind full with the spell of truth-consciousness-bliss.

Freeing of Mind

The bleeding in delightful aspiration of the divine presence in human abode makes God even more willing to taste the spirit of the presence in human conditions with human form. Thus, he takes it up as the consecrated urge of minds to get on to the cause of human aspiration to be in a position to feel the divine presence in the empirical sense.

Therefore, the reasons behind God's getting onto the human abode for the salvation of human being on Earth remain as the emergence of the divine spirit in human abode, made two broad aspects as it reveals to the World. As explained in the *Bhagavad Gita*:

> *Yada yada hi dharmasya glanih bhabati Bharatah*
> *Avyuthanam audharmasya tada aatmanam srijamiaham.* (Gita 4-7)
> Arjuna, whenever righteousness is on the decline and unrighteousness is in the ascent, then I embody myself in material form, in human form in the world.

Whenever darkness prevails upon the creation in the form of unrighteous dominance on the spirit and consciousness of human society, the cause occurs in the domain of God, the Supreme, to create and take care of the cause and help the human world through all kinds of the possible support to take the cause of dharma or the righteous principles ahead. Establishing the righteous principles in the human order sometimes requires the spirit of war.

It was the climax of events in the context of the Mahabharata when the spell and strength of evil forces rose up to the level of victory and reorganised the society in accordance.

The emergence of God on Earth apparently carries these two reasons. However, God's emergence in the world was actually to restore the primordial truth that was there in the early Vedas. The Vedic truth in the early Vedic period was that of the divine truth. The creation had the basis of truth, and the divine urge was to maintain truth in the lives of all created. The supreme Divine had in his urge as remaining void and in conditions of formless, timeless, speechless. He made himself the atman for all in future.

> *Aatma vai idam ekah eva augrae aasit*
> *Na anyat kimchana na mishat*
> *Sa ikshatah lokan nu srijah iti* (Rig Veda, Aitareya Upanishad)

He was present in the form of the entire creation. He is himself the truth embodied. He is the supreme soul with embodiments of the truth of his original creation. The wish that had gradually developed in him took shape in the form of the truth in the context of divine wish, and that is why the formless absolute Lord of the lords started expanding the wish. His original state of truth was void of the indescribable conditions of the spell of this creation and the void, and the divine spirit that was the seeding condition and the living spell of the truth of the emergence. The transformation thus took shape in the creation of the supreme soul in the realm of the divine emergence on Earth. From the absolute void in this creation, it started rolling forward to the spirit of the emergence in factual details and conditions of having realization of the state of truth. The fundamentals of creation thus got structured and formed in the sequence of things that have occurred in the process of gradual progress. The supreme self is initiated by God, the formless God, the God of all forms of God: *devadideva* – the principal form of the Lord. Thus, the wish of the supreme divine took up the challenging shape of being into illumination for the creation to provide light-heat-energy throughout the entire span of the creation. The divine creation propelled the void through emptiness, leading to the formation of the solar world—the sun, moon, and stars—the cosmic pathways, the world, Earth, water, air, fire, light, and nature, all amidst the call of time. Time initiates everything. Life had emerged. It was the human form that came on Earth first, and along with it, all other lives.

The purposeful appearance of God on Earth involves man being picked up based on the attributes, based on the criteria as identified as distinctive and at the same time fits into the divine.

> *Sah iman lokan ausrijat. Ambha marichin maram aapah.*
> *Audah ambhah yat pranae divyam douh pratishthah.*
> *Antariksham marichiyah Prithivi*
> *Marah yah audhastad ta aapah.* (Aitareya Upanishad 1-1-2)

It's the divine intent in clear terms that made the cause of life happen and thrive. The super infinite spell of void had the appearance of ever emptiness and nothingness. In the judgement of a scientific and rational mind, the emptiness and void cannot contain any matter or any other thing in any way. Void or emptiness is regarded as having no matter. However, whether it can have any energy content or not can be analysed or judged from the perspective of emptiness. The study of David Bohm as expressed in his work 'Wholeness and the Implicate Order'- that even in the spectrum or the spell of emptiness or void, energy may remain present in the form of light or even some indescribable way that would cause the senses of human organism thrive in a way that attempts to balance the concerns of the creation with its supportive causes in the original conditions of it.

Sah ikshatah imae nu lokah lokapalan nu srijae iti
Sah ambhah eva purusham samah uddhritah aumuchhayat.
(Aitareya Upanishad 1-1-3)

The question arises, as to how do you understand that in this journey through the phases of the creation may a sense in the set of things that makes it happen in the manner we visualise and understand now through the support of technologies and the aspects of the universe that we understand in our own way having applied the multiple tools of the technology to have its notion in the process of occurrence, physical or the mental world could catch hold of from the germination of the universe.

Yatah vai imani Bhutani jayantae
Yena jatani Jibanti; yat prayanti abhisambishanti iti.
Tat bijijnasasya tat Brahman iti. (Taittiriya Upanishad 3-1-1)

The creation of humans has the strength of justification of a higher order and also a higher degree, once the observations or the inferences are supported by the ground realities of life that have grown on Earth. In the early Vedic period, sages realized the essence of human existence: its deep connection to the cause of creation and the fundamental seeding of that cause. This understanding made the journey through human life incredibly creative, empowering individuals with the ability to be self-driven. As it has been visualised by the sages of the Vedic period, it is the supreme Divine himself who had the desire to create a cause for creation and progression of life that has spanned into the focus of the future on a scale of time, given a start by the Lord of lords, the Supreme in the abode of Lord Shiva. Lord Shiva is the *Mahakaal*, the great cause and passage of time; he owns the causes of life to make it happen and allows it to pass through the passage of time. In the design of things of the Lord Supreme it was just the infusion of divine potent that has caused into the process of the passage of time the going-growth-decline-shinning-darkening-potentialising-burning-acquiring-destroying, and finally contributing to the cause of creation and then thriving on and throughout with a spell of the cause and the effect of the same in a way that attempts to create further prospects in life.

The Vital

The causative factors for the creation are coordinated in such a way that they connect the living soul of one kind and form with that of another. The living soul is one that allows its paradigm to get connected to the other in the sense of the terms that it moves the horizon of connecting network to have it in the best possible manner. In the process of its survival and growth, each element of the creation thus creates pathways of connections.

> *Annam Brahmah iti byajanat.*
> *Annyat hi eva khalu Imani Bhutani jayantae.*
> *Annena jatani jivanti.*
> *Annam prayanti avishambishanti iti tat vijnayay.*
> (Taittiriya Upanishad 3-2-1)

Food itself is the nectar of life with divinity inbuilt in. The entire creation is nurtured and sustained through the appropriation of food for lives. Every element of creation grows and survives on the strength of food and maintains itself with that. The wisdom of creation supports the view of continuity of life in the form of reciprocity of the eternal food among all elements of the creation.

Thus, the essential ingredient and vital input for life enters the realm of the other. In its journey, life's strength and power—the vital force—then integrates into the creation and maintenance of life itself. *Anna* is the food for survival and growth. Each life has its own requirements as to the kind of food. Also, within a particular species, an individual's life has a unique demand on the type, quality and patterns of the food chosen for taking up for consumption. Food thus taken up for consumption makes a unique identity for a person in the flow of the living of lives in a particular pattern. Anna occupies a cardinal role in the entire gamut of things in the world.

> *Pranah Brahmah iti byajanat.*
> *Manah Brahmah iti byajanat.*
> *Vijnanah Brahmah iti byajanat.*
> *Anandam Brahmah iti byajanat.*
> (Bhrigu Valli, Taittiriya Upanishad 3-3-1)

The sages had realised the individual life as a gift of the Divine and a representation of the Divine. The Supreme takes up different forms and abodes and infuses life within to make it functional, and also gets deluged in the material content of the universe at an appropriate point in time.

The vital energy drawn from *anna* or the kind of food is such that it sustains a life into the process of living as it aspires. Human life usually maintains a pattern that orients itself to the kind and pattern of food that begets in life the energy to survive and grow. This energy, as an input to living, is known as the vital force or the *pranah* in the human system. The sage says pranah is Brahman. This means, as life goes on sustaining itself in perpetuity, it is the 'pranamoya kosha' or the vital sheath in human life that takes care of living and at the same time, the energy for the survival of the concerned life. It is such that the survival needs are vital, and again, the growth and sustenance need the vital energy. Vital energy for an organism is such that it makes the thinking-intellectual abilities-abilities to work-the power of embracing life as a force, all depend solely upon it.

Anandat hi eva khalu Imani Bhutani jayantae.
Anandena jatani jibanti.
Anandat prayanti abhisambhishanti iti.
Tat Brahma iti.   (Bhrigu Valli, Taittiriya Upanishad, 3-6-1)

The secret of creation lies in the bliss drawn from the process of creation and the happiness earned therefrom. The entire creation multiplies in its own way, driven by the intrinsic bliss lying within each living entity and always graced by the Divine.

Vital energy also sustains the mind in its urge to have the strength and energy of mind work and function in a way that helps the mind to work in not only usual normal pattern but any creative, meditation and spiritual activity of the mind that works as the input to the spell and series of work in the manner that the spirit that allows the mind to unfold in right sense of the term. The mental sheath is the *manomaya kosha*. It integrates the entire set of things covered by the mind with the kind of impact that the physical mind attains in terms of the influences of the inner consciousness and the kind of bio-physical and psycho-spiritual functioning that the mind is tuned to do. Thus, the mind is a connection between the physical functioning and the spiritual dimension that it connects with. Mind acts as the connecting cord, invisible, non-material, but substantial in terms of its conscious presence. It is that element of life which not only makes and keeps life vibrant, but also positions itself as the driver of consciousness in relation to the world's work, enabling the sense and work organs to perform. Mind analysis has shown the human mind to exist in five different states.

These are:

1. *Kshipta* or Scattered mind

2. *Mudha* or Dull mind
3. *Vikshipta* or Turbulent mind
4. *Ekagra* or Concentrated mind
5. *Niruddha* or Poised mind

These are the states of mind that have been enumerated by the Vedic sages. 'Kshipta' mind is that state of it when the mind is driven by the kinds of desire that human being usually possesses. In the usual sense of the term, the scattered mind is restless like a monkey. At this state of mind, it cannot focus on or have a single-pointed view of things, like a monkey, which, because of its inherent nature of restlessness, travels and jumps from one place to the other. Thereby, the entire scenario of being one with any subject or matter of learning any object of focus and the intuitive function of the mind gets lost as a kind of process in any context.

The 'Mudha' mind is one-sided and does not have its content nurtured because of its ignorance. A dull mind does not contain the power of discrimination between good and bad. It does not have the ability to see beyond the things of the current period. It remains dull until the urge to attain the realization of eternity spans beyond the current flow of time. When the awareness of the divine perspective of life arises, it attains the condition of a settled mind and gradually sets on to understand the purpose of life.

'Vikshipta' mind is turbulent in nature. The condition that offers similarity with the restlessness of a monkey actually gets further aggravated if the same monkey is made to drink intoxicated liquor; then the monkey, under the influence of the liquor, becomes aggressive in its urge to possess and acquire. Such becomes the condition of the person. Driven by the strong ego of the person, the mind behaves in the true 'Vikshipta' way. Gradual understanding of the concern of goodness, noble attributes, or the aspects of divine attributes inculcated in life through the phases of the spiritual practice, the person gradually becomes capable of drawing themselves towards becoming 'Ekagra' mind.

'Ekagra' mind is concentrated. Gradual spiritual practice would instil the belief that the spiritual mind is superior and good for the person and the world. Not only that, the spiritual mind would be in a position to have a central focus of God realization in life, with a focus on spirituality, the functional dimensions of life get coordinated in such a manner that calmness and poise of mind are attained through the final state of mental attainment. This state of mind is known as 'Niruddha'. This is the state of mind that becomes tuned to the spirit of God in life.

'Niruddha' mind thus remains free from mental impurities as categorised under the term 'Sharahripu' or six enemies to God-realization. These are known as: anger, desire, lust, greed, delusion, jealousy and ill feelings about others.

Divine Spirit

Niruddha mind creates a condition similar to have realization of God. When the niruddha mind adopts the spiritual process of realization, it reaches a context that helps in the gradual unfolding of divine truth that was hitherto in an undiscovered condition. The first phase of this realization gets revealed as that of the spirit of wisdom. This is known as *'Vijnanamaya Kosha'* or the spiritual sheath of divine wisdom. All faculties and organs connected to this remain linked with the inner spirit of realization.

'Vijnanamaya Kosha', thus, helps in the process of getting onto the wheels and parameters of truth in life. In this journey of the good self, thus, the parameters of the good attributes of life would be in the realm of things, the urge to have the sense of divinity understood begets the spirit of divinity in life. This begets the wisdom of God as per the spiritual way of things to the complete understanding of the essence of the spirit of God. Now the spirit starts God-realization through the gradual but steady state of having the 'ananda' or bliss in life.

'Anandamaya Kosha' gets on to have a gradual unfolding into life. 'Ananda' is the spiritual variety of happiness. The spiritual view of happiness is the bliss in life. The bliss as a condition of life is the conditions and thus the aspects of life that have emerged in the conditions of the horizons of the world in a way that the graceful presence of God is thus determinant to the perspectives of the world. The condition of 'ananda' or the blissful sheath is flowered when the wisdom mind starts understanding life in its own way. As has been clarified, the happiness that is oriented to the factors of human consciousness gets tuned to the realm of God. It is the touch of God in life that helps in realising the fact that life is but the endowment of God in life. The sages had realised this condition of 'ananda'. 'Ananda' is the state of the mind that makes the world turn into a place free from all vices of life, and thus the spirit gets connected to the extent that the presence of God in all aspects of life on an ongoing process.

The Vedic sage has mentioned this 'ananda' as the Supreme. Without the gradual realization of divine bliss, it is not possible to have the divine spirit in life. The divine spirit gradually enables unfoldment by opening up to the cosmic truth. This is the phenomenon of the microcosm opening up to the macrocosm in the most liberal way. Life attains truth within the limits of the world. It opens up horizons of realization. God realization happens when the reality starts unfolding for the spiritual aspirant, so far as her or his aspiration gets on to a journey into eternity, what the empirical thinks around happens only in a noble way.

The spirit of bliss was explored by a very young sage, Shukhdeva Goswami Maharaj. He was the son of the great sage Vyasa. Vyasa was one of the most revered sages in the Vedic period. The Vedas were coordinated by the sage Vyasa. The Vedas have four segments. These are: Rik Veda, Saam Veda,

Yajur Veda and Atharva Veda. The Rik Veda was coordinated by a senior sage, Paila. The essential message of the Rik Veda was:

'Prajnanam Brahmah'- Brahman, the supreme state of God, is known through the wisdom that is earned through spiritual ways and deep meditation. This is the dimension of realization when the sage makes a solemn call and prays to God, the Supreme, to get into this human condition and transform that into the conditions of divinity, when everything turns noble and holy.

The Saam Veda was coordinated by the great sage Jaimini. Jaimini was an associate of the great sage Narada. Narada was known for the cause and spread of devotion to God in his own way. The spirit of the Saam Veda was thus devotion to God. The essential message of the Saam Veda was:

'Tat tvam ausi'- 'You let your cosmic soul merge in me'. Thus, the stream of the Vedic Truth, where God appears in form. God in the form is recognised with the senses as:

1. 'Tat' and 'Tvam'- 'That' and 'You in existence'- this again merges in the concept of 'You' in 'Me'. Getting the divine merged in his spirit with the *'jivatman'*- the living soul housed in the abode of the spiritual person, aspiring for the same. This is for every person; however, only those who have the right aspiration for that.
2. The separate identity or duality in existence is that which is the apparent reality. When devotion matures, going beyond the limits of the individuality of the person, then she or he realises the spirit and essence of God and that of God on Earth.
3. Through the concept of God and devotee as dual in the initial understanding, a seeker of God realization then aspires to have the spirit of God, gradually creating the impactful conditions of delusion in the mind of the devotee. A time and condition arrive when the lid over mundane vision is gradually removed, helping a person realize God in the true spirit. This merges the empirical identity of separation with the flow of cosmic and eternal identity.

The Saam Veda stands for the existence of God in various forms. His being into his own creation could be in any way and form. However, the journey and passage of the supreme truth thus come down in spirit and elevate the human spirit to divinity.

This was greatly discussed between the great king Parikshit and the very young sage Shukhdeva Goswami. Parikshit, a king of repute and values, was the descendant of Arjuna, the great personality of the Mahabharata. The war of Kurukshetra, where Arjuna, the greatest warrior ever, would remain just as a warrior but with the lesson of the *Bhagavad Gita* learned from Lord Krishna, Arjuna has turned into a person of the highest level of human yet noble character and the power, capacity and knowledge of the war in all its ramifications thereof. It is the way that has the mix of wisdom of God, devotion to God and finally the surrender to God in the form of consecration. Parikshit was the grandson of Arjuna, who was identified by Lord Krishna as his own dear devotee-friend. King Parikshit, by mistake, had killed a holy man while on a hunt for animals. This had destined a strong curse by the son of the holy man, who was again a sage of spiritual attainment and had earned through spiritual process from his father the methods of spiritual attainment. Parikshit was cursed to death initially, and continuation of the curse continued throughout. He was given a recourse of being relieved from the curse provided he had the knowledge of the Lord on Earth. Parikshit had that chance by the appearance to him of a bright young sage, Shukhdeva. Shukhdeva had taught Parikshit the life, work and values in the philosophy of Lord Krishna. Bhagavatam has its roots in the Saam Veda. The spirit of devotion and love for God gradually culminates in the spirit of surrender or consecration in life.

Yesham sam smaranat sadyah shudhayanti vai grihah.
Kim punah darshanah sparshah pavasevanah eha aasanat andivih.
(Bhagavatam 1-9-33)

Parikshit had the realization after having heard the concept of Lord on Earth and that of Lord Krishna with all the actions during the period of his being visible in the activities of the world, he could develop a comprehensive view about the realization of the spirit of God. Parikshit states that personal relations of a divine nature are essential to understanding the essence of divinity on Earth. With God's descent to Earth in a physical abode, the cult and process of devotion are enhanced in many ways.

Parikshit came to the conclusive realization that the vision, touch, smell, and words uttered by the Lord are all guiding principles in life. We can always get into the realm of that when we earn that realization in spirit. Arjuna had that life of being a companion friend of God on Earth, taking the spirit of self ahead of situations where the factors of transcendence were made to happen through the combinations of actions induced by the factors of devotion. The inheritance of the *Bhagavad Gita* is somehow connected with the Bhagavatam so far as the spirit of devotion is concerned. Lord Krishna guided his devotee-friend Arjuna through the process of dedicated action, which means action without any speck of egoistic bondage to it, and that of devotion engrossed in it. Lord Krishna's culminating message during the Kurukshetra war in the Mahabharata was devotion-centric action dedicated to God. Arjuna, already groomed in the highest art and technique of warfare, was thus blessed with the Lord's support and guidance to win the war on behalf of the divine. As a devotee-warrior, Arjuna therefore had the Lord's blessed support in his life.

The *Bhagavad Gita* is a universal text available now in more than 50 recognized languages of the world. The original source of all of this is one and the same, with the text in Sanskrit, assigned chapters (including numbers and names), and numerically signified verses within each chapter. These original Sanskrit verses were not composed by anyone and are not subject to copyright on Earth. However, various analyses, elaborations, descriptions, and comments on these verses are attributed to their respective authors.

The original verse of the *Bhagavad Gita* is one and the same without any identity with the author of any kind.

The Sanskrit verses used in this text are rendered in English by the author, and no translation by anyone whatsoever has been included here. The semantics using the original Sanskrit verses make a difference in the presentation of the verse in other languages than Sanskrit. The author has used his way of mentioning the Sanskrit verses based on more than 40 years of meditative culture of the original text in Sanskrit, and also supporting vast literature in Sanskrit of the four Vedas by the author, whereas the Vedic texts, including the books *Corporate Leadership – The Vedic Way, The Vedic Economy, Stress Management Through Mind Engineering,* are all original texts written by the author based on the knowledge acquired from the original Sanskrit texts of the Vedas, Upanishads, and the *Bhagavad Gita*. This book, *Gita for Work and Life* has uniqueness not only in terms of the theories coined out of it, but also the principles of application in life and the works of an individual human being on Earth. It contributes to the coining of thoughts and ideas, on one hand, and depicts the ways to live a righteous life and maintain the righteous ways of actions for reaching excellence and achieving rightful victory in life, on the other. The problems, turmoil and hindrances to the progress or excellence of a person in general, and that which inflicts the minds and inner consciousness of the person, in particular, can be easily walked over if someone possesses the mental energy and consciousness through the current book *Gita for Work and Life*.

Though a book drawn from the thoughts of spirituality, *Gita for Work and Life* is:

- a book of knowledge leading to wisdom
- a book of principles of actions inspiring the person to do the action with perfection and highest achievement
- a book of inspiration to create a society of individuals with divine attributes which extends mutual hands to each other, helps in collective growth, prevents the evils from overriding and makes the divinely oriented, be victorious in life and work, and
- makes the person receive the blessings of life with a mind full of poise, peace, and divine bliss within.

1 Depression Management

Arjuna's journey through Depression to Winning Action

Journey through the weeds of emotions made Arjuna a winner in all aspects of all age groups. The war of the Mahabharata was identified by the ruling emperor as the war at a place, 'Dharmakshetra — Kurukshetra. The place, as mentioned, Kurukshetra, was a sacred place. Any evil action or wrongdoing at this place was destined to end either through transformation or annihilation. That is why the title 'Dharmakshetra' was given — the meaning of which stands as the 'Holy Place'. Any culmination of action at this place would be a realistic journey in that life, either through the pathways of transformation or through annihilation.

Arjuna was considered a dear friend of Lord Krishna. Krishna, being the embodiment of God on Earth, descended in the human context with a purpose. The central purpose, as mentioned by Lord Krishna himself, was the cause of allowing the elements of truth in the lives on Earth to have smooth and peaceful living, within the fair context of living. The fair context is that of righteousness in spirit and values of existence. Departure from the righteous context creates problems for a good and peaceful living. The purpose of the descent of God in human form has been very clearly mentioned by Lord Krishna in his advisory deliberations to Arjuna in the context of the war at Kurukshetra. The declaration of Lord Krishna runs as:

> *Yada yada hi dharmasya glanih bhavati bharata.*
> *Abhyuthanam adharmasya tada atmanam srijami aham.* (G.4/7)
> Whenever righteousness is affected and unrighteousness dominates the creation, I take birth in the world
> *Paritrianaya sadhunam binashaya cha duskritam.*
> *Dharma samsthapan arthayah sambhabami yuge yuge.* (G.4/8)
> I manifest physically in the creation at times to protect the righteous people and destroy the evil

The meaning of this is whenever the righteous principle and way of living is defeated or problems in life abound and hurt peaceful and honest living people, when wrongdoers start dominating the society, making the lives of good people difficult, then the Supreme decides to create his embodied personality to be at the helm of lives on Earth. Lord on Earth protects those maintaining honest and righteous ways of living, and those following the pathways of divine qualities in life are given protection by the Supreme, and those wrongdoers and those having adopted unrighteous principles on Earth get deluged in life.

The purpose, as mentioned, is maintained throughout the phases of the human journey on Earth. As Lord Krishna mentioned, in the ultimate situational contest, those noble-hearted people would experience their place of peace, tranquillity and ways of honest living on Earth.

The war at Kurukshetra was a conflict between the ruling blind Emperor Dhritarashtra, represented by his son Duryadhana, and the oppressed Pandavas on the other side. Not only were the Pandavas oppressed, but, as a matter of fact, even though faced with lots of debacles, insults, tortures, murderous attempts and continued harassments for all five brothers, the mother and a wife, they had continued to practise tolerance and endeavoured to adhere to righteousness.

Arjuna Turns Depressed

The war of Kurukshetra was the ultimate and final objective of a divine descent on Earth. The purpose was to protect the noble and good ones from the atrocities and onslaughts of the wicked and demonic persons. That set of people who have acquired authority, power of muscles and worldly components are the enemies to those living in peace, happiness and tranquillity. These are the situations when the dominance of wrongdoers occurs. Purposeful presence of the Lord on Earth thus takes up the issues of agony, sufferings of the good people and puts across the right set of values to see that those wrongdoings are either abolished or the people who are identified as the wrongdoers are made extinct. Usually, in the design of the Lord on the Earth, the wrongdoers are given opportunities to stop doing wrong things and live good and decent lives. The good and decent ones thus get support and a lease of life to continue doing good things on one hand, and take proper care of everyone in the world.

> *Arjuna ubacha*:
> *Senayah ubhayah madhyae ratham sthapayah mae achyutah* (G.1/21)
>
> Arjuna spoke:
> Place my chariot in between the two warring forces so that I can get a feel of the fighters on both the sides of the war
>
> *Yabat etam nirikshae aham yoddhukaman abasthitan*
> *Kaih mayan saha yoddhavyam asmin ranasamudrame* (G.1/22)
> Keep my chariot here until I have a proper view of the arrangements of the forces on the enemy side with whom I have to fight

> *Yohutsamanan abekshae aham yah ete samagatah atrah*
> *Dhartarashtrasya durbuddheh ete yuddhae priya chikirshabah.* (G.1/23)
> I shall understand the arrangements of forces from the side of King Dhritarashtra and also our well-wishers

The *Bhagavad Gita* starts with Arjuna's intent to see the arrangements of the army on the other side of the war. Arjuna was the main hero in waging this critical war against the other side. On the side of Arjuna, the number of soldiers in the army was fewer. But in a way, the potential strength of the Pandavas was enough. The side of the Kauravas, who represented the wrongdoers, had a larger number of soldiers and many captains widely known for their valour and might.

It is in this context that the main warrior of the Pandavas, Arjuna, wanted to have a view of the context of the war. The chariot in which Arjuna was riding was being driven by Lord Krishna himself. Arjuna urged Lord Krishna to place the chariot in the middle of the two warring forces to have a direct view of who was there on the other side and form his mind accordingly. Arjuna was curious to see the heroes who were present on the battlefield in support of the evildoers, represented by Duryadhana, the son of Dhritarastra.

> *Sanjay ubacha:*
> *Ebam uktah rishikesha gudakeshenah bharatah.*
> *Senoyoh ubhayah madhye sthapaitwa ratha uttamam* (G.1/24)
> Sanjay said, hearing the words of Arjuna, Lord Krishna had placed the chariot between the two armies

Arjuna had the notion that these heroes had the wrong perception and view of things, as having taken the side of the wrongdoers, unrighteous criminal forces. With this purpose in mind, Arjuna urged the Lord to place his chariot close to the opponent.

The entire scenario was in the vision of Sanjay, who was the chariot driver of the main emperor Dhritarashtra. The emperor was blind at birth. His father had endowed the power to his brother Pandu. Pandu's wife, Kunti, was the mother of the five Pandava brothers. After the death of Pandu, the kingship was supposed to be transferred to the eldest son of the family, Dhritarashtra. That was done, but with some reservations from the kingly court, as Dhritarashtra was blind at birth. The next generation had all the problems surface. Dhritarashtra became the emperor, though blind. Most of the work of the emperor was being done by his eldest son Duryadhan. Duryadhan was greedy and power hungry. Gradually, all powers effectively did vest in him. He had created a team of strong and powerful warriors around him. The other side was the Pandavas. There were five brothers, each one had a distinct identity. Yudhisthira, Bhim, Arjuna, Nakul, Sahadev were Pandavas. They were collectively known as good people, oriented to the masses and truthful in their individual characters.

The war had been the result of many attempts by Duryadhana to kill and destroy the Pandavas. Moreover, they were denied their right to live alone in the royal context. Even small measures of areas for living to survive were denied to them. Duryadhana did a gross insult to Draupadi – the wife of Pandavas – so much so that she was drawn to the office of the king, and an attempt was made to forcefully disrobe Draupadi. With constant ugly effort to disrobe Draupadi forcefully was slumped by the graceful miracle of the Lord. Draupadi had sought refuge in the grace of Lord Krishna, and thus happened the miracle of having an endless length of the cloth on her body, foiling the demonic act of the ruler to disrobe Draupadi in the official court of the king and in the presence of a large number of seniors.

The context was thus humiliating and extremely bad for the Pandavas. All options were over. The only thing that remained was to survive or not. Arjuna was the person whose power of war with weapons was the focus. Another brother, Bhima, was very strong and powerful on a physical scale. Duryadhana was scared of these two persons from the camp of the Pandavas.

> *Drishtae iman swajanan krishna yuyutsunah sam abasthitan*
> *Sidanti mamah gatrani mukhancha parishushyatih* (G.1/28)
> Arjuna's mind was captured by compassion and affection, seeing many close relatives on the enemy side of the battle

> *Baepaethuh cha sharirae mae romah harshah cha jayate*
> *Gandibam sramsatae hastad tvak cha eva paridahjatae* (G.1/29)
> After witnessing the context properly, Arjuna found his task was to annihilate close relations and respectable persons on the enemy side; his body started trembling, the entire human energy was unavailable to him, and even his favourite weapon, *Gandiva*, had slipped from his hand

Arjuna, since the war was not for his personal gain, never intended to become a king, nor was there any personal intent to gather wealth. He was a person dedicated in his mind towards a cause. The cause that Arjuna had was the principal agenda of Lord Krishna. His purpose of being here on Earth was to establish that cause.

But the problem started here. Arjuna's mind had the cause in his understanding of the basic responsibilities. Once the cause was identified as that of the Lord, there was no such chance or scope for personal emotions to have a play. Even then, Arjuna had fallen in the grip of personal emotions and became thoroughly depressed at the scene of all his close relations as enemies to be killed.

> *Na cha shaklami abasthatum bhramati eva cha mae manah*
> *Nimittani cha pashyami biparitani keshabah* (G.1/30)

Seeing the condition of arrangements on the other side, my mind is so hurt that I am unable to stand firmly, and I found a huge disaster on the offing and was unable to stand even

Na cha shreyah anupashyami hatwa swajanam aahabae
Na kamkhshae vijayam Krishna na cha rajyam sukhani cha   (G.1/31)
I don't see the outcome as good for all or the world from the kind of killing that has to be done to win this war; I don't aspire to win the battle through this kind of killing and enjoy the pleasure of becoming a King through victory

Arjuna became bewildered, depressed and effectively lost his senses as a warrior and a person having a mandate to do the work of God through the phases of war. It was his solemn duty to undertake the responsibility of the war. Many things of the destiny depended upon the actions of Arjuna. However, Arjuna had fallen prey to the material orientations of the mind. The materialistic instinct of the mind captured the mind of Arjuna. He started narrating his position and voiced it to Lord Krishna. He became a person having lost his power of the mind to think and act in the way of a common person. He said he could not do the war and that his body and mind were depressed. His hands and the entire body were trembling. He was so lost within that no mental energy was left. Also, his body and mind lost their synchrony. The person is now reduced to someone having no physical or mental energy to look into it.

The warrior, Arjuna, had lost his consciousness, got depressed within and was overtaken by the spirit of disappointment, dejection, withdrawal and escape. The special godly weapon, Gandiva, had fallen from his hand, and Arjuna was shaken so much by the emergent thoughts within that he was unable to stand on his feet and fell on the floor of the chariot. Still, he was giving arguments which are befitting for social individuals in a human context wherein the empirical view of relation, transaction in life, orientation of mind and spirit of individuals had captured his overall consciousness to a great extent. He even had this argument that in a war, killing the nearest ones begets sins, and therefore, he should not be a party to the war, rather leaving aside everything he should escape from the current assignment of waging a war against the devil forces to support the cause of God in the field of the battle.

It was almost a situation of renunciation or giving up. Arjuna was the main force behind the spirit of righteousness. As has just been mentioned, the Earth system or the living world is a unique gift of the Divine. This gift is for the human world to survive and grow as required. There stands the cause of the fulfilment of the divine wish towards making the living world and the entire creation spend their lives and work in smooth sequence. Lord himself takes a specific abode and establishes his divine work in this world. The orientation of the Lord's purpose is to create a living context that would take care of each and every life on Earth. Over a long period of time, the creation may suffer from the dominance of evil. Evil force stands a strong chance of stripping through the phases of human lives, and thereby the world gets overshadowed by the dominance of evil.

> *Kim no rajyena Govinda kim bhogaih jibitena bah*
> *yesham arthae kamkhitam no rajyam bhogah sukhami cha*   (G.1/32)
> Arjuna said to Krishna, 'What's my need for a kingdom. I don't feel enjoyment, happiness in life, as also in this condition, I don't want to keep my life because the very purpose of living is getting lost.

Arjuna was made to grow with special support from the Supreme. The Lord had a special wish in design to bring back the social situations to control and have effective development of the force of goodness, so much so that the force of goodness be superior in valour, strength of character, values and be spiritually oriented. In this design of the Lord, the Pandavas were different forms of God on Earth to take care of the good spirit on Earth. Goodness prevails on Earth through practices in the lives of people lined through. The forces of goodness need the support and protection from the different types of onslaughts of the world on the lives of those who are poised to act as the agents and forces of goodness on Earth.

> *Tah imcha abasthitah yuddae pranan tyaktwa dhanani cha*
> *Aacharyah pitarah putrah tathae eva cha pitamaham*
> *Matulah Swashurah poutrah shyalah sam bandhinah tatha*   (G.1/33)
> Those very people for whose sake we covet the kingdom, luxuries and pleasures, teachers, uncles, sons and nephews, and even grand-uncles, great-grand-uncles, maternal-uncles, father-in-law, grand-nephews, brothers-in-law, and other relations, are there, arranged on the battlefield, staking their lives and property.

Arjuna was the first chosen person in the design of the Lord for making the role of the Lord on Earth effective and decisive. Arjuna was born of a special boon and heritage of the king of the forms of Gods, Indra. His basic and built-in intrinsic power, the godly lineage and the transmission of the strength of the divinity within made him the special make for the role of the central and most important warrior in the design of the Lord.

Arjuna had not only the intrinsic lineage but had the design of a support system in the process of his being and becoming. Arjuna became the symbolic centre for the growth of the appropriate breed to become someone having the highest of knowledge on one hand and a composite of all different types of expertise to grow into the ultimate position of the personality. Arjuna had received the initial learning of knowledge, and the art and science of the wars from one of the topmost sage-teachers, Guru (Master) Dronacharya. Guru Dronacharya was appointed by the king as the teacher-trainer for all the princes. Large in number, the princes were all made to do schooling with Dronacharya. The practice and learning lessons were common to all students, but Arjuna had a special inclination to learn and the teacher, Guru Dronacharya had liked the student so much that he had opened up the entire stock of knowledge of his possession to Arjuna and at times the creative contribution of Arjuna had made the context of learning even more unique. Arjuna had the scope to develop things further to add on to the pool of knowledge and the entire learning, such that the art and science of war of difficult types and in difficulties of situations could be tackled by Arjuna most effectively, converging to win.

> *Etani hantum na ichhami ghnatah api Madhusudanah*
> *Api trailokya rajyasya hi etah kim nu mahikritae* (G.1/34)
> O Krishna, the slayer of Madhu, I do not want to have sovereignty over the three worlds or even just this world, if I leave the war and they kill me.

Arjuna was the only learner who had proved his excellence with personal values, commitment, determination, dedication, respect and intense love for the teacher. Arjuna had the fortune to receive from different forms and identities of God to receive their boons and respective powers, and different types of weapons and input powers to combat, destroy enemies to win the war with a cause to establish the righteous state through annihilation of the evils that stand and come on the way. Thus, Arjuna had gathered and endowed with the power in hand those who would be in a position to annihilate those creating wrong and evil things in the world to help establish God's design for man.

> *Nihatya dhartarashtran nah ka pritih syat Janardanah*
> *Papam aashrayayet asman hatah aatatayinah etan* (G.1.35)
> O Krishna, I do not want to kill them because killing them will put me to rigorous sin in life

With such all-source supports, endowments and boons on the crown Arjuna

> *Tasmat na arhah bayam hantum Dhartarashtran sa bandhaban.*
> *Swajanam hi katham hatwa sukhinah syam madhavah* (G.1/36)
> Krishna, how can we hope to be happy, slaying the sons of Dhritarashtra, killing even these desperadoes, sin will surely accrue to us.

Apart from giving reasons from a personal point of view, Arjuna also presented certain social arguments, highlighting the disastrous consequences of war and the kind of conditions the world might be forced into as a result of such destruction. The personal reasons were usually sensitive to the social position and demographics for the future. It was, thus, the constant orientation of Arjuna towards selfish concern or a persistent concern about the human settlement. He had thoroughly forgotten the fact that he was bestowed with the responsibility of being a support to establish the objective of the Lord to make a transformation in the values of human civilization. Thus, Arjuna got diverted. He had lost the power of mind, the strength of his own consciousness. He forgot that he had the fundamental role to help and serve the Lord, and the urge to dedicate his life to the cause of the Divine.

The ancient society had a structure which is quite different from the structure of modern society. In our modern society, the nucleus is the individual. Selfish interest and the consideration of the individual remain at the core and the centre of gravity of society. It is not only the personal choice and preference of the individual, but the changing context and design of the person's wishes and expectations play a dominant role in the design of things.

> *Yadi api ete na pashyanti lobhah apahata chetasah*
> *Kulakshayam kritam dosham mitra drohae cha patakam* (G.1.37)
> Therefore, Krishna, it does not behove us to kill our relations, the sons of Dhritarashtra, for how can we be happy by killing our own kinsmen?

The modern society banks on the emotions and fulfilments of the wishes, though temporary and situational. These are the elements of the emotions of the person which are variable to external factors. The external factors do have a constant impact on the spirit and emotions of the person. Society values the individual highest, however, norms and standards are available to smooth and balance the evil aspects of the emotions and thus be at the level of acceptable play of emotions, expectations and requirements. The standard of the society is attained through balancing mutual self-respect and recognition with the rights evenly distributed across.

> *Katham na jneyam asmabhih papat asman nibartitum*
> *Kula Kshayam Kritam dosham prapashyadbhih janardan* (G.1/38)
> The war of destruction will kill the plans, inviting large-scale social hazards and pollution in the minds of the people.

Rights orientation of the society repeatedly connects with the core selfish concern and consideration of the society for the matching of the individual rights with the rights of the larger group of people. Usually, it is the number of people in the group of people that determines the vector dynamics of the rights. Usually, the right is chosen through the prioritization of the rights of the larger group over those of the smaller group. However, the democratic norm of the victory of the larger over the smaller does not eradicate the right of an individual or a smaller group of people. Individual human rights, at their core, cannot be killed or suppressed at the crossroads of the broader group. The concern for one's own rights is effectively the one with the spirit of things at a nominal scale or an approved level, as against that of the collective spirit or the combined collective right of the larger group of people.

Kulak shayae pranashyantih kuladharma sanatanah
Dharma nashtae kulam kritsam adharmam abhibhabhavatih (G.1/39)
O Krishna, who sees clearly the sin accruing from the destruction of one's family, think of destroying, deterring them from this crime?

Modern society revolves around the core attributes, which are oriented to the rights of individuals and groups to fulfil either an individual's selfish considerations or the group's selfish fulfilment. Therefore, the core attributes of modern society can be construed as those of individual rights, and several other segmented rights across which the societies are thus structured. Social institutions are gradually slicing down to the level of the individuals. Family, as a social institution, is gradually getting reduced to the fragmented pieces of a nuclear unit and even at the level of one person, the individual. The attributes of mutually shared living were absent from that domain. Whereas the individual values, selfish considerations, and the notion of concern for other members get missing. One of the most important reasons is that the definition of membership in the social unit of family has undergone a lot of changes and transmutations. The roles being separated out, it is the general recognition and concern of a person that matters.

The ancient Vedic society was structured in a different way. dharma or the spiritual attributes, were in a cluster and network of attributes. This cluster was structured on the basis of certain attributes. The attributes have a space and meaning in the attributes that were valid and enduring over a long period of time. The spirit of living was fundamental in the make-up of a collective setting. The collective spirit was based on the philosophy of *'Bahujana hitaio cha bahujano sukhaio cha'* – the meaning of which stands as 'for the well-being of many and for the happiness of many' – each person was actually poised and determined for others and many. Thus, the welfare of others and not selfish concern was the core philosophy.

Adharma abhibhabat Krishna pradushyanti kulastriyah
Strishu dushtasu varshenyah jayatae varna shankarah. (G.1/40)
A society where women are unprotected is subject to character crisis and social disaster, leading to the mixing of blood in the progeny.

The modern approach to finding happiness through living life is through satisfying the identified need of a specific set of varieties. The Pyramid of Need, as specified by the Behavioural Scientist Abraham Maslow, stands good for the modern society. Construed man as a needy animal, this model, named the Pyramid of Need, has an invisible impact of unholy attributes of human society, like desire, greed, jealousy, envy, anger, gluttony, etc., in the context of daily living and accrued habits of human beings. The silent play of all vices in the garb of the need for survival, growth, achievement and fulfilment of ego, all are cardinal in the average modern mind. It is thus important that the modern society gears up to get rid of all the invisible forces and fits into the design of transformation in the context of human society. For the transformation to happen, fundamentals need to change.

> *Shankaro narakayaeiva kulagnanam kulasya cha.*
> *Patanti pitoro hi esham lupta pinda udaka kriyah* (G.1/41)
> Age-long family traditions disappear with the destruction of a family, and virtue having been lost, vice takes hold of the entire race.

The ancient Vedic society had the fundamental view of life that this life is essentially a gift of God and that the quality of living can be transformed altogether or changed with the help and gift of the kind and the attributes of the work done in the life lived. Life, thus lived for others, is actually the life lived as a service to God. Good quality of work based on the principles of virtues would drive the course of life in the pattern and pathways of goodness. It is thus something that counts and maintains the spirit of goodness, whereas the return from the work thus accrues to generate further spirit of goodness. Service to the spirit of goodness transforms into the service towards a recipient is actually considered as the service patterned to the diverse ways of living, but in a way broad-based to see that all kinds of meanness, pettiness and smallness are made to disappear from the lives of the individual. When the work is endowed with the spirit of the Divine and whenever it reaches the context of the desired level, it tries to maintain that throughout. This is known as the Jiban Yajna or the sacrifice involving the best contribution of the person on the strength of his or her being aligned with the spirit. Then the power of the person becomes outwardly directly connected, maintaining parallelism with the remote work or coordinated through the potential of the person. Thus, the person would identify the role as that of a role guided by the Divine.

The ancient Vedic spirit was a very comprehensive impetus and philosophy for living a good life. Life was structured across four aspects of living doctrines. This was known as *Chatur Varga* – the four facets of living a total and comprehensive life. These were: *dharma – artha – kama – moksha* – or, the righteous ways of living – making life meaningful through creation or earning of internal and external wealth – to fulfil any desire that is tested and having inbuilt way-ahead by the principles of righteousness and finally the culmination of life should be into the context and attainment of ultimate liberty. Therefore, the spirit of living was the foundation of the principles of righteousness with an ultimate goal to achieve the state of moksha. Moksha is the process of making the consciousness free from the transient and illusory states of truth or utter falsehood that human society in the modern period has created for its own.

Dosshaei eteih kulagnanam varnashankarah karakaih
Utsadantae jatidharmah kuladharmash cha saswatah. (G.1/42)
With the preponderance of vice, Krishna, the women of the family become corrupt, and with the corruption of women, O descendant of Vrishni, their ensues as intermixture of cultures and castes.

Principles of dharma are essentially ethical and moral principles with a central belief factor added to them. The belief factor is true belief in God and the factors that are related to and drawn from that basic belief. Therefore, the person believes that she or he is the creation of God with a purpose. Similarly, others are construed to have a similar belief. Not only that, the world is a creation of God, and for that matter, every human being is a creation of God. Therefore, in this world, each person has an intrinsic relationship with each other. The wealth, content and nature are gifts of God. Therefore, a person should not have a selfish habit in life. The wealth of intrinsic capacities, mental and physical energies are gifts of God. Therefore, each person should have an iota of ideas and a basis of thought for action, such that others get chances similar.

Utsanna kuladharmanam manushyanam janardanah.
Narakae niyatam basho bhabati anushukram. (G.1/43)
Progeny, weighing to promiscuity, is prone to destroy the race as well as the race itself, deprived of the offering of the rice and water, *shraddha*, *tarpana*, etc., the names of their race also fall.

The principles of dharma become built-in values in the lives of each person as she or he grows up through age and experience. Life begets experiences of different kinds and categories, but the fundamental values of life, if developed at a very tender age. From this point of view, the context of each life could be made into an acceptable level of homogeneity. This principle would develop the views of togetherness, compassion, caring, friendly orientation to living with others. Thus, acceptability and beyond would be taken up as the dominant principles for actions and applications.

Dharma infuses certain basic values, such as truthfulness, honesty, sincerity, cooperation, integrity, respect for those who deserve and the attitude of giving. The principles of dharma keep on encouraging the spirit of giving and sacrifice, and denounce the mental orientations to the approaches to grab things and to garner wealth only in that way, which is not only accommodating and accepting but also extending respect to others who actually matter in the journey of life. Thus, each person develops a concern for others. Causing harm to others becomes a distant factor, and people would refrain from causing harm to anyone else in the world, whatsoever.

That was the fundamental spirit inbuilt in the personality of Arjuna. His thoughts and arguments were clustered across this central view in life; thus were to be thought in broader terms. Selfishness was not the doctrine in the being of Arjuna; rather, the doctrine that had driven Arjuna down here is his mental sensitivity towards society, the larger human mass, and the contexts of the world in perpetuity. His thought had centred around the issues of future society. A great war, of which he was the main personality, had lots of devastating consequences. Arjuna's mind had picked up issues which were pertaining to the conditions of usual living and the well-being of the future society. If the great war is waged, the consequences would of course lead to the destruction of men and property. Post-war society is limited to a shattered form.

> *Aho vata mahat papam kartum bybasita vayam.*
> *Yat rajya sukham lovenah hantum swajanam udyatah.* (G.1/44)
> With these evils bringing about an intermixture of castes, the age-long caste traditions and family customs of the killers of kinsmen get extinct. O Krishna, we hear that men who have lost their family traditions dwell in hell for an indefinite period of life.

Arjuna gave a few reasons behind his urge to give up. He was foreseeing the future society as something where men have lost their lives and reduced to a level where the dominant values of the society get ruptured. The dominant values would be to protect and maintain the principles of dharma in life. Principles of spirituality are construed as those of sattwa guna. Sattwa guna stands for the good attributes in life. Some of these attributes are those which count for the current period or the present period, and the others are those which are eternal in their appeal and spread. The eternal principles were uttered and practised by Vedic Sages through the constant promise mentioning: 'Satyam Vadishami, Ritam Vadishyami' – the meaning of which stands as 'shall speak truth and maintain truth in life'. Speaking the truth is a matter of habit through practice in life. This requires continuation.

> *Yadi mam pratikaram ashastram shastrapanayah.*
> *Dhartarashtram ranae hanyuh tat me kshematam bhabet.* (G.1/45)
> O, what a pity, we have set our mind on the commission of a great sin, in that due to lust for the throne and enjoyment, we are intent on killing our own kinsmen. It would be better for me if the sons of Dhritarashtra, armed with weapons, kill me in battle while I am unarmed and unresisting.

Arjuna's concern for society was the deviation of the social dynamics from the vectors of the journey in life. Journey in life, thus enables a person to have the spirit of truth in eternity and truth in practice. When the factors are for one individual, it is actually done through the personal efforts of the individual, but when it comes to the understanding and concern of a nation, a society or the world as a whole, a broader canvas of thoughts would take care of that in principle. It may or may not see the light of translating into actions in life.

Arjuna's concern was true in itself. He visualised a situation where the forces of dharma would also diminish along with the forces of Adharma. A handful of evil-minded people can cause havoc to a large gathering of good and morally driven people. Evil forces practice and culture the strengths of muscles and bits; whereas that of the Dharmic people goes in favour of extending helping hands to others and focusing mental and physical energies towards the cause of welfare for all and others. Thus, the people with Dharmic values would give priority to cultivating wisdom within rather than being focused on building muscle power for dominating others.

It was truly the bent of mind of Arjuna. Until now, his mind has been focused on the empirical identities of human persons. At this level and condition of mind, external identity comes into focus for the person, whereas the intrinsic values of the same are explored to be there. Arjuna was thus the torch bearer of the society in terms of thinking of its sustainability and that of the protection of weaker entities on Earth. Arjuna's thought focused on the weaker condition of the society where, after the war, the men force being destroyed, the women would lack protection. In this situation, a handful of evildoers with demonic and animal habits would do injustice to society and its women. this would lead to the disruption of the future society and create an imbalance in that. Arjuna was concerned that the war of the Mahabharata would again prove fatal to agriculture, nature and human beings at large. Thus, the perspective of Arjuna was not based on individual selfishness at all.

Sanjoy ubacha:
Ebam ukta arjunah shanghae ratho upastha upabishat.
Bisrijya sashram cha apam shokasam bigna manasah. (G.1/46)
Sanjay said, Arjuna, whose mind was agitated by grief on the battlefield, having spoken thus and having cast aside his bow and arrows, sank into the hindered part of his chariot.

Rising much above the constrained spirit of individual selfishness, Arjuna had argued for the society. He argued for the women and talked about those who would lose their near and dear ones in life to have spent lives after the war like deracinated orphans on one hand and have-nots through the war of destruction. Arjuna gave lots of thoughts on other aspects. His thoughts were focused on the world that would lose some of its great personalities who are teachers and sages in society. People like Visma, Drona were otherwise assets for the human society. Though they had clustered around the evil forces, their wisdom was a strong asset for the human society. This was also proved through the facts of the war. After Visma was made to lie on the bed of arrows by Arjuna, Visma contributed yeomen's wisdom to Yudhisthira on the request of Lord Krishna. Visma's wisdom advice was very essential and effective in managing the post-war society. The would-be king, Yudhisthira, had the privilege to have learnt lessons of raj dharma – the attributes of state-leadership from Visma. Visma, on the condition and state of taking the bed of arrows for some period, was the repayment in life, the toils and troubles having been experienced and absorbed in him. Visma had maintained the spirit of empirical dharma, but could not be aligned with the spirit of God, which is why the suffering.

Arjuna was conscious about it. He did not want to enjoy life through avoidance of the war, rather, he was ready to sacrifice his life to protect the society and the world from destruction. The final issue was that this would not establish righteousness in the society. God's design was to establish dharma and to save and protect people on Earth. That is why the *Bhagavad Gita* transforms into as the final spirit of life.

2 The Awakened Spirit

Journey through the Pathways of Time for Ultimate Victory in Life

Time Impacts

The creation has been designed by God to pass over the spells of time in sequence. The Lord of lords, Bhagavan Shiva, made the beginning of the spells of spirit, forming the pathways of time. It was all void and super infinite space in the creation. Time was given the impetus of the intrinsic connection with the infinite source of energy. With the progress of the wheels of time by the Mahakaal – the Lord of lords, Bhagavan Shiva, began to spread the seeds of life in the sky, the air, water, soils, forests, oceans, underneath, surfaces and for that matter, everywhere. The seed of existence, drawn from God, was pure in its own intrinsic forms and ways. It was the infinite span of goodness all around the creation. The world of humans, the world of varied creatures, all put together, developed the homogeneous, unified conditions of the creation. The senses within a human person were given liberty to work and operate. Problems occurred with the emergence of emotions.

> *Sanjay ubacha*:
> *Tam tatha kripaya aavishtama ashrupurna aakulah ikshanam.*
> *Vishida antam idam vakyam ubacha Madhusudanah.*   (G. 2/1)
> Sanjay said, 'Sri Krishna then addressed the following words to Arjuna, who was, as mentioned before, overwhelmed with pity, whose eyes were filled with tears and agitated, and who was full of sorrow.'

Sanjay had said, at this point, that when the power of depression had captured the mind of Arjuna. His physical and mental condition was such that he was overwhelmed by the attitude of grace and sympathy of Lord Krishna. The eyes of Arjuna were full of tears, he became fully influenced and obsessed by the sense of severe grief and sadness; Arjuna's eyes were covered with an outpouring of thick streams of tears. Witnessing this scenario, Lord Krishna opened up with his words addressed to Arjuna.

The stream of lives required a kind of independent process with the options and power to have the pathways of forward movement in this creation. The forward movements could be somewhat progress in the positive direction, and could also take the impacts of the other options. The associated forces that try to penetrate the focus of light are those of the patches of darkness. It is the vibrant darkness that chases light. This is a part of the human journey on Earth. The journey, as undertaken, goes beyond the standard and logical expectation of God on Earth. It is in this context; there was a need for the war of the Mahabharata. Over a long period, the gradual dominance of evil did occur. Symbolic of this was the blind king Dhritarashtra.

Sri Bhagaban ubacha:
Kutah tvah kashmalam idam vishmae sama upasthitam.
Anarya jushtham asvargam akirtikaram Arjunah. (G.2/2)
Sri Bhagavan said, 'Arjuna, how has this infatuation overtaken you at this critical hour? It is shunned by noble souls; neither will it lead to heaven nor bring fame to you.'

Lord Krishna had said at this point to Arjuna that at the time of a great crisis, which the human society was facing (because of the dominance of the menace created by the forces of demonic character). He said, 'The ways you have been reacting and responding to the situation will surely lead to the identity loss of yours from the spirit of goodness and getting severely influenced by the illusory impact of those negatively oriented factors.'

With the gradual emergence and logical spread of the evil spirit that had overpowered the existing span of goodness of the spirit, the good and honest gradually got depressed, and the power of the state was used to oppress everyone. The set of good people got deprived of the stream of lives, losing not only the wealth, powers and positions, but also the fact of honest living and the inbuilt prestige and dignity of the lives of people.

The facts around the culminating situations are the gradual oppressions of good and honest people by the oppressors. Evil forces are dominated by the greed to capture all power, all wealth and annihilate the forces of goodness. This would remove resistance and threats to the power of any kind. This mind would perpetuate in the acts of animosity; such was the background motive of the war at Kurukshetra.

The war of Kurukshetra, as depicted and featured in the Mahabharata, was the culminating war to fix a course between the evildoers and the righteous on Earth. It was essential for human society as the power and span of the evil forces grew to a proportion beyond the tolerance for normal healthy living for humans in the world. It was at this crossroads of human society that some intervention from the Supreme became essential. The objective of this intervention was to give a lease of good life to the forces of society who are good and oriented to sattwa guna and annihilating the forces of the devil nature. In the context of the Mahabharata, the forces of goodness were identified with the Pandavas, in general, and Arjuna, in particular. Arjuna had the strength of character to withstand the alluring calls and gestures of the best of the heavenly beauties. The power of the integrity in the character of Arjuna was so high that the highest form of enjoyment, considered by most, did not impact his mind.

> *Kleivyam masmah gamah Partha na etad tvayi upapadatae.*
> *Kshudram hridayah dourbalyam tyaktam uttishthata*
> *parantapah.* (G. 2/3)
> Yield not to unmanliness, Arjuna, this does not become you. Shaking of this has faint-heartedness, stand up, Arjuna, you are a person with strength of mind.

Lord Krishna said to Arjuna: 'Do not allow smallness to your mind and heart to figure out at this time when commitment and valour are essential. This kind of weakness in character and personality is unbecoming of a great, strong personality like yours. Throw away this weakness of mind, Arjuna, and indulge in the war to establish righteousness.'

Arjuna was a warrior in the true sense of the term. It was his entire personality that was remarkable. The superior-most person as warrior-force on Earth, as Arjuna truly was, had a very strong mental, physical and spiritual basis in him. A warrior of his design of things, required to possess mental and physical autonomy. Arjuna was known to possess that autonomy in his character. However, the sudden spell of delusions had pushed him down to the conditions of bewilderedness and fall into the grips of depressions of the highest order.

> *Arjuna ubacha:*
> *Katham Vishmam aham samkheyh Dronam cha Madhusudanah.*
> *Ishubhih pratiyotz ashwami pujahi bairi Madhusudana.* (G.2/4)
> Arjuna said, 'It is better to live on alms in this world without slaying these noble elders, because even after killing them, we shall, after all, enjoy only blood-stained pleasures in the form of wealth and sense-enjoyments.'

Arjuna was rebuked by Lord Krishna his having reduced himself to utter smallness in his mind and actions. Arjuna had the knowledge that the divine intent and purpose of being in the world was to protect the good ones in the society by way of annihilating the evildoers on Earth, on one hand and encouraging the people with good attributes to sustain and grow in the context of the world. This basic objective of God was known to the people, in general and those connected with the activities and processes, known as those chosen by God, in particular. Lord Krishna wanted to train Arjuna through the pathways of the actions desired by the logical sequence of things connected with the actions of people. Having received words of noble intent from God, Arjuna could have some kind of reconciliation within and submitted to God.

Gurun ahattwa hi mahanubhavam
Shreyah bhoktum bhaikshyam apiha lokae.
Hattwa artha kaman guruna iha eva
Bhunjiya bhogan rudhirah pradigdhan. (G.2/5)
It's better to live on begging alms than to kill the seniors, respected relations and enjoy a happy life.

Arjuna was behaving in his own context with the sense of possession of his own self, and the authority of actions or behaviour was being driven by the agenda and sense of drive within. He was making decisions about participation in the war as well. The entire span of learning and training for Arjuna was that he had the destined role of waging war for the establishment of righteous principles in the world, that of the rights and privileges of the good people on Earth. Arjuna had the clear idea that the major warriors by the side of the oppressive prince Duryadhona were all his seniors and revered people. Persons like Vishma, Dronacharya were the highest symbolic personalities in case of any involvement by the government in any kind of war or warlike situations. He knew about the promise of Vishma that he would dedicate his life to support the king in all situations. In this commitment, Vishma had never referred to any particular quality of decision or the actions of the world. It was evident thereby that Vishma, Dronacharya would stand firmly by the side of the king. The most unethical person, Duryadhana, though he was the prince, was endowed with all the powers of the king. And that is why Duryadhana, became the king in the real sense of the term. This is why all warriors and soldiers were to stand by the side of King Duryadhana, the evil-doer, to do the war, if required.

At this point, Arjuna had lost the power of discrimination in his mind and consciousness. This shows that Arjuna, at that point, was overwhelmed by the spell of depression in such a manner that it had covered the senses of life.

Na cha etat vidmah katarat gariyoh
yat va jayemah yadih va no jayeyuh.
Yaneva hattwa na jijibisham
esha tae abasthitah pramukhae Dhartarashtrah. (G.2/6)
We do not even know which is preferable for us, to fight or not to fight, nor do we know whether we shall win or whether they will conquer us. These very sons of Dhritarashtra, killing whom we do not even wish to live, stand in these enemy ranks.

This can lead to a point of a depressed and obsessed mind that no longer has the power of understanding what is good and what suits his dimensions of personality.

Arjuna had lost his consciousness. He became unable to choose between the good and the bad. That is why he had expressed that he did not know which was preferable to him. The choice was whether to do the war or surrender to the forces of oppression. He was not in a mood or a position to clearly decide whether it was good for him to fight or to give up his life as an alternative. As a warrior, it is the generally accepted rule that if war for any cause or purpose is declared, it should be taken forward. In the case of the war at Kurukshetra, there is a strong background of experiencing continued onslaught by the ruling clan on the Pandavas. Even more important was the fact that the seniors who were described by Arjuna as respectable people were silent witnesses to the atrocity on the lady, Draupadi, in the presence of all those seniors. By allowing the ruler to continue with the atrocities, they had aligned themselves with the lowest of the low criminals.

Karpanya dosha upahatah swabhavah
Princhchhami twam dharma sam mudah chetah.
Yat shreyah syat tat nischitam bruhi me
Shidhyah tae ahm shadih mam tvam prapanyam. (G.2/7)
With me being very smitten by the vice of faint-heartedness, and my mind puzzled with regard to duty, I beseech you, tell me, what should be my role, which is decidedly good? I am your disciple, pray instruct me, who has taken you in.

Apart from his confusion about whether to indulge in the war or not, Arjuna lost confidence in his own ability to drive the war towards a winning position. Arjuna had on his head the crown of having achieved the position of the best warrior. Arjuna was never afraid of any war with anyone on Earth. More so, he was never a person with any element of cowardice in mind. His own consciousness had lost its power and integrity. That had pushed Arjuna down to a new situation where he became bewildered and had his strength of life lost. He became depressed and stressed mentally. The stress and depression of Arjuna had reached the pinnacle when he had lost not only his mental energy but the physical energy as well in addition. That is why he could not remain even standing on the chariot for war in the field of war. Arjuna had lost hold of his own consciousness. He was a prey to the questions of the masses, in general, to prove the integrity of his character.

Na hi prapashyami mama anupadyat
yat shokam ut shoshanam indriyanam.
Abapyam bhumou asopatnam ridhvam
Rajyam suranam api cha aadhipatyam. (G.2/8)
For even upon obtaining undisputed sovereignty and an affluent kingdom on Earth, and lordship over the gods, I do not see how my mind can drive away the grip that is drying up my senses.

However, at the end of the long series of revealed thoughts of depression, delusions and massive stressful conditions, Arjuna could recall the original purpose of his being in the company of God. His bottom of consciousness had reflected to the arousal of the fragment of consciousness. Arjuna, at this point, had expressed his inability to decide and take a call on the matter. Arjuna was full of depression with an element of life lit in his mind. The intrinsic mind had sensitized Arjuna's surficial mind. That is why Arjuna could find at the corner of his mind the memory of his past and his role in the entire episode of things. This is again a factor that triggered the glimpse of facts that focused on his role as the associate of God in the functions of him as acts of establishing

The righteous principles of life by way of defeating the forces of evil doers and demonic in character.

Arjuna's mind had reflected the fact that he was the companion and friend of God and an instrument in the hand of God to perform the desired role as a companion on Earth. That is why good thought had prevailed over the deluged mind, and thus, Arjuna could find his realistic position in the chain of things. Arjuna, thus, surrendered to God with an urge to accept himself as the disciple of God. Arjuna wanted to know the true perspective and receive guidance from Him as to what his role and functions should be in the war.

Arjuna's condition of mind was thoroughly distressed. He decided not to do something which, according to his empirical understanding, would in any way affect the chord of his relations with the society in general and his revered persons in particular. In this condition of his mind, it revealed to Arjuna that it was his utter ignorance that he did not and could not understand the ultimate truth. His position was somewhat like a person who does not possess any element of realistic intelligence. It is again a situation where a host of rubbish arguments cluster together across the intellect and its behavioural aspects as applied to the causative factors which construe the framework for a new structure of things in the realms of creation in the world.

Sanjay ubacha:
Evam uktva Rishikesham Gurhakeshah parantapah
Na youtsya iti Govindam uktva tushnim babhubah ha. (G.2/9)
Sanjay said, O King, having thus spoken to Sri Krishna, Arjuna again said to him, 'I will not fight and became silent.'

The description of the sequence of events was made by Sanjay, the support person and the driver of the blind king Dhritarashtra. Through this narration, Sanjay was actually narrating the entire episode, including the conversation made by and between Lord Krishna and the devotee warrior Arjuna. After having talked continuously for a long period, and through that narrating the utterly depressed condition of mind. Arjuna narrated not only his own physical and mental conditions but also raised some of the very important social issues. If the entire context is looked at from the aspects of the world and the empirical perspectives of the world, arguments put across by Arjuna are not only pertinent but essential for the social and worldly context. Looked at from the ordinary perspective and rational analysis would establish the fact of importance of those issues for human society, at large.

Tam ubacha Rishikeshah prahasat aniva bharata.
Senayo ubhouh madhyae bishidam antam idam vachah. (G.2/10)
O Dhritarashtra, Sri Krishna, with a smile, told Arjuna the following words, having placed in between the two warring armies.

After hearing all these narrations and arguments from Arjuna, Lord Krishna was surprised and reacted to the incident. Lord decided to suggest and advise Arjuna in a series of different sets of advice. In fact, Arjuna's arguments in the beginning are, in a sense, the representative of the same from the so-called rational world. The world of rationality gives the highest importance to the causative concerns of the world, even ignoring fully or in part the presence of the wrongdoers, or even having the favoured view to coexist with the wrongdoers. It is believed that this way, the veracity of wrong actions by the wrongdoers would be marginalized through this act.

In this phase of depression, Arjuna was not aligned with the righteous people or the principles of righteousness. The concerns for moral and ethical values, which were referred to by Arjuna, were not founded on the principles of justice or the cause of truth. Rather, it was a set of concerns for society, for elders, without the ethical basis in that.

Sri Bhagavan ubacha:
Ashouchan anva shochantam prajnabadam cha bhashase.
Gatasun na gatasumcha na anushochanti panditah. (G.2/11)
Sri Krishna said, Arjuna, you grieve over those who should not be grieved for and yet speak like the wise men. Wise men do not sorrow over the dead or the living.

The climax of the situation had pulled in the context of the war, the intervention of God. Too much of a depressed mind and strong reason to bring the intervention through different sets of lessons.

Lord Krishna had immense love and concern for Arjuna. Arjuna was the chosen devotee-warrior in the design of the Lord. when there is a demanding situation like this, the set of initiatives that Lord undertakes would always be fulfilled. Thus, Krishna began his lesson for Arjuna in a series of well-connected phases, but with a view to bringing the essence of truth to the surface and thus the kind of suggestive reconciling against the facts of lives in the most transforming journey. But the key force of this transformation, becoming stress-stricken, makes the purpose uncertain. Krishna, in his wisdom, thus figured out an ignorant mind. The Lord of life goes into the phases of life, explaining the concepts to Arjuna. Lord had the persons by the way of developing, the inner or the intrinsic focus, the basis of the intent of God, thus made applied.

Lord Krishna reminds Arjuna of the grief that he was engaged in his mind and behaviour for his uncles, grand-uncles, was not right. Arjuna was feeling anxious because of his belief that if the war is allowed to happen, then the society would be into a condition of jeopardy and chaos, resulting in the disruption of the lineage.

> *Na tu eva aham jatu na aasam tvam na ime janadhipah.*
> *Na cha eva na bhabishyamah sarve bayam atahparam.* (G.2/12)
> The fact remains that there was never a time when I was not, or when you or these kings were not. Nor is it a fact that hereafter we shall all cease to be.

Arjuna's idea was clouded by social sentiments. He had expressed that the destruction caused by the great war would tarnish social equilibrium. If he had to kill his master, grandfather and other kith and kin, this would push him to earn a huge store of sins. This is why he had said that even if he earns absolute victory and sovereign control over the world, the sin of killing the respectables and kith and kin would make him bewildered and confused. His life would turn into the life of the traces of hell all through. At this point, the Lord had said to Arjuna that it was the wrong way of understanding the social sentiments placed at the point of choice.

> *Dehinah asmin dehae Koumaram jouvanam jarah.*
> *Tatha dehantarah priptih dhrah tatra na mujhyatae.* (G.2/13)
> Just as boyhood, youth and old age are attributed to the souls through this body, even so it attains another body. The wise man does not get deluded about this.

Arjuna's choice was driven by the spirit and factors of social justice. On the other hand, things that are of a short-term period. In the long run, the concept of eternity, the concept of permanence, has to be kept in consideration. Then the understanding of the permanence of the soul of man would reveal its intrinsic nature: carrying the message of permanence. Lord Krishna tells him that there was never a time when he was not present, nor was there any time when Arjuna was also not there. No place or time was there when the eternal identity of the individuals had a cessation of real existence.

> *Matra sparshah tu kounteyah shitah-ushnah-sukhah-duhkhadah.*
> *Aagamah apainah hi anityam tan titikshanam bharatah.* (G.2/14)
> O son of Kunti, the contacts between the senses and their objects, which give rise to the feelings of heat and cold, pleasure and pain, are transitory and fleeting; therefore, Arjuna endured them.

Lord Krishna mentioned the transition of the appearance in reality of a person through different stages of life, like childhood, through the journey into higher stages of life. Childhood transforms into a youthful, energetic form and then, through the stress and strains of life, into the conditions of later age. Reaching the condition of old age, and person's body degenerates into the grips of diseases, disorders and disruptions of the physical and mental conditions and abilities of the person. The capacity of the body to understand and experience objects of the senses by the sense organs and the power of the mind and intellect go down as natural consequences.

> *Yam hi na byathayantae purusham purusha-rishayah.*
> *Sama sukhah dukhshyam dhiram sah amritayah kalpatae.* (G.2/15)
> Arjuna, the wise man to whom pain and pleasure are alike, and who is tormented by these contacts, becomes eligible for immortality.

Lord Krishna tells Arjuna that things that are perceived through the senses are short-lived and constrained by the influences and impacts of nature, whereas the real identity of a person stands differently. The real identity of the person lies in the eternal spirit and content of the person. this eternal identity stands beyond the impacts of time and space. Whereas everything in life changes over a period of time, the eternal spirit that resides within a person does not get influenced by the factors of nature. Rather, it remains constant and static amidst all changes occurring throughout the span of life of a person.

> *Na esotoh bidyatae bhabho na bhabo bidyatae satah.*
> *Ubhoyah api drishtayah tu anayoh tattwadarshivi.* (G.2/16)
> The unreal has no existence, and the real never ceases to be. The reality of both has thus been perceived by the sages of truth.

When a person develops the position of equipoise, when the spirit within responds to the call of the world but does not get drenched in it, the spirit within starts opening up. The connections between objects of the world and the impacts of that on the person depend on the conditions and approaches of the mind. If the mind is allured to the factors of enjoyments and the qualities of mind, it is said that oriented to the intrinsics, the mind functions as the chord of connections between the objects of the sensory targets and the connections with the factors of eternity and empiricism in the world.

Anything that is apart from God is unreal. Things that are believed to have emerged from God are real. Lord Krishna says that the unreal is transient; it does not have any existence. On the other hand, the real never ceases to exist. The seers of truth, called sages, understand that God is real and remains in existence in its permanence, whatsoever and in every element or creature.

> *Abinashi tu tat biddhi yena sarvam idam tatam.*
> *Vinasham abayasya asya na kah chit karatum arhati.* (G.2/17)

Know that alone to be perishable which pervades this universe, for no one has the power to destroy this indestructible substance.

The unreal turns real when it converses with God. Divine consciousness makes things different. With the divine consciousness in mind, the spirit inside undergoes a huge drift towards the aspirational aspects of the person. Divine consciousness impels a situation where the mind is expected to remain vacant of its usual kind of impurities. Impurities of the mind are those considered enemies to the normal functional approaches of the mind. This makes the point clear that the impacts of anger, lust, greed, selfish desires, aggressive ego, jealousy, envy, covetousness, and the like make it very filthy in its approach. It may be considered a situation when the person needs a rescue from the impacts of these. With these and the like having affected the core of the mind, the person may get support if surrendered to God. This is what had happened with Arjuna. When he understood that the power was lost in a depressive situation, he surrendered to God.

Antah banta ime dehah nityasya uktah sharirinah.
Anashinah apromeyasya tasmat yuddhasva bharata. (G.2/18)
The soul is imperishable while the body is perishable. All these bodies pertaining to the imperishable, indefinable and eternal soul are spoken of as perishable; therefore, Arjuna, you should fight.

Arjuna understood that his mind had got deluged in the bewilderedness of the mind and thus a myopic view had crippled his mind in its approaches to the world. But the most important aspect was that once Arjuna himself understood the same, his course of life and the approaches got tuned towards the divine intent, and thus his initiative to surrender to God was accepted by Lord Krishna in the right spirit. He realized that rescue from this condition was possible only through God. Arjuna offered to God to become His disciple and in the process declared surrender to God. The spirit of righteousness was not adhered to in any way, and thus Arjuna was eager to invite the spirit of God in the utterly disastrous condition of his mind.

Yah enam betti hantaram yah cha enam manyatae hasam.
Ubhou tou na vijanita nayam hanti na hanyatae. (G.2/19)
They are both ignorant who consider the soul to be capable of killing and he who takes it as skill, for barely the soul never kills nor is skilled.

The advice of God came in sequence of things. It was a series of verses, each having contextual reference to the conditions of Arjuna's mind. Arjuna had the mental condition of jeopardy; accordingly, it had the implications of the new situation when the God's grace had a constant show on him.

In the sequence of things, Lord Krishna started narrating about the long-term presence and existence and God. The spirit of eternity was something where a gradual and continuous spell of wisdom had the sphere of eternal truth in the realm of the world. It was the spirit that had contained the supreme truth in the form of wisdom. Wisdom that was the spirit of God at the onset of time and thereby the creation, it was thus the eternal uncovered, so for now, getting open.

> *Na jayatae mriyatae vah kadachit*
> *Na ayam bhuttwah bhabita va na bhuyah*
> *Ajo nityah shashvotoh ayam purano*
> *Na hanyatae hanyamano sharirae* (G.2/20)
> The soul is eternal, omnipresent and omniscient. It is never born nor it ever dies, nor does it come into being on being born, for it is unborn, eternal, everlasting and primaeval. Even though the body is slain, the soul is not.

The search for the real ends when the aspirant realizes the fact that the Lord alone is the truth embodied. Lord Krishna started narrating the position and dynamics that state that the life of a person has two aspects. One is the empirical aspect of life, and the other is the eternal dimension of life. Within the deep core of the person, the spirit of eternity remains in a very small dimension. The dimension talks about a highly condensed form of the spirit. This is the atman within the being. Lord suggests having the invocation of the spirit within. The spirit within thus reveals its true identity to the person's intrinsic dimensions. The spirit emerges from the external factors of life. On the surface, the facts of the spirit get revealed throughout. In a way, the basis of the externality gets into the factors of life in a sequence of things empirical in nature.

Eternal truth is embodied in the truth of the Supreme by nature. He is the embodied presence in all the forms, lives and structures of the world. The Supreme is permanent. He is not only present in the time now; He is the force behind all forces. He is all profound and sovereign. Time starts and culminates with him. He is all profound in all respects. The purpose of His creation is to see that His wish spreads around. The journey in eternity covers the series of acts that arise within the horizon of time. This is because of constantly refreshed approaches to truth. His wish gets reflected in the seeds of noble intentions in the consciousness of humans. The Supreme intends that the human journey transcends human limits.

> *Veda binashinam nityam yah enam ajah abyom.*
> *Katham sa purushah partha kam ghatayanti hanti kam.* (G.2/21)
> One who knows the soul to be indestructible, eternal, free from birth and decay, how can he be killing anyone or makes someone to kill others?

In the process of the aspiration for God realization through whatever method is adopted, the ultimate objective runs as the realization of God in life. The spirit opens up the horizon of the limitless when the aspirant can reach out to the noble self. God's design being the spread of goods and divine attributes to all those who are poised to have the realization of the Supreme in the physical self, consciousness, thus gradually transforming from the human level to the level of divinity.

Revealed to the conscious self that the eternal in his true identity does not get vanquished or extinct, he is void, formless, yet present as the intrinsic self in all being. He is timeless, spaceless, thus eternal. Divine does not allow himself to be limited within the boundaries of real time. Whether present in the present moment or not can be understood only through the realization of the self. He is thus felt or understood by the aspiring conscious mind only in the event of his being graceful.

Basanshi jirnani yatha behayah
Nabani grihnanti narah aparanih.
Tatha sharirani bihaya jirnam
Annayani samyati nabani dehi. (G.2/22)

The embodied soul remains with the body until its end, and at the end of it, takes up a new body suited to its will, the same way a human changes the garments worn out by replacing them with fresh and new ones.

The eternal self resides within each life. It stays inside the hearts of people. This small, dimensionless and invisible entity is not a form of usual understanding. It is but a formless form. Its real nature is in the void. This void carries in it the infinite energy and the spirit that covers life with the content of the eternal self. The eternal self is full of truth. God's truth is that. This is the full truth of the empirical world that covers and follows the laws of cause and effect. Through these implications of the law of cause and effect, the entire world and God's creation have been made to run. God's creation thus operates on the principle of impartiality and impersonality in the world of humans.

Nainam chindanti shastrani nainam dahati pavakah.
Na cha enam kledayantah apo na shoshayati marutah. (G.2/23)

Weapons cannot cut it, nor can fire burn it. Water cannot drench it, nor can air blow it off.

Every individual soul that resides within a human is understood as something subtle. Three forms of existence are construed as the body of a human: the gross body, the subtle body and the causal body. The causal body is the state which gets involved in the actions and transactions of the world in the most subtle way and based on the spirit of the person. The spirit is thus engrossed in the actions of life. Actions in the empirical world are continued through the set of inactions in the world and finally reach the culminating end of the causations. Actions undertaken in life are actually concerned and collected together to have the resultant effect drawn out from them. The self that resides within the human context is *jivatman*, which is also eternal.

> *Acchhedyah ayam adahyajya ayam akieddyah ashoshy eva cha.*
> *Nityah sarvagatah sthanuh achalah ayam sanatanah.* (G.2/24)
> For this soul cannot be cut, nor burnt by fire. It cannot be dissolved by water, nor dried by air. The soul is eternal, omnipresent, immovable, constant and everlasting.

Jivatman carries in it the identity of the Paramatma. The causal body of the person is susceptible to the empirical attributes of life. Three categories of the set of attributes are as such grouped among sattwa, rajas and tamas. Based on the quality of work, the attribute gets imprinted in the character of the person. These attributes are a set of inputs for the character of the person for the period during which the person can adhere to the qualities of life of the person. When jivatman completes the tenure of presence in a life, it carries along the resultant essence of the quality of life lived throughout. In the case of the resultant attribute being the unfulfilled desire, the soul has to come back in life after the span of living is completed. However, the soul that experiences God realization in life is liberated.

However, the soul undertakes the course of journey in life in the form of jivatman again and spends the tenure of a new life. Soul is thus immortal. It has been mentioned by the Lord that as a human person changes the used and torn-out dress, replacing it with a new one, the soul undertakes a journey through the new life. it helps life, even though indifferent, to realize God.

> *Abyaktam ayam achintoh ayam abikaryah ayam uchyatae.*
> *Tasmat devam viditvenah enam na anushochitum arhashi.* (G.2/25)
> The soul is unmanifest, it is incomprehensible, and it is spoken of as immutable. And therefore, knowing this, you should not grieve.

Immortal and formless in essence, the Supreme is eternal and indestructible. No weapon can cut it apart. The fire cannot burn it at all. The supreme self cannot be blown off by air. Nor can it be washed off by the forces of water through its current of flow. The soul is timeless, spaceless. It does not have any identity in form. Yet it has its presence in all the forms and lives in the entire creation. Invisible, unmanifest, constant, yet the soul is present in the cave of the heart. Generally, his presence is as a witness and an accompanying element. He is eternal and immutable. Being present in the cave of the heart, he remains aloof from the thoughts and actions of life in most cases.

> *Atha cha enam nitya jatam nityam va manyase mritam.*
> *Tatha api tvam mahabahu na enam shochitam arhasi.* (G.2/26)
> If you should assume this soul to be subject to perpetual birth and death, even then, you should not grieve like this.

However, when life decides to experience divine realization develops faith in God, cultivates love for God and experiences the realization of God, then the person receives support, inspiration and strength from the intrinsic soul within. Soul does not have a beginning or end. However, when life turns into a devotee and dedicates to God, the gradual incremental or sharp realization of the supreme truth, the condition as such becomes different. Life, in this condition, is on the threshold of moksha – liberation. Moksha is attained by attaining the condition of a dedicated and consecrated devotee. Then occurs the situation of liberation. Jivatman now gives up the essence of truth to paramatma.

> *Jatasya hi dhruva mrityu dhruvam janma mritasya cha.*
> *Tasmat apariharye arthae na tvam shochitum arhasi.* (G.2/27)
> Death is certain for the born, and return is inevitable for the dead. You should not, therefore, grieve over the inevitable.

The soul is not subject to birth or death. Neither does it appear *de novo*, nor does it get extinct. It is permanent, but at the same time, in the identity as the jivatman, it has quite often the eagerness to sensitize life with the sense of eternity and the faith in God. Faith, in realistic terms, is what the soul wants to acquire is the essence in noble terms. Essence of the life lived comes from the core of conscious living. It is thus the assimilation of the resultant effects of the person. The consciousness of human self contains the elements that are sensitive to the creation of a series of emergence. Once lost out of the stream of human life, the soul goes back to its own place.

> *Abyakta adini bhutani byakta madhyani bharata.*
> *Abyakta nidhani eva tatra kaa paridevana.* (G.2/28)
> Arjuna, human beings remain unmanifest before birth, become manifest during life, and return to an unmanifest state at the end of life. Where, then, is the scope for lamentation?

Soul resides in the body and gets connected with the human limits of consciousness. This alone can have a direct impact on the living system. The living system nurtures individual consciousness through the ways in wherein the independence of the mind and senses of the person. Autonomy of mind and senses derived from the divine endowment is supposed to be functioning on the basis of truth and the ideas of cosmic justice, distributive in nature.

> *Aashcharyabata pashyati kashchit anyah va*
> *ashcharyabat badati tatha eva cha anyah.*
> *Ashcharyabat cha enam anyah shrunati*
> *shrutvah api enam vedah nacha eva kashchit.* (G.2/29)

Some people look at the atman with wonder; others explain it with wonder; and still others hear wonders about the atman. However, even by seeing, hearing, or explaining It, these people may not truly realize what It is, because the atman is beyond easy realization.

Consciousness at the human scale does diverse things. It is the way and means to live life in the right way. It is thus the impacts and effects of things originating from the core of a human's own consciousness. Mind driven towards the pathways of selfishness, greed, anger, jealousy, desire, lust, covetousness makes it imperative the anchor in these. Dirt of these gets cleansed to the surface of the soul until these are fully taken in as essence. The essence as such comprises these impurities create the cause of rebirth, pulling jivatman down to life again.

The soul that resides within the abode of a person cannot be known in the ordinary condition of living. However, there are great people who, through their own inspired search for divine consciousness, have been able to realize the real identity of the soul residing within, by God's grace.

Dehi nityam abodhyam ayam dehae sarvasya bharata.
Tasmat sarvami bhutani na tvam shochitam arhasi. (G.2/30)
Arjuna, the soul dwelling in these bodies of all can never be slain; therefore, you should not mourn for anyone.

This soul residing within the existence has the immense power to sustain lives and sustain the world. The soul stays within as a witness. All thoughts and actions of life are under the focus of the soul. All intents and mental formations are within the purview of the soul. The eternal existence breeds eternal truth in the context of the creation. It is thus mentioned that the empirical truth is poised to touch upon the intrinsics of the soul in the flow of life. This is how life in the empirical context asserts its autonomy over the flow.

Svadharmam api cha abekshya na bikam pitum arhasi.
Dharmyat hi yuddhyat shreyat na anyat kshatriyabya
navidyatae. (G.2/31)
Besides considering your own duty too, you should not yield, for there is nothing more welcome for a man of the warrior class than a righteous work.

It is the flow of things in the world, the empirical thoughts and actions accumulate at the level of its own dynamics to take care of the essential elements of life. If life has to progress towards a definite pathway, it needs to fulfil the design of God in the creation. The empirical mind got hold in spirit the mind of Arjuna. It is thus a situation when the divine action needs to be seen as something that overcomes the impact of the worldly mind. In the usual sense of the term, the empirical mind is reflective of the desires of the world. It contains the essence of the desiring mind that is reflected in Arjuna.

Yat shriyaya cha upapanyam svargadwaram apabritam.
Sukhinah kshatriyah Parthah labhantae yuddhavam adrisham. (G.2/32)
Arjuna, lucky are the Kshatriyas who get such an unsolicited opportunity for war, which is an open gateway to heaven.

The uniqueness of the soul residing in life is scarcely understood by a few. Also, in the unique feature of the soul, the supreme power and the energy of the infinite content of God. This could be heard or learnt by many through different means, but the real essence of the soul's knowledge is hardly understood. Only a few truly God aspirants who are dedicated to the cause of God's intent in the creation can have the understanding through the process of realization. This requires a pure mind at the outset, totally disciplined on time, total faith in God, love for God and finally full dedication to the cause of God.

Atha chet tvam imam dharmyam sangramam na karishyashi.
Tatah svadharmam kirtim cha hitva papam abapyasi (G.2/33)
Arjuna, if you refuse to fight this righteous war, then shirking your duty and losing your reputation will surely incur sin for you.

Those who try to realize the essence of the soul in life sometimes try to equate that with worldly energy and resources. While trying to understand the soul through rational, objective ways, one may get its revealed perspective as something that has the nature of worldly objects and elements. However, a person who has developed true faith, who has the real love for God and is sincere in the attempt to have dedication to God, would obviously see that this soul reveals its real identity. This approach is transcendental, and it happens truly in life; the person becomes blessed with the grace of God in this empirical life and activities.

Akirtim cha api bhutani kathaishyanti tae abyayam.
Sambhabitam asya cha akirtira maranyat atih uchhyatae. (G.2/34)
People will also pour undying infamy on you; an infamy brought on a man enjoying popular esteem is worse than death.

It has been observed that the great persons in the world of spirituality who have realized God have understood His essence. But when it comes to narrating the experience to others, they can do that only in parts or fragments. The truth about the soul, in its own reality, is understood only when you get merged in the consciousness of the divine and get immersed in that. The moment you are apart from the divine consciousness, the realization comes down to the fragments of reality. This is why the great seers and even embodied Godly persons, when interacting with people in the world, do so in fragments of truth only. It is also implied that among the billions of people who would honestly take an interest in the matters of the Lord, his realization is based on the degree of love, devotion and dedication of the person to God.

> *Bhayat ranat upataram mamsyantae tvam maharathah.*
> *Ya esham cha tvam bahumatoh bhutva yahasyasi laghvam.* (G.2/35)
> The warrior chiefs who thought highly of you will now despise you, thinking that it was fear which drove you away from battle.

The natural and usual way of functioning in the context of the world is to follow the path of dharma or righteousness. This implies that the person would live life based on the principles of *satyam* and *ritam* – or the ways of eternal truth and ordained functions, conceding to that. Satyam is truth in life based on faith in God and love for God. Ritam is the same in application for the purpose of the intent of God in life. This is what has spread goodness among people on Earth. The span of that in the expense of time in life has that in the design of things.

> *Abachya badan cha bahun badishanti tava ahitvah.*
> *Nindantuh tavah samarthyam tatoh duhkhataram nu kim.* (G.2/36)
> Your enemies, disappearing your mind, they will disparage you, and your mind will speak many unbecoming words. What can be more distressing than this?

The world of actions as such is full of diverse intents for the work. Lord Krishna puts across to Arjuna that in this world of actions, wherever has completed the tenure of journey through the world of work a person understand the true essence of the work when the work is performed based on certain underlying and basic principles. The true properties of the character of a person should be reflected in the life of the doer of the work. The doer has to have the urge to have the intrinsic spirit behind the work to rhythm through the art and act of the work. It is behind that an element of dedication to God, as reflected in the work or a deeper and transcendental approach in the work, would lead to perfection.

> *Hatoh va prapyasi svargam jitva va bhokshyase mahim.*
> *Tasmat uttishthva kounteya yuddayah kritanischayah.* (G.2/37)
> If killed, you will win heaven; if victorious, you will enjoy sovereignty of the art. Therefore, Arjuna, you stand up and be determined to fight.

The amount of confusion that had covered the horizon of Arjuna's mind was embraced by and also captured by the calls of Earth. This call of Earth is to perform things based on the usual normal senses of a human being. However, the senses are usually oriented towards the worldly approaches of selfishness in the flow of actions in life. Whereas the transcending dimension of consciousness is that of the spirit of things which are, in a way, elements of binding forces. Binding to the context of the world in a way is fostered by that identity of mind which has consistently maintained the spirit of goodness in life.

> *Sukhae dukhve same kritva labhalabhou jayajoyou.*
> *Tato yuddvayo yujysva na evam papam abapsya asi.* (G.2/38)
> If you treat victory and defeat alike, gain and loss, pleasure and pain, get ready for the battle. Fighting thus, you will not incur sin at all.

Mind remains the basis of the elevation and transcendence of consciousness in life. If the mind is made to get drenched in the flow of the spirit of God, the divinely energized elemental goodness flows deep inside the factors of life. Lord Krishna has advised Arjuna to try to rise above the levels of the desire-driven factors of life. These are the factors that require a series of flow in the life of the person turned a devotee. The mind that orients fully to God and that which gradually becomes pure at its base is competent to have the realization.

> *Esha teha abhihita samkhyae buddhih yogae tu imam shrunu.*
> *Buddheya yuktoh yaha Partha Karmabandham prahasya asi.* (G.2/39)
> Arjuna, so far, I have shared with you the theory of self and righteous ways of living; now I am going to tell you the yoga of action, which will liberate you from all bondages.

The righteous way of work to serve the Divine purpose in life and the world is to have the mind free from negative emotions, such as anger, jealousy, greed, covetousness, falsehood, hatred, etc. The negative emotions are the killers of good spirit in life. The spirit is thus the creator and preserver of the element of truth and goodness in life. Realization of God happens in the mind that is full of the spirit of God is truly free from the impurities of the mind. Ahead of time is always drenched in the factors of life in the right spirit of the thing in the span of life. Life, when it is oriented to the realization of God, becomes very dear to him and the person becomes a winner in life through excellence and perfection.

3 Eternal Truth in Realized Action

Eternal truth is that which represents divine consciousness. God in life reveals the essence of eternal truth. It is the spirit of divinity which makes the realization of the eternal truth in life. Truth in the world is empirical in nature and by its character and total reflection, it can be construed as the truth in fragments over the designated periods of living on Earth. Truth, thus, makes it vibrant to be into the activities of life through its realization. It is that spirit of God, if drenched in life, the total outlook of life transforms. With most of the quest for the realization, an aspirant gets the trance of it in the process of acquiring the realization as well. The doctrine of formation and assimilation was actually missed by Arjuna in the context of the war of the Mahabharata.

Yat ichhayaya cha upapanyam svargadwaram apabritam.
Sukhinah kshatriyah Parthah labhantae yuddhavam adrisham. (G.2/32)
Arjuna, lucky are the Kshatriyas who get such an unsolicited opportunity for war, which is an open gateway to heaven.

Throughout the period of his making and becoming, Arjuna was fortunate to have divine company. Though not really aware of it, Arjuna had the perception of God having been with him in the form of his friend, but a constant source of inspiration and the indicator of right approaches to life. Arjuna's valour, courage, and strength of mind were so special that his name was considered with a lot of esteem. Arjuna had some idea of the spirit of goodness, which he had the opportunity to acquire from his mother, Kunti, and the values built in the lineage he belonged to. The environment of his upbringing was kingly but fully driven by the heritage of values of goodness. That is the reason why Arjuna had developed a strong character. The strength of his mind and that of his character were revealed many times.

Atha chet tvam imam dharmyam sangramam na karishyashi.
Tatah svadharmam kirtim cha hitva papam abapyasi (G.2/33)
Arjuna, if you refuse to fight this righteous war, then shirking your duty and losing your reputation will incur surely sin for you.

At the end of twelve years of forest living and one year of hiding, Arjuna had the opportunity to prove the strength of his mind, valour and power as the best and the most powerful warrior. At the end of the period of hiding, the place of hiding was somehow revealed to King Duryadhana. This was under the kingdom of Virat. At that time, the king's position was taken care of by the son in the absence of his father. Considering this as their opportunity, the savage king Duryadhana came with all his powerful warriors and attacked the kingdom of Virat to capture the Pandavas.

> *Akirtim cha api bhutani kathaishyanti tae abyayam.*
> *Sambhabitam asya cha akirtira maranyat atih uchhyatae.* (G.2/34)
> People will also pour undying infamy on you, an infamy brought on a man enjoying popular esteem is worse than death.

The initial stipulation, as accepted by the Pandavas, was that after twelve years of forest living and an additional year of hiding, if, in any way, they were traced down, they would have to take up another period of forest living for another span of twelve years. Thus, at the point in time when the Virat Kingdom was attacked by the forces of the savage king Duryadhana, it was very important for Arjuna to protect the Kingdom. It was on the last day of the hiding period of one year. Also, the time of attack was sunset. According to the almanac of Vedic heritage, which was very prevalent at the time, when the sun starts setting down, it marks the end of the working span of the day. It was then twilight.

> *Bhayat ranat upataram mamsyantae tvam maharathah.*
> *Ya esham cha tvam bahumatoh bhutva yahasyasi laghvam.* (G.2/35)
> The warrior chiefs who thought highly of you will now despise you, thinking that it was fear which drove you away from battle.

Son of King Virat, who was out there to face the enemy with his army, took Arjuna as his chariot-driver. Arjuna, in hiding, was performing the role of an art teacher, mainly teaching and training the king's daughter with rhythms and dancing. But he was taken along by the son of Virat to drive the chariot, assuming some help and courage from him on the battlefield. In the war field, a dramatic incident happened with the son of Virat becoming squarely scared and unable to stand up before the host of famous warriors of the attackers. This had pushed Arjuna to take over. This is an incident when Arjuna had struck a single but comprehensive firepower that had fainted everyone in the army of the attackers led by the savage king Duryadhana. This incident clearly proved the ability and power of Arjuna as superior to the collective power of the enemy.

When the situation of war arises, the conflicting parties' use of unbecoming words becomes rampant. Infamy and public spreading of unfair words create a lot of stress, confusion and sorrow in life. Words of reproach and denunciation uttered in any context of conflict create disruptions in mental poise. If the delusion of Arjuna continues leading to the abandonment of the initiatives to the war, he is likely to receive immense filthy words from the other side of the war. The withdrawal of Arjuna from the war would have led to such a context.

> *Abachya badan cha bahun badishanti tava ahitvah.*
> *Nindantuh tavah samarthyam tatoh duhkhataram nu kim.* (G.2/36)
> Your enemies will speak many unbecoming words, disparaging you and unsettling your mind. What could be more distressing than that?

While imparting the lesson of eternal truth to Arjuna, the Lord mentioned that the eternal truth is transcendent in nature, but it remains with the existence in its perpetuity. The soul that resides within the human body is permanent and eternal in nature. This soul cannot be destroyed. It cannot be slain in any situation. The soul may appear diverse in the situations of diversity in the world. Whereas humans are different based on the differences in the making and growing of people in the world. This makes the sources of differences in creating differential identities in the world based on the set of attributes drawn and developed primarily from the tenets of inheritance and the impacts of the surroundings in the world. However, the intrinsic quality of the soul remains the same and constant throughout all situations of the present time.

> *Hatoh va prapyasi svargam jitva va bhokshyase mahim.*
> *Tasmat uttishthva kounteya yuddayah kritanischayah.* (G.2/37)
> If killed, you will win heaven; if victorious, you will enjoy sovereignty of the art. Therefore, Arjuna, you stand up and be determined to fight.

The soul remains constant in its approach, pattern and core attributes. Whereas the approach, pattern and core attributes contribute to the making of the physical and in most cases the mental horizon of the person, the spirit and strength in the form of the eternal self, the soul, remain the same in all situations. The situation thus resembles a context where the factors-external keep on changing in the midst of the changing time frame. The soul not only remains constant and the same always, but remains constant with the same potency in all lives all over. Thus, the lives all over may prove diverse on almost all visible and external parameters.

> *Sukhae dukhve same kritva labhalabhou jayajoyou.*
> *Tato yuddvayo yujysva na evam papam abapsya asi.* (G.2/38)
> If you treat alike victory and defeat, gain and loss, pleasure and pain, get ready for the battle. Fighting thus, you will not incur sin at all.

The parameters which are visible, tangible and may appear to be widely different may be found out and experienced as unique to each life. Though the soul is thoroughly magnificent in its approach, it remains workable in its own unique way. The approaches of dharma and karma that an individual may find out would approach the ultimate content of the personality, its behaviour and character. Though the soul remains apart from the spell of lives and activities, the impacts of lives and activities would be felt in the context of the overall functioning of the world. The world of incidents, world of events, thus, impacts the intrinsics of the person.

> *Esha teha abhihita samkhyae buddhih yogae tu imam shrunu.*
> *Buddheya yuktoh yaha Partha Karmabandham prahasya asi.* (G.2/39)
> Arjuna, so far, I have shared with you the theory of self and righteous ways of living; now I am going to tell you the yoga of action, which will liberate you from all bondages.

Even though the soul is eternal, it is immutable – unchanging in all situations, it clings to the effects of the work and total actions having taken up and pushed across in life. The work, habit and character of a person provide an essential element through each of the actions at each phase, and thus it will offer a set of imprints to be associated with the soul in a quasi-permanent and semi-constant approach of the continuations and the flow of time. The flow of time on an eternal scale would thus make the journey in life unique in its approach, and thus also in its different phases. In this phasing of life's activities, the imprints of the essence and eternity get absorbed. This impacts the thoughts and actions of the person. The soul turns into jivatman – the soul positioned in the flow of an empirical life. jivatman is not separated from the paramatma or the supreme soul. Both are the same in the intrinsics, in the potentials and the qualities in essential terms. However, as the jivatman, the soul accepts the essence of the impacts from the life lived by the person. The impact comes in the shape of an impersonal, non-attributive entity, invisible and untraceable, still having the power to impact the life now, or in a way for the new life after the present one fulfils its terms and objectives. Thus, the essential summative and atomic essence is brought to transfer to the next life as the *samskar* – the intrinsics of life.

The germination of the next life begins with choosing the biological stream that adheres to the tendencies of the life and self. Tendencies that match with the residual desire stored in the jivatman turn into the same identity of jivatman in the new context. Jivatman that had a breeding in the context of the new world order would thus take up a course of growth into the aspects of the new realities available with the new set of people who would carry the mantle in the company of the rest.

> *Na iha abhikrama nasha asti pratyabayo na bidyatae*
> *Svalpam api asya dharmasya trayatae mahatoh bhayat.* (G.2/40)
> In this path of nishkama karma, disinterested action, therefore no loss of effort, nor is there fear of contrary results. Even a battle practice of this discipline saves one from the terrible fear of birth and death.

In the new context, the jivatman, thus picks up the tendencies, characters and dominant attributes. Thus, the new life begins with new types of things, sometimes being much advanced in goodness, orientation to the good spirit in life of life has been worked out with a basis that is based on acquired inputs of the knowledge of life. Thus, the essence of the acquired goodness and the summative impact of the good thoughts and good work done in the previous span of life impact the new spell in the new phase of life. It is thus the carried forward attributes of life that are slowly but effectively giving gradual shape to the new life. The new life is, thus, a sum total of the inputs that are carried down to the new life and the combination of impacts of the effects from around and that of the seeds of the new set of its life and the influence of the relevant part of the world. Samskar does not dictate terms but creates slow and incremental impacts in life.

Vyabasayitimka buddhih eka iha Kurunandana
Bahu sakha hi anantah cha buddhi avyabasayinam. (G.2/41)
Arjuna, nishkama karma or desireless action, the intellect is determinate and directed singly towards one ideal, whereas the intellect of the undecided, ignorant men, moved by desires, wanders in all directions after innumerable aims.

As is usual in human nature, the mind usually remains confused and disintegrated. Conditions of mind usually vary with the conditions spelt out, conditions prevailing around. Mind tuned to the situations prevailing around and everywhere, the conditions of the mind become somewhat tuned to the externalities. Externalities that impact the mind may make life on Earth diffused and scattered. A diffused mind is considered to be the mind that gets upset with situations of unacceptability. Thus, it breeds in the spells of sorrow. It may beget the spell of happiness and delight. This may bring question marks to life itself. It is thus inherent in the basic propensity of life carried down to a forward period.

Yam imam pushpitam vacham prabadantim bipaschitam.
Vedah vada ratah Partha na anyad asti itivadinah. (G.2/42)
Arjuna, those who are attracted to the worldly desires and guided by the superficial ideas of the Vedas and consider heavenly place as the supreme goal of life are unwise.

However, if that moment can be achieved with the basic understanding of those situations, it may become equipoised. An equipoised mind is one that responds to the situations leading to happiness and sorrow with the same conditions of response of the mind. Equipoise is attained when the ignorance of the mind is removed; the dualities and multiplicities of the mind arise because of the ignorance that persists in the person. Ignorance is the lack of understanding and realization of God. Through the true realization of the intrinsic truth of the soul, it happens that the ultimate nature of supreme truth is the matter to be realized at the poise of the mind.

Kamah atmanoh svarga parah janma-karma-phalo pradam.
Kriya bisheshah bahulam bhoga-acishvarya gatim prati. (G.2/43)
The utterly cloudy space, recommending many rituals of various kinds for the attainment of pleasure and power, with the revert as their fruit.

Consciousness of the individual self connects with that of the universal consciousness through the process of realization. Realization requires a condition of the mind when, in the state of poise of the mind, consciousness of the individual flashes to the point of attainment of the light from the realm of eternity. The light of eternity attempts to remove ignorance from the mind and consciousness of the person. It is the reciprocity of consciousness that would reveal the fact of the wholesome truth. The reality of situations was spelt out by God as revealed by him.

Bhog aeisvaryah prasaktanam taya apahrita chetasam.
Vyabasayitimka buddhih samadhou na bidhiyatae. (G.2/44)
Those whose minds are carried away by such words and who are deeply attached to pleasure and worldly power cannot attain the determinate intellect concentrated on God.

Jivatman is the embodied soul that differentiates between the good and the bad and through that at the level of human soul the imprints of the works of the life touches the jivatman, even when the fruits of the work get clinched to the virtuous aura of the jivatman, it shrugs off the effects and induces the life to orient itself to the works of the world and the demands of divinity in life. A deep-rooted understanding would induce the words of God in a spell. This would ultimately lead to the aspiring minds attaining realization of the supreme truth.

The attitude of a person towards her/his life and work creates a unique set of things for the person. It is the mental orientation that determines the course of action in a particular situation. A person's transformation occurs through the attitude and orientation to the same. The usual human approach is to reckon with the selfish orientation of life. However, once the selfish orientation changes, things change.

Traigunya bishayah veda nihtrigunyoh bhaba Arjunah.
Nih dandoh nitya sattwastha nih yoga kshemah aatmavanah. (G.2/45)
Arjuna, the Vedas thus deal with the evolutes of the three *guna*s, modes of the attributes, namely the worldly enjoyable, the means of attaining such enjoyments. Be thou indifferent to these enjoyments and their means, rising above pairs of opposites like pleasure and pain, and so on, established in the eternal existence of God, absolutely unconcerned

about the fulfillment of wants and the preservation of what has been already attained and self-controlled.

Transformations occur through the changes in the orientation and its approach, not only for a short while but for things in perpetuity. When the divinely set of qualities set in the core of a person if the person reckons to certain values of goodness like, honesty, truthfulness, integrity, cooperation, compassion, caring, sacrifice, selfishness and the like, are imprinted in the intrinsic aspect of the personality, are considered as the personalities with divinely attributes of the eternal choice. It is thus the set of divine attributes that gives shape to the making of a personality for the creation of a new set of things for the human society. The new set of attributes would make new types of personalities.

Yaban arthah udpanae sarbatoh sampluto udakae.
Taban sarveshu vedeshu brahmanasya bijanatah.   (G.2/46)
Just as small water bodies are deluged by the vast floodwaters, so too does a person who has realized the essence of the Vedas experience the bliss of Supreme Consciousness, having transcended the realm of the results and effects of action.

A transcendent mind elevates the person from having engrossed by the material factors of life to the state of eternal freedom. Faith in the spirit of God makes the person oriented to the godly attributes. If the person nurtures in life the seeking of God's grace, then the imprints of godly qualities get tagged to the lives of people. Thus, getting tagged to the context of the divine devotion and that of the fundamentals of the situations leading to the development of devotions within. Thus, the devotions conceived in the mind of a person get mixed in the consciousness of the person in that situation.

Karmanyae vah adhikara astae ma phaleshu kadachanah.
Ma karma phal heturbhu ma tae samgatoh karmani.   (G.2/47)
Your right is to work only, but never to the fruit; therefore, you do not be the party to beget the fruits of the action, do not hanker after the fruits of action, nor let your attachment be to inaction.

With the incremental induction of a certain set of divine qualities in the life of a person, the attitude towards the works in the world thus undergoes gradual change, leading to the factors of transformations in the acts of persons. The factors of work thus make a unique present with a new set of attributes. If that new set of attributes works for life, apart from transforming the qualities of life, it helps in transformations.

Yogasthah kuru karmani samgam tyaktah Dhananjaya.
Sidhho asiddhou samo bhutva samatvam yoga uchhyatae.   (G.2/48)

Arjuna, perform your duties established in yoga, renouncing attachment and being even-minded in success and failure; the evenness of mind is called yoga.

In the context of the war of Kurukshetra, Lord Krishna thereby advises Arjuna to be oriented to those godly qualities always. Thus, in his design of things, Arjuna should view the war as his action induced by the divine spirit and righteous assertion. The righteous assertion thus would induce Arjuna to be duty-bound to do the work with a selfless approach and thereby devote the entire conscious attention towards making the entire energy, creative faculty, and strength of the brain so that the outpouring of work happens without any selfishness.

Durenah hi abaram karma buddhiyogat Dhananjayah.
Buddhou sharanam ichh kripanah phaloh hietavah. (G.2/49)
Action with a selfish motive is far inferior to this yoga in the form of equanimity, you do speak refuse in this equipoise of mind, Arjuna, for poor and wretched are those who are instrumental in making the actions bear fruit.

Work is done with the spirit of doing duty and oriented to the service. The spirit of work is thus selfless dedication to the cause of God. Arjuna understood that the work he is destined to do is not just doing a war successfully, but helping God in his design of things on Earth. God's intent is to fulfil the objective of the divine on Earth. Whenever the living society is pushed to a situation such that the noble and good ones in the world get oppressed by the demonic forces on Earth, whenever the principles of righteousness are pushed down by the wrong doers, whenever the lives and activities of the good and noble ones are at stake, the Supreme descends on Earth, in human abode, to rescue the good ones and to establish righteousness in the world.

Intellect with a positive inclination and intent tends to make the transformation of the life and activities of the person. Thus, the person looks into the set of works from the perspective of the divine intent. Whenever the person considers the work as an action of essential devotion and dedication to God, goodness prevails.

Buddhi yuktoh jahatih iha ubhae sukritae dushkritae.
Tasmat yogayo yujyasva yagoh karmashu koushalam. (G.2/50)
Desireless action, endowed with equanimity, one sheds in the battle both good and evil; therefore, strive for the practice of this yoga of equanimity. Skill in action lies in the practice of this yoga.

With goodness as the mental orientation, the facts of life now undergo a dramatic response; the course of actions would turn into a set of duties performed for the service of God on Earth. Work with a good intent, which is again dedication to God, breeds good values, and at the same time, the character of the doer transforms into the character of the godly set of qualities. The world then becomes the place for equality, fraternity, connections, and homogeneity. Thus, there is an initiative to allow the people to unfold.

Karmajam buddhi yuktah hi phalam tyaktva manishinah.
Janma bandhah binih muktah padam gachhanti anamayam. (G.2/51)
Wise men possessing an equipoised mind, renouncing the fruit of action and freed from the shackles of birth again, the blissful supreme state.

The results of actions become obviously of the order of special perfection in the context of the changing scenario of the world. The doer now does the work to perfection, having shrugged off personal interest from either the context of work, the flow of the work and finally the realm of the work. Thus, the work of the world no longer remains the work of the person. Selfless work is termed as nishkama karma. It is on the selfless premise of the work that the fruits of the work get transmitted to the entire world. The sages of the Vedas have urged the human being to cling to the devotion of God and unify with the fact of life and activities of the person in society.

Yadah tae moha kalilam buddhi byati tarishyati.
Tada gantasi nih vedam shrotabasya shrutasya cha. (G.2/52)
When your mind is fully engrossed in the spell of delusion, you will then grow indifferent to the enjoyments of this world and the next that have been heard of, as well as to those that are yet to be heard of.

In the context of the world and its empirical activities, it is very difficult to do nishkama karma. Each work has its own objective to fulfil. While trying to fulfil the objectives, the doer either gets or achieves a target for accomplishing the work. Now, while the doer proceeds with doing the work, the agenda must be centred on the targets aligned with the objectives. If the work has to be accomplished, then just fulfilling the objective would make that happen. However, a doer who has the core orientation in mind to perform with perfection has to make a difference in this. Perfection in orientation transforms the view.

Shruti bipratipanna tae yadah sthasyati nishchalah.
Samadhou eva achala buddhi tada yogam abapsyasi. (G.2/53)
When your intellect, confused by hearing conflicting statements, will rest steady and undistracted in meditation on God, you will then attend yoga that is everlasting union with God.

The doer now does not depend upon any of the external parameters. Rather she or he does the work to fulfil the objective of the work with elements of perfection. This element of perfection cannot allow the fulfillment of selfish desires; rather can do the work for meeting the objectives. When the work as such is done to the fulfillment of the objective and goes without any selfish intent, the person is said to be in the nishkama karma. This is driven by the honest intent of the person to do the work, with utmost perfection, but without personal motive.

> *Arjuna ubacha*:
> *Sthita prajnassya ka bhasha somadhih tasya keshabah.*
> *Sthitadhih kim prabhasheta kim asitah brajact kim.* (G.2/54)
> Arjuna said, 'Krishna, what are the characteristics of a God-realized soul, stable of mind and established in samadhi or perfect tranquillity of mind? How does the man of a stable mind speak? How does he sit? How does he walk?' Lord said, 'Arjuna, when one thoroughly casts all cravings of the mind and is satisfied in the self through the joy of the self, then he is called stable of mind.'

Arjuna wanted to understand what the stable mind stands for. The stable mind is known as the soul and symbol of a particular condition of the mind and the soul. The mind can attain the condition of stability and become uniquely positioned only when the mind is allowed to focus on a particular point or a particular thought. Lord has already mentioned that when the mind rises above the phases of delusions and illusions of the world, understanding of a superior principle in life would reposition life into the context where the world converges into a point of illumination to shower light into life.

With the teaching of godly attributes so far, Lord Krishna wanted purity of mind and dedicated karma from Arjuna. Also, he had mentioned the equipoised mind, which is single-pointed and follows the impacts from God based on the context.

> *Sri Bhagavana ubacha*:
> *Prajahati yada kaman sarvan Partho monogatan.*
> *Atmani vah atmana tushthah sthataprajna lat ucchyatae.* (G.2/55)
> The Lord spoke:
> The person who is indifferent to worldly gains and is always satisfied with the condition of life as a gift of God and doesn't have any desire, greed or negative emotions in mind is a person of wisdom.

Lord Krishna responds to the point raised by Arjuna by saying that the fundamental issue is desire. When the mind and intrinsics of the person get completely free from the spells and tenets of desire, it attains the condition of equipoise of mind. In the state of equipoise, the mind behaves and performs in a way that single-pointedness is attained through the consecration to godly values in a situation of flowing of worldly materialism to dominate. The patterns thus emerged may have been useful to minds.

Duhkheshu na udbighna manah sukheshu bigatasprihah.
Bita raga bhaya krodhan sthitadhi munih uchyatae. (G.2/56)
He, whose mind remains unperturbed among the sorrows and whose thirst for pleasures has altogether disappeared, and he who is free from the passion, fear and anger, is called a sage of a stable mind.

The factors of mind, their management in the context of the work and profession, while the doer performs the action in the field and context of the world, the person should have developed mental equilibrium in all situations. The person should be free from anger, free from fear, free from delusions. Mind thus remembers the carry forward impression of this world in general, and in particular contexts it has to operate from. The general pattern of life is thus important to conceptualize in the true context of life on Earth. The Earth system restricts its response to the extent of being neutral in life.

Yah sarvatra na avisneha tat tat prapya subha–ashubhyam.
Na avinandanti na dveshti tasya prajna pratisthita. (G.2/57)
The person who is equal and the same in pleasurable things and doesn't allow the mind to get swayed by temporary pleasure and is free from all delusions is established in wisdom.

The condition of equipoise is not an easy state to attain. It requires the bent of mind and the approaches of the character wherein the person understands the basic fallacy behind the happiness and sorrow in life. The usual human response is to be thoroughly perturbed by the impacts of sorrow and maintain the view in life that sorrow and happiness have alternate spells of play in human life; also, that the spell of sorrow in life cannot be for an infinite period; it comes to life also goes off from life. Sorrow has an impact on the body and mind. It may touch the jivatman also. Whenever the body-mind-soul are under the spell of sorrow, it not only creates a situation where even a creative mind may turn non-productive. It gives immense strength to the person once that spell is over.

Yada sam harantae cha yiyam kurumah angani eva sarvashyah.
Indryani indriya arthebhyah tasya prajna pratishthita. (G.2/58)
When, like a tortoise which draws in its limbs from all directions, he withdraws all his senses from the sense objects, his mind is considered to be a stable mind.

Each functional organ of life has its unique way to correspond with the next. Whenever a functional organ becomes spellbound by the spirit of the sorrow or its course, the effectiveness and efficiency of that organ drop, and thus it attains the height of fulfillment once the spell of sorrow is gone. The same response occurs with the impacts of happiness. Happiness may create a deluge by getting swayed. When happiness grips a person, there is a tendency to believe that the happiness continues and does not end. The churning of things at the time of happiness is what a person is usually involved in. In this process of churning things, it appears that it may not last long.

> *Bishaya binibartantae niraharasya dehinah.*
> *Rasabarjam rasah api asya param drishtva nibartatae.* (G.2/59)
> Sense objects turn away from him who does not enjoy them with his senses, but the taste for them persists. This relish also disappears in the case of a man of a stable mind when he realizes the Divine Supreme.

Happiness is a sense of continued satisfaction with somewhat fulfillment or, in some cases, achievements in life. An element of fulfillment or an achievement begets in the person a sense of sweetness inside, which may sometimes appear as the nectar of life. The usual contexts of ups and downs are forgotten by the person. Even the person may develop a feeling of getting drenched in the phase of life with the fluid of nectar and thinks this phase to be of a certain permanent variety and remains continued for a fairly long period of time. Thus, whether it is the spell of happiness or sorrow, it has to continue for a period expected to be longer than the impact of usual emotions in life.

Happiness or sorrow are the results of the sensual satisfaction or on the other hand dissatisfactions wherein a person may attempt to have the sensual satisfaction fully for a particular period and thereby attains a kind of fulfillment which is powerful enough to deluge the mind with the variety of ingredients, each of which would turn into a task-oriented objective, and thus, the objective gets either denied or fulfilled. In either of these cases, the most important would be assigned to the spirit of things and not the detailed material facts leading to that. However, in the process, a person's mind may create an imprint of the powers to enjoy the gift.

> *Yatoh hi api Kaunteya purushasya bipaschitah.*
> *Indriyani pramathini haranti prasabham manah.* (G.2/60)
> Turbulent by nature, the senses, even of a wise man, who is practising self-control, forcibly carry away his mind, O Arjuna!

In the extreme conditions of the repulsions to the world, when a person may go for fasting by choice or by compulsions, it may so happen that the good senses that are normally likely to function over minds, may go deep inside the factors of life and thereby make the factors of living vibrant. At times, sensual enjoyments or the tendencies to have that get spoiled by the impacts of the results of too much enjoyment. The person may end up in a situation of incapability. This could be physical, mental or any other way. Inability creates the constraint for certain kinds of joy-making, wherein many of the factors of joy-making depend upon the physical-biological and mental domain of the person. If someone, under certain perceptions, give up the activities of the world including the actions that are only personal, the cluster of senses in the person, get a kind of support so that its domains are of quite strong and thereby can absorb much of the heat that the world contains that of the spirit of the forces of the empirical life. A person would catch up with a true positive motivation. The master of the situation is the conscience of the person that may transform.

> *Tani sarvani samyamya yukta aasitah matparah.*
> *Bashae hi yasyae indriyani tasya prajna pratishthita.* (G.2/61)
> Having controlled all the senses and concentrating the mind, one should sit for meditation, devoting herself or himself totally with full heart and soul to the Divine. For he whose senses are under his control is known to have a sthita prajna, or the stable mind.

The process of transformation in this case starts with the process of attaining realization of God. In this way, the quintessence of the realization of truth starts. In the realm of the mental energy and vital energy of the person as present within may get the impetus for revealing the spirit and accomplishment in the field space of the world it is involved in the creed. Thus, a gradual process of getting out of the impediments is just in a way. Inability-driven abandonment of sensual enjoyments is not the real giving up of the path of enjoyments. Most people would experience the somewhat negative impact of the general symptom and the possibility of creating balance.

> *Dhyatoh bishyan pumsam sangatae eshu upa jayatae.*
> *Sangyat Sanjayatae kamah kamat krodhat abhijayatae.* (G.2/62)
> The man who dwells on sense objects develops attachments for them. From attachments develop desires, and from desires, which in most of the cases remain unfulfilled, develops anger, which causes harm to everyone.

Whenever the expressions of the general mind take a consolidated shape, it appears that the forces of desire for material and things of the world are higher than any other driving force. The markets across the world are made to be vibrant based on the transactions in the market. Products and services all pass through the process of transactions between products and value or services and value. The common parameter, value construed in financial terms, does occur and adds to the forces of markets in its own unique way.

It is the basic need or desire that takes the shape of the demand function in the market. With the changes of the parameters of demand, the pattern of demand and supply aligns. Work done, in this context, is full of demand and supply-side alignment. Work done in this context is full of demand driven by selfish desire. Desire-driven demand, thus identified, contributes to the motive of the person in the macro scenario. In the macro scenario, thus, the issue is to choose the selfless way of accomplishing the work in the moral conditions.

Attachments to the material objects and functions of the world beget a deluged condition of the doer. This world paves the way for a new option of perfection. Works done this way contribute to beget the good response back for the source as spelt out. In this way, it would create wealth of happiness when the performer is at the optimum level of performance. It is thus the condition of mind, equipoise of consciousness, that becomes one of the most important aspects of the work. A calm and cool mind that is thoroughly settled makes a difference.

> *Krodhat bhabati sam mohah sammohat smriti bibhramah.*
> *Smriti bhranshad buddhinasho buddhinashat pranashyati.* (G.2/63)
> Anger begets delusion. A deluged mind loses its memory, with this loss of memory, the intellect is lost, loss of intellect leads to the destruction of the person.

The person who is driven by the sensual instincts and looks for the pleasure in life through the ways of possessive enjoyments the person shall remain confined to the limits and barriers of the short term. The character goes through a process of gradual contamination. Thereby, the long-term objective gets a shock of being confined within. Sensual attractions, thus, create a hope which comes true in the process. However, once the awareness is created, the factors of progress in life can be clinched into the effective making of a valid and rightful career.

The usual worldly pattern of life usually gets trapped by certain factors and emotions of human scale that are prone to anger, and some other factors of the mind that colour lives with the impacts of these. These are some of the known areas of influence which are powerful enough to bend the mind from the pathways of fairness. Fairness of the mind is ensured once the pattern is examined carefully and the factors of fairness are brought into it. Greed, lust, envy, jealousy, desire and strong selfishness grip the minds to take possession of life in its unique context. Thus, the factors of fairness would have to struggle to regain their position in the profile of the personality. It is thus important to understand that anyone who resorts to these negative emotions in life does, partially, cause harm to their own potential in life. Also, these are the emotions which cause harm to the balance of the social fabric.

> *Raga dvesha biyukteshu astu bishaya indriyai nischaran.*
> *Atma bashyacih bhi bidheyah atmah prasadam adhigachhati.* (G.2/64)
> The self-controlled person who is on the path of God is called a *sadhaka*. A sadhaka is self-controlled while enjoying the various sense objects through his or her senses, which are disciplined and free from the choices, tastes and preferences of the ego; the person attains the blessings of the Divine and the condition of complete tranquility and poise of the mind.

Anger is a typical case that, when stored in one's mind, gradually leads to the end of the epitome of human progress. Human progress in the right direction and the right ways need a condition of the mind that is strong enough to behave unperturbed by the events and incidents of the society, thus being able to get back to the call of the situation to augment through the counteractive impacts that are prone to be the add on factors for life in the continued context. It is thus important to understand the impacts of anger in the lives of individual human lives. Lord Krishna suggests that Arjuna ought to be careful about anger and not be prone to it. As he says, anger breeds the conditions of delusions in life, against the backdrop of the stored anger.

Prasadae sarvadukhanan hanih asya upajayatae.
Prasnna chetosho hi aashu buddhih parya batishthatae. (G.2/65)
With the attainment of such complete tranquility of mind, the person is away from sorrows and the infliction of sorrows. The intellect of such a person arises out of the tranquility of mind, and she or he soon withdraws from all sights and becomes firmly established in God while fully involved in the work of the world.

Delusions that arise out of anger, continued in life, help in the making of a situation of loss of memories. Memory plays an important role in the empirical aspects of life. With memories lost, the person loses the strength of intellect. Intellect thus gets grossly affected. It is said that with the loss of memory, a person loses everything.

Nasti buddhih yuktasya na cha yuktasya bhabana.
Na cha abhabayatah shantih ashantasya kutah sukham. (G.2/66)
The person who has not controlled his mind and senses can have no determinate intellect nor contemplation. In the absence of contemplation, he can have a condition of turbulence and lack of peace of mind and therefore, happiness in realistic terms does not occur to the person. The person loses peace of mind.

The situation, when intellect is totally lost, pushes the person to a condition of loss of life. It's like, everything is lost because a single factor of anger proves to be the all-profound killer of resources contained in a personality. It may even push the person to the end of life and create examples for society.

The proper management of anger and related destructive emotions can be formulated as follows:

a) Whenever you experience anger generating within, apply your conscious choice of will force to get aligned with the strength of consciousness within.
b) Never act in haste.
c) Calm down in mind.

e) Do introspect.
f) Review, reaccess, reconstruct, reorient and reengineer in mind.

> *Indriyanam hi charatam yat manoh anubidhiyatae.*
> *Tat asya harati prajnam bayuh ambhosi nabam iba.* (G. 2/67)
> The organs of the individuals of any kind are like a boat on water, which is carried out by the strong blows of air and therefore senses moving among sense objects, the one which the mind is attached to takes away his discrimination.

Rational analysis of the cause of anger would reveal that, in most of the cases, the cause of anger has some kind of root within. If you transact with the root that you have identified, then you may have an easier way of overcoming the spell of anger within. If you are unable to locate any root within, contributing to the cause of anger, even then, you have a recourse. There are situations when the factors which have led to the creation of anger are all external and not connected with the things within. In this scenario, it happens that the spirit of the action leads to the formation of the quality and character of the action. With some kind of realization earned by a person, the spirit of action changes. Sometimes the change is marginal, and at times an occasion occurs when this change turns into a kind of transformation. God realization brings forth with it the spirit of sattwa guna. Sattwa guna represents a set of qualities that are instrumental in making the person truthful; the person, in this context, develops the profile of integrity, honesty and a combination of the qualities of the like. It is thus the spiritual basis of life that makes the enduring in her or his life with respect to the actions and tasks assigned to.

> *Tasmat yasya mahabaho nigrihitani sarvashah.*
> *Indriyani indriya arthebhyah tasya prajna pratisthitah.* (G.2/68)
> Arjuna, therefore, keep in mind, a person whose senses are completely restrained from the attachments to objects and selfish considerations or attachments to material sensations is a person who has developed the wisdom and the stability of mind.

Organs have their specific roles in life. However, each organ operates on the basis of the principles of coordination by the central coordinating system. From a biological point of view, the central coordinating point is located in the brain. It is one of the lobes or segments of the brain which coordinates the functions human organs undertake. In the event of the functions undertaken by the different lobes of the brain, it is made clear through the pathways of our journey in life that the system functions based on the directions of control from the brain; however, there is another factor which lies behind everything, not only as a catalyst, but as the basic guidance and energy provider. This factor is the consciousness of the person.

Consciousness of the person could have two varieties: the empirical consciousness and the spiritual consciousness. Whereas the empirical consciousness is material in nature, the spiritual consciousness is beyond the purview of the material.

> *Ya nisha sarva bhutanam tasyam jagarti samyami.*
> *Yashyam jagrati bhutani sa nisha pashyoto munaeh.* (G.2/69)
> The person who has a stability of mind understands the true nature of truth and that which is night to all beings in that stage of divine knowledge and supreme release. The God-realized person always keeps awake and remains ever-changing to transient worldly happiness, in which all beings keep awake, is night to the seer.

Consciousness shapes the quality and direction of control of the brain. And then the functional realities of the brain pour into the basics of the micro and macro details of life. In both the macro and micro contexts, the directions converge into a realistic description of the work. Thus, the thoughts of work constrain the type of consciousness. And consciousness, in turn, further remains a guiding input towards the details of the action. Empirical consciousness is calculative, rational, and from a material perspective. But the spiritual consciousness is beyond material rational and attempts to bring human attention to its core. Spiritual consciousness would thus teach life to be oriented to the spirit of God. It is either God directly or the divine attributes that lead to the divine orientation of life. In this context, when the spiritual consciousness is unfolded in life, the work the person performs would count to be the work for God. God does not have any work to perform. Nor does he have the intent to perform. However, whenever the impetus for any action occurs that intends to perfection, the doer, in this context, endows the effect of the work to God.

> *Aapuryamanam achalah pratishtham samudram aapah prabishanti yatvat.*
> *Tat vat kama yam prabishanti sarvae sa shantim aapnoti na kamakami.* (G.2/70)
> As the water of different rivers enters the ocean, which though full on all sides, remains undisturbed, likewise a person in whom all enjoyments mark themselves without causing disturbance attains the poise of mind, and it's not the person who hankers after such enjoyments.

Work, thus offered to God, not only multiplies to get the person rid of the impels of the work but also, in a sense, enhances the power of the work in the context of the world.

Usually, the markets and economies across the world behave on the basis of the collective pattern of response of individuals. Individual dynamism in the market works in a penetrative manner whenever there is a true transformation in the basis of work.

Whenever the person's attitude towards work turns into a kind of dedication, the work that is performed receives a qualitative boost. Its quality turns upright. Thereby, the work heads toward perfection in the context of the many approaches to rationality in life. Dedicated work creates the possibility to work towards perfection. On the other hand, when the work is done with a view to dedicating to God, the doer advances in her or his endeavours of God-realization. Work itself turns into an item of meditation on God and begets goodness in life.

Bihaya kaman yah sarvan pumam cha charati nishpriya.
Nirmamo nirahamkarah sa shantim adhigachhati. (G.2/71)
The person who has given up all desires and moves free from attachments, egoism and thirst for worldly enjoyment attains the condition of supreme bliss, peace of mind and stability of wisdom.

The best principle of work is thus the principle of nishkama karma, and more intensely, the element of sacrifice which is made to be inbuilt in it. Thereby, the doer turns into a giver. She or he does work continuously, but with the belief in mind that no work is being done by them. It is the work of the divine that he or she has a chance to do. Therefore, the doer does work for a purpose. In this case, the purpose of the work serves a noble cause. This noble cause could be the momentary well-being of some people through some kind of physical service with a material outcome. This could be to do some good to the people on Earth through support and service of righteousness. In the case of the war in the Mahabharata, Arjuna finally conceded to the notion and action or war. The war had passed through severe destruction.

Esha hi Brahmi sthitih Partho na enam prapya bimuhyati.
Sthita hi asyam anta kaleho api Brahma nirbanam hichchhati. (G.2/72)
Arjuna, such is the state of the God-realized soul having reached this state, one overcomes the delusions and the destructions which occur in the mind and is established in this state even at the last moment; he attains the supreme bliss of the divine existence and divine knowledge.

In the war of the Mahabharata, Arjuna finally fought the war, and the ultimate victory was for them. Though at the beginning he became obsessed with worldly emotions and thus had fallen into the grip of depression, he could win that phase of his mind. Arjuna's winning the war was not for himself, but for the Lord. Victory was achieved through a huge sacrifice – loss of thousands of lives and huge damage to the properties. It was the context where the joy of victory could not be celebrated. There were the potentials within, there are the potentials that these could yield much better or much poorer results could have been more implicit. However, after the entire *Bhagavad Gita* was narrated by Lord Krishna and after the cosmic view of the Lord's presence was made to revealed, Arjuna understood that he was engaged in the war of righteousness. Also, he realized that Lord Krishna was the embodiment of the divine, and his view on any matter should be the ultimate. Anyone who doesn't do the work for selfish gain, but does it for the benefit of humankind, achieves devotion to God.

4 The Atman

Transcending Barriers of Impossibility through Realization of True Self

It was at the dawn of civilization of human society, when a boy of ten years approached his mother to express his urge to learn. He had heard of a great teacher of his time from friends in society. The boy had urged his mother to get him enrolled in the learning school of the great teacher. His mother, though, was hesitant. The teacher was such a formidable personality that reaching out to him was difficult. The mother was also unclear about the kind of questions she might be bothered with, even if she could make her son reach the core connection of the great teacher. However, this did not stop the boy. Therefore, the mother had to concede. The scenario was such that the boy had to proceed alone as the mother was hesitant about facing unfavourable questions, if any. However, it was widely known that this great teacher's students or a would-be disciple were inducted on the basis of certain satisfactory answers from the incumbent. These questions included personal dimension, family dimension and finally, the core or basic objective of life.

Vedic sages were primarily the teachers. They all had one thing in common: the quest for the supreme truth in life and spreading the same quest across. The quest developed in the mind of the boy was to have wisdom in life, about that of God. This made him approach his mother. The usual social custom of learning the truth at an early age and trying to maintain that in life was so widespread that even the small boy wanted that.

> *Brahmabhutah prasanna atuma na shochati na kamkhati.*
> *Samah Sarveshu bhuteshu mat bhaktih labhatae param.* (G. 18/54)
> A truly realized person is placed in the bliss of the Supreme Divine in terms of truth consciousness and bliss solidified. The person maintains his cheerfulness in mind and does not at all fall into the trap of grief and nor craves for any pleasures. The person remains the same in all beings, and such a person who maintains this condition in life is a person who is very dear to the Divine.

In his teaching to Arjuna, Lord Krishna said that the soul that is immersed in the spirit of God and wants to earn the knowledge of God alone, turns very dear to him, such that he offers the precious quality of devotion to him. Devotion is something which connects God with the spirit of the aspirant in such a way that the aspirant gets the elements of devotion within her or him that ultimately makes the person achieve the realization of God in the sense of the term. The person is then free from attachments.

Arjuna ubacha:
Sannyasa asya mahabaho tattwam ichhami beditum.
Tyagah asya cha Hrikesha prithak keshi nishudan. (G. 18/1)
Arjuna said, O Lord Krishna, O my Lord, O Hrishikesa, O slayer of Keshi, O the Supreme, I wish to know, in classified and several clear terms, the truth of a person having attained the ascesis and having disowned the world or having become neutral to the world.

Lord Krishna has explained the fundamentals of spirituality. As he has mentioned, spirituality in life is a constant quest for the supreme truth. God himself is the truth. The truth that we perceive in the world is just a fragment of the supreme truth. Any aspirant of the supreme truth is thereby an aspirant of God-realization. Lord Krishna has answered questions put forth by Arjuna. In one such question, Arjuna was eager to understand the true nature and approach of a person undertaking *sannyasa*. Sannyasa is a state of the aspirant wherein her or his mind is free from the impacts and impositions of the material world. Krishna says sannyasa is not the giving up of the connection of relations with the world.

Kamyanam karmanam nyasyam sannyasam kaboioh beduh.
Sarbo Karmaphala tyagam prahuh tyagam bichakshanah. (G. 18/2)
One view of the Vedas is that the power of ascesis is given up all actions motivated by desire, and other discerning thinkers declare that this giving up consists in relinquishing the fruit of all actions.

Matters and elements of desire are widespread in the world. The limits of human desire are enormous; each one of them has its usual imperatives. Desire once fulfilled usually does not get exhausted. Desires breed desire. One ends to bring forth the other. This being a matter of fact in the human context, it's said that spirituality demands a desire-free mind of a person.

Thajyam dosham eva ekah iti karmah prahuh manishinan.
yajnah danah tapak Karmah nah tyajam iti cha aparae. (G. 18/3)
However, some wise men declare that all actions may breed evil and are therefore not worth giving up; while there are actions which lead to the act of sacrifice, charity, penance and creating goodness for the world, should not be given up. Good actions should be retained; bad actions should be given up.

In answer to the point of difference between giving up and sannyasa, Arjuna had asked Lord Krishna, who narrated, explaining that the concept of tyaga or giving up is to give up things of the possessions of the person. Most of their possessions are acquired in the process of life. Whereas a person attains sannyasa when she or he has renounced the very basic ego of the person and have aspired to get the spirit of God within. The spirit of God once thus aspired and endowed with, the person falls in love with and begets and divine spirit to embrace.

Even when the person attempts to give up or does, that expectation does prevail. Each element of giving up gets associated with a specific magnitude and degree of giving, and the connected point with this idea talks about the magnanimity lying in the act of giving. When given the idea of the material value of the gift, the expectation is generated therefrom.

> *Nischayam shrinuh mae tatra tygal bharat sattwam.*
> *Tyagoh purusha byaghrah tribidah sampra Kirtisahah.* (G. 18/4)
> Between the spirit of ascesis and becoming a monk and the giving up, the first lesson, O Arjuna, is my conclusion on the subject of renunciation. Arjuna, you are the tiger among men, you are so strong in mind and body, and you are so special in the human world. Renunciation has been declared to be of three kinds: *sattwika, rajasika* and *tamasika*.

In the realm of God-realization, the idea of giving through the process of life begets expectations broader in its purview and larger in the context of human expectations. Material items of gifts are all indexed with a range of material identities that go really beyond the human assessment of things. It is another approach where the principle of giving really turns into the principle of the lives of the giver, who acts and behaves in a realistic reciprocity. This kind of reciprocity is associated with the process of a transaction that is usually identified as something that augments the social spirit.

> *Yajnah dana tapah karma na tyayya karyam eva, tat.*
> *Yajnah danam tapah cha eva pabanani manishinam.* (G. 18/5)
> Sacrifice, charity, and penance are not worth giving up. They must be performed for sacrifice, charity and penance. All these are purifiers of the wise. In short, the sattwa-guna-based karma or the truth-oriented actions have to be adhered to. Others may be given up.

In the case of sannyasa, the person has two dimensions in life. First is the choice of God in life. Choice of God may breed love for God. Love for God makes a decisive inroad in the consciousness of the person. This may make the person oriented towards God with a basic faith, dedication and love. When the person attains faith, respect, and love for God, the mind acts and that the mind this is the mind's gradual, simple pointed attraction and orientation to God. The person in this condition of mind does not like to review the mind and the attraction of the spirit of God.

> *Etani api tu karmani sangam tyaktah phalani cha.*
> *Kartavyani iti me partha nischitam matam uttamam.* (G. 18/6)
> Hence, the acts of sacrifice, charity and control of senses and all other acts of duty too must be performed, but without any expectations of reward and attachments. This is my well-considered and supreme verdict, O Arjuna.

The person now develops a dedicated personality. Dedication to God and the orientation of the mind of the person now connect with the spirit of truth within the work performed by the person. This becomes work of a different type and variety, since the person has developed one of the quietest, simple pointed orientations of mind that makes the person perform the work in the world with utmost honesty and sincerity of purpose in life. Thus, the work that she or he takes up no longer remains an ordinary pattern of work. This pattern is known as the destined work or the approach that work is the ultimate salvation.

> *Niyatasya tu sonnyasah karmano mah upapadyatae.*
> *Mohat tasya parityagah tamasah porikirtitah.* (G. 18/7)
> The acts which are prohibited and those which are motivated by desire should be given up, but it is not advisable to abandon prescribed duty. Such abandonment out of ignorance has been declared as *tamasika*.

The dedicated karma in this context becomes the work which the performer would be in the wider sense of the term, making it the nishkama karma. Nishkama karma thus focuses on the kind of work-driven spirit of action that comes in a single form. The single pointed karma makes the work also best expected, possibly takes towards perfection.

> *Dukhyam iti eva yat karma kaya kleshan bhayat tyajyet*
> *Sah kritva rajasam tyagam na eva karma phalam tyagam*
> *labhyet.* (G. 18/8)
> Should someone give up his duties for fear of physical strain, thinking that all action is verily of the nature of discomfort, practising such rajasika from renunciation, he reaps not the fruit of renunciation.

When the spirit of God thus stays in life, the person realizes the strength of it and understands the work not for any personal gain but for the world and the broader benefit of life. Thus, it is now oriented to the spirit of God that gets more intensely twined with life and effectively associates with things which are more of his selfish focus, rather which begets priority in thoughts, aspirations and orients life to sattwa gunas. Thus, life transcends from its material worldly identity to the divine identity. This person is a *sannyasi*, no matter where she or he lives or stays.

The best principle of work is to dedicate oneself to the cause of the work. Work is best performed when the body and mind are tuned to the spirit of work. On the other hand, the person calculates on the fruits and results of the actions, part of the mental energy is spent on calculating and cherishing the idea of the same. Therefore, the mental energy gets divided among many things other than work alone.

Karyam iti eva yat karma neyatam Kriyatae Arjana.
Sangam tyaktva phalam cha eva sahtyagh Svattwika matah.   (G. 18/9)
A prescribed duty which is performed simply because it has to be performed, giving up attachment and fruit, that alone has been recognized as the sattwa form of renunciation.

Thus, the thoughts and calculations about the consequences and the result of the work disrupt the flow of work in this context. The flow of work demands thoughts and consciousness to go along with the work, and finding out the best ways to accomplish the work.

The boy who had approached his mother was named Satyakama. Satyakama used to live with his mother Jabala. They did not have any other relation to mention or talk about. Mother Jabala used to work in different places as a domestic assistant, and in the process, had probably come in touch with someone biologically who deserves the identity of the same.

No dwestyah, kushalam karma kushalae na anu shajjatae
Tyagi swalla soma bishtoh medhans chhinna Samshagah.   (G. 18/10)
Action haters do not bring lasting happiness, nor does he get attached to that which is conducive to blessedness, imbued with the quality of goodness, he has all his doubts resolved, is intelligent and a man of true renunciation.

For reasons of social constraints, therefore, Jabala did not want to mention the same to anyone. When she was asked about the father, Jabala did not say anything to her son. Rather, she suggested that her son should mention this in his own way, if that calls for. Satyakama went to a great master, Goutama, to fulfill his objective of learning there. The master usually takes the identity of the students who wish to join his group. He asked the boy about his credentials or identity. Satyakama just followed his mother's advice and said that the only thing he could share was: I am Satyakama, Jabala is my mother.

Na hi dehabhrita shakyam tyaktum karmani asheshatah.
Yah tuh karma phala tyagi sa tyagi iti abhidhiyatae.   (G. 18/11)

Since all actions cannot be given up in their entirety by anyone possessing a body in the physical world, she or he alone who renounces the fruit of action is called a man of renunciation.

The truth of the context as revealed in the utterance of the boy Satyakama had impressed the master, Goutama. Goutama saw in the boy the firepower of truth. He was thoroughly impressed by that utterance of truth. This led to the induction of the boy into the learning system of Goutama. But then an issue was created. Having gained the strength of mind, Satyakama was given an assignment by the master. This was a part of the learning system.

Anishtam jishtam mishrancha tribidham karmanah phalam.
Bhabati atyaginam pretya na tu sanyasinam kah chit. (G. 18/12)
Agreeable, disagreeable and mixed, threefold indeed are the fruits that accrue thereafter from the action of the unrenouncing, but there is none whatsoever for those who have renounced.

The modern education system considers self-learning through projects and assignments as one of the best ways to impart teaching. It is said by many scholars that this learning method has been a contribution of modern scientific society. This view is wrong. The learning method during the Vedic period was based upon two basic principles: *Swadhyay* and *Adhyasyh* – which means self-learning and self-unfoldment, in sequence. The learning system during the Vedic period was very advanced in its pedagogy, approach, orientation and objective. The Vedic Civilization was oriented towards creating the basis of likes of the people across the principles of stimulating wisdom in people and thereby, creating a social infrastructure that would not only value knowledge but nurture that towards the unfoldment of individual worth to generate wisdom. Wisdom-centric life contributes to the formation of a society based on the values of truth, integrity, honesty and freedom.

Satyakama was given an assignment which was described by some leading scholars as a very impossible one. Because of this there has spread a view that the sage Goutama was one of the most cruel teachers the human civilization has witnessed so far! Indeed, the view makes sense, considering his age, the context and the content of the assignment given.

Pancha imani mahabaho karonani nibodha me.
Samkhaya krita ante proktani siddhayae sarvakarmanam. (G. 18/13)
In the branch of learning known as sankhya, which prescribes means for neutralizing all actions and concentrating the mind, five factors have been mentioned as contributory to the accomplishments of actions. Know them all from me, O Arjuna.

At the time when Satyakama had approached the master Goutam for his learning, he was around ten years age. Goutama said, 'I am happy to give you an assignment'. This was the task of taking along a team of cows consisting of two hundred and fifty. Most of these cows were not well. Many of these cows had walking difficulties, and they were having various kinds of diseases. The master had announced that Satyakama would carry all these cows to the forest. Satyakama has to nurture the cows such that once the number grows to one thousand and each cow is back to good health, the student can return to the learning school of the master.

> *Adhishthanam tatha karta karanam cha prithak bidham.*
> *Bibidha cha prithak chesta daivam eva cha atra Panchamam.* (G. 18/14)
> Factors operating towards the accomplishment of action are the body, the person acting, the organs of different kinds, different functions of manifold kinds, and the fifth one is the endowment from the divine and destiny as well.

The impossibility or absurdity of the assignment was evident as the student or disciple was only around ten years old. He was alone to nurture two hundred and fifty cows. More so, it was never thought in any way by an adult person that such an impossible task might ever be made possible. The forest region where he had to take the cows was full of different types of wild animals: lions, tigers, elephants, serpents, and bears. Even saving the lives of the cows was a question mark, to forget about their growth in number.

> *Sharirah vak manovi yat karmah prarabhatae narah.*
> *Nayam ba biparitam ba pancha etat tasya hi etad.* (G. 18/15)
> These five are the contributory causes of whatever actions, right or wrong, a person performs with the mind, speech and body in the context of the world.

On top of everything, the question of the safety and security of the ten-year-old boy Satyakama was very important. The boy was pushed to the shelter and the mercy of Mother Nature. His food, stay, health concern, welfare and studies or practices all were dependent upon and left to the choice of Mother Nature. The task given by the master to Satyakama was exclusive. If the number grows to one thousand, only then can Satyakama come back.

> *Tatra evem sati Kartaram atmanam kebalam tuh yah.*
> *Pashyati akritah buddhi tvat na sa pashyati durmatih.* (G. 18/16)
> Notwithstanding this, however, he, who has an impure mind, regards the absolute, taintless self alone as the doer and that person of perverse understanding does not view or write.

The most important part of this learning assignment was the attitude of Satyakama that was expressed in the process of receiving the assignment. Satyakama, the boy, was so delighted with this assigned work that he was almost dancing in joy. His joy was because of two factors: one, his studentship or discipleship was accepted by the master. Secondly, and more importantly, the master had taken him to trust.

Yasyah na et ahamkritao bhabo buddhi yasy na lipyatae.
Hatvaapi sah iman lokan na hanti na nibadhyatae. (G. 18/17)
He whose mind is free from the senses of doer and whose reason is not affected by worldly objects of activities does not really kill, even having killed all those people, nor does any sin accrue to him.

The attitude of the small boy Satyakama was so positive that he started believing that since the great master had given him the assignment, it was something achievable by virtue of his grace. So, the work should be accepted with full faith in the master and the system. Satyakama started for the woods also started the willed and joyful interest in the work. It was indeed a great success for Satyakama at the end of the assignment, many years later. Satyakama was happy being in the company of the cows, and the ultimate analysis, the love for work and nature, was established by Satyakama.

Satyakama had a positive outlook on life. As soon as he got the rare opportunity of his life of having got the blessings of the guru or the master he had dreamt of, he accepted the master with full faith and devotion. Satyakama had the feeling that the blessings of his master were the winning power.

Jnanam Jneyam parijnatah tribidha karma chadona.
Karanam Karma Karta eti tribidhah karma shangrahah. (G. 18/18)
The knower, knowledge and the object of knowledge, these three motivate action. Even so, the doer, the organs and the activity are the three constituents of the action.

The attitude to work of Satyakama being so strongly positive, he started having the feeling that the power of wishes of the master was with him, so making the impassibility turn around to the possibility was within his ownership. Thus, with this faith in him, his journey started as a kind of long-term adventure in the deep forest. This noble and simple faithful boy was never caused harm to by any of the jungle animals. Rather, even the deadly and cruel ones were sympathetic and supportive to him and his team of cows. The entire team was now full of joy at being in the midst and company of friends of the woods.

Jnanam karma ca karta cha tridhaiba gunabhedatah
Pra uchayatae guna to samkhanae yathabat shrinu tani api. (G. 18/19)
In the branch of knowledge dealing with the *gunas* or the qualities of life or modes of nature, knowledge and action, as well as the doer, have been declared to be of three kinds according to the gunas, sattwa, rajas and tamas; this is available in each.

Satyakama saw elements of knowledge from every incident that happened. His mind was keen towards making the spiritual practices. He received the message of wisdom borne by air. The flowing water in rivers also imparted elements of wisdom to him. The lightning from the sky one day passed on wisdom to him. The matter of some special wisdom was passed on by some animals as well. Satyakama drew wisdom in him over that period of his enduring and devoted work towards fulfilling his cherished objective identified in life.

Sarvabhuteshu yena ekam bhabam ikshatae abyayam.
Abibhaktam bibhakteshu tat jnanam biddhi swattikam.   (G. 18/20)
That which a person perceives as one imperishable divine existence as undivided and equally present in all individual beings, is known that knowledge to be swattika.

Satyakama had received wisdom that was marked as Chatuskal Brahman, four different ways of realising the truth of creation and endowing life with the same. It was the spirit of the Vedas that Satyakama had earned the knowledge of Brahman from. Four different Vedas - Rig, Sama, Yajur and Atharva have their distinctive ways to earn the knowledge of Brahman. Satyakama had earned all of these. While being in the forest, the entire range of learning of Satyakama fitted in the framework of the Vedas.

Prithak tvena tu yat jnanam nanabhavan prithak bidhan.
Betti sarveshu bhuteshu tat jnanam biddhi Rajasam.   (G. 18/21)
A rajasika person holds differentiated knowledge. The knowledge by which a person recognizes the many existences of various types, as apart from one another in all beings, knows that knowledge is rajasika.

Satyakama had received elements of wisdom completely from nature. The trees, animals, air, and water in the forest each had their contributing elements to the pool of wisdom that Satyakama had earned. He never developed the egoistic affirmation that his power of faith or his power of devotion contributed to the making of the positive approach towards any functionalities. Satyakama was one day told by a senior cow, that they had reached the landmark number.

Yat tu kritsnavat ekasmin tat karyae saktom ahaitukam.
Ata tattwartha badala alpam cha tat tamasem samasitam.   (G. 18/22)
Again, that knowledge which clings to one body as if it were the whole and which is irrational, has no real grasp of truth and is trivial, has been declared as tamasika.

The landmark number for the cows was to reach & collective strength of one thousand, which they had achieved. Not only that, the lap of nature through different varieties of the forest setting had provided remedies to the ailing cows. Now, the cows are in good health. Therefore, having fulfilled all conditions of the assignment, it was time for them to tell Satyakama to go back to his master, which they did. Satyakama with his entire team, now a thousand cows, started their return to the guru.

Niyatam sanga rahitam raga dweshatah kritam.
A phala prepsura na karma yat tat swatta uchyatae. (G. 18/23)
That action which is ordained by the scriptures and is not accompanied by the sense of worship and has been done without any attachment or aversion by one who seeks no return is called the swattika action.

Yat tu kama apsuna karma sa ahamkaran ba punah.
Kriyatae bahulam ayasam tat ryasam udahritam. (G. 18/24)
That action, however, which involves much strain and is performed by one who seeks enjoyment or by a man full of egoism, has been spoken of as rajasika.

Anubandham kshayam himsam anapeksham cha pourusham.
Mohat arabhyatae karma yat tat tamasam uchyatae. (G. 18/25)
That action which is undertaken through sheer ignorance, without regard for the consequences or loss to oneself, injury to others, and one's own capacity, is declared as tamasika.

Mukta sangah na ahamvadi dhriti utsahah samananitah.
Siddhah asiddhah nirvikarah karta swattikah uchyatae. (G. 18/26)
Free from attachments, un-egotistic, endowed with firmness and zeal of unswayed by success and failure, such a doer is said to be swattika.

Ragi karmaphala prepsu lubdhah himsatmakah ashuckitah.
Harsho shokanihtah karta rajasah parikirtitah. (G. 18/27)
The doer who is full of attachment seeks the fruit of action and is greedy, who is oppressive by nature and of impure conduct and is affected by joy and sorrow, has been called rajasika.

Satyakama returned to the place of his master. As he was approaching his master, the great sage Goutama could see from a distance the vibrant and glowing face of Satyakama. The sage understood that Satyakama had achieved the Supra wisdom, the Brahmagyana. With the attainment of the very coveted wisdom, the person got completely drenched in the elements of truth. Satyakama appeared to be that boy now transformed into a total man with the sacred wisdom of God fully attained.

Ayuktah prakritaha stabdhah shathoh naishkritik alasah
Vishadi dirghasutri cha karta tamasah uchhgatae. (G. 18/28)

Lacking pity, self-control, uncultured, arrogant, deceitful, inclined to cause harm to others, rob others of their livelihoods, low-thought, downhearted and procrastinating - such a doer is called tamasika.

The guru was curious and asked whether Satyakama had taken up any kind of oration or discipleship under any other master. 'Who has provided you with the supreme wisdom? Have you been to any hermitage of any other sage?' Satyakama replied, saying that he has learnt everything from his master Goutama and no other person. However, he explained the sequence of things that happened to him. He explained how he was the fortunate recipient of spells of wisdom from the sources of nature. He believed that it was all God-sent for making him equipped with the knowledge of all four Vedas. The concept of the four aspects of the revelations was elaborated to him in different ways. It was God's design that he earned the wisdom in the context of nature. Animals became his friends in life. The lightning, the air the void all turned into friends to him. Therefore, to Satyakama, the total truth of the entire cosmic system got revealed. The knowledge of the Supreme thus became evident to Satyakama.

Buddhih bhedam dhritih cha eva gunatah trividhaham shrinu
Prochhyamanam asheshenah prithaka tena Dhananjaya. (G. 18/29)
Arjuna, now hear from me the threefold division based on the predominance of each guna of understanding and firmness. I shall explain in detail one by one.

The learning of Satyakama was directly from the cosmic sources. He was thoroughly drenched in the spirit of truth. Journey in the natural content happens with the truth as realized and understood in the context of the world. However, the mental equilibrium of Satyakama was achieved through the entire process. He was a true sattwa guna person. Whenever the guru used to tell him anything, Satyakama did not hesitate to make a movement to affirm that he was going to comply with the same. Thus, in the process, the devotees had only got in his mind to follow and accomplish. Satyakama understood the fundamentals of the causative factors of God realization in life.

Pravgittim cha ninsitim cha karya akaryae bhayo abhoyae
Bandham moksham cha yah vetti buddhih sa partha Swattiki. (G. 18/30)
The intellect which correctly determines the path of activity and renunciation, what ought to be done and what should not be done, what is fear and what is fearless, fearlessness and what is bondage and what is liberation, that intellect is swattika.

Lord Krishna has affirmed the need for that kind of character in life. He narrated to Arjuna that human tendencies are actually either binding or liberating elements in life. The fundamental properties, as expressed in three categories sattwa, rajas and tamas, make and build the characters and thereby, the basic tendencies. For a person who has been into the continued sattwa variety or gunas or attributes, would tend to liberate life from any kind of bondage. Bindings to the factors of desire and the related pettiness, smallness, are removed with sattwa guna in life.

> *Yaya dharmam adharmam cha karya akaryam eva cha.*
> *Ayathabat projanati buddhih sa partho Rajashih.* (G. 18/31)
> The intellect by which man does not truly perceive what dharma or righteousness is, and what is adharma or unrighteousness, what ought to be done and what should not be done, is rajasika.

Maintaining sattwa guna in life would instill strong faith in life. In the case of Satyakama, that factor was also dominant. As soon as the master had endowed Satyakama with a task, he accepted that task with a smile on his face and a genuine delight inside. He did not think of any hazard that might appear in the process. The task given was indeed something in equilibrium with nature, but almost an impossible task on a human scale, in general and for a small boy, in particular. However, the honest and strong faith in Satyakama acted as more of a strength of mind and consciousness for him.

> *Adharmam dharmam iti yah manyatae tamas abritah.*
> *Sarba arthan biparitan cha buddhih sa Partho Tamasi.* (G. 18/32)
> Stepped in ignorance, the intellect which imagines even adharma to the dharma and seeks all other things perversely, that intellect is tamasika, Arjuna.

The entire tenure and journey of his trying for the realization of God and in the process earn brahmagyana, Satyakama had the purity of faith and the strong intent that made him pass the days in the difficult context and still earn the wisdom of God in the same ways as that of a person who are into the process of meditation for years. He was thus graced by God with the ability to interact and transact with animals, even dangerous ones, and the others in the deep forest, which were even doubtful in their usual behaviour and transactions in life for the fulfillment of his spiritual journey.

In the context of the war, it was mentioned by Lord Krishna that a person with the sattwa guna goes ahead with consecration to God in all situations of life. The person being oriented to truth always sticks to the principles of right actions and justice to all. Right actions as perceived by the person may not be accepted by others as truly right actions; however, actions that result that are positive to most people or for every person are always righteous.

> *Dhrityah yaya dharayatae manah pranah indriyah Kriyah.*
> *Yogen abyabhicharinah dhritih sa Partho Swattiki.* (G. 18/33)

The unwavering firmness by which man controls, through the yoga of meditation, the functions of the mind, the vital areas and the senses, that firmness is swattika.

A truthful, sincere person who is also having integrity in life, somewhat devoted acts along the course of work, making it more acceptable. Accepted, when the person undertakes and follows the principles of complacency. A winner through any means may win a context for a period, but in the next sequence, the previous winner would face challenges in other contexts. A sattwa guna person, if unable to come out victorious in the short term, would have occasions to have scopes for a superior position or result in the course of the journey in life. It is thus an imperative for the cause of sustainability to be sattwa-oriented.

Yaya tu dharma-kama-arthan dritya dharayatae Arjuna.
Prasangena phala akamkshi dhritih sa Partho Rajasih. (G. 18/34)
The perseverance, however, by which a person seeking a reward for his action clutches with the extreme fondness of wrong values, earthly possessions and worldly enjoyments, that perseverance is said to be rajasika.

Sattwa gets merged with the personality of the individual. Once a person gets involved in the process of the competition in the market, diverse forces of the world get entangled. It is the same context where the person is construed with diverse impacts; the easy solution or a short-term remedy would be to get swayed by the forces and dynamism of the market. However, in this way of getting together and jointly doing things, a sattwa-oriented person always has to stick to the eternal principles of truth, honesty and integrity. When the person has to perform in the market, it is always advisable to be oriented to the principles of goodness and that is to achieve sustainability.

Yaya Swapnam bhayam shokam bishadom madam eva cha.
Na bimunchati durmedhah dhrih sa Partho Tamasi. (G. 18/35)
The firmness by which an able-minded person does not give up sleep, fear, anxiety, sorrow and vanity as well, that firmness is tamasika.

Human qualities are abundant in societies and the nations, mostly with a combination of tamas and rajas breeds of qualities. The tamas variety of attributes are basically those who are akin to sleepy, drowsy, always fearful, get easily soaked by the impact of sorrow, are prey to depression and addiction in mind. These are the people who lack the power of anger, causing harm to others, but always construct the devil's thoughts in her or his mind. The tamas person is thus someone who constructs evil things in the mind and consciousness. This is how the person becomes the messenger of an evil spirit and spoils the spirit of goodness in human society.

Sukham tu idanim trividham shrihu mae Bharat Rishava.
Avyasad ramatae yatra duhkhyah antah cha nigachhati. (G. 18/36)
Now hear from me the threefold joy too, that in which the aspirant of spiritual attainment finds enjoyment through the practice of adoration, meditation and service to God, etc.

The spread of an evil spirit thus makes the person a messenger of evil in such a way that, as if the factors of untruth are presented as the factors of truth and the factors of goodness are doubted, thereby passing the factors of evil as the factors of goodness. Factors of goodness thus get into lives that are totally embraced by the elements of untruth. A tamas personality thus causes or tries to cause harm to society and the human world. The most important impact of the tamas personality causes permanent harm to the progress of humans.

Yat tat agrae bisham iva parinam iha amritam upamam.
Tat sukham sattwikam proktam atma buddhi prasadajam. (G. 18/37)
The person reaches the end of sorrow, such a joy, through appearing as poison in the beginning, just like nectar in the end, hence that joy born as of, it is of the plasticity of the mind brought about by meditation on God and has been declared as swattika.

The rajas personality always engages itself in activities. Rajas is known for its dynamism. The intrinsic dynamism which takes the person to actions, but the orientations of those actions would be to get into the factors of somewhat good and mostly bad outcomes for the society. The bad outcomes are due to two reasons; one, the orientation of the work is bad and, on top of that, the dynamism inbuilt in the system makes it more strong and powerful. Evil with more power then begets greater problems for the world.

Once the rajas and the tamas are properly identified, the person should be made to be serious about it and gradually understand the impact of that on human society or the human world. Rajas and tamas personalities easily come out of the context once they resolve to be oriented to the sattwa attributes. People choosing truthfulness in life would get into sattwa.

Bishayah indriya samyogat yat tat agraha amrita upamam.
Parinamae bisham iva tat sukham rajasam smritam. (G. 18/38)
The delight which follows from the contact of the senses and their objects is eventually a poison-like, though appearing at first as nectar, hence it has been spoken of as the rajasika.

The human tendency to aspire for happiness may lead to happiness or sorrow in term. The element of happiness that actually sustains for a short while but brings in shadows of gloomy conditions thereafter is a kind of happiness that breeds sorrow forthwith. This kind of happiness is actually a rajas variety of happiness. The rajas variety of happiness is that of a short term. It provides the desired happiness, but at the same time, the person invites problems or perils in the connected areas of life. Therefore, the assertive position of the gunas is important in shaping life. The rajas happiness has an action component that creates inroads in the understanding of the person in the context as the prevailing realities of the concerned life.

> *Yat agre cha anubandhae cha sukham mohanah atmanah.*
> *Nidra alasya pramadoh uttham tat tamasa udahritam.* (G. 18/39)
> The happiness that is for the short term and gets deluged in indolence, sleep, wrongful actions and the like is termed as tamasika happiness.

The rajas variety of happiness has the action component. The person strives to attain things of choice and desire. However, it goes beyond the limits of her or his understanding if the person attempts to transcend the line limits of rajas and adopts the sattwa orientation, which would be embodied through that process of transition. If, however, the person lacks the action component and gets involved in idle thoughts of the attributes, it gives immense impetus to the person to address the attributes that are exhibiting some kind of look-similarity with the tamas set of attributes. Tamas stops progress.

> *Na tad asti prithivyam va dibi debeshu va punah.*
> *Sattwam Prakritijaih muktam yat evih syat trigunaivi.* (G. 18/40)
> There is no being on Earth or in the *akash* or the sky, even among the Gods or anywhere else, who is free from the three gunas born of *prakriti*.

Happiness in a tamas mind is actually that for a short while. In this short while, tamas may have to remain in the form of a messenger of some change or a transformation. That transformation, thus, may reposition the person to the track or sustaining the same, looking at the final objective. Intent stands as the most important component. When a person is determined to lead a truthful life, their mindset becomes unified and begins to understand the fundamental behavioural aspects of life and thought.

> *Brahmana kshatriyah bisham sudranam cha parantapah.*
> *Karmani prabibhaktani swabhabs pravaabai gunaih.* (G. 18/41)
> The duties of the people having attained God realization, the people who are into the actions with energies, and the people who are into the business in life, as well as those who are working for others, have been divided according to the qualities with which they are born.

The power of discrimination, once developed in a person, contributes a lot to the design of things. Once the power of discrimination is developed, the person understands two categories of things in the world, broadly speaking. This is what makes the person choose goodness in the long term. If, in order to attain goodness for the long term, even if experiencing somewhat reverse conditions for a shorter period, it stands more advisable.

> *Shamah damah tapah shoucham kshantih arjabam eva cha.*
> *Jnanam vijnanam astikyaham brahmakarma swabhabojam.* (G. 18/42)
> Control of the mind and senses, enduring hardships and riches of one's sacred obligations, external and internal impurity, giving up the faults of others, uprightness of the mind, senses and conduct, beliefs in the Vedas and other scriptures, God and life, after death, etc., study and teaching of the Vedas and other scriptures, and realization of the truth relating to God, all these constitute the natural duties of a Brahmana.

The two varieties have their identified categories. One of them is called *shreya*, which means the electable dimensions in life. It may be somewhat unpleasant for a short while, but it eventually brings pleasure and happiness in the long run and continues to be so. Shreya could be anything of human choice or identification. While taking any matter for life in its own way of journey or its own aspects of choice, shreya is in the position of the person in the context of the world. It is thus one of the most formidable and effective guides in the life of a person. Shreya is the welfare or the good one. Shreya is something that continues to be good for a person.

It is not easy for anyone to understand and identify the spirit of goodness in all situations of life. Human tendency is an orientation to the other aspect of life, the *preyas*. Preya is the item of choice that is always attractive at first sight or notice. The true spirit of Preya is pleasurable. It is the elements that attract delusions.

> *Shouryam tejoh dhritih daksham yuddhae cha apalayanam.*
> *Danam Iswarah swabhabatcha kshatram karma*
> *Swabhabajam.* (G. 18/43)
> Exhibition of valour, fearlessness, firmness, diligence, dauntlessness in battle, bestowing gifts and lordliness, in all constitute the natural duty of a Kshatriya.

Preya is something that is attractive. If we try to understand the right kind of distinction between shreya and preya, we can do so in the context of items of food. If a person is made to consume a glass of sugar juice every day or many times a day, they would find that the sweetness of the sugar juice tastes good. It provides pleasure. This is good for his moment. It gives him a feeling of the pleasure of sweetness. The sweetness of taste is pleasurable. However, if the pleasure of drinking glasses of sweet juice lasts for some period of time, it may invite hazards and diseases of a deadly variety. The habit of drinking sugar juice frequently may lead to the person having diabetes in their life and thus making it a point that the person is affected by the disease and replaces the pleasures with the pains of the disease.

Krishi Goroksham banij'yam vaishya karma swabhabajam.
Pari charya atmakam karma shudrashya api swabhaabajam. (G. 18/44)
Agriculture, rearing of cows, honest trade or merchandising, these constitute the natural duty of a Vaishya, a member of the trading community, and the service of other classes is the natural duty even of the Shudra, a member of the labouring class.

Shreya could be the other way. If instead of taking the sugar juice, the person drinks neem juice every day in a small amount, the result comes somewhat different. On consuming the neem juice, the person develops a situation that actually attempts to provide difficulty now but begets results different from the previous. Neem juice consumed in some logical volume on a regular basis makes it unpleasant to consume, but helps to make certain vital organs of the body become stronger while developing the habit.

Sve sve karmani abhirasah same siddhihim labhatae naarah.
Svakarma niratah siddhim yatha a bindati tat shrinuh. (G. 18/45)
Keenly devoted to his own natural duty, a man attains the highest perfection in the form of God-realization. You hear from me that the mode of performance whereby the man engages in his inborn duty reaches that highest realization of God.

Shreya habit is not easy to develop, but it brings forth the context where the entire system draws in vital strength, enough to help the organs of importance become stronger than the normal situations, Thus, life sets a longer lease of existence. Shreya does not provide the pleasures of having the sugar juice; however, the long-term good health and span of life. Shreya offers that goodness in life by way of infusing more vitality into his life for the sustainable journey.

Yatah probrittwi bhutanam yena sarvam idam tatam.
Sva karmana tam avyarchah siddhim vindati manabah. (G. 18/46)
A person perfectly committed to his/her own *prakriti* or the innate nature and carrying out actions in accordance is offering divine submissions to the Supreme.

It is not only in the context of goodness in life it happens so that the identification of shreya in all aspects of life makes the person reasonably balanced. Shreya orientation makes the person come out of the spell of the impacts of the devils or the falsehood in the context of life. The mental orientation thus brings in some changes in the context of the world. Thus, the context is made to change forthwith when a repeat choice of the shreya brings in a habit that is tuned to the process of transformations.

Shreyan Svadharmo bigunah parad harmyat sva anushthityat.
Swavava niyatam karma kurbam na apnati kilbisham. (G. 18/47)

Better is one's own duty, though devoid of merit, than the duty of others. All performs the duty ordained by his own nature, man does not incur sin.

The habit of goodness creates the spirit of goodness. The person now develops an inclination towards the knowledge of the spirit. The spirit thus makes the person inclined to the goodness of life and the world. Goodness emanates from the core spirit of life. It is the core spirit which, if oriented to God and the approaches of living through its habit, is dedicated to truth, that sattwa personality now develops the quality to realize God. Wisdom develops in the person. The spirit once opens up; the person knows and realizes that the Supreme resides within as the atman in the cave of the heart. Atman is the truth and light in itself. Atman is the supreme truth and bliss in the world.

Attainments in life depend on the way life is lived. A person creates her or his impressions through the quality of work that she or he perform. It is the person's behaviour and the orientation of the person's karma in life that gives shape to her or his personal character, which identifies their life.

Sahajam karma kounteyah sadasham aapi na tyjyet.
Sarva arambha hi doshenah dhumenah agnih iva abritah.   (G. 18/48)
Therefore, O Arjuna, you should focus on your intrinsics, for even as fire is covered with smoke, all unacceptable things are beset with some imperfection or the other.

The work performed according to the character and the essence of the karma that the person undertakes makes a clear breakthrough and sets the idea towards what the resultant effect of the work is determined on Earth. The person, thus, fixes the course of life, orientation and the future course of things based on the attributes and attitudes in the inherent dimension of life. Wisdom accumulates and gradually grows in content with the urge of the person to have wisdom. Knowledge and the urge together make the aspect in life that shows the ways towards the attainment of God's knowledge in life. A person who orients the work towards the objective in life, as winning things in life, gradually wins the love of God and the wisdom in life.

Asaktah buddhih sarvatra jitatma bigata sprihah.
Naishkarmya siddhim paraman sannyasenah adhigachhati.   (G. 18/49)
A person unattached, whose thirst is enjoyment, has altogether disappeared, and who has subdued his mind, reaches through *sankhya yoga* or the path of knowledge, the extreme and the supreme consummation of actionlessness and realizes God.

Work that does not have any item of desire hidden in the design of life has direct pathways open, and thus, this type of person develops a connection with the world. However, on the other hand, if the person has developed a strong time orientation and, thus, through this desireless karma, the person now does the constant innovation, also continues for a reasonable period of time. Nishkama karma, or desireless work, brings in divine realization.

> *Siddhim praptoh yatha Brahma tatha apnoti nibodha mae.*
> *Samasena eva kounteyah nishtha jnanasya yah parah.* (G. 18/50)
> Arjuna, know from me only briefly the process through which man, having attained actionlessness, which is the highest consummation of jnana yoga, the path of knowledge, reaches Brahman.

Divine realization forms an important component in the design of things that are essential for making a life on Earth. This life remains God-connect. God-connect happens primarily through the meditative and devoted condition. The values undertaken by a person act as determinants to the character of the person.

Nishkama karma is possible in a soul that is tuned to the sattwa guna. A life that has taken in vows of satyam and ritam can be the one that would be true to the spirit of divinity. Spirit of divinity is an element of the eternal qualities of the spirit of atman. It is the transcendental in human conditions.

> *Buddhya bishuddhayah yukoh dhrithi atmanam niyama cha.*
> *Shabda adin bishayam tyaktva raga dwesho budyt asya cha.* (G. 18/51)
> A person endowed with pure mind and pure intellect, having concentrated on the spirit of God within, devoid of material attractions, anger, delusions and emphatic ego is swattika.

The course of sattwa in the truth in the material universe. Wherein, the realization of the fact that God is eternal, can be the guide of a life. God is the creator, maintainer and the destiny of humans on Earth. If the human society can affix faith in that universality of the wholeness of God, then the person perceives the truth in this material life on Earth. An ideal life that is sattwa in all attributes but adopts rajas for dynamism and strength, and a bit of tamas to stimulate it.

> *Bibikto sebi laghu aashi yata bak kayamanasah.*
> *Dhyana yoga apora nityam bairagyam samup upashritah.* (G. 18/52)
> A person who prefers a pure place of stay, purity of things in mind and heart, and always focused on the spirit of God is a swattik person.

The life that would actually be in a position to have the spirit of God on Earth. The spirit of God would instill love for God in a form. the spirit of God would thus make the person oriented to the eternal truth and light. The person would develop a love for God on Earth. The ultimate call is given by Lord Krishna by urging Arjuna to have God in mind alone, to seek God in all aspects of life, to dedicate the desire-free work with perfection to God and to consecrate fully upon God. While the person is engaged in thoughts, works, sleeps and dreams, she or he should have God in their consciousness; this person would thus be the one with complete realization of atman.

5   Work for Fulfilment and Liberation

Bhagavad Gita is the song of God realization, which helps a person to attain the state of oneness and live a life of bliss. Lord Krishna was himself involved in the entire process and the spirit, so that humans understand the nature of the Supreme Truth and maintain life full of actions of the right variety. The theory of self was narrated by Lord Krishna to make the point that mental constructions for any work should not be the guiding principles of life; rather, the continuum of the acquired result of each element of work should. Work thus becomes an instrument towards making life; something that would lead life to be simple but full of wisdom. This life realizes the eternal nature of living based on the realization of the spirit of divinity. Work in life can provide the eternal truth. Though the spirit of the divine remains altogether, virtues of life through the passage of time are the true path of life. This life is built on the foundations of divine qualities.

Knowledge of God is connected with the work of life. There are people who become disillusioned in the context of the life they live. While different types of work and life profiles may lead to societal rebuff, it is the varied work individuals perform within the flow of actions—as a stream of things in life—that not only fulfills the dimensions of living but also contributes to a rigorous social and human system.

Knowledge of God leads to the making of wisdom in life. Wisdom sits in a context where the factors of life are coordinated and synchronized to the tune of making life oriented to the spirit of things. The spirit of a human being is that of the spirit of matter and nature combined. It is the essence of the human spirit that needs to be judged against the backdrop of universal values for human living.

Lord Krishna has driven the thoughts and infused them into the spirit in the sense that a person needs to appreciate and adopt the universal spirit in his or her personal life, and at the same time extend the universal spirit to the nucleus of the society and the treasured spirit to spread the same across.

The War of the Mahabharata, which was held at Kurukshetra, is considered very important in light of the conflicts or the crossroads between the righteous spirit of life and the evil spirit, which is on the opposite side of the righteous spirit. The empirical reality, which is a part of the total truth, includes things which are perceived and understood by our senses in the human context. It is something which can be called visible, measurable and electable, and could be sensed by our sensory organs. However, that's just a fragment of the total truth. The remaining part of it is vast and enormous. The creation by God has been two-pronged. One is the eternal component of the creation, and the other is the empirical component of the creation. While the empirical component, as has been mentioned, is visualized, sensed, understood, measured, calculated, and can be ascribed with numerical and other parametric points, the eternal can't be understood and sensed through that. The eternal component of truth is related to the truth of God. Lord Krishna has mentioned to Arjuna that it is the soul which is present in the human condition in a human profile in the form of atman. Atman is a representation of the supreme consciousness. God is understood by the term Supreme Light, Truth and Consciousness. In other words, He is mentioned as *sat, chit* and *ananda*. Sat is truth, chit is consciousness, ananda is bliss. Therefore, the Divine is truth in itself. The Divine is the origin, source and the entire Consciousness of this creation, and the Divine is also the blissful aspect of this creation. The Divine Himself is Bliss. He represents the Truth, the Consciousness and the Bliss. It has been mentioned to Arjuna by Lord Krishna in the context of the war of Kurukshetra that the Divine is eternal, the Divine is ageless, and does not have any origin or destruction. Therefore, it is called *shaswata, sanatana*, meaning it is primordial, a continuation through the scale of time and eternal in its own identity. The Divine may be present in a form, precisely, in a human form. When the Divine appears on Earth in the context of the world, the Divine is termed as Avatar or the Incarnation of God. Lord Krishna is such an Incarnation of God, and Lord Krishna, as an incarnate, has undertaken certain responsibilities at that point in time. It was His destined wish to be an individual part of the war between the evil forces and the righteous forces. Arjuna was the representative figure and the fighter on behalf of the righteous forces. When Lord Krishna talked about the consciousness in the form of wisdom and the knowledge of the Supreme Atman, it was understood by Arjuna, primarily, that it is something which is connected with the knowledge of the world. That is the reason why, in the mind of Arjuna, a very pertinent question had arisen. That was, if Krishna was talking about the goal of life, then which one should be or should have been the real goal of life? The real goal of life should have been the way of wisdom or the way of karma, the action. This is why Arjuna had raised a question to Lord Krishna. The question was very pertinent, and it was very important for Arjuna to get a proper answer from the Lord. This is because he was considered the pivotal and most important fighter to establish the cause of truth, and if he chose not to fight, then what may happen in the context of the war was also his concern. However, Lord Krishna started explaining this point to Arjuna in the form of a yoga, called *karma yoga*. Karma means action. Yoga means connection. Karma yoga is an action that connects the actor with the divine.

Krishna wanted the spirit to get spread universally. T.S. Eliot keenly observed and explored Krishna's message to Arjuna on the battlefield. Eliot's reflection conveyed a powerful admonition: rather than dwelling on farewells or the outcomes of their deeds, those embarking on a journey, whether literal or metaphorical, should simply press onward. It was a call to advance, to "fare forward," embracing the continuous movement of life without attachment to results.

The concept of nishkama karma was narrated by the great poet T.S. Eliot in his *The Dry Salvages*, where he mentions the human being as someone who is passing through the pathways of life, something like crossing the sea of life. And in that, he is mentioning that the ups and downs through the waves of life, as it is there, are experienced by different persons in different ways. The message that Krishna gives in the *Bhagavad Gita*, addressing Arjuna to the world, is a message which talks about moving forward and doing the work of the world without expecting the fruits of the world or aspiring for anything in terms of those fruits. The fruits of the world, arising out of the work contributed by a person, should be considered a contribution to the world and are not to be enjoyed by the person as a personal benefit. As Eliot has mentioned, you are not those who are at the harbour, you are still passing through the sea. And then he advises to forge forward. Addressing the voyagers and the seamen, he advises that once we land on the shore, we don't need to stop there for the benefit of having peace and calmness. But to face the challenges of the life, travelling through the ups and downs of the sea and continuously facing the realities of the world, sufferings may come; the judgment of the sea is a judgment based on the work that you contribute and that could lead to good reaping from the travelling through the sea or somewhat of backlash or bad element in the benefit out of that as well.

Krishna, having been the idol of Arjuna, advises Arjuna on a constant basis. Here, Eliot identifies Arjuna as a representation of individual persons of the world and suggests that the Arjunas of the world take the advice of Krishna as a form of conscious input to live a better life.

The marvel of human civilization lies in the work of humans at the individual and at the collective levels. It was an autonomous point to understand by Arjuna, whether conceptual knowledge or action—if they may be considered as mutually exclusive to understand and drive in mind. The facts of living thus require being dressed up in the context of knowledge and spirit of life, giving the highest importance to work based on contextual wisdom.

In the battlefield of Kurukshetra, the bewildered Arjuna had lost his power of thinking, the strength of his body and mind. He was pushed down to a situation where his body was trembling. Unable to stand, Arjuna could not hold the famous Gandiva, the unique weapon that was associated with his name and valour. Arjuna even fell down on the floor of his own chariot. Having abandoned the urge to fight, Arjuna was constrained by his depressed mind and unable to think of the war to fight in Kurukshetra. However, having lost everything of a personal human possession, Arjuna could maintain a glimpse of his consciousness and the personal intrinsic goodness in life. Arjuna did not forget that Krishna was with him in continuation. His mind, even after having lost the power to stand up in the empirical material sense, could retain an attraction for Lord Krishna. Eventually, Lord Krishna was driving the chariot of Arjuna wherein the later had developed the sense that Krishna was God-embodied, yet his own friend. That is why Arjuna was curious about certain elements of truth. In the mind of Arjuna, there is also an impression that Krishna is the source of wisdom. That is why whenever any crisis of decision or crossroads in making the right choice comes, it is good to hear God.

Eliot had developed a curious sense of trying to understand the appearance of light in the context of darkness of any kind in life. Eliot understood that the light of life has to emanate from the light of eternity.

Arjuna understood the concept of eternal life and that of the Supreme, having been present in the form of light and energy. Now, Divine is symbolically and essentially condensed in the human personality of Krishna is somewhat understood by Arjuna. Arjuna asked the Lord:

> *Jayasi chet karmani astae matah buddhih Janardanam*
> *Tat kim karmani ghorae mam niyojayasi keshavah.* (G. 3/1)
> O Krishna, if you consider knowledge as superior to action, then why do you recommend and ask me to do the action, which I think may have a terrible consequence.

> *Vyamishrana eva vakyena buddhim mohaya asiva mae*
> *Tat ekam badah nischityam yena shreyaham apnuyam.* (G. 3/2)
> You are, I guess, putting me into confusion in my mind by these expressions, which are involved in creating that same confusion. Therefore, please clear my doubts and tell me which is a definite discipline by which I may obtain the highest good.

Arjuna had the confidence that he could get the best and truthful response from Lord Krishna. He asked Lord Krishna questions, the answers of which were not only pertinent but also very much pressing, essential to him. Arjuna wanted to know that if knowledge of the soul is Supreme in understanding and realization, then what is the need to have karma or actions in life. Precisely, he wanted the answer which leads to certitude. Arjuna requested Krishna's answer in certain terms so that whenever he becomes convinced of the true pathways of life to follow, he will essentially do that in the light of the cause-and-effect relations that emerge in the context of the conflict of choice in life. Arjuna made a request to Lord Krishna for his response in certain terms so that he can follow that in life and make the facets of actions in life. Arjuna was the main person in the war of righteousness in Kurukshetra;

if he dropped the war, the evil would rule the world. However, if he leads, supported by Lord Krishna, victory comes on the side of the virtue drivers, which is the purpose of the appearance of the Lord on Earth.

It was in this background that Lord Krishna had thought of responding to the essential points as raised by Arjuna in the form of questions. It was crucial for Arjuna to know the way of living the best life according to Lord Krishna. Lord Krishna spoke about the Theory of Self or *Atmatattwa* at length. In the theory of self, the concept of eternity had surfaced. Truth, according to Lord Krishna, is the holistic reality in this creation. The holistic reality includes the facts and factors of the empirical and the eternal. Whereas the empirical has aspects which are perceived by our sensory organs, the eternal needs to be realized through the method of internalization. When the person gets back to her or his own internal context, the process of internalization starts with the proper recognition of the internal world and orienting it to the world outside. Human emotions and factors of character appear here.

The curious question that Arjuna had expressed was actually realistic and pertinent to the people who have a real agenda to contribute to the society and the world. Whenever there is a choice between work and wisdom, for a person with an inclination towards work, the natural choice would be work. However, others, who are attracted to the orientation of wisdom, would identify wisdom as the core factor or the objective of life. This life and its future are thus subject to the factors of life that are the usual objectives of each life. However, the way Lord Krishna is driving the scenario is to actually establish the factors of universal choice for an ideal life based on the righteous attributes.

Arjuna was shown the eternal principles and the core truth of life by the Lord. The essential truth in this creation is the universality of life. In essential terms, the truth explains the universal truth for life and the entire creation. The true identity of each created is that it is in the continuum of a journey that is truly unending. This life is a fragment of life in eternity. The cosmic source of life is like the eternal candle of light, offering illumination through flames. It provides the inputs for vital energy in the elements that usually compose life. The universal source of life is that of an infinite source of energy that usually construes life and its material-biological compositions.

The compositions carry forward and multiply the seed of life and take it forward towards creating a series of lives and thus, maintaining a balance in the human settings and formations. The supreme soul is the origin of existence. It divides itself into the lights of wishes and inclinations that truly oversee, and want to experience in the backdrop of changes and transformations happening in the course of the journey of time in the world. The Supreme fragments itself into trillions of lives and maintains its existence in each life, irrespective of the nature of the life that it ought to be. Each fragment thus impacts life as its own in terms of the qualities and attributes. Qualities of each life are thus patterned by the set of karma or actions, orientation of mind and the factors of the essential wish of each soul. Thus, each fragment resides in the abode of life as the element of the Supreme rests in the same fashion and way that the Supreme desires, in its original form and the wishes maintained for the creation.

Arjuna's questions, on the choice in life between the ways to seek wisdom and that of the set of actions or karma which is destined in life, were good enough for Lord Krishna to respond.

Sri Bhagawan ubacha:
Lokaeh asmin dwividha Nishtha pura proktya maya anagha.
Jnayogena samkhyanam karmayogena yoginam. (G. 3/3)
Lord Sri Krishna said, 'Arjuna, in this world, two courses of spiritual processes have been mentioned by me in the past. In the case of the yoga of self, the meditative process proceeds with the path of knowledge, whereas in the case of the yoga of action, it proceeds with the causes of action.'

Lord Krishna said to Arjuna that in this world, those who aspire for knowledge gradually receive the knowledge, and those who like and love to do the work of the world are destined on the path of yoga. These are the two different aspects and ways in life that people in the world may choose from. The way of knowledge gets fulfilment once the spirit of things and the aspects of divine intent are gradually fulfilled with the true element of knowledge of the Divine, and at the same time, that of the empirical aspects of the world. The person in this situation would devote her or his time to the roots. Meditation or the ways of practice like yoga would support the fulfilment of the person. Similarly, the other person has the orientation to participate and devote to work, making it desireless or nishkama karma.

Eliot profoundly explored the concept of individual liberty, asserting that it must be rooted in the unique importance of each soul. He posited that the recognition of ultimate personal responsibility for one's salvation or damnation naturally obligates society to foster every individual's full human development. However, Eliot warned that if humanity is not considered in relation to God, it could lead to an excessive devotion to created beings. This, he suggested, could paradoxically result in a humanitarianism that oppresses individuals based on what others perceive as their best interest. A person who achieves divine realization understands this by honouring individuals and performing their duties as if towards God.

Lord Krishna was clear in his utterance about the choice of the pathways in life and made it the urge and genuine choice of the person. Eliot, in his quest to find out the humanitarian context of life, finds the essence of spirit in the journey. Krishna continues for the benefit of people and to highlight the desire of the person. He says,

Na karmanam arambhyat naishkarmam purusho ashnutae.
Na cha samsyanat eva siddhim samah adhigachhati. (G.3/4)

Man does not attain freedom from just the action. Without entering into the action, nor does he reach perfection. Merely by ceasing to act, the perfection lies in a different area.

Without performing the destined karma or action, a person cannot achieve complete success. Not only should the work that someone does not get into the core of the work, alternatively, the person gets caught up in the addictions either in the work or its outcome. Fulfilment comes through the way of karma. The work can be driven to perfection under the impact and sustained drive of the person. The work, as its message in the world, carries forward the result that may have some iota of expectations of being desired in the work, and requires desireless or non-expectation from the outcome of the work.

Na hi kashchit Kshanamapi jatu tishthati karmakrit
Karyatae hi abashah karma sarvah prakritijai gunaei. (G 3.5)
Surely none can ever remain inactive, even for a moment, for everyone is helplessly driven to action by the very innate nature of human beings and the nature with which the person is born.

Everybody has to work. No one can continue in life without doing any karma. Each one is different, yet connected in the chain of things. It is the stream of karma that helps in connecting one with the other. People would prefer the type and attributes intrinsic in the person. Three broad types of personalities would be the basis of performing individual work or duty based on the intrinsic mix of attributes in him or her. Depending upon the basic attribute of a person, karma would take form and shape in accordance.

Lord Krishna has mentioned that till people are in the context of work, the flow of work would create attractions. It is through the attractions for the right attributes that a person would undertake karma. Lord Krishna gives a hint to Arjuna that the type of work that is awaited and fitted in the context, along with the quality of the person would lead to the best accomplishment in life. Krishna advocates for work, thus creating the ground for the journey towards God-realization.

The unique concept for nishkama karma as the final view of God realization in the *Bhagavad Gita* is that the work of a very special kind and in a special context leads to attaining a unique position of poise, acquiescence in all situations and neutral to each and all connections, relations, interactions and identities in the world. The factual position is that the very purpose of the sayings of Lord Krishna in the context of the war at Kurukshetra, as depicted in the Mahabharata, is to motivate and inspire Arjuna to get fully involved and wage the war to help protect the people who are in the path of righteous principles and to try and annihilate those who are opposed to righteous people and actions. Arjuna is urged to create and elevate himself to a personality where he understands the real purpose of life. In the process,

Arjuna would have the fortune to receive the grace of God. This is because Arjuna is involved in the fight for righteousness is that of noble variety. It is not the fulfilment of his own desire that Arjuna has to fight for, but it's the divine intent.

It was understood by Eliot that calmness of mind begets a unique experience in life. If someone can organize her or his mind in a way that the impacts of people around and, as a whole, the impacts of the varied types of influences from across, would make the person diffused, scattered or even chaotic in mind. However, a cool mind can settle down deep inside to dig out things which are otherwise involved in varied objects and subjects. This is how the crucial point is going to focus on the core of the consciousness of a person.

Lord Krishna is driving Arjuna to the point of stillness, where the mind is neither deluged nor diffused by factors of the world, in general, and the connected ones, in particular. Krishna says:

Karmani indriyani samyamya yah astae manasa smaran.
Indriyah arthan bimudha atma mithacharah sa ucchatae. (G.3/6)
He who outwardly restrains the organs of senses and actions, cultivates mentally the objects of senses, that man of deluded intellect is called a hypocrite.

Even when a person conceives certain ranges of unacceptable or unfair elements in mind and conceals them from the world, it is a falsehood. The organs of action may not have been involved here, but the mind, having got involved in that rotten aspect and maintaining a wishful context, and also the work that is performed by the person in this context, is that which is admixed with dirty elements of the mind. This work cannot provide good to the world, nor can it be good to the person.

Yah tu indriyani manasa niyamya aarabhatae Arjuna.
Karma indriyih karma yoga asaktah sa vishishyatae. (G.3/7)
But he, who is controlling the organs of senses and action by the power of his will and remaining unattached, undertakes the connection to God through the action using the organs of his life, and this person excels in life.

The person who is in a position to apply conscious choice towards doing some work, without getting deluged in the affairs and the results of the work, is equipoised. Even if sometimes it may happen that the person has chosen a path of work that is unworthy, the entire work and its context cannot be proven as a falsehood; rather, it is somewhat better. What appears and can be derived from here is that even if the person is unable to make the conscious choice for the work and towards the right direction of life to accomplish work, being open and fair to the context of the work would be fruitful.

This is thus the context wherein the person should choose to do work with conscious choice and guidance of a good spirit.

Actually, it is not the karma as such, but the attitude, orientation and the mental formations across karma that matter. If a person is not seen or identified as having done something that is not true or fair in the spirit of things, it may appear that the person is one among those good and fair people in the world who think and act good for others. The situation may turn out differently. It is the totality of the revealed work, thoughts and the mind of the person that matters in this process. Fairness and goodness should prevail at all levels: mental, physical and conscious. If at any of these three levels, one is in touch with, under the influence of or in collusion with any dirty things or untruth, then the work would take a shape that would essentially spoil the destined and expected poise or the expected to be of the person. These become very important in a case when the person is of the kind of Arjuna, in whom the destiny and the Divine had already identified a course of life to support the divine cause to fulfil the objective of God on Earth.

It has been a part of the observation by Eliot in his *Burnt Norton*, III, II, 114, also, that the person or persons with the ground realities properly known and understood, the aspects of the orientation, objectives and ultimate contributory purpose of the life of a person would involve the subjective, as well as, the objective dimensions of life. As Lord Krishna says:

Niyatam kuru karma tvam karma jyaoh hi akarmanh.
Shariya yatrapi cha tae na prasidhyat akarmanah. (G.3/8)
Arjuna, you do the allotted work, you perform the duty, for action is superior to inaction. Getting away from action is not good. You cannot even maintain your life, keeping yourself away from action.

Lord Krishna gives the practical advice to Arjuna that if a person does not do the karma required in life, how will the person gather a livelihood? On the other hand, he continues explaining a rational analysis between doing work and not doing work in a particular given context. It is always understood that doing work is the factor and the approach in life, which is always better than not doing work.

Yajnarthyat karmanyae hi anyatra lokaeh ayam karmabandhanah.
Tat artham karma Kounteyah mukta sangah samacharah. (G.3/9)
Man is bound by his own action, except when it is performed for the sake of God. Therefore, Arjuna, you do diligently the duty and perform it based on the principles of desireless action. You should be free from attachments, and for the sake of sacrifice, you should practice the kind of action which leads to that sacrifice.

The work, that is done with a view to fulfilling the objective of God on Earth, is the one that is liberating in its intrinsic character. Work done with personal or broader selfish interest would spoil the essential spirit of it and usually create a sense of bondage in life that is always oriented to the material, emotional and human context in the world. As in this advice, Lord Krishna gives a hint that a variety of work accomplished with a view to being a part of God's design of things, work itself is fulfilling for the person and for the world.

Karma liberates from the impacts of delusions and mental problems of a wide variety when its purpose is noble. Karma, that suits the purpose and objective of God, makes the performer fulfilled in many respects. It is, thus, the objective and the orientation of the karma that create the base of doing things and take things forward in the light of the Divine intent and objective. As Lord Krishna says,

Saha yajnanah prajah shrishtwa pura ubacha Prajapatih.
Anena prashavidyam esha vah ista asya kamadhukah. (G.3/10)
Having created mankind with their duty specified at the beginning of creation, the Creator, the Lord Supreme, said to them, You shall prosper by this. May this yield the enjoyment you seek.

Lord Krishna said that when karma is turned into the quality of a sacrificial fire or yajna, it provides a person with the realization of the true identity of God. The person understands that God is himself eager to offer divine attributes and resources for lives when the life develops the attitude of sacrifice and comes into contact with God, in terms of the living context of people. It is thus the prerogative of the person to resort to such a set of actions that would actually work as elements and forces of invocation. In such a situation, the honest wishes and initiatives of the person are taken into consideration, and at the same time, the ones that construe the wish and ways of the Divine on Earth get transformed into accomplished actions. The Lord offers a suggestion to the people on Earth for the fulfilment of worldly objectives. He says:

Devan bhabayatah anenah tae devah bhabayantu vah.
Parashparam bhabayantah shreyah param abapashah. (G. 3/11)
Adore the gods through this sacrifice in the form of action, and let the gods also be gracious to you, if you are into the actions, each fostering the other disinterestedly, you will attain the highest good.

When the person performs this yajna or sacrificial work, the offerings of conspicuous elements of enjoyment constrain the fundamental resources for living. It is thus a way for the person to make a turnaround in the world, in the context of their mind and consciousness. The divine endowment of provisions for food and materials essential for living a good life is on offer in this kind of situation. The people doing this sacrificial work would thus bring about some kind of initiative that connects with others and creates a situation of collective attainment.

Ishtan bhogan hi ho devah dasyantae yajnabhabitah.
Taih dattwan apradayah ebhoyoh yo bhunjtae stena eva sah. (G.3/12)
With your sacrifice, the gods will surely bestow on you unmatched desired enjoyments. He who enjoys the gifts bestowed by them, without offering anything to them in return, is undoubtedly a thief.

Whenever the sacrificial work is finally accomplished, it is a pleasing factor to the divine entities. The doer and person doing sacrificial work and thought would, thus, reach out to the consciousness of the gods as a whole. However, there could be some people who are opposed to this way of doing things, maybe undertaking the work of theft. This is because of the factors of the collective approach.

It appears that there are time zones, as well as those where, on a different time scale, things offer their hidden orientation. This is one reason why it's longing for such a mixed approach. This is a way out for the world and human beings to meditate with a view to having God's grace for a good life on Earth.

Annad bhabanti bhutani parjannayat annah sambhabah.
Yajnayat bhabati parjanya yajnah karma samat udbhabah. (G.3/14)
All beings are evolved from food, production of food is independent of rain, rain ensues from sacrifice, and sacrifice is rooted in prescribed action.

Anna or food is not only essential but primordial to life. When the sky showers with rain, it creates the right condition for the Earth's ecosystem to be in a position to produce. Therefore, anna or food maintains life and thereby does the great connect with work. Work of the right kind, therefore, depends on the providence for the maintenance of lives. It is an essential part of life that sustains it. The one who performs the right kind of work without imposing conditional constraints and without expectations from, is doing the right kind of work.

However, prior to talking about the sequence of processes leading to the perfection in karma, Lord Krishna had narrated to Arjuna the essence of doing the yajna in the context of the world. He elaborates on the power and essence of the yajna in the form of sacrificial work.

Yajnashishtha ashinah santoham uchhyatae sarva kilah bishau.
Bhunjatae tae twagham papai ye pachanti Atmakaranam. (G. 3/13)
The virtuous who partake of what is left after sacrifice are absolved of all sins. Those sinful ones who cook for the sake of nourishing their body alone partake in sin only.

The food in its pure condition, as dedicated to the Gods, is powerful with its intrinsic nature and purity. If any person with a pure and dedicated mind takes it, the person is now endowed with the blessed power of having got rid of any kind of sin stored within. The food which is already presented to God in the Yajna is thus the purifier of the world within, of the person who has taken that within.

Karma Brahmo udbhabham viddhi Brahmah Aksharah Sama udbhavam.
Tasmat sarvagtam Brahma nityam yajnae pratishthitam. (G.3/15)
Know that prescribed action has its origin in the Vedas, and the Vedas were produced from the indestructible godly head; hence, the all-pervading, infinite, the Supreme God, is always present in sacrifice.

Lord Krishna says to Arjuna that karma of all kinds, varieties and descriptions emerges out of the wish and grace of the Supreme Lord. This is a pathway of fulfilling the wish of the Supreme through the process of the entire creation. Therefore, when the sacrificial work is thought out and attempted to it begets the blessed position of the Lord and thus, the karma makes a continuity in the flow of lives of people on Earth and the entire creation.

As Lord Krishna mentions, all varieties, types, descriptions and categories of the work have their own legacy and inheritance in subtle intrinsics of each karma, and thereby, each karma is blessed by the divine consent for a performer to take it forward, but with a difference. The destined karma should always carry forward a broader message and perspective, and exist beyond the narrow limits of personal selfish interests of the person.

Evam prabartitam chakram na anubartayati iha yah.
Agha aayuh indriyah aaramah mogham Partha sah jivatih. (G.3/16)
He who does not follow the wheel of creation, thus set in motion in the world, that is, the person who does not perform his duties, O Arjuna, that person leads a sinful and sensual life; he lives in vain.

Karma of the right kind is introduced in the creation by God. However, some are unaware or careless about what passes on to another spectrum of karma. This other spectrum of karma is low in its quality and filthy in its contents and characters. People are there who are fond of this and get tuned to this. These are the people who are guided by the wrong and negative senses within, and are guided in the system they foster, wherein the organs catering to the lower intrinsics get stimulated and are dominated by the lowness of the mind in certain emerging contexts of life. This type of karma thus reduces the spirit of living to very low and loses the purposeful existence of lives on Earth.

Yat Atmah aarati eva syat Atmah triptasya cha manabah.
Atmani eva cha santusta tasya cha no karyam vidyatae. (G.3/17)
He, however, who takes delight in the self alone, and is gratified with the self, and is contented in the self, has no duty to perform.

However, Lord Krishna continues to say that a person blessed with knowledge of self is contented and happy with the spirit of atman in life, and thus, the person resides in the sense and spirit of God in its form as atman, residing within the cave of heart of the person. Thereby, the person does not have to look for any karma for her or him in the empirical sense of the term. Rather, the person is free from the impacts of the world of empiricism. This is how the person needs to be accommodated in the realm of life. Karma with dedication is thus the karma leading to God-realization.

Lord Krishna elaborated on the nature of the karma that helps to show the ways to God-realization. A person who keeps away from the realm of karma reduces herself or himself to a position of aloneness. Usually, the person not engaged in karma falls prey to the emotional factors of life like dullness, depression, deprivation, delusions, dejections and factors which generate and enhance stressful situations within. Their mind may turn indolent and deluged, making itself a prey to the attractions of the evil forces scattered across and pulling the mind down from the fairness and ethical standards of life. As Krishna puts emphasis on the concept of the eternal foe, it is the human desire that stands as the eternal foe. He emphasizes by saying:

Aabritam jnanam etena jnanino nitya bairinam (G.3/39)
The eternal foe is the enemy of knowledge and realization. It is the process of realization that requires purity. Desire kills the purity. He has stressed the point further by giving the example of fire.

As Lord Krishna continues saying,

Kamarupena Kounteya duhh purena analena cha (G.3/39)
The enemy to human purity is the desire of any kind, in general, and the biological desire, in particular.

It destroys the stream of good wishes and the spirit of goodness to approach the destiny of purity and truth. The central problem in life is desire. It is that central problem which needs to be taken care of. The spell of desire is the killer of goodness in life. It is that fire which, by nature, consumes and destroys the fuel of goodness and purity of human life. The fire of desire has an enormous capacity to burn. It, thus, needs to be contained. The fire of desire, by nature, has so much capacity and strength that even if the item and focus of the desire is made to fulfil, it is never totally exhausted. The roots of desire help and allow it to grow further, maybe in a new form and with new dimensions.

Waging the war was not the sole concern of the Lord. It was actually the art of controlling senses and then undertaking the task. Once the senses are within the limits of control, the person is competent to represent the forces of divinity. Lord Krishna had clarified by saying:

'Tasmat tvam indriyani niyamya Bharatarshava' (G.3/41)

Calling Arjuna the best person, Lord Krishna had asked him to control all sense organs and be neutral in spirit to the cause, but at the same time drive the cause towards success and fulfilment.

Krishna repeatedly mentions, with huge emphasis, that 'desire' is the root of all evils. He explains that desire arises out of the ego of the person. Desire captures the organs of the senses and tries to dominate over other tendencies of life. Once desire is in a position to capture the senses, it takes control over the faculties of the human mind. Once the mind is under the spell of desire, it attempts to contaminate the intellect of the person. Jivatman, residing within the existence, gradually accepts those impacts on the mind as the experience of this life. Senses become obsessed with the elements of desire. The person then develops the conviction of the primacy of desire. That means the mind goes on to craft and design things in such a way that the perception and conviction are developed across the elements of desire, considering those as essential to achieve and fulfil the objective of life. A person develops attractions and passions towards enjoyment in fulfilling the objective in life. Once the person understands the futility of the enjoyments in life through the fulfilment of the desires, their perspectives undergo change. Devoted to God, a person develops the best conditions for life and work. Thus, it is an imperative that in the interest of the spread of truth among the traditional and other ways power of the mind combines with the power of the vital to accomplish mind choice.

The Vedic observations are also, in a way, synchronized with what Lord Krishna, as a guide, tells Arjuna. The Krishna Yajur Veda connects the senses with objects and organs through a series of talks, as mentioned by the Godhead Yama, to a very young spirit and soul, Nachiketa. Nachiketa had, among others, the quest for atman. He wanted to know from Yama the nature, character, features and descriptions of the atman. The role of the mind in the process of understanding the spiritual truth was narrated by Yama. He was talking about the connection or relation the mind has with the organs, systems, the objects and above all, the Earth consciousness. While narrating the relation to Nachiketa, the godhead Yama said that senses are the drivers of the human system, but the objects are always greater than the senses. The mind is greater than the objects of the senses. The intellect of the person is more important than the mental power. However, human intellect is limited by its own boundary and horizons of things: the divine intellect, which is sometimes considered as the cosmic intellect, is the Supreme and the governing intellect for the cosmic system. The Vedic sages have called it m*ahat-tattwa* or the Noble Existence, the Truth. The identity of God in the form of purusha is above all. The cosmic consciousness, human consciousness or the individual consciousness all converge to a point where the original creation or the primordial creation of matter and life were driven by the Spirit of God. As Lord Krishna narrates this sequence in clear terms:

Indriyani parani aahu indrievya param manah
Manasha tu para buddhih yah buddhae paratah tuh sah.   (G.3/42)
The senses are said to be greater than the body, but greater than the senses is the mind, greater than the mind is the intellect, and what is greater than the intellect is the self within, the self within is the connection with God himself.

The sequence, things, organs, forces and inputs that collectively govern the life force and make it suited to the growth towards God-realization. It is thus pivotal in the sequence of things to understand the role of each and, in the process, to identify the nature of things which are not only primary but are instrumental in the making of the vehicle of life move forward in the direction of the divine light.

The mind remains an invisible and otherwise untraceable organ in the human system. The eyes see with the power of vision, and all the mechanisms of the human visual functions are aligned with. However, viewing occurs only when the entire process of vision is supported by the elements of the mind. Mind added to the process of vision makes the view happen. Similar is the case and the situation with all other functional activities of the human system. The mind plays a central role in making functional organs respond and act in such a way that it is a part of the entire human system, connecting and influencing the functionalities of the organs in a way that connects with the universe, within and without.

The point is, however, driven to the purity of mind. Generic function of human mind connects with the inputs and guidance from organs of senses. However, in a spiritual journey human mind is attempted to get connected with the internal consciousness with God as the central objective to realize. In case of the objective of the functionality of one organ or one particular system in the human organic or functional activity, it is the wisdom acquired by the mind that talks about the priorities of one against the other would be the important elemental focus. Wisdom is developed by the pure mind. Purity of mind is possible to attain through realization of God and being in the God consciousness. Mind, free from all elements of desire, anger, delusions, greed, jealousy, ego and elements of life, is in a position to earn realization of God through continuous churning and invocation of the spirit of God within the personality. This mind is endowed with the wisdom and the spirit that truly gets in touch with God. The devotee, thus, gets the wisdom of atman residing within.

6 Art of Knowledge-driven Work

Journey from the empirical to eternal Knowledge

Spirit of Work

The doctrine of work or action is very explicit in its objective, approach and the impact which could emerge from it. Work has its own dimensions in the world. It is a functional entity that has connections with the world of thoughts, aspirations and actions of individuals and entities. Actions that are undertaken in the process can transform the world of thoughts in a way. On the other hand, the process of thought can also have generative and formative dimensions in the frameworks of the things relevant to the work. It is, thus, the orientation to the thoughts and work that needs the appropriation of focus in its becoming and realistic functioning in the world. Work that is realistic with the focus and orientation in the context of the work makes its impact in the world as a new generative idea or input to the next round of action. It is this round of thought and orientation that makes the work habitable in its own way and dimension. The world of corporations has its own approach to work. This approach has a few dimensions. One of such dimensions is to be compatible with the focus and the vector of the actions. The corporate functions can be classified as follows:

Sharhaprakriti Karmani (The six functional natures of work):

a) *Viswatmakam* (विश्मात्मकम्): Universality in the corporate functional approaches
b) *Visheshattwam* (विशेषत्वम्): Particularity in the corporate approach to the work chosen for it
c) *Gatimayam* (गतिमयम्): Dynamism in the scopes for and the objectives of the work for it
d) *Gunannwitam* (गुनान्वितम्): Quality and Quantum of the work per unit of the invested time and resources
e) *Samartham* (समार्थम्): Effectiveness of the work in the context of available unit of resources
f) *Samani Vyaptam* (समानि व्याप्तम्): Compatibility of the work with the contextual and factual realities prevailing

(a) *Viswatmakam* (विश्मात्मकम्): Work of any description, dimension or profile catches the identity of universality through its nature and exposition. Work done by a person in a particular context, whether defined or undefined, may prove to be ideal before the world. This can be in a way that anyone in the world, from any of its corners or boundaries, may prove to be an ideal to bring out the best output possible in that particular context or in different ways out there. It is, thus, the spirit of the work and not just the features of the work that creates the difference in the context of things. Dimensions of the work prove to be unique and special, whereas the spirit of the work proves to be the guiding force towards accomplishing any work.

(b) *Visheshattwam* (विशेषत्वम्): In the context of a particular work, the power of the work gets associated with the performer of the work, the nature of the work and the intrinsic spirit of the work. In each case of a work, a particular dimension of the work is created by the uniqueness of the context, nature and the objective of the work. The factors of work would include the specifications and details of the work. The work that the performer is induced to has a tune and also specific ingredients. The truth of the work is located in the spirit of the work. The work and its dimensions get deluged in the functional dimensions. these are the particularities of the work. Every work can transcend the limits of its particular identity once the work is drenched in the spirit and truth lying within its intrinsic dimension. However, the *Visheshattwam* gives the work a new identity once it is done with the right perspective.

(c) *Gatimayam* (गतिमयम्): Displacement from the position zero is an indicator of work. When an amount of force (f) is applied to a body at total rest, the amount of positional shift that the object makes is a measure of displacement (s) that makes work done (w). To put it in a formula, it works out as: $w = f \times s$. This means work done is a measure equal to the product of the magnitude of force and the magnitude of displacement taken place. It has been said: *'Tat ejati sarvashah tat bhi na ejati'* — which means the supreme entity, Brahman, is the abode of the Mahakaal — the creator of time, is in the mood of either moving or may be sometimes averse to any movement. The abode of the Devadideva — the primordial god or the god of all gods had created this universe as an entity with inbuilt diversity. However, this undertakes another form — that of Nataraj. Nataraj is the dancing form of Lord Shiva. With the onset of the dance of Nataraj Shiva, time started clicking in the world. This world is akin to doing something in line with the original desire of the creator. By way of inducing the cosmic dance of Lord Shiva, he pushes up the energy within the creation. Whereas the scientific definition of entropy focuses on the amount of thermal energy per unit of temperature that goes to waste and remains unavailable for work. This also indicates the degree of disorder in a system. In a way, it leads to the estimation of the amount and degree of randomness in a system. Scientifically, it has been shown primarily as: $S = K_s$. In R. Where, S is the measure of the entropy of the system, K_s is the Boltzmann Constant, which has been calculated as 1.380×10^{-23} Jules per Calorie of temperature unit and R stands as the measure of the affected random particle at its nuclear description. Boltzmann had visualised that in the case of even the extreme randomness, there remains an element of constant within the particle. When in the solid form, let's take a cube of ice. Now, the particles are at rest. When it is heated, the particles start moving apart, the input energy leads to a situation where the particles start moving apart; the input energy leads to a situation where the particles, which were at rest, now make movement and take up the profile of water. Following further heating beyond the boiling temperature, the small constituting particles start moving in a random manner, leading to a gaseous form. At this point, the energy released is enormous. It was thus the normal static situation, made to be dynamic through the infusion of energy. Whether in a static or dynamic situation, the intrinsic energy remains as a constant factor in the system.

This creation is thus the one where the Supreme Brahman remains in full energy in the creation, even at the most minute level. For the living entities, he remains inside the abode of a person in the form of an invisible and very minute spirit in the identity of the atman. Atman is the symbolic, material and spiritual existence of entities. He exists without being noticed. His presence is thus understood as the energy, potent and the spirit that contains goodness, all the noble qualities of the Supreme. The revelation of the Supreme through the eternal truth as Sat, the cosmic consciousness or Chit and the underlying spirit of bliss or Ananda are collectively possessed by the atman residing within. The Lord has designed this universe in such a way that every element thus created carries the potent energy of the Supreme. The Lord has also designed this creation with elemental consciousness within each entity, having similar or the same kind of potency as the largest or the most potent one could have in the process of living their lives on Earth. Life has carried forward the energy and the spirit which are in its attributes, having the same or similar focus as that of the superior objects and entities, which carry larger and wholesome potency on the matter or the living substance. The atman that rests within the human abode is thus the unique presence of the supreme truth, consciousness and bliss. In this process, life and even non-living entities of material nature do have energy within. Initially stored as static energy, it may be revealed in the dynamic form at any point in time.

With the inbuilt potential of dynamism, the living entities exercise their power of intent to be dynamic and, at the same time, to generate energy in other forms in life. Thus, when an entity with the potent may lead to having a unique realization of the supreme truth in life and at the same time can help the creation to come up with new and creative things, it serves as the backdrop of the requirements of new creative power and the process triggering into the continuity of the same.

The entire universe is said to be in a dynamic equilibrium. The equilibrium is to maintain the movements and relative movements of the objects, lives and things. It has been identified by scientists in the modern era, as well as previously, that each item of matter is comprised of small particles which are in a dynamic form. Each matter may be broken down to its basic molecule. Within molecules are atoms. Within atoms are the particles. At this level, the particles are sub-atomic particles - protons, neutrons and electrons. The position of subatomic particles is arranged in such a pattern that a nucleus exists around which the electrons are continuously moving, following certain pathways that are roughly circular but actually have oval shapes. It makes the electrons move across the nucleus in a particular manner. At the center or the nucleus, the neutrons and protons are grouped under a particular category called hadrons. These are particles with intrinsic mass. Protons and neutrons are heavier than electrons. Neutrons would be roughly 2600 - 2700 times heavier than electrons, and neutrons would be slightly heavier. Hadrons, because of their mass and elemental contents, would exert the power of gravity on the lighter element, electrons. These powers of attraction are sometimes linear forces and at times skewed or curved in their trajectories. The fact remains that the subatomic fundamental particles are in constant movement. Electrons are moving around the nucleus, where protons and neutrons remain. However, within the nucleus, protons and neutrons are also constantly changing their positions with respect to each other. It is a kind of intimate mixing between them. Thus, they are intimate co-particles with protons having positrons as their fundamental. Positrons are positively charged and electrons are negatively charged in terms of their electromagnetic identity, whereas neutrons consist of neutral particles.

(d) *Gunannwitam* (गुनान्वितम्): The quality of a work depends on various factors of life and the context of the work. A work is said to be performed in a given context and situation. Whereas the context of the work is mostly unique. The performer's uniqueness added to that makes it happen in a way that stipulates the relation and the match of suitability between the work and the performer. However, the situation thus created would be one and unique when the work attains a level of accomplishment to the satisfaction of the performer, and the inputs which were ordained for accomplishing the work. The structural aspect of the work gets the touch of efforts by various other performers of a similar kind of work. Any action that follows the structure would thus lead to a similar kind of situation where, because of that generic structure of the work, when oriented in a way that it remains impersonal in nature and approach, the process reduces the burden on the person to do a unique way of the functional reality of getting a particular work done.

Uniqueness is an essential attribute of the work where the human component remains important. However, in each context, the human component remains as one of the most important and vibrant aspects of the work, whatever the prevailing situation for the work. It is thus the degree and quality of involvement of a person in a work that may attempt to redefine the context of the work, even in a mechanistic system.

Mental orientation of the performer plays an important role in the shaping of the work, thus making it part of the system to have an in-depth review of the work. Thus, it is the combination of the domain of work and the human elements in the work which makes up the quality of the work. Quality, as a factor, thus focuses on the intrinsic nature of a person in a way that breeds the derived and recommended elements of the work and its context.

A person dedicated to the cause of the work, on one hand, and connected with the outcome of the work, makes the work, by and large, accomplished. Demand for things in the purview of the context would make it directly linked to the making of the work. It is, now, the perspective of the person in the work and its performer that an amount of dedication would create the most valued context of work that would be good for society, the person and the world.

Quality, thus ensured in a system, would push the realities in a context that would benefit the work and make its impact in the world better. A context where the highest achievable quality is possible is thus the one in which certain dimensions of the work would benefit and fulfill the world of work.

Imperatives of the quality of work can thus be segmented into some kind of fragments or components of required attributes that make it happen in a way that makes the work better. This would include the following dimensions:

(a) Empirical knowledge about the approaches, objectives, methods, any sequence of things and the modes of the work, tools, technologies and instruments, facilities may make the work incrementally better.
(b) Intrinsic knowledge about the work remains the force behind the most successful, sustainable, rewarding and other related things in the work. Thus, the divine source of intrinsic value would be the most accomplished for the work. Belief is thus a factor which is important here to understand a few fundamentals:
  - Who is the real owner of the work?
  - What is the set of things that the performer has to maintain?
  - Which aspect of the work proves to be more indicative of the authority over the work or its result therefrom?

With the possible response to all these aspects, the usual way of work can be accomplished as the possible functional design of the work.

Intrinsic or the inner dimension of work, in a way, removes it from the context of it and thus remains an intrinsic multiplier of the design, thus proving the best outcome that could emerge from any source. A work dedicated to its own cause signifies the transcendence in the scope of work and its resultant impacts in the world of work. Eternal possibilities in a work thus make it happen within the categorical selfish expectation of the work in the context.

Science of Work

(e) Samartham (समार्थम्): Human quest is basically the quest to fulfil the internal desires and, at the same time, to make revealed to the world the fact of fulfilment. Meaningful life is considered to be that which is a life of success in the context of the rolling of the wheels of time, and at the same time, drawing satisfaction in the incidents and things that are allied with the spirit of life.

Success and fulfilment have differential meanings in the lives of different sets of people. However, a common and usually perceived meaning is one that brings to life whatever is dreamt of or whatever is expected. However, while aspiring for something in life, all the consequences of getting those things in place may not have the identical meaning in life. The examples for such dichotomy may be obtained from different aspects of lives of different people. It will not be out of place to mention the same in the context of the great scientist, Sir Albert Einstein. The Theory of Relativity, or Special Theory and the Mass-Energy Equivalence Theory, are all remarkable ones. The atomic experiments of the Manhattan Project during the Second World War and the contribution of the team of scientists, including Rutherford, were remarkable. But the idea triggered by the relation $E = mc^2$ was remarkable in its power to create energy at the point of the act of convertibility. Process of fusion or that of fission, either way goes ahead to release an enormous flow of energy from the explosion. The discovery of the power of the huge quantum of energy released through the explosion of atoms made some scientists happy that the shortage of the supply of energy for activities related to or targeted at human progress can be made to happen through some device or system considered suitable for the same.

Supposing some entity has plenty of thorium in stock and a handful of the required element, uranium. The atomic configuration of uranium shows having 238 electrons in the orbits of the nuclear structure, whereas thorium has 235 orbiting electrons in the structure of the atom. The real capacity to have an explosion, being at the level of uranium, the first task would be to elevate thorium from its level of 235 electrons at the outer orbit to 238 electrons. Through this process of elevation, additions of electrons do happen in a context that makes a transformation in the element to make it into the property of uranium. This matter, at its elemental level, can release a good amount of energy. Albert Einstein's idea was such that the amount of the large flow of energy that occurs through the fission of the particle of U-238 would help in generating electricity for human living, in different ways. However, the requirement of the Pentagon was different. The situations that had emerged in the later part of the Second World War made getting a destructive atom bomb more important to them, as a kind of emergency need of the nation at that point in time. Thus, the idea had developed to help human beings to live better, have better ways of satisfaction in life. But the reversal did actually happen. Rutherford could become successful in the act of getting the fission energy released through the process of explosion when dropped from above onto an unacceptable object on any part of the Earth system. The objective of getting huge energy released through bond of the mass of atoms for human good had turned into devastations of humans in the world.

Perceptive understanding, in most of the cases, may not provide the truth of the context and the situation thereby may be booked into from different perspectives including the facts garnered through perceptive understanding. However, there are situations where perceptive understanding plays not only an important role, but also the most dependable guiding parameter. Even though we find some experimentation limits, the facts and knowledge of the subject of observation or research are limited to its boundaries of time, space and context. It is thus a proven imperative that the idea of the focus, the total truth can be understood when we combine the empirical observations with the entire context with the perceptive understanding. *Samartham* is the process when the entire contributory elements of the focus of the object become one and the same in all situations to in all places. It is thus the situation when the objectives of the focus have to be realized in the context. Only then are we observing the situations and the emerging dimensions of context. Truth is thus revealed through a combination of the elements of functioning; truth as identified through the empirical realities of the situation. The empirical part of truth is important, but it is just a part of the entire truth, which can be understood through perception.

"So, we cannot take the functional freedoms we find in classical physics, in the wave functions, despite the fact that the wave function has clear influence on direct physical behaviour." Functional freedom still has a key role to play in quantum mechanics, but it must be combined with the critical idea introduced by Max Planck in 1900 with his famous formula: $E=h\nu$. (E is the energy bundle; ν is radiation frequency; h is Plank's Constant). And further, with the deep insights that Einstein, Bose, Heisenberg, Schrodinger, Dirac, and others later provided. Planck's formula tells us that the kind of field that actually occurs in nature has some sort of discreteness about it, which makes it behave like a system of particles where the higher mode of frequency of oscillation that the field might indulge in, the more strongly the energy in the field would manifest itself in this particle–like behaviour."

> Roger Penrose, *Fashion, Faith and Fantasy, In the new physics of the Universe,* Princeton University Press, Princeton and Oxford, 2018, p. 192.

The scientific understanding starts with the material content of the thing and, at the same time, the perceptive dimension of the function. This perceptive dimension can yield some understanding when the perception develops through an inner penetrative dimension of the situation. The perceptive dimension varies with the degree of penetrative focus, with the context and the realities prevailing across. It is thus the degree of penetrative view which becomes an important determinant in the process of realization of the context. Contextual understanding translates into a situation where the material elements in the object of focus, its contextual understanding and the physical dimensions of the content together focus on each other to understand the factors that have impact on the physical description of mass, and also on the conditions like whether the object is having any movement or not, whether it has clear dimension and different types of focus or the force equivalents.

The mass of an object is something that has an autonomous relationship with the Earth and the cosmic system. Gravity cannot be stopped. Gravity is the act of the heavier object exerting the force of pull over the other objects, large or small. Gravity of the entire cosmic system has endless power to be felt even by the smallest object. Thus, the smaller objects will receive a smaller force of pull while the heavier ones have a larger force. Apart from this, in the event of dynamism, as encapsulated by the observer, the object in a position of vector becomes important. The velocity and speed make it revealed. However, at the core of every object, there lies an intrinsic truth which stands beyond the observational or measurable facts. This is understood only through realization.

Art of Work

The Cosmic Colony: The King's Colony

One of the most important ingredients of empirical identity is the gravity of the element or the entity. Gravity as a force is present everywhere within the Earth system, around it in the solar system and within the universe. Everywhere, gravity is a common presence. However, the magnitude and overall vector of gravity vary from object to object and time to time. The structure of the universe is such that everywhere there stands a central entity enforcing its power of influence on the things around. This makes the colony of the entity at the centre be called the King's Colony. The King's Colony creates a kingdom with certain fundamental features built into it. The King's Colony, in the cosmic context, may be finally termed as the Cosmic Colony. For example, the cosmic colony of the Sun is the provider of vital energy to its fundamentals, to the lives lived and grown under the aegis of the solar system. It may not be the same pattern always and everywhere, but there is a pattern where every element has a reciprocity with the king, in this cosmic colony. In the solar system, the Sun, being the king, shoulders the major responsibility of making the destined things that happen. God has made it in such a way that once the colony takes a step, the king has to assert its responsibility to take charge of the colony, remaining in the destined conditions, maintaining the standards of existence throughout.

"Max Planck was confronted with the problems of granularity in 1900. Here we have a state which we now consider to be composed of coexisting components, where each component involves different numbers of those filled quanta that we now refer to as photons. For any particular frequency v, Planck's revolutionary principle implied that a photon of that frequency must have a corresponding particular energy as given by $E = hv = 2\pi h'v$.

It was, in effect, by using such a counting procedure, that the previously little known Indian physicist, Satyendranath Bose, in a letter he sent to Einstein in June 1924, provided a direct derivation of the Planck radiation formula (without appealing to any electrodynamics) where in addition to $E = hv$ and the fact that photon number would not be fixed (Photon number not conserved), he just required that the photon have two distinct polarization states and most importantly would need to satisfy what we call Bose statistics (or, Bose Einstein statistics) so that states differing from one another merely by interchanging of pairs of photons would not be counted as physically distinct. These last two features were revolutionary at the time and Bose is deservedly remembered today in the name of Boson that is attached to any basic particle of integer spin (which is thereby subject to Bose statistics)."
Roger Penrose, *Fashion, Faith and Fantasy, In the new physics of the Universe,* Princeton University Press, Princeton, Oxford, 2018, p. 194.

God has created this universe in a sequence of things in existence, so as to have the positions of identities of each entity remain uniquely defined, in a way that they maintain a kind of reciprocity in the cosmic system. The cosmic system has its own king's colonies of infinite number. Human life as ours is in a perpetual bond in the colony maintained by the solar king. It is thus the solar king's functioning and reciprocity that make things happen. This is a pattern that is followed by the elements remaining within the system. The relationship of entities within the king's colony thus connects each other physically.

Scientific understanding of this pattern has been explained by the great scientist Roger Penrose, taking reference from the relevant others. Scientists depict gravity as an autonomous force that arises out of the presence of contents in essential material terms called contents of the mass. Gravity arises within the mass contained, responding based on variations in the mass of materials and the position of the material. The position could be static or dynamic. This refers to both the level of the gross matter and the level of particles comprising the matter. The structure of this cosmos is such that a basic dynamic equilibrium exists in terms of the velocity, frequency, spin and magnitude of materials, which connect each with the other and make the system functioning and vibrant. God designed such an independent system operating through an exchange process of karma or actions initiated in life.

Gravity is inbuilt in the elements that have some mass in their content. However, if the particle is massless, then gravity cannot work on that. In that kind of situation, the kind of forces that operate are points of concern. In case of the accumulated massless particles, some kind of force other than that of gravity works. The concept of having energy identified in a vacuum works here. The vacuum energy arises out of something apart from the material ingredients available in the form of mass. Here, the issue of mass and energy having a reciprocal relationship of equivalence does work. Although the empty space in the cosmic system called the cosmic void does not have any content of mass, by virtue of having energy content within, it connects with the cosmic bodies. The connection is not necessarily on the strength of the gravitational pull, but it is because of the magnitude of energy that is contained within the vacuum space. The creation has a wide diversity of this kind and other varieties that make the cosmic system keep going. It is the outpouring of the energy content that creates a pool of attractions, and through that, mutual connectivity is established in our cosmic system.

God's wish has been the causative factor behind the entire creation. It is the type and the destined character of the entity that matter in the gamut of things. Each entity in this creation has some connectivity with the other entities through mutual connections of the forces of nature or forces created from within the entities. This means even if a particle is massless and gets treated as a part of the void, it may still create connections through the elemental character that is still in the process of nature.

The scientific view stands as

According to the cosmologist George Gamow, Einstein once remarked that the introduction of the cosmological term was the biggest blunder he ever made in his life. However, from our present understanding, as witnessed by the 2011 Nobel Prize winner Saul Perlmutter and others, had observed the phenomenon that the cosmic system maintains an inherent dynamism with continuous acceleration in most part of the system and a possible retardation at some place as well. This accelerated expansion is most directly explained by Einstein's cosmological constant Λ. Einstein's cosmological relation is $G = 8\gamma T + \Lambda g$, where Λ is the cosmological constant, g is the metric tensor, and the vacuum energy which should permeate all empty space. The reason that physicists expect the vacuum to have a non-zero (positive) energy, therefore a mass (in accordance with Einstein's E=mc²), comes from some very basic considerations of Quantum Mechanics and Quantum Field Theory (QFT).

> "It is common practice in QFT to resolve a field into vibrational modes, each of which would have its own definite energy. Among these various vibrational modes (each oscillating with its corresponding specific frequency in accordance with Planck's E=hv) would be one that has the minimum energy value, but it turns out that the energy value is not zero, and is referred to as Zero-point Energy. Even in a vacuum, therefore, the potential presence of any field leads to it manifesting itself in at least a minimum amount of energy."
> - Roger Penrose, *Fashion, Faith and Fantasy, In the new physics of the Universe,* Princeton University Press, Princeton, Oxford, 2018, pp. 285-6.

The scientific view tries to explain that the phenomenon happens within the entire system, that the continuous and discrete functions coexist in the universe as a process of diversity. When the discrete process is focused on the aspects of the content on one hand and that of the possibilities on the other, combined, it creates an impact on the cosmic bodies in the existence of different aspects of the cosmic forces on the other. Looking at it, one can come to an understanding that nature has provided the creation with profuse options and connections for each element to connect with the others. This makes it possible for the elemental material object to connect with the objects of the vacuum as well. This King's Colony in cosmos, or the cosmological colony of elements, focuses on the elemental constant as the cosmological colony for the same. The cosmological colony is thus connected with the king of the colony; thus, it is connected with some kind of force, either explicit or implicit. It is, therefore, the main focus of the cosmic order that the king's cosmic colony makes a composite presence happen. In this context, one understands that the system, which happens to be available, is to be made visible as a kind of option in the game of things for the benefit of existence. On this issue, the basic idea of going ahead with the process of life connects with the king of the cosmic colony. Thus, God's intent is truly realized in the context of the cosmic progress of life and other forces across.

f) **Samani Vyaptam (समानि व्याप्तम्):** The spiritual understanding of the universe makes the wider coverage of truth perceived by the individuals. Scientific quests reveal the empirical and physical realities, but the spiritual understanding makes things revealed at a higher degree and in larger dimensions. For example, when we talk of the reality present in our solar system, the scientific understanding makes it such that the sun, which is at the centre of the solar system, makes the planets and other bodies revolve around it. The entire solar system keeps on receiving energy through its rays and radiation. The rays and radiation thus remain and function as the next-level connect, apart from the gravitational connect in between. On one hand, the cosmic colony of the Sun maintains life on one hand and then fosters the inputs for living in the form of energy, light and the confidence for positivity. The scientific view of the cosmos is that it is an entity which has arisen out of a factor of chance at the time of the Big Bang. The Big Bang has a starting point; it is assumed that the entire world was in a state of heavily condensed, rather infinitely and absolutely condensed, in a form which is infinitely small in size. Nothing had existed before that. It was the beginning of everything that we come across, or which we consider to have been present or anything present before. All have arisen from that initial infinitely small mass of material that works out to be a part of the original, carried down to the future as a kind of ancestral input to life.

"In my opinion, in view of general relativity's remarkably large-scale observational support, we should take on board the Einstein perspective, this being extremely likely to be ultimately more in accordance with nature's ways than the Newtonian perspective. Then we find ourselves driven to the viewpoint that superimposition of two gravitational fields under consideration, both fields must be treated in accordance with the Einsteinian perspective. This involves us in trying to superpose states belonging to two different vacua, i.e. two incompatible Hilbert spaces, such superpositions being considered to be not allowed.

Strictly speaking, the notion of alternative vacua is a feature of QFT, rather than of the non-relativistic quantum mechanics, but the issue has a different relevance to the latter also. Standard quantum mechanics requires that energies remain positive (if, that frequencies remain positive) but this is not normally a problem in ordinary quantum mechanics (for the technical reason that normal quantum dynamics is governed by a positive-definite Hamiltonian, which will preserve this positivity). But the situation arising out here is not like that and we do appear to be forced into violating the condition unless the vacua are kept separate; that state vectors belonging to one of the Hilbert spaces are not added to (superposed with) those of the other."
- Roger Penrose, *Fashion, Faith and Fantasy, In the new physics of the Universe,* Princeton University Press, Princeton, Oxford, 2018, pp. 285-6.

The scientific view of life thus has the fundamental question to face, which is that the entire universe has risen out of a sudden burst of that infinitely condensed form of matter, but it is at the same time tuned to the requirement of the new reality to take a shape? Once the basic input was formed and existence was in place, the rolling forward of lives and material movements takes place through the transactions in the physical world.

The spiritual traditions as stipulated by the Rig Veda say that the creation is the result of the intent of God to experience the beauty and pleasure of being in the company of many of a similar identity. In the beginning, God existed in an infinitesimally small, non-material form. It was the form in spirit. God was present in the form of a spirit that was not noticeable by any other entity, if it could exist. However, the existence received the input, energy and the vital force of life. The first form of existence was non-form, non-structured, and non-material in shape. The spirit was revealed in the form of the atman, which is an embodied entity of God himself. Atman had all the potential within itself; it has the energy required for having a cosmic system in place. He got the intrinsic potency of the divine creator in the form of the cosmic bodies. Lives lived require the vital energy in their place to develop and grow lives in their own trajectory of lives. Living thus becomes something which progresses along the lines of the types and identities of living. He thus created human life and set all the arrangements of nature which can nurture the potential of humans to remain and then grow to a further extent where the potential becomes self-revealed in the process.

Life in place requires the support of air to breathe in and out, and water to sustain and grow. And the light of life is essential to show the ways that life can be traced forward. It is in this context that the lives of people on Earth have received the context of adequate and profuse air to breathe and sustain life on one hand, and help lives to focus on the thoughts and acts of growth in existence. It is, thus, showing the ways the cosmic light offers life to pave through pathways of life. Thus, God created the sun to give light and energy continuously, and plenty of sources of air and water. Water got stuck beneath the soil of Earth, present to provide support to the soil to breed life of plants, herbs, shrubs, trees, vegetation and other items that create the basic and ongoing food to make life grow through the process of germination, generation and also regeneration. The combined presence of air, water, light, and energy could make life on Earth not only possible to exist but to grow to its full potential in terms of the possible dreams of human society. It was thus required to have a system of reciprocity and mutual dependence through which the cosmic ecosystem got itself gradually established. The ecosystem is such that air carries the reciprocity in the system of living and gets absorbed in the process. Mutual support and dependence are, therefore, the fundamental attributes of Mother Nature.

Roger Penrose, in his work, discusses a fascinating proposal for achieving quantum superposition in a macroscopic system. He describes a scenario where the quantum state of a single photon is initially divided by a beam splitter. One part of this photon's wave function then repeatedly impacts a tiny mirror, delicately suspended on a cantilever. Penrose explains that the photon's momentum would cause the mirror to move minutely, perhaps by a distance comparable to an atomic nucleus.

Because the photon's state is split, the mirror itself would consequently enter a superposition, simultaneously existing in states of both displacement and non-displacement—a kind of miniature Schrödinger's cat. Penrose notes that for a visible light photon, a single impact wouldn't suffice; thus, the same photon would be made to strike the mirror around a million times by reflecting it back and forth from a fixed mirror. This cumulative effect, he suggests, could displace the tiny mirror by the diameter of an atomic nucleus or more, within a few seconds.

The cantilever would then cause the mirror to return to its original position within a set time frame. To determine whether the mirror's quantum coherence was preserved or if spontaneous reduction occurred during the photon impacts, the photon would be released from this reflecting cavity and sent back to the beam splitter. Meanwhile, the other part of the photon's wave function would have been kept in a time-marking state within a separate, stationary reflecting cavity.

The dilemma of the particle and the wave form of reality is resolved through the spiritual understanding of life and the process of the universe. This life and the process of life require some kind of focus on the system. The spiritual realization would reveal that when the time started life, the creation was entirely spirited to flourish in the process. The Supreme Lord took up a form to experience the essence of creation. It is the creative energy which was taken up by the Lord of the lords, Shiva. Devadideva— the primordial form of the Gods, Lord Shiva himself, appeared as the Mahakaal— the creator-mentor of time. As he launched time, the Mahakaal took the form of Nataraj-Shiva, the form of the Lord, manifesting in the cosmic dance. It is the cosmic dance of the Nataraj-Shiva that had initiated the process of vibration in the creation. The creation, thus, had received the impetus of vibration. It is the eternal spirit injected into lives through the process of vibration, where the movement started within and without the material objects. The cosmic dance of Lord Shiva provided endless input energy to the particles, atoms and fundamental particles that always maintain an intrinsic dynamism. Within the matter, atomic level, the nucleus continuously mixes and emits energy by protons, neutrons, and is always encircled by electrons. The cosmic colony of the cosmic king also have a similar kind of dynamism. It is not gravity that fosters it, but the energy input provided by Lord Shiva through the vibration of his cosmic dance.

7 Divine Wisdom for a Better Life

With the cosmic dance of Lord Nataraja Shiva, the emergence of life occurs and grows through evolution. Wisdom remains the central force of life. Based on the empirical wisdom of life, living on a human scale gets the impetus for work. Work thus requires inputs for living and re-engineered inputs for better living in a context that keeps on changing on a continuous basis. Sustainability and emergence require continuity in terms of the forces of life in the conditions created therefrom. It is thus the original input that begets the potential for the growth of life and helps in its total blossoming into the beauty of the Earth's ecosystem.

Cosmic vibration being the primordial input into the energy system, the entire cosmic system actually dances within and without. This is why the cosmic energy in the system makes it a point to converge with the unitary position of a static system drawn into a dynamic equilibrium. The dynamics of this equilibrium is thus made into a process and an orientation that conduces to the convergence of the eternal spirit into factual empirical identity. This convergence is continuously contributing to the spirit of emergence of the individual human spirit to the entire stream of things happening in the world, at the real-time occurrence of incidents contributing to the progress and emergence of the spirit within the core of the living entity on eternal principles, but at real time.

The Lord says in the context of the war at Kurukshetra (Lord Krishna to Arjuna):

Imam vibaswatae yogam proktovan aham aryoyam.
Vibaswan manabae prahu manuh Ikshakuh eva arabit.   (G.4/1)
I taught this immortal yoga to the Sun-God Vivasan, and Vivasan, the Sun-God, conveyed it to Manu, his son, in the human form in the beginning, and Manu imparted it to his son, Ikshaku.

The knowledge of the eternal truth was spelt out by the Lord to the earliest revealed creation, the *Vibaswan*, about it. Vibaswan was the first identity of this empirical Sun revealed to people on Earth. The Sun, as mentioned in the Vedic text, is the Sun-God in a form. The eternal knowledge can be transmitted through a procedure where there is an intent on the part of the recipient of the knowledge, with the intent having arisen to the extent of its culmination. The eternal knowledge was permeated through the strong and energetic soul that wishes to connect with God on a real-time journey in life through a series of occurrences in the spirit of things connected. Thus, the Lord's intent would imply that the issues converge with the systematic approach of connecting with God. Lord Krishna, thus, makes a point that the original Sun-God, in the name and identity of Vibaswan, was actually inclusive of the spirit and his own role. The Sun God was in continuous connection with the Supreme Lord and carried the message of this divine entity down to the relativistic position of the creation. Thus, it was needed that God truly transmit the same eternal wisdom to the next creation— the human form. The first human form, the Manu, was connected to God himself to transmit the eternal knowledge. In the context and background of this, Manu had started his journey through the trajectory of life. It is thus a point to reckon that the eternal principle of having the thing on run accomplished the recipient of the knowledge gets into the elemental composition of the being, such that, the entire span of living on Earth, the wisdom of spirituality as realized from God, directly gets properly assimilated in life, so that the lives lived can perform the function in a way that fulfils the objective of God on Earth.

Knowledge, such as transmitted by the divine sun to earthly entities, deserves the inclusion of knowledge in the framework of the making of the new system of lives to be lived. The Lord had announced the different aspects of life's new attainments, where life begets the fruits of the best wisdom, which God had expected the revelation of eternal truth. This is possible when the empirical objective of life connects with the core principle of the intent of God. The creation had been endowed with the gradual realization. With God's creation, it would reveal that God remains present in the abode of the ancestors of Manu. That is why He is present in all, in the formal making of the person and remains vibrant throughout the lives of man.

It is the sequence of lives lived through millennia and the things that it has been created out of, and at the same time, the effective presence of the spirit of wisdom transmitted, that makes a significant approach to the issues and challenges over the phases of time. Wisdom, originally shared by the Lord, required adequate support in terms of acceptance of the same and adoption of the wisdom in the action of the period of time. It is thus a kind of adaptability that talks about the application of knowledge in the process of living life across the stream of inputs, prompted by wisdom.

Evam Parampara praptyam imam raja rishayo veduh.
Sah kalena iha mahata yogah nashtya parantapah. (G. 4/2)
Thus, transmitted in succession further to son Arjuna, this yoga remained known to the Rajarshis or the sages and sage-kings, through a long lapse

of time, this yoga got lost to the world; now I am preaching the same to the world again.

The lineage from the earliest flow and period of time until today makes the theme of knowledge gradually more evident and imperative in the lives. The idea that divine wisdom gets revealed to the individual soul makes people converge with certain things, which are considered for the purpose of the collective setting. The new areas of understanding of the same wisdom in the context of life have gone in favour of the issues of sustainability on Earth. In order to maintain the flow of things, as mentioned in the pool of knowledge, it was evident that the contents should be made as inputs to good life, which would make the forces of living aligned with the contents of the living. So, having faith in the Divine being one of the most important areas, the endeavours should have progressions in the elements of faith in the process of adopting the Divine.

Sah eva ayam maya tae adyah yogan proktyam puratanah
Bhaktah asi mae sakha cha iti rahasyam hi etad uttamam. (G. 4/3)
Arjuna, you are my devotee and friend; that is the reason why I have shared with you this ancient yoga for the benefit of all.

The classical age was characterized by its ability to hold on to the best ways; maintaining faith in the activities of life requires the acceptance of the spirit of the divine entity. The acceptance of divine entity from its perspective makes one a spirit-driven person on any issue of survival, talks of the intrinsics of life. Thus, in order to focus on the core divinity in life, it is established through the space and process of life lived. Thus, in this context, it becomes important that a relationship is developed between God and the person. The best way is to develop the idea of devotion to God. In the process, when devotion starts as a devotee, the task of getting the required realization leads to the continuity of devotion. Devotee understands the context properly and gets its meaning.

Arjuna ubacha:
Aparam bhabatoh janmaya param janmah vibaswatah.
Katham etad vijniyabaan tvam aadoh proktravana itih. (G.4/4)
Arjuna said, 'You are of recent origin, while the birth of Vivaswan dates back to remote antiquity, how then am I to believe that you taught this yoga at the beginning of the creation.'

While having learnt the basic inputs from the Lord, Arjuna had developed a few questions in this regard. The eternal knowledge in the realm of the flow of life and thus considered the meaningful understanding of the eternal knowledge. It is important that eternal knowledge is understood on the universal inputs of knowledge. The positions of such devotees in the framework of the different expositions of the differences the person has developed for their lives in the continuity of the process. Thus, in a process where the endowment of God is properly revealed, the devotee is now engaged in devotion to God. The person develops proper attraction and reorients life towards the empirical aspects and makes the context free from the intrinsic pool of life as revealed. Wisdom of God gets revealed to this life in the proper sense of the term.

Thus, it is the prerogative of the devotee that the knowledge of the life lived with the wisdom of God becomes important in all respects. When the knowledge about God is instilled in the minds of the devotees, then the dimensions of work get transformed into a new dimension, where the focus of the work in life becomes different. Work in this context becomes a kind of consecration to the divine entity, and with that kind of consecration in life, the person's work transforms into an act of divinity. This work becomes selfless and is endowed with the spirit of the Divine, where the spirit would be totally different.

Sri Bhagavana ubacha:
Bahunih mae byatitani janmani tava Arjuna.
Tani aham vedah Sarvani na tvam bethhu parantapah. (G. 4/5)
Sri Bhagavan said, Arjuna, you and I have passed through many births. I know them all, and you do not remember. You are the winner in the battles, you are the superior and perfect warrior, you don't remember, I remember.

The devotee understands God in the context of the present time; however, it is that of the time eternal that the devotee has to keep in mind. The journey of the atman through different forms of life thus makes it like the perpetuity in the appearance of the spirit of life. In the design of this creation, the eternal knowledge remains with the Lord only. He is the truth himself and maintains truth throughout. The fact of the relation between God and his devotee remains understood on a real-time basis. Memory of the devotee may get shaken or lost through the act of passage through the lives on Earth in such a way that once reminded of the relationship, the devotee gets back the huge pool of knowledge of the wholesome truth, in the empirical sense of the term. The devotee now regains the memory of the real sense of the relationship between them. It is being said by Lord Krishna that whenever, in the previous cases of human journey, there appeared a need, he and his devotee, Arjuna, were always present with the same set of relationships.

Aujah api sat na abyayh aatmah bhutanam Iswarah api san.
Prakritim svayam audhisthanam sambha hayam aatma
mayoyah. (G.4/6)
Through birthless and deathless conditions I have passed and I remain and I am the Lord of all beings, I manifest myself through my own yoga maya or divine potency, keeping my nature or the *prakriti* under control.

Though the true identity of God is that he is omnipresent, it is the eternal wish that makes him appear in the creation at the stages, states and conditions required for that. Lord is actually unborn, but at the same time, when time arises, He takes up the root of birth and appearance, good for living and growing through the context which requires the divine presence most. In this act of the Divine on Earth, the spirit of divinity is somewhat deterministic in the realm of creation. The creation thus makes it a point to receive the touch of God in its journey through life. Thus, it happens that the spirit of God, as required on the Earth system and the lives, is maintained thoroughly. Divine truth thus gets unfolded on Earth this way.

Yada yadah hi dharmasya glanih bhabati Bharatah.
Aabhyuthanam adharmasya tada aatmanam srijami aham. (G.4/7)
Arjuna, whenever righteousness is on the decline and unrighteousness is in the ascent, then I embody myself in material form, in human form, in the world.

However, the cause that stimulates the need for the appearance of God remains challenging in view of the required perspective in which it occurs. God's intent thus becomes one with the requirements in the human context. It is thus the perspective when the appearance of the intent of God becomes urgent in the interest of the perpetuity of truth on Earth. Righteous living or righteousness defeated in situations generates agonies and cries. Whenever the agonies and the facts of sufferings become significant, such that they affect truthful living in general, the principle of the stream of living gets affected. In this situation, the Lord promises that he will take a vow to stop the forces of untruth from winning. The victory of such untruth makes a tremendous amount of impact. Lord himself decides to appear in the world with a predestined cause in mind, so that the notion of coexisting with the wrongdoers is thrown away. Lord now takes up the cause of cleansing the human context with a definite set of actions against the forces of untruth. He rescues the good souls from the inflictions by the wrongdoers and finally tries to establish peace and contentment in life for those who have virtues in life and are supportive of truth in life.

The appearance of God on Earth on the agenda of protecting the culture and tradition of the world is, essentially, to protect the functional and cultural identity of people. Whenever the righteous principles are affected by the unfair and unrighteous attributes dominating the lives and societies on a scale that is worrying, then God himself descends on Earth to take care of that trend of winning the negative forces, thereby trying to establish the conditions of truth and integrity in the lives and societies. This is the core reason for God to have incarnation, for saving the lives and societies from the evil dominance and infliction.

Paritranayao sadhunam vinashayah cha duhshkritam.
Dharma samsthanarthayao sambhabami yugae yugae. (G. 4/8)

For the protection of the virtuous and for the act of dominating or removing the ill-doers or ill-forces from the world, for establishing the righteousness in the world, on a firm footing, I manifest myself from age to age.

The other reason for God to descend on Earth is to annihilate the wrong-doers and, at the same time, to protect the lives of those good people and establish a truthful society. The purpose and objective are to establish a truthful society and to resolve the issue in the best possible way. God is thus directly interested in establishing the practice and system of truth in the thoughts and actions by virtue of his presence. It is assurance provided by the Divine that those who are honest and truthful will be protected or rescued, as the case may be. This assurance is to those also having faith in God, and at the same time, to prevent atrocities against the honest and truthful people. The honest and truthful also have faith in God. Some of these people, having faith, may also have love and devotion for God in their lives.

Janma karma cha mae divyam evam yoh betti tattwatah.
Tayaktavah deham purah janmah na iti nam eti sah Arjunah. (G.4/9)
Arjuna, my birth and activities are divine; he who knows this is in reality not reborn on leaving this body, but comes to me or gets the ultimate moksha or salvation in the process of life.

The knowledge and understanding of God's position with respect to the creation is also for the entire span of knowledge that tries to reflect upon God's work in a context that connects the creation with the Supreme, the creator. God has created this entire world, the cosmos, all the stellar, non-stellar objects, lives within and without; thereby, he is thus associated with each entity in a way which makes a part of it or a small fragment. Lives, living things all come along at the same time. It is God's wish that led to the creation; however, he himself remains aloof from all these. Though God's appearance on Earth connects with the conditions and realities, in the true sense of the term, he is hardly involved in any of the incidents of happenings. He is, thus, always apart from his creation, but enormous love and concern for his own creation, the Divine, are involved and not visibly connected in the affairs of the world at the same time. Knowledge of God's presence is a true realization of him.

Bita ragah bhayah kradhaah man maya mam upashritah.
Bahabo gyana tapasya putah mat bhabam aagatah. (G. 4/10)
Completely rid of attachment, fear and anger, wholly absorbed in me, depending on me and purified by the penance of wisdom, many have become one with me even in the past.

The knowledge through realization of God requires a particular state of mind and a unique condition where the depiction of the spiritual reality makes the person uninvolved in the negative emotions of life. Vices that are usually common to the minds need remedies in a way that the person's voluntary choice goes against having those negative emotions in life to play a role. Anger, fear, greed, desires, all such emotions, among many other sets of negative emotions which stand as resistant and deterrents to the growth of spiritual realizations in life. Once the mind of a person is free from these emotions and negatives in life, he or she attains the realization of God in life.

> *Yae yatha mam prapadyantae tvam tatha eva bhajami aham.*
> *Mama bartah anubartantae manushyah parthah sarvashah.* (G. 4/11)
> Arjuna, I gift fulfilment and be with the person; however, men seek me in whatever manner, I appear and approach the person the same way and support the person the same way, even so do I approach them in the same manner, for all men follow my path in different ways.

God is omnipresent, being present in every entity; he has his presence in all aspects of life. Lives remain vibrant with individual identities widely spread and distributed across. Individual identity creates individual choice everywhere. It is thus the focus of individuals to have the specific idea she or he generate from within based on individual choice, taste and preferences. Each individual thus has his or her priorities, personal view, and philosophy of life and thus, shall have the focus on each of them. The focus is thus to have the basics of the presence, and then gradually scale up. The choice may be based on the need, possibility, and the makeup of the entire framework that visualizes the effective position of the views of life. Thus, people may have and, in fact, do have different views of God. Some may even think that God does not exist. Some may, however, think that he exists in a particular form and way that the person likes and loves to think of the presence of God in that form only. Some may not be fixed about the idea of God and thereby, accept God in any form or any pattern or as formless. God has a liberal view to accept all the same.

Whatever the idea about the form or presence of God, it is his solemn promise that God will always stand by and be by the side of the devotee, holding hands with the devotee. In his chosen fight against the unholy spirit and the evils on Earth, he welcomes the participation of each individual inclined to the goodness of life. It is this goodness that acts as the invocation of God on Earth. The divine presence on Earth thus acts as the turnaround force, and the scenario not only changes for the period but gets transformed in a way that acts as the root to the salvation of human beings in general on Earth.

> *Kamkshantah karmanam siddhim yajantah iha devatah.*
> *Kshipram hi manushaelokae siddhih bhabati karmajah.* (G 4/12)
> In this world of human beings, men seeking the fruition of their activities, worship the gods for success, born of actions, follow quickly.

With a mind that is free from the negative factors and vices like anger, jealousy, greed, envy, ego, lust, desire, gluttony, the aspiration to have God realization would lead to the proper understanding of divine presence. When the mind becomes free from those negatives, it is considered a pure mind. A pure mind can go a long way to generate realization of the supreme truth. With a pure mind, when a person initiates karma or starts doing work, the work turns into a puja or an offering to God. In this situation, the work leads to its perfection in the work. Perfection in the work is the ultimate objective of any entity. This work also takes the person to success.

> *Chatur barnam maya srishtam guna karmah bibhagashah.*
> *Tasya kartaram api mam viddhya kartaram abyayam.* (G. 4/13)
> The four orders of society that means Brahmana, Kshatriya, Vaishya and Shudra were created by me classifying them according to the gunas or the types of the person or the types of the character predominant in each and appropriating corresponding duties to them through the originator of this creation, you understand and know me that I am immortal Lord and to be a man doer, I remain immortal always.

For the work to be accomplished in the right sense of the term, segmentation is the best possible way to proceed. In the modern scenario, we have hierarchy and, in most cases, classification or segmentation. Segmentation for the effective accomplishment of the work of life and society was thus done. The basis of classification or segmentation in modern society is market potential, concerns for the market, leading or managing functional areas and overall hierarchy in terms of decision making and application for the same. It was thus the effective accomplishment of work, but the concern for it does have connections with the rewards for the work in terms of financial gains, corporate salutations and positioning of people in the hierarchy. The four Varna or the clans were created only for the betterment of the works.

> *Na mam karmani limpanti na mae karmaphalae sprihah.*
> *Iti mam yah abhijanati karmabhi nah sah badhyatae.* (G. 4/14)
> Since I have no craving for fruit of action, actions do not taint me or touch me, even he who does knows me in reality is not bound by actions.

The classifications in the society were based on the principle of equality and the spirit of best accomplishment of the work based on the fundamental view of the dignity of each work. It was the spirit of equality, fraternity and freedom based on which the classifications were done. The principle of equality was echoed in the Rig Veda, which urges us to cultivate an equal and collective mind, thereby fostering a proper and cohesive understanding of the existing scenario. It does not state that any of the Varna or clan is superior and the other one is inferior. This notion has arisen in many places in India and is being profusely highlighted by some people who have an ulterior motive of ridiculing the Indian culture and traditions. Thus, the four Varnas or clansa, such as Brahman, Kshatriya, Vaishya, and Shudra, are four different categories of work performers. The Brahmans are those who are involved in the cultivation, streaming, spreading and inculcation of knowledge among all in the world. They are learners and teachers in life.

Evam jnatva kritam karmah purveh api mumukshaebhih.
Kuru karma evah tasmatvam purbaih purbataram kritam. (G. 4/15)
Having known that those actions were performed even by the ancient seekers for deliberation, therefore do you also perform, you also perform such actions as have been performed by the ancient sages from the beginning of time, you will also attain me.

The Kshatriyas are the managers, functional leaders, warriors, kings and others who are into providing security to nations, regions, states, organizations, entities and people at large. Kshatriyas do maintain the disciplines and law and order on one hand and create strategies for kingdoms, regions, areas and organizations, for people, governments and others. The Vaishyas are the people involved in commercial activities, business, trade, and commerce. They create, operate and maintain markets for trade and commerce. These are the set of people who have knowledge of business and markets. They create the products and services to offer better facilities of living standards. They connect with the people with knowledge for the research developments, ideas and procedures to develop or create a new generation of products and services, new technologies, new ideas of business, new set of knowledge for markets and societies. On the other hand, the value generated through business or in order to do business, various kinds of plans, procedures, the mission, vision, and policies become essential. These were supposed to be done through coordination between the Brahmins and the Vaisyas. The functional ideas required people who are experts in the production facilities in the fields of agriculture, on the shop floor of companies, in the factories and in the areas and zones of productions, manufacturing, distributions, output maintenance, transportations and the human services offered to complete the business process, in the act of defence, public and private services and so on.

Kim karma kim karmaeti kabayoh api atra mahitah.
Tat tae karma prabakshyami yat jajnatva mokshasae
ashubhyat. (G. 4/16)
What is action and what is inaction: even men of intelligence are puzzled over this question and unable to determine, therefore I shall tell you how to, what is the truth about the action, knowing which you will also be freed from all the effects of the binding narrative.

The works and services thus identified used to be carried down by human involvement, either in manual mode or in technological mode, and were done by the experts, called Sudras. They are one of the most important segments of the population who maintain the lives and progress of societies and kingdoms smooth and developing. The class of people who are in this category, called Shudras, were never considered in any of the Vedic texts as lesser or inferior compared to others. It was mentioned in the scripture that in the positions of the imagined or the visualized abode of the Lord, the Supreme, considering him as the human person with infinite and magnanimous dimensions, the Brahmins are considered as the outcome and connections with the brain and heart of the Supreme personality. This is obvious because of the fact of cultivation of knowledge by them.

> *Karmano hi api baddhyabyam boddhabam cha bikarmanah.*
> *Aakasmanah cha boddhyabyam gahana karmanoh gatih.* (G. 4/17)
> The truth about action must be known and the truth of inaction also must be known, even so the truth about prohibited action must be known, for mysterious are the ways of the action.

It is never mentioned with a highlight that this category of people, called the Brahmins, are superior and they have exploited the society through dominations and the dictating terms for social, familial and personal living. This is not based on facts. Also, the hereditary identity of being a Brahmin does not remain valid if the generations go for a function which is apart from gathering, disseminating and sharing knowledge in the society. It is acceptable that when the generation maintains the function in any way, it remains a person of the varna. If that does not happen, then the person would fall under a different 'Varna' altogether. The same thing applies to all other categories of the Varnas. Thus, getting confined within the domain of birth identity does not make a person perpetually belong to that throughout the generations of lives lived and worked for.

> *Karmani akarmah yah pashyaet karmani cha karmayah.*
> *Sa buddhimana tmanushyeshu sa yuktah kritsa karma krit.* (G. 4/18)
> He who sees inaction in the context of action and action in the context of inaction is wise among men; he is a yogi performing on perfection.

Therefore, the four broad divisions of the human society across Varnas are not to divide the society across clans, but to sharpen the social forces to get a new kind of homogeneous society to emerge out of this system of managing the society. In this scheme of things, social cohesion occurs; however, when India was under attack and got wrongfully dominated by the Mughals, Pathans and later by their lineage, the social autonomy was broken. Consistent attack on the temples of God, the Vedic ideas, ideals, systems, rituals, culture and also tortures and wrongful impositions on the custodians of the Vedic lineage, the social structure got disrupted, and conflict of clan positions and disharmony among different *varnas* had arisen.

Some historians have used their consequential situation to malign one *Varna* against the other.

> *Yasya sarvae samah aarambhah kama samkalpa barjitah.*
> *Jnajngni dagdhya karmanam tvam aahuh panditam buddhyay.* (G. 4/19)
> Even the wise call him a sage whose undertakings are all free from the desire and thoughts of the world, and those whose actions are burnt up by the fire of wisdom.

In the view of Varna, homogeneity is needed to establish a winning position of the society where peaceful coexistence, mutual cooperation and so on are required. The supreme abode is referred to as positions of their Varnas, like Sudras are compared with the legs, Kshatriyas with the heart and Vaishyas with the mix of calculating or a particular function of the brain supported by the *indriya*s, the vital organs. Some have narrated saying that the Sudras are subdued as they are compared to the legs of the supreme personality. These people have forgotten the fact that the legs are not only very important but are fundamental in the structure of the human system. In fact, legs are the pillars of life. Without legs, life becomes constrained and full of incapacity. At times, this leads to the meaninglessness of life.

Lord Krishna has brought in the view of a balanced and comprehensive life force where an individual will cultivate bearing, disseminate knowledge, be strong enough to have the art and faculty of interactions, transactions and be self-mover and self-doer in life.

The Lord has created this classification of people based on the types of karma or actions they think of. Actions are thus tuned to the objectives of the action. If a person is tuned to the action with the knowledge and understanding that the work is being done by him only, he is not tuned to the fruits of the actions or any benefit that accrues out of that action. This happens only when God descends on Earth as an incarnate to protect those who are righteous in their thoughts, approaches and works. Because he is indifferent to the work and the design of it, whenever he is involved in any work.

> *Tyaktva karma phala aasangaham nitya triptya nirashrayah.*
> *Karmani abhi prabrittwoh api na eva kimchit karati sah.* (G. 4/20)
> He who, having totally given up attachment to action and its fruit, no longer depends on the world and is ever contented, does nothing at all though fully engaged in action.

Real work is that which begets and enhances the work and its thoughts. Thus, any work that would not be associated with personal gain or the thoughts about selfish gain is the situation when this kind of mindset and urge for action is in the intrinsic dimension. In a way, desireless work with possible involvement of the person in the domain of the work is dedicated to God. Lord himself, when in the endeavour to have the objective on

Earth, is in the framework of the creation. This work is considered as one in which the person is not involved, and at the same time has a high concern for.

> *Nirashih yata chittwa aatma tyktah sarva panigrahah.*
> *Shariram kevalam karma kurban na aapnoti kilvisham.* (G. 4/21)
> Having subdued his mind and body and having given up all the objects of enjoyment and being free from craving, he who performs sheer bodily actions does not incur any sin.

The best way to accomplish this is to work by not being involved. However, the contents of the work won't be fulfilled if the involvement is lacking in the process of the work. This means in the process of doing the work, one has to be fully involved and try to perform the work to the best possible completion. However, the fruit of the work should not be the focus of the performer as long as that means a personal escape. A person who is in a position to do nishkama karma or the desireless action attains the condition of being able to contain all sorts of negative, then devotion for God generates in the person in the real sense of the term. Whatever the term of reference for the walk, a serious look into it would reveal that the person would do the walk for only survival and not for the purpose of attaining realisation.

> *Yat icchwa labhoh santushtoh dandatitoh bimatsarah.*
> *Samah siddwah eva ashiddhou cha krita api na nibadhyatae.* (G. 4/22)
> The karma yogi who is contented with whatever is got unsought is free from jealousy and has transcended all pairs of opposites like joy and grief, and is equipossessed in success and failure, is not bound by this action.

Whenever a person generates true interest in the realization of God and exercises the issue for the same, he is not perturbed by the extreme situations like extreme heat, extreme cold or any extreme situation of any kind. With these conditions or appropriations, the idea of such a situation may cause some difficulties, but with tolerance and a goodness of feeling, the person then attains realization of God. Desireless work enhances the spirit of realization in the right sense of the term. The work that leads to the cleansing of the mind is the basis for all different types of spiritual understanding. The time for final liberation or moksha occurs in that condition of mind.

> *Gata samgasya muktasya gyana abasthitah chittwasya.*
> *Yajnayah aacharatah karma samagram prabiliyatae.* (G. 4/23)
> All his actions melt away who is free from attachment and who has no identification with the body and does not claim it as his own, whose mind is established in the knowledge of self and who works merely for the sake of sacrifice.

Being devoid of all associations with karma makes a person directly spiritual when karma becomes free from the clutches of desire and the problems of consciousness. This form of karma is not only liberating, the inbuilt elemental influences of the liberation, but also becomes very much connected with the wisdom of Brahman. The essence of the results, it is action that should be truly associated with the core of the work. In this context, this awareness of selfless work opens. The person now realises that God is omnipresent. With this meaning and understanding, the Brahma Jnana occurs in the life of the person. In this situation, the Brahma Jnana becomes open to the person as well as to the world. Selfless karma leads to the core of the devotion and thus, to the situation of non-discriminative situation in all contexts. This kind of devotion begets the realization that he and his God are of the same origin and as such, that discrimination on every aspect of life goes off. Neither the colour, creed, religion, education, nor any other parameter can be the basis of discrimination; rather, the collaborative view is developed in him.

Whenever any karma is undertaken, the performer needs to have a belief in the Supreme, and have to be in the consciousness of the person. Conscious understanding of the relations that one has with the divine is essential to keep in mind that the work one tries to have in their understanding is a kind of input to the continuity in the *yajnyaen* of the person at the crossroads of the work. Any hazards or restrictions across work can be undertaken, or known for certain that the goal set for the work usually has two different dimensions. One is the goal that is usually or generally associated with the work, the other is the intrinsic offer of inner realization of truth through work.

Brahmarpanam Brahmah habeh Brahman agnou Brahmana aahutam.
Brahmah eva tena gantavyam Brahma karma samadhinah. (G. 4/24)
In the practice of seeing Brahman everywhere and the form of sacrifice the God Supreme is there into the fire of your expectation, God Supreme is in the oblation, he is the fire, he is the fire of the sacrifice, he is the fire of determination, he is a fire of goodness, he is a fire of oblation into and finally Brahman is the goal to be reached by him who is absorbed in the concept of Supreme as the act of such sacrifice.

Thus, it is advised to consider each work and the set of activities which would be undertaken in life be considered as that of God's work. It is also advised to dedicate the consciousness of the performer that the fruits or any positive outcome of the work and the elements of the work are considered as something of utmost importance. The segments or elements of work thus requires to be identified in the right sense of the terms. The quality of work to be driven towards the highest standard of it, called perfection. Work is being dedicated to God. It is like the fire of a sacrificial yajna where they want to add *ghritam*, the qualified butter, in the altar of fire to make the flames burn further and receive continuity to drive the work towards its logical completion.

Daivam eva aparae yajnyam yoginah pari upasatah.
Brahma agni eva parae yajnagm yajnenad upajuhvahati. (G. 4/25)
Other yogis duly offer sacrifice only in the form of worship to God, while others perform sacrifice by offering the self by the self himself in the fire of Brahman.

With the sense and belief that this work is going to have its basis of functioning rooted in the action and its principles, the work generates into the fulfilment of its material objective and its spiritual orientation. The spiritual dimension of a work is what it aspires to become and perpetually remain. Thus, with the fulfilment of its immediate objective, it attempts to accomplish the work for a larger cause. This broader objective of work could connect the facts and whereabouts of human society. The accomplishment of this serves the cause of the work in a broader sense of the term. This is how the focus of the work can be made to get oriented to God and, at the same time, to take care of the work of the world.

Shratra aadihih indriyani anyae samyamah agnishu juhvati.
Shabdah dina bishyan anya indriya agnishu juhvati (G. 4/26)
Others offer a sacrifice of their senses of hearing, etc., into the fire of self-discipline; there are some yogis again who offer sound and other objects into the fire of the senses.

Basically, concentrating on the factors of karma, the doer needs to find out ways for the act of consecration to God. Consecration is endowing it to the divine spirit and thereby, to act in the same way, and doing the work for the best output of the same. This type of work is destined to offer service to many. Any work has the potential to satisfy its objectives of the organization where the work is endowed and, at the same time, can perform the sacrifices to a great extent. Work thus becomes *puja*.

Sarvani indriyah karmani prana karmani cha aparae.
Aatma samyama yaga agnou juhvati jnajnadipitae. (G. 4/27)
Others sacrifice all the functions of their senses and functions of the vital layers, prana, into the fire of yoga in the form of self-control and kindled by wisdom.

The performer does the work with her/his organs. However, the doer continues with the same agenda for the duration, which is essential to accomplish. For example, when the hands or legs are involved in doing the work, the mind and senses of the person get tuned to that as well. Organs are direct or apparent tools to perform, but none of them can really perform without the intervention of the mind and consciousness. The idea of work, its performing ways and extents, its strategies - all are set and settled by the intervention and guidance of the mind. The mind is also tuned to the consciousness of the person. The idea of God's work being performed would impact the consciousness of the person. If atman is present in the human form and if, in the form, atman stays with vibrant consciousness, then the divine connection is automatic in the system. Atman, thus remains confined within and does not intervene in the life and activities of the person. In the life and activities of human scale remains the only way unless the support from the atman is received in the life of the work.

When inspiration comes from the atman, it creates a holy condition over the entire context. The Supreme, along with all his support, helps the doer in finding or identifying the right directions in the ways of the human spirit. It is thus very important to understand that the work is accomplished in the context of the same, with the support of the Divine seated within. If the person does the work without the guidance of the Divine, the quality of the work thus erodes to a large extent. To take care of the situations, focus on the intrinsic remains vibrant.

Dravya jajnyah tapah jajnyah yoga jajnyah tatha aparae.
Svadhyah jnana najagnayas cha yataoh sam shita bratah.   (G. 4/28)
Some perform sacrifice without material possession, some offer sacrifice in the form of austerities, others sacrifice through the practice of yoga, while some striving souls observe both austerity and perform sacrifice in the form of wisdom through the study of sacred texts.

Whenever the performer does not recon the context and intrinsics, the work remains an empirical work. Empirical work takes care of the targets, plans, and objectives, as set by the function or the department. However, with the addition of the Divine, it remains the work with new potential to perform yajna or sacrifice. Without the dedication to the Divine, the work remains that of the continued endeavour to convert the work to the divine work. In this case, the performer is induced to the world as the divine aspirant.

Apnae juhvati pranam pranaeh apaneh tatha aparae.
Pranah apanah gati ruddra pranayam parayanah.   (G. 4/29)
Other yogis offer the act of exhalation into that of inhalation, even so others the act of inhalation into the exhalation, there are still others given to the practice of pranayama, the breath control system.

The presence of an attentive mind and a single-pointed mind is essential to cultivate thoughts of God in life. With thoughts of God in mind, being deeply focused, the person attains connections with inner consciousness. The spirit within needs to be retrieved or sensitized to have the single-pointedness developed within. It is possible with the coordination and control of different types of air within. When we inhale air from outside and when we release air to the outside, it makes a difference. Air has five different characteristics and formations, each with a specific agenda and functional identity. This is actually seen from the usual empirical angle of view, is the same, but the Vedic sages have identified five different characteristic features of the air, as applied to the biological system prevailing within. Air drawn in the body and its systems gets distributed to different sets of organs. One of these is most vital and begets the sensitizations required to get the vital force regained or stimulated. Vital force thus stimulated creates factors positive to life.

> *Aparae niyatah aaharae pranan praneshu juhvati.*
> *Sarvae iha apyatae yajnabidoh yajna kshapita kalmashah.* (G. 4/30)
> Who having regulated their diet, control the process of inhalation, exhalation, both and put their vital layers into the vital layers themselves, and all these have their sins consumed away by the sacrifice and understand the meaning of sacrificial worship.

The Vedic sages have classified air into five types and five different ways to support life. According to this classification, the five different identities of air are collectively called *Pancha Vayu*— the five different properties of air. Pancha Vayu, or the five types of air, are *Prana, Apana, Samana, Vyana,* and *Udana*. The Vedic sages in the later period, during the period of Atharva Veda, were inclined to identify and offer methods to the human society for living an ideal life and have the capacity developed to see that the realization turns effective in the process of life. Thus, the Vedic sages were trying to develop a process develop developed which is effective, universal, realizable, available at the discretion of people and at the same time supportive to the process of attaining good realization.

> *Yajnah ashishthah amritah bhujah yah anti Brahma sanatanam.*
> *Na ayam lokae astya jajnasya kutoh anyah kurusattam.* (G. 4/31)
> Arjuna, yogis who enjoy the nectar that has been left over after the performance of a sacrifice attain the eternal brahman. To the man who does not offer sacrifice, even this world is not happy; how then can their world be happy?

The act of coordinating and controlling Pancha Vayu is achieved through a process known as *Pranayama*. The meaning of the term is to revive the prana, the vital energy of the person. The Vedic description of human science is deeply rooted in the science of spirituality pertaining to individual human beings. It was a general practice during the Vedic period to have pranayama practised by everyone and consolidate the effects of that in life.

Out of the five types of identity of air, the Prana Vayu begets the vitalizing elements carrying up to the brain and strongly energizing the brain to get into functions that would get aligned to living. It generates the natural stimulation to brain cells, once energized; it arouses the functional activities of all the major organs of the system of body. A haemopoietic stem cell, which is actually empirically the functioning stimulus of the entire governing faculty of the body, thus arouses the functionalities of the biological functions of the entire biological system. It is the Prana Vayu which governs, triggers, and connects the vital energy in the body to the best benefit of the person.

Pranayama (Invocation of the Life Force)

Pranayama is a process of invoking the life force for the best use and application of the same. This process involves coordination and control over the breathing functions and maintaining the functional implications for the body and mind. Basically, it is exercising control over the mind in order to tune it to the desired functions. The effects of the same would be on the mind, primarily, and then on the body and the system.

Process and Steps

Step 1: Pranayama attempts to harmonize the entire physical, mental, and spiritual aspects of the functioning. Hence, it tries to have certain positions of the physical and connect them with the mental functions. So, it has to have a definite posture; the sitting posture for pranayama is straight.
    a) Sitting: Straight on a chair (no cushion). No leaning in the back. Feet to place on the floor, parallel to each other. Hands on the respective knees, eyes closed.
    b) Breathing through alternate nostrils with straight sitting, eyes closed, hands placed on respective knees to start alternate nostril breathing. Press the left nostril with the left thumb. Inhale air slowly but steadily. Close both nostrils for some time. Now release air through the right nostril. Pause for a few seconds and do the reverse cycle. The ratios of duration ideally would be 1:4:2. This means if inhale by counting 4, then holding air inside by counting 16, and exhale by counting 8. The same applies in the reverse cycle also.

Step 2: After alternate nostril breathing, have normal breathing through both nostrils. With eyes closed, try to consolidate the thoughts and the mental process.

Step 3: This step involves willed imagination. Apply your will force to take the consciousness up, on top of your body and on top of your head.

Step 4: Try to visualize the rising sun in the backdrop of a clear blue sky. If the clouds of thought appear, try to get rid of them by way of allowing them to pass over. All these with your eyes closed and sitting posture remaining the same.

Step 5: Explore and experience the power of cosmic light first at the forehead in between the two eyebrows and then within the cave of the heart, sitting the same. Eyes remain closed.

This five-step pranayama should be done in a calm and restful state. No concern or awareness should be left for the outside. Logical period at the beginning of practice may be 10 to 15 minutes. After that, make it normal. Eyes opened. Practice gets over with awareness brought back.

The effect of Pranayama shall be direct to the physical function of the body, and then on the mind of the person.

1. Prana Vayu
   ↓
   The Vital Air – a stimulating, sensitizing force that coordinates.
   ↓
   This is reinforcing the vital energy in the body and allowing it to get connected to the cosmic order. The balance of life with the unseen, unknown factors of spiritual understanding leading to spiritual realization is usually stimulated by the *Prana vayu* when it's done in the context of *pranayama* in the background of a pure mind. Pure mind is one which is free from the impacts and drives of negative emotions like greed, anger, jealousy, envy, desire, lust, arrogance etc.

⟶ The Brain (responsible for arousal of cells, stem cells, connecting and coordinating cells, the central nervous system, etc.)

⟶ The Nervous System (Passing the message through the vertebral column – 'Irha', 'Pingala', 'Susumna')

⟶ The 'Pancha Gyanendriyas' (Five organs of direct sense) – eyes, ears, nose, tongue, and skin – meaning the functions of vision, audibility, respiratory, taste and skin.

⟶ The 'Pancha Karmendriyas' (Five organs of action that make the person functional in the empirical world. These are the two hands, two feet, and the external mind. All these receive stimulation by virtue of the *pranic* or vital air drawn in.)
Mind, Intellect, Memory, Self Awareness:
The creative, intuitive, intrinsic faculty of the mind gets stimulated. Intellect obtains new inputs through the opening up of functional realities and connecting them with the domains of the mind to have proper activation of the creative faculty. Ideas, realistic position of dreams, and retrieving memory to support new elements of knowledge emerge.
Activates the functioning of the cardiac system, the respiratory system, the digestive system, the nervous system, the muscular system, etc.

2. *Apana Vayu:*
   - Stimulates the actions of purity through the process of cleansing.
   - Makes the process of reproductive functioning activated. This has the control with Vyana Vayu, which helps in restricting the wrong path of the reproductive energy from getting lost and functionally makes it most effective for having the best creative forces of reproduction.
   - Excretory system is activated, organs of renal and excretory functions find better cohesion and perform sharply.
3. *Samana Vayu:*
   - Connects and coordinates to create and maintain a cohesive balance among major organs like the liver, heart, lungs, kidneys and all related and connecting systems.
   - Maintains purification flow and balance of the blood and muscular system.
4. *Vyana Vayu:*
   - Maintains the balance of endocrines, hormones, enzymes, and all types of secretions.
   - Maintains and stipulates the autonomous system of response, autonomous connections and the functionalities which are tuned to the overall connectivity of this body.
   - The muscular and dermal systems of the body.
5. *Udana Vayu:*
   - Maintains the sharp functioning of the skeletal system.
   - Overall balance, strength, response level and the dynamic faculties of life are stimulated and maintained by this.

Thus, the prana vayu triggers the entire system; however, each one has been assigned to have its own potency to be made use of in the functioning of life. It is thus the best option to have the functionalities of Pancha Vayu in the realms of the human living system. It is this functioning that helps in the entire living process, contributing impacts for the new set of things suited to the lives of people.

Evam bahubidhah yajnana bitata Brahmano mukhae.
Karma janah biddhi tana sarvani evam jnavtva bimokshasae. (G. 4/32)
Many such forms of sacrifice have been set forth in detail in the Vedas; know them all, involved in the action of mind, senses and body, thus knowing the truth about them, you shall be freed from the bondages of action through the performance of desireless action.

The method of Pranayama, if followed properly, helps in vitalizing the entire system of the body towards its best and optimum performance. When, through such a process, the person is ready with the input factors and the categorical imperatives, the person becomes ready in the true sense of the term. The accomplishment becomes a fact of the entire scenario to have the same achieved in life. It helps the system to acquire the factors and forces which are a part of the entire making of the system. The knowledge of reality and truth, which stands beyond the visible and tangible dimensions of life, attains a true homogeneous spectrum for the best output of things in life. The potent that remains dormant in life becomes energized by virtue of the actions of Pancha Vayu, consciously.

> *Shreyan dravya mayad yajnajah jnanayajnah parantapah.*
> *Sarvam karma akhilam partho gyanae pari samapyatae.* (G. 4/33)
> Arjuna, sacrifice through knowledge is superior to sacrifice performed which is material things, for all actions without exception culminate in knowledge.

The factors of life are all residing and resting within. And according to the descriptions given by Lord Krishna to Arjuna, it stands as a general lesson in life for those who aspire to the same achievements as well. Though in this context, Arjuna had no intent, actually. Arjuna had been destined to function as the force representing God. Meaning, Arjuna was bestowed with the duty to perform, having the unrighteous forces annihilated. The context of the war of the Mahabharata was that Lord Krishna, the incarnate of God, had a definite purpose to descend on Earth. He visualized that only words, advice, suggestions, good ideas and offers to guide in the right ways did not yield any result. As Lord Krishna had the objective of descending on Earth as an assurance to help the truth survive.

> *Tat biddhi pranipatenah pariprashnena sevayah.*
> *Upadekshantih tae jnanayam jnaniha tattwadarshinam.* (G. 4/34)
> I understand the truth, you understand the true nature of that knowledge by approaching an illumined soul, if you prostrate at their feet, render them service and question them with an open and greedless heart, then the wise seers of truth will instruct you in the knowledge.

The declared objective of gods having descended on the Earth was that, when life gets spoiled by the impacts of the wrongdoers, when the lives, prospects of good people and all values of goodness and fairness are affected, there arises a cause for the Lord to come on the Earth to perform two broad functions of life. He is destined to support the fairly lived people who follow the truthful path of living, who are righteous in their spirit, usually do not cultivate and practice power; rather, they believe that if they cultivate strength and power, that may impact their goodness by way of reducing the potency in life. God has promised to save these good people.

> *Yat gyatna na punah mohah evam yah asyasi pandavah.*
> *Yena bhutani asheshenah drakshya aatma anyatoh mayih.* (G.4/35)

Arjuna, when you have reached enlightenment, ignorance will delude you no more; in the light of that knowledge, you will see the entire creation within your own self, and then you will understand and realize me totally.

On the other hand, if the good, honest, truthful and righteous people have to be protected and saved, the basic way is to end the onslaughts on them by way of annihilating the forces of evil intent and actions. Thus, God on Earth has two core aspects of activities, which are actually to be performed through war. The devil force is always with muscle and power. Therefore, in order to justly annihilate them, persons like Arjuna are essential. Arjuna is a person with integrity of character. Arjuna is honest, truthful, and fair in his behaviour and character. And on top of everything, Arjuna is the most powerful warrior among all. This unique combination of the spirit of life is what Arjuna possessed. Therefore, Lord Krishna had chosen Arjuna as his friend to do the war against the evil forces and establish the righteous rule and condition of the world. Thus, Arjuna cannot and should not give up the destined work. Arjunas of the world should work hardest and at the same time maintain faith in the spirit of God for the well-being of the world.

8 The Corporate Sadhu

Modern society is driven by the corporate spirit and the functional implications in the life and orientations of the persons in the societies. Corporate culture and the mode of functioning work out to be the fundamental choice of the aspirants of career from different perspectives. It is thus one of the most important and attractive dimensions and elements in the run of career in the urban societies of the world. To make a career in the corporate, one has to be tuned to the call of the corporate needs and expectations. It is thus the corporate affair which makes realistic attractions to the societies and economies of the world. Thus, the leaders and managers of corporates prove important and essential for career pursuance in our world.

> *Shreyam dravyamayat yagnyat jnanayajnyah parantapah.*
> *Sarvam karma akhilam parth jnanae parisampyatae.* (G. 4/33)
> Arjuna, sacrifice through knowledge is superior to sacrifice performed which is material things, for all actions without exception culminate in knowledge.

Any action or karma that is initiated by someone to perform continues to be identified as work, as well as just a generic service offered to the company or an entity which works or creates the basis for human process. It is this process that, when the right time occurs, becomes very important in life. Lord Krishna is suggesting here that the quest for knowledge remains very important. In fact, he suggests that the amount of learning from the karma or set of actions becomes very important as a consequence of working in the context for a reasonable period of time. Thus, when karma is undertaken, the doer is expected to get involved to such an extent that instead of being a burden on the person, it acts as the input energy and the stimulus to work in such a way that it contributes to the creation of additional knowledge, which is associated with the work and its various aspects. Thus, simple churning of knowledge is good, but the knowledge that one garners through the process of work proves wider and better.

Tat viddhi pranipatena pariprashnena sevayah.
Upadekshanti tae jnenam Jnaninah tattwa darshinah. (G. 4/34)
You understand the true nature of that knowledge by approaching an illumined soul, if you prostrate at their feet, render them service and question them with an open and greedless heart, then the wise seers of truth will instruct you in the knowledge.

The knowledge of God for an aspirant is also subject to that method or orientation. Thus, the learning is better through this process of orienting to God and at the same time, the core elements of knowledge in the human context require some basic understanding. It is thus under a certain set of preconditions that the work is undertaken, in a context that requires maintaining conditions appropriate to the context of the world. This is always true in the context of the world; also, at the point of adoption, the attitude of the learner remains ultimately connected to the system of sequential learning.

God realization as such also remains the focus of learning for a person who wishes and tries to have it. It can be attempted in many ways and routes. Apart from garnering intrinsic spiritual realization through the process of meditation, it could be achieved through consecration, a deep intrinsic quest for God or being able to offer service to God in the way that satisfies him most.

Yat jnwatah na punar moha evam yasyasi Pandava.
Yena bhutani ausheshenah drakshya aatmani anyoth mayae. (G. 4/35)
Arjuna, when you have reached enlightenment, ignorance will delude you no more; in the light of that knowledge, you will see the entire creation within your own self, and then you will understand and realize me totally.

God realization makes a high and intense factual quest, making it possible to be blessed by the many spiritual ideas and objectives. The way of knowledge once garnered continues to mature in its own process of becoming the realized truth, the truth of realization to the world. The way of knowledge requires *Swadhyay* by the aspirant. Swadhyay is the practice of self-study. It is usually when the meditation reveals a stream of truth that needs to be realized. In the process, what an aspirant attains is also where the association of the society may trigger the process of creation; the spiritual aspirant would be away from the scenario, but the knowledge realized within. This may be in the realm of impersonality. This knowledge remains true to the context. The pattern of knowledge remains the same throughout the spiritual journey.

The knowledge of Brahman is real wisdom. It is always endowed with the blessings of God. Once the wisdom is attained by someone, she or he turns into a devotee of God. With this, the divine intervention and support would be available to the person whenever the need arises. Thus, any kind of sin which may crop up in any way to the person would thoroughly dissolve, and the person will be free from the same, even if it is due to their own fault. The wisdom or spiritual realization thus helps the person in the journey through the pathways of life. This applies to the context of the corporate corridors in a big way as well. This may be tuned to the values one would get involved in life.

> *Aupi chet ausi papebhyah sarvebhyah papakrittwam.*
> *Sarvam jnana plabena eva brijinam santarishyasi.* (G. 4/36)
> Even if you were the worst of all sinners, this knowledge alone would take you out of the sin, and it's like a raft which would take you out of the waves of turbulence. And this is how you save from your sins.

Divinely person by virtue of his or her orientation to the goodness of life is always attracted to good values. He would be a sattwa guna personality. This means, in the realm of things, the spirit of good values and fairness of things would always be associated with a personality with him. The corporate advantage with this person lies in the possession of good values like honesty, integrity, cooperation, sacrifice, commitment, etc. They are tuned to fully dedicate the work to the cause and objective of the world. This implies a gainful context of the entity. Each manager or leader of corporate functions may be advised to follow this path. Sattwa guna in a person induces her or him towards dedicated service and work to the benefit of the organization. Through the rendering of services truly, in the honest path and with the spirit of selflessness, would enhance the mileage for the corporate to have its run in the right direction. This resembles the God realization in the context of work.

> *Yatha edhansi samiddhvah agnih bhasmasyat kurutaeh Arjuna*
> *Jnanagnih sarva karmani bhasmayat kurutae tathah.* (G. 4/37)
> For the blazing fire turns fuel to ashes, Arjuna, even so the fire of knowledge turns fruits of all actions to ashes.

Wisdom of Brahman acts like a fire that can burn most impurities or things which are not in the lines of action of truthfulness. Thus, for a spiritual aspirant, it is always the journey towards establishing the context of truthfulness. This is something that goes against the spirit and dominance of wrong values in life. Taken in the corporate context, it applies as a vehicle to garner a higher degree of sattwa attributes. A higher degree of sattwa guna among people in the organization would be good in terms of gains by the organization, attributed to a higher degree of human energy in the company. Obviously, these higher degrees of collective manpower would mean more revenues and profit for the entire organization.

In the world of spirituality, the higher degree of production means a more intense journey towards reality in life. So, this applies primarily to individuals. However, a group of people experiencing collectively the truth in their collective and group performance is considered a situation where there has been a values upliftment in the entity, and it shall reap the results thereof.

> *Na hi jnanena sadrisham pavitram iha vedyatae.*
> *Tat swayam yoga samsiddhih kaalena aatmani bindati.* (G. 4/38)
> In this world, there is no purifier as great as knowledge. He who has attained purity at heart through a prolonged practice of karma yoga automatically sees the light of truth in the self, and over a period of time he realizes God.

Values that an organization may undertake are a set of input factors or contents of an organization that serve as the governing principle of the same. As such, Lord Krishna puts across the issue of jnana or knowledge of self as the purest one. With the knowledge of the self realized, the person rises above the domains of pettiness and meanness. A person remaining within the shell of selfishness is actually a deterrent to the real growth of the organization.

Knowledge of the Supreme brings in the jnana. This is incremental in nature. The knowledge spreads in diversity through various aspects of life. Living a life in a way that helps in the process of revitalizing the spirit within is the way of knowledge. This is pure. This knowledge is attainable only in the condition of a pure mind, a pure mind is one that is free from the contaminations of the negative emotions of life. That means it should be such that the mind is free from the entire range of selfish considerations and selfish orientation. This mind is a golden mind with the golden habits in consideration throughout. This golden mind with golden habits is tuned to the issues and potency of eternity. This mind is God-centric in nature. The orientation of mind, including the tenets of intrinsic belief, is very much essential for the knowledge of the Divine. The mind should be free from its impurities as reflected in the transactional, behaviour and character of the person. It is thus for acquiring divine knowledge, the human mind must train itself to get rid of the negative emotions and adopt the positive.

> *Shraddhya vana labhotae jnanam tat parah samyatae indriyah.*
> *Jnanam labdha param shantim auchirena adhigacchati.* (G. 4/39)
> A faithful person attains the wisdom of god, a person with control over senses, the next in sequence with attaining the wisdom, the person gets poise of mind and a supreme bliss at the end.

A person should cultivate and have the required objective in life for knowledge. Certain attributes, like respect and love for the Divine are essential attributes for initiating the process of learning in this system of realization. Shraddha is a term that includes respect and love together in the framework. Respect for the divinity as the way of life and love for God and divine qualities together make a way out for the best way to look forward and to get connected to the system. Thus, the basic attribute being shraddha, the element of love and respect, needs to be combined. In the absence of either of these, the conditions being prelude to the process are not fulfilled. The process of realization, therefore, does not take place. However, through a process of rigorous cultivation, if that element of respect can be developed, this goes a long way to transform the life of the person. If a person attains divine knowledge, then their life transforms to a life of peace, harmony, and becomes tuned to the spirit of divinity in life. Realization of God brings in peace and happiness.

> *Ajnah cha aushraddhaadanam cha sanshaya aatma binashyati.*
> *Na ayam lokaeh asti naparo na sukham samshya aatmanah.* (G. 4/40)
> He who lacks wisdom is devoid of faith and is at the same time possessed of doubt; is lost to the spiritual path. For the doubting soul, there is neither this world nor the world beyond, nor even happiness.

On the other hand, the element of shraddha should not be missing from the personalities of the spiritual aspirant. Shraddha is a strong element which requires faith in the mind and consciousness of the person. Consciousness would consider cultivating faith in two ways. The people who are actually rationally oriented, the rational dimension of life is focused on the rational dimension, thus examining every aspect. If faith needs to be explored, then the person should look into different dimensions of that faith. It is a kind of testing in the given context; this may be in the rational framework of the scenario. Rational analysis of the scenario may or may not fit into the model of the framework of the expectation of the person; however, the expectations may be considered as that of an unusual framework of choice. The world of spirituality functions in a different manner. Here, the subjective dimensions of the quality-based module prove very essential. When we talk of mind purification, the factors of certain negative emotions have to be grouped as impure things.

> *Yogah sam nyastya karmanam jnanasam chhinna samshayam.*
> *Aatmabantam na karmani nibaddhananti Dhananjaya.* (G. 4/41)
> Arjuna, actions do not bind him who is dedicated all the actions to God according to the spirit of karma yoga, whose doubts have been dispelled by wisdom and who is self-possessed.

Desire is considered a quality which proves a vital requirement for the corporate world. For example, the corporate world is actually based on demand for the products and services in the market. Demand arises out of the need and greed, among other factors. To a certain extent, need is justified in life. However, beyond the basic and chosen dimension that maintains need, one may equate the needs of a certain magnitude to desire. However, once it is identified as the basic requirement of products and services, it may not remain bound by the barriers. The quantity that exceeds minimum demand is constantly required to be associated with the dynamics of the market for the making of additional demand.

Tasmat aujnana sambhutam hritasham jnana aasina aatmanah.
Chhittwa enam samshyam yogam aatishtha uttistha Bharata. (G. 4/42)
Therefore, Arjuna, destroying ignorance with the power of wisdom, this doubt in your heart, born of ignorance, establish yourself in karma yoga in the form of even-mindedness and stand up to fight.

The spiritual understanding of things thus differs from the empirical ideas. Empirical ideas thus accommodate many elements considered as negative attributes in the spiritual domain. Thus, the spiritual idea proves to be testifying to most people. It is particularly pertinent to consider when a person chooses the elemental spirituality in life, while at the same time, some of those elemental attributes are essential to consider for the journey into the world of spirituality.

When a corporate personality aspires to have the realization of God, she or he has to create and maintain a proper balance between the positive factors. Greed is destructive to a person. Here, the balance that is needed to make a peaceful journey into life is achieved through the balancing between the spiritual concern and the material concern. A simple, straight philosophy and outlook of living life is essential for the growing and grooming of life. Looking into the spiritual dimension would thus embrace the rational dimension in life; it would embrace rationality and have an intuitive dimension also.

The set of activities related to rituals proves good in maintaining a habit of a God-seeking spirit in human life. But the chances are strong that in such cases that even if the rituals are in place, the core purpose of the rituals is either forgotten or takes a backseat in the agenda of serious activities in life. The focus of life is settled within the mind as achieving a purpose empirically chosen, for then it is all good that rituals serve.

Arjuna ubacha:
Sannyasam karmanam krishna punah yogancha shamsasi.
Yat shreyah etayoh ekam tat mae bruhih sunischitam. (G. 5/1)
Arjuna said, Krishna, you extol both sankhya yoga, the yoga of knowledge, and the yoga of action. I pray to you, tell me which of these two you decisively consider more conducive to my well-being.

The pertinent question that Arjuna asks is about the condition and real characteristics of Sannyasa. Sannyasa is a term that refers to a state of ritualistic living, ideally in a detached way. A person having adopted the life of a monastery and living there, detached from the affairs, connections or places of the families and societies, is usually termed as a sannyasa. It is actually the position of a detached monkhood. The detachment is considered as that from the set of activities, stream of thoughts and set of actions in the context of the world. It is thus a state of things where the person is someone who is not having any kind of binding in the affairs of the world. On the other hand, the person is tuned to the quest of God, in possible or impossible ways, and to explore the realization of truth.

Sri Bhagavan ubacha:
Sannayasah karma yogah cha nihshreyasakarou eva ubhou.
Tayoh astu karma sannyasat karmayoga bishishyatae. (G. 5/2)
Sri Bhagavan said, The yoga of knowledge and the yoga of action both lead to supreme bliss. Of the two, however, the yoga of action, being easier to practice, is superior to the yoga of knowledge.

Arjuna was hearing Lord Krishna speak about the concepts of eternal truth being seated in the form of atman. However, he had learned also that karma or action is most essential. Without the karma or action in life, truth remains far from being the focus of life. Thus, the advice imparted is that karma needs to be continued to perform in the best possible way to fulfill its objective of accomplishment. But at the same time, to get rid of the desire of the person, if any, connected with the karma as a kind of resulting benefits out of the set of karma undertaken in a given context or a set of boundary conditions, karma needs to be performed, but the intention is not to nurture the results out of it.

Jneyah sa nitya sannyasi yah na dweshti na kamkshatih.
Nihdando hi mahabaho sukham bandayat pramuhchatae. (G. 5/3)
The karma yogi, who neither hates nor desires, should ever be considered a renunciate. And for Arjuna, he who is free from the pairs of opposites is easily liberated from bondage.

Out of two broad categories of karma, the sannyasis usually perform the one called ritualistic, and the other one is any karma pertaining to the world. However, the first one is given the name: karma for puja and yajnya karma, and the work of the world is empirical in nature. It's not the empirical work that is looked at here, in the context of the work of the world. The ritualistic karma is aimed at serving God, whereas the empirical one serves the world. The person who does not aspire for empirical enjoyments in life and is free from the impacts of anger, jealousy and the like is unattached to the usual worldly bondages and can attain the realisation of God freely.

Samkha yogoh prithak balayh prabatanti na panditah.
Ekam api aasthitam samyak ubhouh bindatae phalam. (G. 5/4)
It is the ignorant, not the wise, who say that the *sankhya* and *karma* are divergent in result. For one who is firmly established in either, gets the fruit of both, and which is the same as God-realization.

Yajnya karma, as such, does not provide any direct or eventual support to a certain set of things like puja, which are no longer the realm of the work or the focus of persons concerned. The work of the world such as the inputs for living support system for living, products and services that are tuned to the total idea of living, all such activities of creating machines, using machines, having the resources created as such that the system would bring down to the task of organizing, making, arranging things, supporting the cause of life. It is thus the fundamental tenet of human civilization that a total free hand is offered to the human process of innovation, creativity and generations in terms of the new products, technologies, and being tuned to the elevation of human comfort, reach, control and learning, because the world will be engrossed into the aspects of creating one after the other marvels for human society.

In his response to the question asked by Arjuna, Lord Krishna presents an answer which says that in the realm of God, if the endowment of things of the world whether one performs the Yajna karma or the Jivan karma does not differentiate from each other, as long as they are usually focused on the rational dimension of the same. However, the difference occurs in the orientation of each work's objective.

Yat samkhayaeh prapyatae sthanam tat yogou apih gamyatae.
Evam samkhyam cha yogan cha yah pashyatih sa pashyatae. (G. 5/5)
The supreme state, which is reached by shankha yogi, is also attained by karma yogi. Therefore, he alone sees who shankha yogi and karma yogi are as one, so far as their result is really seen.

Thus, it is not the karma that a person undertakes that distracts from the spirit of sacrifice, but the focus of the work that becomes the most important in the gamut of things. The objective of karma, once identified as the selfless one, is known as nishkama karma, which means a karma that is in no way connected with the selfish desire of the person. It is the same selfish desire which is present in the actions and thereby acts as a deterrent to the initiative of the person to have a spiritual journey in the truest sense of the term.

The designated spiritual practices of sankhya and yoga make up the mind of the aspirant of God-realization to induce him or her in the ways of God ahead in life and activities throughout. Both of these ways lead to the same perspective in their journeys in a future spell of realization. Both streams of practice lead to the realization of the Supreme in the context of personal attainment.

Sannyasah tu mahabaho duhkham aaptum yogatah.
Yoga yuksah munih Brahmoh na chirena adhigachhati. (G. 5/6)
Without karma yoga and sankhya yoga or the renunciation of doership in action, the activities of the mind, senses and the body are difficult to

accomplish, whereas the karma yogi who keeps his mind fixed on God, which is Supreme Brahman, in no time, Arjuna.

However, in the pursuit of knowledge, once the person attains the equilibrium condition of the mind, the person is now thoroughly connected to the spirit of Brahman. Sannyasa yoga with a practice of the sankhya and yoga in life, the person can have complete achievement of things if dedication, as a specific and focused element, takes place. In the process of sankhya, the aspirant practices the habit of the impact of eternity as a kind of input factor in the course of action and creating the premises for bringing in or invoking the spirit of God in life. This creates the inputs for knowledge of the person and finally may lead to the realization of the Supreme. But this is always on a personal scale.

Yoga yuktah bishuddha aatma bijita aatma jitendriyah.
Sarva bhuta aatma bhutatma kurban na api na lipyatae. (G. 5/7)
A spiritual practitioner, having attained purity of mind and is blissful, has mastered his senses, whose heart is pure, and who has identified himself in the self of all things and also in God, remains untainted even through performing actions.

The issue arises when the practice of yoga also leads to the same consequential end. Achieving the realization at the personal end contributes to self-satisfying in all respects. It contributes to the retrieval of the intrinsic knowledge of the person in a situation that, through both ways, reaching a state of God-realization is possible.

However, the intent of God is different. Lord Krishna focuses on the context where going beyond the personal gains in terms of self-satisfaction is good, but if one can have a way where the personal limits are transcended, she or he contributes to the wellbeing of the world.

Na eva kimchit karomi iti yukto manyaeta tatvavit.
Pashyan shrinvan jighran ashnan gachhan svapan svashan. (G. 5/8)
The yogi, he who knows the reality of things, must be the one to believe that he does nothing, even though seeing, hearing, touching, smelling, eating and drinking, walking, sleeping, breathing, speaking.

Personal limits are possible to transcend through karma. Karma or action in life should be oriented to the position of doing the same karma in a way that it is considered as the act of giving. This means the karma that focuses on the emergence of the spirit of this world. The emergence is possible through karma only. Service to mankind, service to the creation and service to mankind specifically are possible through the kind of karma that is not to serve the selfish need alone, but the karma that requires to be undertaken in the context of the world. This is best done by the work done in the possible manner. The work could be any that adheres to the context of the global system. One can connect with the world with any kind of work, provided the work done is above the limits of human domain and the spheres of understanding and where the services of the system are accepted throughout; but the work should be free from selfish understanding and selfish knowledge of the person.

In the act of the choice of dedicated work, any of the functional areas of the realistic ways of performance is that the work should have the dimensions of one of the most important ideas of the series of activities in the process of having the required realizations in life. It is thus one of the best ways to perform the act of dedicated work. This also acts as an important dimension in life.

Pralapan bisrijan grihnan unmishan nimishan api.
Indriyani indriya artheshu bartantan iti dharayan. (G. 5/9)
Answering the calls to nature, grasping and opening or closing the eyes, holding that is also the senses alone that are moving among the other objects.

Thus, the individual choice determines the aspects of the world. The dedicated personalities are those who are just one of the best choices and ingredients that yield and lead to the fulfillment of the world, and in that context, proper fulfillment through perfection in the world, as that of the realistic identification of the same, contributes to the welfare and benefit of the world. Alternatively, the nature of the functional aspects of the world thus elevates the world to a context where the entire set of works dedicated to the cause of the world. This dedication, the wide opening of the same, thus serves as the core aspect of the work: the scientific innovations of any kind, technological gains of any kind, of the conceptual framework of the same. This set of works is supportive of the cause of human progress.

Brahmani aadhyayah karmani samgam tyaktva karoti yah.
Lipyatae na sa papenah padma patram iva ambhosah. (G. 5/10)
He who acts offering all actions to God and shaking up attachment remains untouched by seeing and is like the lotus leaf of water.

It is thus the most optimum way to contribute to the scheme of things. However, the kind of things that are included in the forward orientation can be considered that the whereabouts of the perspectives of the world and are focused on the context of the entire set of things. This can be so encouraging within the realistic realm of things in the world. However, this contribution to the world by an individual may be termed as nishkama karma if the work remains selfless in the truest sense of the term. Selfish interest could arise in various ways in life. Thus, if the initiator and the person do the work of the world with no personal agenda in any way fulfills the divine intent in the world.

Kayena manasa buddhya kevalah indriyai api.
Yoginah karma kurbanti samgam tyakta aatma shudhyae. (G. 5/11)
The yogi performs actions only with their senses, mind, intellect and body as well, without the feeling of mind, and shaking up attachment simply for the sake of self-purification.

Calculations for personal gains in monetized terms or a set of things that arise out of the context may involve indirect gains in power, positions, name, fame, recognitions, etc. Any of these associated with the work in any way spoils the spirit of sacrifice. Therefore, that kind of karma cannot be termed as nishkama karma in the context of the work and the world.

Basis of the nishkama karma, thus, requires a particular way of tuning of mind. This tuning of the mind should be such that giving away things and not grabbing in any way is not at all the approach of the mind in the context of work.

Yuktoh karma phalam tyaktva shantim apnoti naishthikam.
Ayuktah kamakarena phalae saktoh nibadhyatae. (G. 5/12)
Offering the fruit of action to God, the karma yogi attains everlasting peace in the form of God-realization, whereas he who works with a selfish motive, being attached to the fruit of action through desire, gets tied down.

The identity of a sannyasi truly becomes a logical way of looking at it, a true set of the elemental consciousness of the person in a definitive perspective in the world of actions, thoughts and practices.

In the corporate context, this stands as a very unique point and approach. Companies can rise above their individual contexts and barriers to offer a pure contribution to the world of work, thoughts and processes. Empirical approach to creativity and innovation is the spirit of work beyond logical dimensions that add value to the contextual reality and have somewhat contributing points to the realm of the new set of contributions to that. A new set of realities thus needs to be ensured to benefit the stream of things in its own ways. This mechanism is associated with reward management. A combination of financial and non-financial rewards, where names, fame, rewards, gains and positions acquired through various means would make more things happen.

Whenever the question of reward management occurs, it involves the individual. This point was very intensely and carefully dealt with by the sages of the Vedas. One of the most important Upanishads covered under the Shukla Yajurveda has elaborated this concept through the process of Vedic analysis of the human personality in the context of the world. It is thus a kind of broad classification of human personality based on the true patterns and corresponding types of the same. This can be explained through classification.

Sarva karmani manasa sam samnayasya astae sukham bashi.
Nabadwarae pure dehi na eva kurban na karayan. (G. 5/13)
The self-controlled shankha yogi, doing nothing himself and getting nothing done by others, rests happily in God, the embodiment of truth, knowledge and beliefs, mentally relegating all actions to the mansion of their mind-gates of the body.

It has been mentioned by the sages, as explained in the Brihadaranyaka Upanishad of this Shukla Yajurveda, that personality types are classified into three broad types. These are: Demonic, Human and Divinely. In the Vedic parlance, these are mentioned as the *Aasuric Manava, Manabic Manava* and the *Daivi Manava*. The Aasuric Manava has characteristic similarities with the animals and demons. They are fond of or are tied up with the dimensions which are common features connected with the lives and activities of animals. Common factors that are actually pertinent and relevant to the context of human society are: anger (roaring like tigers), greed (hunger, driven like almost all animals including lions, bears, jackals, dogs, cats, rats, etc.), envy (like lions, elephants), and the likes.

Na katritvam na karmani lokasya srijati prabhuh.
Na karma phalam samyogam svabhaba astu prabartatae. (G. 5/14)
God determines, not the doership, not the doing of men or even their contact with the fruit of action, but it is the nature alone which functions.

The demonic attributes are translated into other fine-tuned terms by human beings in several ways. However, a few of these in a context would be depicted in the following terms, each or most of which are logically known by people in their regular transactions and the explorations or quests to find out the best out of the scenario, in all possible ways. The highlights of these are: jealousy, backbiting, covetousness, gluttony, conspiracies, love for the falsehood in life in general, in all contexts and situations.

Na aadatyae kaya chit papam na cha eva sukritam bibhuh.
Ajnanena aabritam jnanam tena muhyanti jantabah. (G. 5/15)
The omnipresent God does not receive debauchery or sin from anyone. Knowledge is enveloped in ignorance; hence, beings are constantly falling prey to their delusion.

The demonic approach primarily governs not only the majority of human set of actions and transformations of the mind and spirit of the persons concerned, but also almost all aspects of the corporations. Whereas none of these are the set of attributes which the manpower functions in the organizations are concerned with, the demonic attributes not only dominate but also maintain the show of human games in the corporate organizations. From this perspective, we find that the human journey through the actions of the world has lots of similarities with demonic qualities.

Jnanena tu tadjnanam yesham nashitam aatmanah.
Tesham aadityavad jnanam prakashayati tatparam. (G. 5/16)
In the case, however, of those whose said ignorance has been destroyed by virtue of knowledge of God, with that wisdom shining like the Sun reveals the Supreme.

The idea and theory that human beings are needy animals fits in the theory of demonic personality. This theory talks about various kinds and categories of needs through the depiction of a pyramid. This pyramid of needs thus has some kind of hierarchy according to this theory. The first of the series is known as physical need. This has various components like hunger, thirst, sex, etc. Physical need, when it crosses its logical and fair limit, turns into greed. It is actually driven by desires in life. Desires of different kinds have to be processed through different factors of life. Certain biological components are actually the elemental aspects of the physical need in life. Most of the elements of physical need are animalistic in nature. Having lots of similarities, the physical needs when in the process of fulfillment or meeting needs squarely through its processes, develop identity with the animal nature in many ways.. The approach and behaviour represent an animal type. With this, having the spirit and functioning in place, the physical, if allowed, unbounded, leads to chaos and disruption in the human context. It is thus a kind of description in the context of human society that the physical is contained.

Unbounded physical need causes disruption in human society. The issues of economic disparity in human society thus make it possible for the scale of things to create societies within the global society. Thus, a non-cohesive society, of the high and low, rich and poor, living on abundance and living on deficit, forms. This disrupts not only cohesion but harmony, cooperation, friendship, and concern for others are all lost in the process, and societies become skewed and fragmented.

Tat buddhayah tat aatmanch tat nishthah tat parayanah.
Gachhantih punah aabrittam jnana nidhuh ta kalmashah. (G. 5/17)
Those whose mind and intellect are wholly merged in him, who remain constantly established in the identity with him and have finally become one with him, their sins being wiped out by the wisdom and reach the state of oneness with the Supreme.

However, the theory of human needs proceeds further to coin the safety and social needs in the context of the human journey. Safety, in terms of the elements of living being available at discretion, is something that works out to help human beings in terms of the activities that would ideally safeguard eventualities in the world. Thus, safety in terms of economic existence boils down to income, safety, finance, revenue, opportunities, availability of work, etc., in the functioning of the person. Safety needs fulfilled, then comes the issue of social needs. It is like having a position of choice, maybe a speciality, which is a part of the person's aspiration. Safety needs, along with the social, create a kind of uniqueness in the stream of activities in life.

> *Vidya vinayah sampannah Brahmanae gavi hastini.*
> *Shunih cha eva svapakae cha panditah samadarshinah.* (G. 5/18)
> The wise look with equanimity in all, whether it is Brahman endowed with gleaning and humility, a cow, an elephant, a dog or a pariah, everything now sees the equality in everything.

Even when the physical safety, social aspects of the needs are fulfilled, the human need doesn't stop. Rather, it rolls down to the best output in the world and the unique concern to have uniqueness in the general kind of identities. This refers to the esteem of the person. In a way, this esteem has unique methods of experiencing and enjoying an identity in the world, which stands out from the others. This need of human esteem can be equated with the perceived kinghood of a lion in the woods, a jungle. Esteem is a kind of individual attaining the positions of recognition in the context of the society where the real spirit of things is denied or equated to the position of esteem.

> *Iha eva taih jitah sargoh yesham samyae sthitam manah.*
> *Nih dosham hi samam Brahman tasmat Brahmani tae sthitah.* (G. 5/19)
> Realised person has his or her consciousness fixed on god, mind is established in equanimity since the absolute is untroubled by evil and is the same to all, hence they are established in Brahman and have attained the Supreme.

The theory of need flows down to the pinnacle of human need in the context of work and life. Each life lived is thereby one of the various sets of attributes, either revealed through behaviour or through practice. It is the point of achievement, a part of which is revealed through actions, perceptions and values of life. At this stage, the person wishes to elevate from the human conditions and attempts to work out a scheme in life where the felt potentials of the person, which had remained very unique but contribute to the schemes of human society. The theory of need describes this stage of need as that of self-actualization.

> *Na prahrishyet priyam prapya na dwijet prapya cha priyam.*
> *Sthira buddhi sam muroh Brahmabid Brahmani sthitah.* (G. 5/20)
> He who with reason form and free from doubt rejoices not only in obtaining what is pleasant and does not feel perturbed on meeting with

the unpleasant, that nor of the supreme Brahman lives eternally and identically with the Brahman.

Many people have tried to explain this stage of self-actualization as the spiritual dimension of life. However, this proves to be the tuned peak of the various types of needs and may be looked at as an apparent discovery of the real personality within. This real personality thus goes a long way to rebuild the structure of human nature in the society and at the same time to ink forward the message for the future of the world.

Elemental rationality at the individual level is, in most of the cases, remains selfish. It is thus that context of the society where the fundamental view of the cause and the desired way forward of human society does not lie in the selfishness of individuals, but rather it talks about the tenets of the person who wishes to join the stream of good things for the human society. This demands rising above personal selfishness.

The theory of need, or in other words, the pyramid of need, cannot create a better society; it drives towards breaking the society further with the projections of stimulating the needing animal and demonic habits within human beings in the global society.

> *Bahya sparsheshu asaktva aatma bindati aatmani yat sukham.*
> *Sah Brahma yoga yukta aatma sukham akshayam ashnutae.* (G. 5/21)
> He whose mind remains unattached to the sense objects, derives through the meditation of the sattwa joy and dwells in the mind, then the yogi, having completely identified himself through meditation with Brahman and enjoys eternal bliss through the realization of God.

Lord Krishna suggests to Arjuna that human excellence lies not in the act and art of a person being selfless in philosophy, habit and focus. A work performed by a person in society transcends the limits and barriers of human capacity when she or he understand that grabbing yields good results for the moment is temporary. But invariably invite or cause damage to the cause of human growth: homogeneity, collective living, cooperation, cohesion, tolerance, friendship, equality, fraternity, individual freedom and above all, the power of capacity to accept others in the journey of individual life. It is thus the situation and position that Lord Krishna suggests the way of life and the fundamental attributes of life of an individual in a given context. This life is not based on the animal spirit, but on the divine spirit in life.

> *Yae hi sam sparshaja bhoga duhkhya noyah eva tae.*
> *Aadi antah bantah kounteya na teshu ramatae budhah.* (G. 5/22)
> The pleasures which are born of sense contacts are verily the source of suffering only through the appearance of enjoying what the selfish-minded people, they have a beginning and an end. The end comes and

they come and go. Arjuna, it is for the reason that a wise man does not indulge in them.

Lord Krishna has suggested to Arjuna that intensely doing the *aarabdha karma* or the divinely bestowed karma is what is needed for people with full dedication to God. This makes the person elevated from the existing level of human attributes to the level of divine attributes. The divine attributes, thus, would make the human attributes tuned to the noble attributes in life for the emergence of human society. It is thus the spirit of good values in life lived that can make it happen. The Vedic sages have thus passed on the tenets of this spirit in the form of a kind of self-undertaking. This says: *Ritam Vadishyami, Satyam Vadishyami*. This means that a vow is taken to be always truthfully oriented in thoughts and actions.

Shaklotih hi eva yah sodhum prak shariram bimokshanat.
Kama krodha udhbham begam sa yaktah sa sukhinarah. (G. 5/23)
He alone who is able to withstand in this very life before casting off his body the urges of lust and anger is a yogi, and he alone is a happy man.

The Vedic utterances for all different qualities of life are such as: *Da-Da-Da; Dayddhamah – Dattah – Damyatah*. These are the utterances for the demonic, humanistic and divine qualities of people. For the demonic, 'Da' – 'Dayaddhamah means hold on, take care, no further sin be committed in life, or else the obvious end would be destruction. For the person, the Vedic voice suggests that: 'Da' – *Dattah* - be a giver, give it up to the extent required and possible. Practice giving in life. To those who are 'sattwa guna' persons: 'Da' – *Daymatah* - control your ego in life. Thus, the Vedic voice offers clear guidance to everyone in society.

Yah antah sukhah antah aaramah tatha antah jyotih eva yah.
Sa yogi Brahma nirvanam Brahmabhutoh adhigacchatia. (G. 5/24)
He who is happy within himself enjoys within himself a delight of the soul and even so is illumined by the inner light, the light of the soul. Shachi yogi identified with the Brahman attains the supreme realization and rests in peace.

Lord Krishna has suggested to Arjuna a sanguine way of this realization. He advocates that, at the end of everything, a sense of pleasure is what can induce one towards happiness. This is somewhat begetting the impacts of the parameters in life that would create a stage for human beings to chase and achieve the condition of perfection in life. Whether the person is now tuned to the journey through empirical material quest in life or a journey for the work of the world, it is the attempt to have a quest in life that is constantly with a pure and unselfish mode. The same applies to the concern for God-realization. With selfless but intense work, if a person drives life in such a way that his or her work contributes to the well-being of many in the world, the person surely attains the vision and realization of God, as advised by Lord Krishna. It is both in the context of the work of the world and the work for God that nishkama karma contributes the highest attainment of truth and sustaining the organizations at the same time.

As an aspirant of spiritual attainment needs selfless work to grow into the stage of perfection, so is the condition best suited for corporates to win and sustain.

> *Labhantae Brahma nirbanam ishayah kshina kalmashah.*
> *Chhinna dweidhah yata aatmanah sarvabhuta hitae ratah.* (G. 5/25)
> The person with desireless work, unattached, shall overcome all sins, whose doubts have been dispelled by knowledge, whose disbelieving mind is firmly established in God and who is actively engaged in the service of all things, attains the Brahman, shall enjoy peace of mind.

It is thus a prerogative of corporates to foster the spirit of noble attributes in life and at the same time to push forward the work given to be rendered in the best possible manner. Whether a manufacturing company, a services company, a non-profit company or an organization of any type, description and objective, the functional managers or the strategic corporate leaders should cultivate in them and push forward the idea of these noble spirits to cover things together for achieving the goal and fulfilling the purpose of victory and sustainability. These are obviously among the core focuses of corporate dynamism in a given context. The functional strategic or corporate leader thus needs to practice in life sattwa guna or truthfulness in thoughts, policies and actions in life.

> *Kama krodhah biyukta aatmanam yatinam yatachetasam.*
> *Abhitoh Brahma nirvanam bartatae bidita aatmanam.* (G. 5/26)
> To those wise men who are free from lust and anger, who are subdued in their mind and have realized God, the Brahman Supreme, the God and its spirit offers the eternal peace and understands that God is present in all and all around.

A corporate manager or the leader is expected to be an impersonal personality in the true sense of the term. This implies that a corporate Sadhu is what the manager or the leader is supposed to become. The corporate Sadhu will be the real Sadhu. This means the person needs to cultivate sattwa guna very rigorously in life. A sequence of Pranayama would always cleanse the mind of the regular layers of impurities. Desires and selfishness are regular associates of human beings in all situations in life. The person who can assert the mind power to overcome the influencing power of selfishness and desire is halfway through the journey in work life.

Sparshan kritva bahih bahyah chakshuh cha eva antarae bhruboh.
Pranaapanau samou kritva nesa abhyantaroh charinou. (G. 5/27)
Shouting out all thoughts and external enjoyments with the gaze fixed on the space between the eyebrows, having regulated the prana or the force of air, the *apana*, the five-fold breathing system follows within the nostrils.

In the case of spiritual realization also, a Sadhu also has the same requirement. Regular pranayama removes the impurities that may crop up in life. With a pure or mostly pure mind in place, the manager or the leader of corporate bodies would then gradually practice to perform work without getting it tagged to any gain beyond the usual rewards system for the organization. Thus, the spirit of the corporate leader now turns out to be that of a Sadhu.

Yatah indriyo mano buddhih munih moksha parayanah.
Bigata ichhah bhayo krodhah yah sada mukta eva sah. (G. 5/28)
He who has brought the senses, mind and intellect under control, such a contemplative soul, content in liberation and free from desire, fear and anger, is ever liberated.

In the true sense of the term, as Lord Krishna has explained to Arjuna, the true nature of a sannyasi or a monk is that person who has devoted his or her mind and energy fully to the cause of the work without any distraction for reward or recognition. This would make the point clear that the one with true dedication to the work of the world, full faith in God, and attraction to no amount of reward, return, seeker and the love for God of anyone, whether living in a family, society or monastery, is a Sadhu in the true sense.

Bhoktaram yajnaram jajna tapasam sarvo loko mahesharam.
Suhhridam sarva bhutanam jnwatva mam shantim ichhati. (G. 5/29)
Having known me in reality as the enjoyer of all sacrifices and austerities, the Supreme Lord of all worlds and the disinterred friend to all beings, my devotee attains peace.

Brahman is present anywhere and everywhere. He is omnipresent in all living and material objects. His presence is the noble orientation. However, the fact is that each one who is in search of God and who is pursuing the way of truth in life is the invoker of truth in life. The Supreme reveals himself through the truth of the world, as well as through the ways of truthfulness of individuals in life. Thus, whenever this aspect of life is understood, visualized and enforced in life, the power of life enhances the spirit of truth and light within. In the corporate context, the person has grown into a sadhu. In a real sense, this corporate sadhu is to be the best performer and most sustainable in life.

9 Discovering Inner Reality: Look Within

Reality is experienced in the context of the world at a particular point in time. At times, it is justified through the process of experiment, and sometimes, through experiential ways. The ultimate reality is understood only when God-realization takes place in a person. It is thus the context in which the facts of reality are expressed through the intuitive-perceptive modes. This mode is somewhat similar to the method of meditative realisation. The truth of the Divine is understood when a particular precondition is fulfilled in a human context. Whereas the scientific understanding of reality is material, that of the spiritual is divine.

> *Sri Bhagavan ubacha:*
> *Anasritah Karmaphalam Karyam Karma Karoti yah.*
> *Sah sannyasi cha yogi cha nah agninah cha akriyah.* (G. 6/1)
> Sri Bhagavan said, He who does his duty without expecting the fruit of action is a sannyasi and a yogi both. He is a sannyasi or renunciate who has merely renounced the sacred fire, and also, even so, he is no yogi. He has merely given up all activity.

The person who does not depend upon the result of the work, nor expects any result in his chosen way, is a sannyasi or monk in the true sense.

Leaving aside the concerns for the result of any karma or action undertaken by the person, if she or he wishes to continue performing the karma intensely, that person is a true *Sannyasi cha yogi cha na nih agnih cha*; he or she is not into the desireful work. Lord Krishna has repeatedly suggested to Arjuna about the desire-free karma where the result or the outcome does not necessarily remain the concern of the person. It is not the fruits of the karma that are looked at, but the quality of the work, given perfection for the work, that is emphasized. This would make the person truly tuned to the spirit of the work and devote all faculties of the mind to accomplish that.

The monk or sannyasi has to be in connection with the goodness of spirit in life and abandon the evil effects of that or any evil association in life.

Yam sannyasam iti prahuh yogam tvam biddhi Pandava
Na hi asamhasya samkalpam yogi bhabati kah chana (G. 6/2)
Arjuna, you must know that nyasa is a specific level of yoga which is only possible to attain when the yogi has not given up thoughts of worldly desires.

Nishkama karma is the state of the mind and consciousness of the person who has attained the position of exploring spiritual thoughts and cultivating the spirit of things within. It is the context where the perspective is created for the best creative contribution to the work. It is to be remembered that merely being into the karma with lots of thoughts about the work, the basic point to consider is that selfish gain expected out of the work becomes the focus, and the observations get radically transformed, keeping in mind the fact that psychological energy gets dissipated through the calculations across personal gains through the result of the set of works.

Aarurukshoh munaeh yogam karma karanam uchhyatae.
Yoga aarhurasya tasya eva shmah karanam uchyatae. (G.6/3)
The spiritual practitioner who desires to climb to the heights of karma, yoga, and disinterested action is spoken of as the stepping stone. For the same man, when he is establishing yoga, the absence of all thoughts of the world is said to be the way of blessedness.

When the person is able to accomplish work without a specific work-driven result or output, she or he can now devote their mind fully, as the spiritual enlightenment grows within, to the stream of work. The issue now is to understand how the art of doing the work becomes conducive to the spiritual dimension of life. The precondition to this is the purity of mind, whereas the concept of impurities on the body is detectable through physical viewing or examinations. The impurities of the mind are the negative qualities that can be understood, by observing keenly, the conditions of the body from the character or behaviour.

Yada hi na indriya-artheshu na anusvajyatae karmana.
Sarva samkalpa sannyasi yogah aarhurah tad uchyatae. (G.6/4)
When a man ceases to have any attachment either for the objects of the senses or for actions, then he has renounced all thoughts and worldly desires. He is said to have attained the height of yoga.

Once the person's mind becomes pure, the point in focus is that a sustained effort through meditation can make the mind gradually remove the psychological impurity from the layers of the human mind. A person may undertake the process of meditation following the steps that are considered a prelude to the act of meditation. Meditation leads to the condition of samadhi, the condition where the mind of the person is thoroughly absorbed in the stream of cosmic consciousness. This is the state of God-realization. When the stream of consciousness is first realized, the perception in the condition of awareness is one, and in the next place, the condition of awareness of the cosmic stream of consciousness remains indescribable. With the touch and realization of the cosmic consciousness, the person is in a position to elevate his or her personality to the level of 'impersonal persona'.

Different states of mind have different types of issues. The mind can be classified into states based on its characteristic features and the patterns of response in the world. Thus, the states are identified as 'Mudha, 'Kshipta', 'Vikshipta', 'Ekagra' and 'Niruddha'. Mudha is the dull state of mind. It is a state when the functionalities of the mind have stopped responding properly. The Mudha mind can understand the imperatives of the material world, but is non-responsive to the functions where a creative component is present. This means the creative and intuitive dimension of the mind remains beyond the Mudha.

The person, who is a monk or a sannyasi, keeps away from the mental orientations concerning material satisfaction, remains out of the focus of the divine choice.

> *Uddharayet tad aatmanam na abasadayet aatmanam.*
> *Aatma eva hi aatmano bandhuh aatmaeva ripuh aatmanah.*   (G.6/5)
> One should live to oneself by one's own efforts and should not degrade oneself, for one's own self is one's friend and one's own self is one's enemy. It depends on how you behave with that.

The Mudha, or the dull mind, does not understand and appreciate the spiritual dimension of life. The Mudha mind understands the material instincts and issues arising out of physical need. It understands the issues, senses and requirements of hunger - thirst - sex. The Mudha mind wishes and prefers to be inactive, in practice. This mind is escapist by nature. The Mudha mind is sleepy. It is indolent in nature. Lazy in its approach, the Mudha mind escapes work or any kind of rigorous responsibility. The Mudha mind understands only the direct and simple kind of communication. It wishes to be away from the call of creative works. It is just tuned to be carried away by the current of the waves of issues and things. The Mudha mind prefers to forget the issues of the past, and also does not wish to spend energy towards structuring any kind of strategies for the future.

In a context where the person himself is oriented to the Supreme Truth seated within as a friend, it acts as the factor to understand and accept the divine in empirical life.

> *Bandhuh aatma aatmanoh tasya yena aatmaeh va aatmana jitah.*
> *Anahtmanah astuh shatrutvae vartatae aatma eva shatruvat.*   (G.6/6)
> One's own self is the friend of the self by whom the lower self or the inner self, which is connected with the senses of the body, has been conquered.

Even so, the very self of him, who has not conquered his lower self, behaves antagonistically, like an enemy.

The Mudha mind needs guidance to get up to the level of a normal mind. The Mudha mind can overcome its conditions through the process of practice and energy infusion within the realms of the mind. Energy infusion is the state of affairs of the mind when it arises from the boundaries of the protective realm. When the Mudha mind finds the infusion or energy within it, it gets chaotic. This state of mind turns into restlessness with the becoming of the energy potent mind: the condition that is infused in it is characterized by the factors of being at one point, at this moment, and then moving to the next. This is the identified aspect of the Kshipta mind. The Kshipta mind endorses the idea of being into many things at a time.

> *Jitatmanah prashanta tasya paramaatma samahitah.*
> *Shito ushnouh sukha duhkheyeshu tatha mana apamanoyao.* (G.6/7)
> The supreme spirit is rooted in the knowledge of the self-controlled man whose mind is perfectly serene in the midst of fears of opposites such as cold and heat, joy and sorrow, honour and ignominy.

The Kshipta mind is equipped with input energy for the purpose of its functioning. It requires an engaging process to settle down on a thought. The usual ways to keep the mind in an active state are an adequate load of work of a general nature. This goes a long way to take care of the dynamics of the work. Dynamics of the work takes the mind to the core aspect of the work, with no or few options left for the accomplishment of the work. The Kshipta mind is restless in its profile. The restless Kshipta mind naturally tends towards a slow settling.

> *Jnana vijnana tripta aatma kutasthoh bijite indriyah.*
> *Yuktah iti uchhyatae yogi sama loshtashma kanchanah.* (G.6/8)
> The yogi whose mind is seated with the jnana or the knowledge of the Supreme and the jnana or the direct knowledge of the divinity, he who is unmoved under the circumstances whose senses are completely mastered and to whom art, stone, gold and all are alike is spoken as the God-realized soul.

The Kshipta mind maintains the settled-down condition only when there are guiding parameters for its settling down. Kshipta, or the restless mind, with an opportunity to settle down, may also get scattered at times. The Vikshipta mind, on the other hand, is widely scattered. The scattered mind has attained its energy to function and at the same time collects and somewhat focusses, having received the mental energy to function. However, the Vikshipta condition of the mind gradually becomes a fact. Yogi is a person who maintains equal balance of mind in the context of the conscious choice of practices in life. To a yogi, the valued and trifling things are weighed the same; she or he does not have any attraction for the material value of an object. Rather, they shall have the full orientation of giving and sacrifice, being fully unattached from anything otherwise valued by the world.

> *Suhhrit-mitra-aurih-udasinah-madhyastha dveshya bandhuhsya.*
> *Sadhushu api cha papeshu sama buddhi bishishyatae.* (G.6/9)
> He who looks upon well-wishers, friends and foes, neutrals, as well as the mediators in makers and relatives and debauches and the sinful with equanimity stands supreme.

A yogi shall find and believe in every person as equal and the same. She or he will not discriminate between an outwardly known, holy man and an ordinary person. To her or him, there remains no difference between people based on any physical or qualitative dimension. The Vikshipta mind has contents of energy which are the factors of the reality around. The Vikshipta mind cannot comprehend something properly. This application of the new approach of mind management is essentially the same as forward-looking. However, until the position of the mind settles down, it cannot perform clearly. The condition of *ekagram,* or the mind concentrated, develops through various ways to attain that. The Ekagra mind, or the concentrated mind, focusses on this state. In this state, the Ekagra mind contains the usual dimensions of the mind in the right sense of the term. With the concentration in place, the mind now attains all powers to do so. The concentrated mind minutely covers all rational and emotional dimensions of life in the context of the world. The Ekagra mind gets the realization of God.

A person with the Ekagra mind is a yogi. Yoga is the art of looking within. A realistic review of the same would reveal the position of the mind and where the mind should find the ways of growth and emergence further. Growth and emergence would thus be identified truly as a prospect for a person in a context.

> *Yogi yunjitah satatam aatmanam rahisi sthitah.*
> *Ekaki yata chittah aatma nirashih aparigrahah.* (G.6/10)
> Living in cessation by all himself, the yogi who has controlled his mind and his body and is free from desires and devoid of possessions should constantly engage his mind in meditation.

It is in this context that it is honestly noted that the true state of mind is difficult to understand oneself, because of perceptual imbalance. Therefore, it requires the help of a guide to identify the same and suggest the right pathway for a person. This person is the guru or the master in the wholesome context. The Vedic civilization has projected this guidance to the people, in general, through the activities of masters or gurus. Ideally, the master should be someone who has earned the spirit of realization and offers the same kind of realization as a host to contribute truth in a realistic way, suited to the context of the learner or the disciple. This is why the learner or the disciple was always required to stay with the master for a designated period.

Suchou deshae pratishthapya sthirah manasa aatmanah.
Na auti uchshritam na autinicham chili-aujina-kusha uttaram. (G.6/11)
Having firmly placed his seat in the spot which is free from the dirt and impurities of the mind, the sacred person and the dear skin and the clothes, therefore, one upon the other, neither very high nor very low.

The yogi shall maintain a position of equibalance in all situations. She or he will not be a seeker of anything. The yogi shall maintain the spirit of God, seeking for decades and always maintaining a simple standard of living, avoiding all extremes in life whatsoever. The objective of learning is the first thing to be identified by the master and accepted with a graceful mind by the disciple. In this exercise, the background of the disciple is identified by the master to determine the course of learning for the disciple. Learning stands as a specific course, pedagogy and content for a person. This is because each individual is different from the other. Learning in the Vedic civilization was specific for every person. Each person was offered a unique way to learn. Learning used to have a conceptual as well as a practical component. Concept was obviously oriented to reach the target domain of learning; however, the other component, practice, was oriented to the functional aspects of doing the same.

Tatra ekagrah manah kritvah yatah chittah indriyah kriyah.
Upabishyah aasanae yunjyat yogah aatma vishuddhayaeh. (G.6/12)
Seated on pure spread, concentrating the mind and controlling the function of the mind and senses, he should practice yoga for self-purification.

The Vedic practice was something regular and daily, suited to the context and the essential requirements of learning. The teacher used various methods such as: a) generic practice, (b) practice in place, (c) extrinsic learning as a practice. Out of these three modes, the generic learning was a certain common tool which the sages used collectively on all students or learners. This includes daily yoga, chanting and a general stream of meditation for all. Apart from this, the next practice in place was a specific stream of the learning process. This has a similarity with the present-day terms of specializations.

Samam kayoh shiroh gribam dhrayan achalam sthiram.
Samprekshya nasikam aagram svam dishah cha na abalokayan. (G.6/13)
Holding the trunk, head and neck in a straight and steady way, remaining firm and fixing the gaze at the top of the nose without looking in any other direction and fixing on God, he attains the yoga.

Each area of learning has certain specific segments of choice, which provide a kind of liberty and option to the learner. As it is done in the case of the choice of modern-day specializations, the Vedic sages had actually initiated the process of choice-based learning components in the case of the context of the disciples. Thus, differentiation in the curriculum and the subsequent way to have the component of learning undertaken was one of the ways to make the best out of a person as a learner. The yogi shall continue with the spiritual practice, sitting in meditative posture, with spine and neck erect, eyes closed, doing alternate nostril breathing.

Thus, the yogi orients his consciousness towards God, with the mind fully devoted to God, and is endowed with divinely blissful life thenceforth.

Prashanta aatma bigata bhih Brahma aacharih bratae sthitah.
Manah samyamya mat chitto yuktoh aasitoh mat parah. (G.6/14)
With complete chastity and fearlessness, perfectly calm, and with mind restrained and fixed on God, the vigilant yogi should sit absorbed in God.

So, with the extrinsic learning and practice in place, the student was to undertake self-experiencing within the learning environment and sometimes, also away from that. The learning environment may have certain elements of limitations which were targeted to overcome, and to allow the learner to move out and mix with organizations or individuals outside in society, at the crossroads of things and also in the case of changing scenarios. This method has been adopted in modern-day practices in the manner and ways of doing an internship to understand the nuances of the applications of the concepts which have been taught. This again was an important element of Vedic learning under the guidance of a guru or teacher.

Once the conceptual understanding and the practice components are mastered, the disciple is entitled to receive the acclaim of Brahmagyan, or the realization of Brahman achieved. The disciple now becomes a sage.

Yunjan na evam sada aatmanam yogih niyatah manasah.
Shantim nirvane Paramam mat sthanam audhi gachhatih. (G.6/15)
Thus, constantly appealing his mind to me, a disciplined mind attains everlasting peace and gets absorbed in me in the realization consisting of supreme bliss, and he is always getting a touch of mine.

In the framework of the general learning component, the disciple does meditation in the manner that is prescribed by the master. Usually, yoga is that component which creates the basis and foundation of meditation. According to the sage Patanjali, the components of yoga are many. However, he has coined all aspects together in a collective manner through a method of eight-step yoga or *ashtanga yoga*. This means yoga is essentially having eight different limbs. These are specific to each stage and prepare the aspirant or the disciple through various aspects of yoga. The stages of yoga have two broad segments, Preparatory and Final. The Preparatory is known as that of *prostuti*, and the Final is known as *parinam*. A meditative personality requires a balance in the habits of eating, consuming, should also be active and awake always.

> *Na auti ashnatah yogah astih na cha ekantam na ashanatah.*
> *Na cha auti svapnashilasya jagratoh na evah cha Arjunah.* (G.6/16)
> Arjuna, this yoga is neither for him who overeats, nor for him who observes complete fasting, it is neither for him who is given too much sleep, nor for him who is awake for too long.

Prostuti, or the preparatory to the yogic way of realization, is spread out in five different layers, such as: *Yama, Niyama, Asana, Pranayama, Pratyahara*. The parinam or destiny consists of three layers of spiritual realization. These are: *Dharana, Dhyana* and Samadhi. With achieving the stage of samadhi, the person achieves a complete victory in the journey, and thus the person who has been practising may have self-initiative, coordination or under the guidance of a master. The sage, who has attained this stage of samadhi, is now all set to take her or his spiritual journey forward in a generic or unique way.

A balanced and poised mind is supported by balanced diet, controlled sleep, regulated work and positive behaviour.

> *Yuktah aaharah biharah asya yukta cheshtasya karamashuh.*
> *Yutah svapna avabodhasya yogoi bhabati duhkhyaha.* (G.6/17)
> Yoga, which reads one or both, is accompanied only by him who is regulated in diet, recreation, regulated in performing action and regulated in sleep and wakefulness.

However, in the entire gamut of yoga, prastuti or the preparatory becomes very important. In the process of preparation, the person has to take care of all aspects and take a stand to proceed accordingly. To begin with, the basic prastuti has 'Yama' as the focus. Yama is disciplining the habits and the character. This involves disciplining certain core functions of life. Most of these pertain to the biological functions. This has also been termed as *Samyam*. Samyam refers to the act of maintaining biological discipline. The core material instincts connected with the biological functions are hunger-thirst-sex-desire. A disciplined approach to all of these is suggested as a requirement of yoga.

When the yogi gets rid of all types of desires and does not get involved in any of the illusory factors of life, then the way to God-realization becomes easier.

> *Yada biniyatam chittam aatmani eva avatishthtae.*
> *Nih spriyahah sarvo kamebhyo yuktoh itiuchyatae tada.* (G.6/18)

When the mind thoroughly disciplined gets focused on God alone, then the person who is free from yearning for all enjoyments is said to be establishing yoga.

Samyam is connected with every aspect of life, but it particularly focuses on the basic aspects. Thus, when it comes to considering hunger, it is related to the requirement and greed connected to that. Greedy consumption is against Yama. Food intake should be balanced in its quantity, frequency and quality. Toxic, stimulant, inflammatory or similar kinds of habits in the intake of food are wrong and go against the principle of Yama. Similarly, other components of biological activities would also require strict discipline.

When the condition of mind of the aspirant is steady like a flame that is unperturbed by the blow of air, realization of God sets in that aspirant's mind.

Yatha dipoh nibatsya tastho na ingatae sa upama smritah.
Yoginoh yata chittasya junjatae yogah aatmanoh. (G.6/19)
As a flame does not flicker in a windless space, such is the mind with the state of the disciplined mind, and yogi practice managing is an unfettered flame when you practice the meditation and fix on God.

Yama is to be included in the organic patterns of living and activities. This should be inbuilt in the character of the aspirant. Yama is very basic in the yoga framework. Without having maintained this, the basic orientation of life may make it difficult to get tuned to the yogic principle.

Once the aspects of Yama have been tuned to the process of life, the next phase of prastuti appears. It is to be noted that dispersion in any way or a change of pattern in the basic ways of living, the very objective of yoga in life, gets shattered. One of the most important aspects of this is to be drenched in the practice, such that the biological calendar of the person is easily set out for the same. It is this biological calendar that needs to be maintained throughout in a somewhat uniform manner, such that it helps the person's progress in a yogic way forward without significant disruptions.

The Yama properly coordinates the facts and factors of *niyama* in life. *Niyama* is a principle-centric and time-tuned practice of a person. Principle-centric and time-tuned, such that the same is included in the regular matters of work of the person in the context of the prevailing scenario around and that of the world.

The practice of meditation makes a person accustomed to getting absorbed in the inner realm of the mind and consciousness. The yogi thus penetrates down the inner consciousness and realizes the atman within.

Yatro uparamatae chittam niruddham yogasevayah.
Yatrah cha eva aatmana aatmanam pashyani aatmani
tu ishaati. (G.6/20)

The state in which the mind and the memory are controlled through the practice of yoga becomes completely tranquil and in which realizing God through subtle reasoning purified by meditation on God and the soul, is now fixed on the Supreme Soul.

Niyama has two distinctly differentiated aspects. This identifies the set of principles in life that are required, as well as the time-tuned practices for things in life. A set of principles is the driving force. For example, in the case of a learner or a student, the driving force is the learning of the theories and practices for life. Theories usually have a documented source or are the results of creative development by the master. The practice is usually tuned to the matter of tuning compound of learning as a combination of theory and is attributed to the pathways of the spiritual quest. A kind of regularity may be visualized in the process, and that has been identified as the basis of the guiding niyama.

The intellect sometimes misguides the person towards the world of desires and material gains. A yogi initiates the process to realize the Supreme Truth by way of dissociating from worldly affairs.

Sukham aatyantikam yat yat buddhi grahyam autiindriyam.
Vetti yatra na cha ebayam sthitah cha chalati tattawatah. (G.6/21)
In which the soul experiences the eternal super-sensuous joy which can be instituted through the subtle and purified intellect, and wherein established the said yogi moves from truth, does not move from truth on any account in any way.

Tuning to units of time is another component of *niyama*. It is creating a domain in which the practice of principle-oriented activities and time-tuning occurs as part of the guidance. Niyama is required to be observed and adhered to when the person develops the urge to go ahead with a spiritual agenda. Niyama in an empirical form is maintained by different monasteries in the world. Monasteries have the habit and policy of getting everything done on a scale of time. The day starts with the ringing of a bell. Worship or meditation, or some kind of ritual, happens when there's another bell to ring; food intake again requires a bell to ring at the designated times. All activities are tuned to time.

God-realization in a particular context refers to the state of mind that attains bliss by the realisation, which represents the highest and incomparable happiness.

Yam labdha cha auparam labham manyatae na aadhikam tatah.
Yasmin sthitah na duhkhenah gurunah api bichalyatae. (G.6/22)
Having attained a firmness in mind and let on to other things gains greater than that, the person who is establishing the faith in God in which is never shaken.

However, human response of a kind of regimentation is good for some targeted activity. It is such a targeted activity that focuses on the issue of time-tuned principles in application. The monastic ways of a regimented approach to growth create a kind of environment or a growth prospect to foster creativity among the participants of the system. Also, the individual constitutions do vary. Therefore, everything should not be done through just a collective, timely procedure except for certain programs or occasions that imply a regimented way.

This equanimity of situation, through which the state of ecstasy or samadhi in which the wisdom of the atman is realized, is through this yoga of dedicated consciousness.

Tam vidyat duhkhya samyoga biyogam yoga samgitam.
Sa nih chayena yoktabyo yogoh anirbina chetashah.   (G.6/23)
The state called yoga, which is free from the contracted sorrows and is not under the impact of any kind of changes in the condition, and the person is into yoga who is resolutely practising an unvaried mind and fixed on God.

In the context of work, the life of people, particularly in urban society, the work structure of a particular corporate or organizational function would imply that the same should be process-oriented. Process orientation is impersonality in the work. Impersonality is attempted to make it suited to the diversified impact of people in the context. This diversified impact of the work procedure or the system of work thus fits in the individual inputs in a series of functional inputs that contribute to the performance of the person in a given context.

The yogi does not entertain in mind promises that are important from the world's material perspective. The mind finds a new context where the search for God continues with utmost importance.

Samkalpa prabhaban kaman tyaktva sarvan asheshatah.
Manasa eva indriya gramah biniyamya sama unnatah.   (G.6/24)
Completely renouncing all desires arising from the worldly thoughts and cravings are fully restraining all the senses, all bodies and minds, the yogi remains.

Niyama, for that matter, is always good to practice in the context of work in the empirical perspective. The corporate agenda can be fulfilled to a great extent by virtue of the collective force created out of the principle-oriented and time-tuned activity for the organization, for excellence in its approach to have the objectives fulfilled through the targets and strategic plans set for the same. It is thus a direct and fulfilling agenda for an organization, either with a corporate focus or through the acts of this niyama-centric approach in the field of work of the world. This is again equally applicable in the context of a spiritual journey for a yogi. Niyama thus creates further fortification done by Yama towards the yogic journey.

Once the aspirant and yogic practitioner is through with the founding pillars of Yama-niyama, the question of asana comes. Asana is reflective of a particular way of sitting posture. Asana thus creates the next step to get the basis of the yogic journey. When a person attempts to meditate, she or he has to settle down somewhere. Settling down somewhere is thus meaningful in this context. Asana is usually considered the ancient way of lying something down on the floor. However, the real purpose and objective of asana are somewhat different.

Gradually, with keen patience, one has to be active in consciousness that involves a clear understanding of truly getting connected with the realm of truth within. God-consciousness needs to be discovered there.

> *Shaneih shanei uparamyet buddhya dhritigrihitaya.*
> *Aatmasamstham manah kritva na kimchit api chintayet.* (G.6/25)
> He should, through the grateful practice and attain tranquility and fixing on the mind, on God through reason, control and steadfastness, he should not think of anything else than God.

Though it means a sitting place and a sitting posture as well, the way one looks at the theory of asana stands very important. In the case of *asana*, the usual kind of suggestions that stream down in the field of spiritual practice are using a particular fabric just adequate to be seated by one individual in a squatting position. The alternative to a fabric is a sitting spread is the dried, procured and treated skin of a tiger with a good amount of soft but steady fur in the composition on the outer side of it. This is really interesting as a place to sit on and at the same time to have the same as a spread for doing some mental practice. However, this, as a part of the process, can be reviewed and that for the modern context chosen.

The yogi shall be very particular in identifying factors related to the restlessness of the mind. Those factors he removed from the possession of the person and again set them devoted to God.

> *Yatoh yatoh nischalati manah chanchala austhiram.*
> *Tatah tatah niyamya etad aatmani eva basham nayet.* (G.6/26)
> Drawing back on the restless and scattered form of the mind from all the objects, after which, if it runs, he should repeatedly fix it on God, always think of God and fix on God.

The seating could be on a spread on the floor for the learner or the practitioner to do the mental coordination. It can be a chair also, not with a thick and sponge cushion, but something that has a plain and solid surface to sit on. Ideally, a wooden chair is chosen as the one for the spiritual process of yoga. Thus, the person initiates the spiritual process and proceeds with the process in a way to take on the activity sitting straight on either the floor or a chair. The seating way becomes successful once it is made to suit the inherent procedure to proceed. On the floor, it is the squatting position. The person needs to have a loosely tied dress on the body; she or he is required to sit cross-legged on the floor, in this position.

Thus, the yogi is in a position to create calmness of mind. With this mental calmness and a cool mind, the yogi undertakes the responsibility of focussing on the core of the mind and thus focuses on the spirit of God alone.

> *Prashanta manasam hi enam yoginam sukham uttamam.*
> *Upeiti shanta rajasam Brahma bhuta akalmasham.* (G.6/27)
> Having placed the mind in a perfectly serene state, who is seamless and the passion is subdued, and who is identified with God, the supreme embodiment of truth, knowledge and bliss, supreme happiness comes true to him or her.

In the case of a person sitting on a chair, the pattern and the basic approach to asana remain the same. Sitting on the chair would imply that the legs of the person are placed on the floor. Legs and feet are on the floor, placed parallel to each other.

In both cases of such sitting, the next steps would follow the same way. The person should take care that the posture is not bent. They should sit just straight, with the backbone maintained straight, no leaning in the back in either of the cases. The hands are to be placed on respective knees, and the backbone is to be maintained straight always. It is thus something that needs practice.

Reaching the state of ecstasy or samadhi, the yogi attains a sinless state and thereby the desire for material comfort goes off, making the mind pure. Thus, the yogi attains an equipoise state of consciousness.

> *Yunjan na evam sada aatmanam yogi bigata kalmashah.*
> *Sukhena Brahma samsparsham atyantam sukham ashnutae.* (G.6/28)
> The seamless yogi, thus uniting his self constantly with God, easily enjoys the eternal bliss and oneness with the supreme Brahman.

When the person starts with the practice, and the sitting posture is maintained properly, the eyes are always maintained in the closed position throughout. The person starts pranayama now. After the asana is properly settled, the person is now all set to do the pranayama. Once the position for the pranayama is set, the first prelude to that needs to be maintained. Pranayama is a kind of invocation. It is the invocation of the cosmic spirit that meets the individual soul now. The individual needs to develop a view that this framework of the person has the perception that she or he has not been the one totally different from the cosmic system. However, the cosmic system is the overall reflection of most of the overall reality. The reality is such that an individual is just an element of the wholesome cosmic system. Therefore, the individual can just cultivate the inner consciousness to connect with the cosmic system as such.

Pranayama has three usual components to be followed in three different steps. Each step is partly independent and partly connected in the total preparation. It is thus the initiative that would lead to the condition of the set of things that arise out of the process as the ingredients to the attainment of the oneness of the mind. The oneness thus happens in a way that would really allow and help to proceed in the direction of the objective as understood.

On attaining God-realization, the yogi visualizes the Divine consciousness in everything and, on the other hand, the presence of the God spirit in all creations.

Sarva bhutastham aatmanam sarva bhutani cha aatmani.
Ikshatae yoga yukta aatma sarvatra same darshanam. (G.6/29)
The yogi who is united in identity with the all-pervading and infinite consciousness and whose vision everywhere is even, unfolds the self present in all beings and all beings assumed in the self.

Thus, this entire process runs into three steps. These are the steps known in the unique ways of: *(a) Prana Sancharah, (b) Prana Puran and (c) Prana Vikashah. Prana Sancharah* is the process of invocation of the *pranic* (vital) force within. At this stage, the elements of the vital energy have been spread out in the world and the entire cosmic system. The invocation of *pranah* is thus calling the elemental consciousness that has taken the position of the individual with respect to the universe as it is visualized. Thus, the universal air or the entire *mahapranah* is now taken care of to touch it. The aspirant is thus ready to draw, in her or his living system, the spread-out elemental *pranic* force that is distributed energy everywhere. They are in touch with the cosmic gift of the *pranic* energy, which is the very coveted source of the entire elemental aspects of the process.

Through this kind of samadhi or ecstasy, the yogi now sees God everywhere and understands the presence of God's spirit in all creations.

Yoh mam pashyati sarvatra sarvam cha mayee pashyatai.
Tasya aham na pranashyami sa cha mae na pranashyati. (G.6/30)
He who sees in me the universal self, present in all things and all belonging in me, never loses sight of me, nor do I ever lose sight of him.

The process at this stage is that of alternate nostril breathing, which can be carried forward with the facts and processes combined together to steam through. After the sequence of *asana* is properly done, the procedure would be to coordinate and internalize the impacts and effects of the same. Correct nostril breathing thus effectively coordinates with the internal and the external. Air is drawn in; this is done with one nostril only. Let us have a direct mention of that. The sitting position in the asana remains steady without leaning in the back or in any way thereof.

Lord Krishna says that the yogi who realizes his presence in all creatures and understands the same becomes blessed with the realization of atman within.

> *Sarva bhuta sthitam yo mam bhajati ekamtvam aasthitam.*
> *Sarvatha bartamanoh api sa yogi mayee bartatae.* (G.6/31)
> The yogi who is established in union with me and worships me as dwelling in all things as their own self, abides in me, no matter what he or she does.

Lift the left hand to the nose and press the left nostril with the left thumb to breathe in through the right nostril. Next, do the breathing in or inhale air through the right nostril by closing the left nostril, slowly. After a few moments, close both nostrils so that the air drawn in is what remains within for a while. This is *kumbhaka,* or the containing of air within; this is the stage of assimilation of air within. After a few moments, the air contained within is released through the opposite nostril, and while doing this, the right nostril is kept closed. Now, after the air is released fully, a pause for a second is given to have a similar cycle in the same way.

Lord Krishna narrates to Arjuna, saying the person who considers the sorrows and happiness of others and that of own, is the best yogi,

> *Atmoh upamanyena sarvatra samam pashyati yah Arjuna.*
> *Sukham va yadi va duhkham sa yogih paramam matah.* (G.6/32)
> Arjuna, he who considers the problems of others as his own, looks on all as one and looks upon the joys and sorrows of all equally, such a yogi is deemed to be the highest of all.

The forward and reverse process of this intake of air-holding of air-releasing air, and then reversing the entire procedure, makes one cycle complete. This composite has to be considered as a single item of the pranic invocation done. Journey of the pranayama starts here. It needs to be repeated and continued for several cycles, spreading through a reasonable number of orientation initiatives, so that the process is made to completed in its way. Repeating the pranic invocation is needed with the same way of sitting, same orientation, same kind of focus and similar approach of mind. The underlying stream of thought is ideally inviting or praying the spirit of God to come down to life and encourage or energize the life force to proceed with the agenda of invocation of God in life.

This set of steps thus comprises the first initiative. The next position is the stage of normal breathing through both nostrils. However, sitting posture remains the same. Eyes continue to remain closed. Thoughts also remain the same.

Arjuna ubacha:
Yah ayam yogah taya proktah samyena Madhusudanah.
Etasya aham na pashyami chanchalatvyat sthithime sthiram.   (G.6/33)
Arjuna said, Krishna, weighing to the restlessness of mind, I do not perceive the lasting stability of this yoga in the form of equanimity which you have just spoken of.

Arjuna, being curious, asked Lord Krishna about the stable, deterministic calm and poise of mind, which Krishna has mentioned is difficult for him to comprehend because of his mind being restless.

In the next focus, the act of willed imagination is what is identified. While the yogi is now closed-eyed and remains in the same position, in the same way. In this stage, awareness is attempted to be worked on with active will force. The awareness is now taken to the top of the head, gradually. At the top of the head, the awareness focusses on the view of the sky at dawn with the rising sun in it. Meaning, the person tries to visualize that the awareness allows the person's internal power of vision to focus on a scenario where the rising sun is viewed in the backdrop of the vast and clear blue sky. The aspirant is now viewing the golden sun at the point of its rising in the sky with energy and illumination.

Arjuna says that the mind, being restless, is difficult to calm down. It is less of the poise and calmness of mind, as it is very difficult to dissociate from desires in life.

Chanchalam hi manah krishna pramathi balabad drirham.
Tasya aham nihgraham manye bayah iva sudushkaram.   (G.6/34)
For Krishna, the mind is very unsteadily turbulent and tenacious and powerful; therefore, I consider it difficult to control this mind.

The inner vision now sees the rising sun in its golden bright lustre. The Sun is now out to offer its energy and illumination to the world, and helps in sustaining and maintaining all life on Earth. The vision of this golden bright Sun is somewhat similar to a causative element to use in the perspective of the functional elements on Earth. The rising sun is full of potential; it has the power and intent to distribute its light and energy to the world to benefit life and the living ecosystem. Yogi now finds it stimulating to receive the light and energy for respective utilization on Earth. Thus, the Yogi is now connected with a cosmic system as such. The focus of the person is to obtain the spirit within without being grossly involved.

Sri Bhagavan ubacha:
Aushamshayam mahabaho manoh duh nigraham chalam.
Aubhyasena tu Kounteya vairagyena cha grihyatae.   (G.6/35)
Lord Krishna explained to Arjuna, saying that the mind is restless, no doubt, and difficult to carve, Arjuna, but it can be brought under control

by repeated practice of meditation and by exercise of dispassion to others and having focused on God.

Lord Krishna mentions that unaltered faith in God and continuity in the practice of meditation shall develop the competence in the person to have God-realizations.

Now is the issue of connection. With the vision of the golden Sun, the vision induces energy and attempts to develop a perception of the cosmic identity of the Sun. The vision now induces the thought that God is connecting with life, with the Sun as the agent and provider. This is again out to the individual to accept in the perceptive design the connection with the cosmic sources and that of the universal spirit of God on Earth to actually and finally benefit the creation.

Lord Krishna continues saying that those who have no discipline and lack control of the senses and are prone to greed, desire, etc., thus go away from God's spirit.

Asamyata aatmana yogoh dusprapah hi iti mae matih.
Vashya aatmana tu yatata shakyah abyaptum upayatah. (G.6/36)
Yoga is a difficult achievement for one whose mind is not subdued by him; however, he who has the mind under control and is restlessly trying and striving, it can be easily attained through practice, this is my conviction.

Willed imagination and the vision of the same in life are equated to the Divine spirit in him as a person. Therefore, the feeling is that a kind of connection is established in the design of things, such that the yogi now may be fortunate to receive the message of the Divine in some form. The task is to understand and make out that the usual way of this focus in the spirit is to have it. The faith of having the realization of God residing within makes the person understand the presence of Divine within.

Arjuna ubacha:
Ayatih shraddh aupetoh yogah chalati manasah.
Auprapyam yoga sam siddhim kan gatim krishna gachhati. (G.6/37)
Arjuna said, Krishna, what becomes of the aspirant who, though endowed with faith, has not been able to subdue the passions and whose mind is, therefore, diverted from yoga even at the time of death, he who thus fails to attain the perfection in yoga, what happens to God-realization of the person.

Arjuna was curious to know the real destiny of a person who has deviated from the path of purity and truth. Even if this person does meditation, what would be the real outcome of the same?

After giving sufficient time to spend at this stage of willed imagination, the person may now focus on the somewhat detailed focus of the entire process.

With the willed imagination experiencing things in the right sense, the carry-forward impact of this would entail that the cosmic energy is now connected with and can be invoked in life to have the impact in the thoughts, acts of life, having the spirit elevated to the same. The task now is to be directly tuned to the cosmic energy and get that aligned for life at an enhanced level of realization.

The devotee now develops a true attraction for the cosmic spirit. Now, in a way, this is taken care of by the broad view and openness of mind of the devotee. What exactly is now the position of the mind of the aspirant? This mind is now different from the perspective of the world. Thus, the cardiac center, deep in the cave of the heart, is where one should visualize the Supreme's presence.

Arjuna had further questions in mind. For instance, if a person deviates from the way of divine action and that of rightful meditation, would that invite a partial or total disaster for that person?

> *Kah chit na ubhoi bibhrasutah chhinna abhrama iva nashyati.*
> *Apratishtho mahabano bimurahah Brahmanam Pathi.* (G.6/38)
> Krishna strayed from the path of leading to God-realization and, without anything to stand upon, is he not lost, like a scattered cloud deprived of both God-realization and heavenly enjoyments?

The vision of the golden Sun is soothing and gives in its own spirit. It needs to be contained within. Again, activate the will force and apply it to the conscious vision of the Surya Deva - the Sun as God. Invocation for him to come inside, creates possibility of spirit of God's presence within. Gradually the soothing light is drawn to the cardiac centre. And now position it inside your heart. This is your supreme illumination in life. The divine light is now within your entity. Concentrate on that for a while or as long as you can visualize the color, the formation and the aura of that divine light. If you have love for God in any form now see Him within this cave of your heart as He has undertaken having been housed in you.

Arjuna was certain that the kind of questions and doubts that had arisen in his mind, as spelt out, cannot be fully cleared by any sage or anyone other than Lord Krishna himself.

> *Etat mae samshayam krishna chettum asya asheshatah.*
> *Tvat anyah samshayah asya chhettwa na hi upapadyatah.* (G.6/39)
> Krishna, only you are capable of / this doubt of mind from me completely, for none other than you can dispel this doubt from me.

The devotee is now in touch with God, the Supreme. He is *Sat, Chit* and *Ananda* himself. Having his vision within the cave of the heart requires welcoming him within and taking care of him through the spiritual ways. The yogi will now have the option to continue in the worship of God through having him in mind and containing him in the chosen message, words, visions or any kind of *lila* or play of actions in the world. The best option is to identify a relation or connection, or interaction with him or his consciousness. This begins with the spirit of realization of God within the empirical personality.

> *Sri Bhagavan ubacha:*
> *Na eva iha na amutra binashah tasya vidyatae.*
> *Na hi kalyanakrit kah chit durgatim tatah gachhati.* (G.6/40)
> Sri Bhagavan said, Dear Arjuna, there is no fault for him either here or hereafter, for none who strives the self-redemption and God-realization ever meets with evil destiny.

Lord Krishna, while responding to the questions raised by Arjuna, said a yogi remains on the pathways of wellbeing and remains chosen even if fallen to certain lower mindsets.

God is not away from his devotee as Lord Krishna offers suggestive hint to Arjuna that God is here, with the devotee, within the devotee. The question boils down to the point that how do the devotee understand that God is here with the devotee or God is present within the devotee as his eternal friend in life. God is his/her 'Sakha', the true friend. God has so many identities. Consider him as father. He is your father. Consider him as your mother - he is your mother. Consider him as your friend - he is your friend. Consider him as any other relation - he is that. He has so many identities to present.

Lord Krishna continues saying that a devoted yogi achieves the heavenly shelter and then enjoys divine company of spirit as a subtle consciousness, and if rebirth occurs, it comes in a nice family in the context of the world.

> *Papya punyakritam lokah anushitva shashvati samah.*
> *Shuchinam shrimatam gaehae yoga bhrashtah hi abhijayatae.* (G.6/41)
> Such a person who has strayed from yoga obtains the higher worlds or the heaven and the seat of God, to which men of meritorious deeds alone are entitled, and having resided there for many years, takes birth of pious and prosperous parents.

Whatever thoughts the devotee might be having about God, whatever be the consideration for him, be that way connected to him. If the devotee considers him in any particular form, it is God's way and grace to remain with the devotee in that form in all situations, in all contexts. If the devotee believes that he/she is his/her father or any other relation, he/she stands as that. The way one develops his/her faith and love for God should maintain that.

Alternatively, the rebirth takes place in the house of a great sage or a person with the spirit of God-realized mainstream flow of consciousness through the wisdom of life.

Athaba yoginam eva kulae bhabati dhimatam.
Etad dhi durlava taram lokae janma yat idrisham. (G.6/42)
If a person is possessed of dispassion, then not attaining to those regions, he is born in the family of enlightened yogis, for such a birth in this world is very difficult to obtain.

The first phase of meditation is over, with the identity of God being within and with the perceptive understanding of the same, most of the time. God can be and should be kept in mind in work, thoughts and interactions. He is always there as the spirit within. He is always a companion of the person amidst the functions of life. It is difficult, but needs to be achieved as a stage of attainment. God is the true spirit within. He is the true guide from within. He shows the pathways for life from within. He is a realistic and empirical identity. He is the soul and the real self within. God is aligned as an invisible force within. He is eternal and does not have a beginning. He will not have any end as such. He is present within the system, and in the case of the world, his presence is felt, as if he is the energy in the form of the heat of your body. He is there in your vision, with his view as the cosmic memory. You try to remember God in all situations, actions, and thoughts of life.

Now, the yogi needs to proceed to the next step of the session. In the next step of internalization, the yogi needs to follow the spiritual pathway of the course. The spiritual pathway is now open for the yogi to follow and achieve the point.

Lord Krishna continues saying that the knowledge of previous life and the purposeful orientation make the person advanced in spiritual attainment.

Tatra tam buddhi samyogam labhatae pourba dehikam.
Yatatae cha tatoh bhuyah sam siddhoh kurunandana. (G.6/43)
Arjuna, he automatically regains in the birth and latent his even mindfulness of his previous birth, and through that he strives harder than ever before for perfection in the form of trying to have God-realization.

Transcendence: It is now the course of transcending the objective and material barriers in life and attaining the spiritual consciousness as the focus and objective of life. The entire process is one which begins at the beginning the repetition of the entire process of pranayama. Thus, the yogi needs to do the pranayama in a way that shall do the enriching of the entire state of the spiritual process and then allow the consciousness to undertake the principle of having been adapted to the spirit and facts of living, and then inculcate it in life in a long-term journey. The course of action initiated as such is that the life and actions of individuals form the composite core of the person and make up the existential ingredients. The elements which have already been tuned to God are already factors of the spells of realization at each plexus of learning in a way that is adaptive.

The yogi attempts this manner of inner awakening, knows about the salient features of God realization and performs yoga to attain fresh realization faster.

Purba abhyasena tena eva hriyatae hi abashah api sah.
Jijnasuh api yoga asya shabda Brahma atibartatae. (G.6/44)
The other one who takes birth in a pious and rich family, through under the sway of his senses, feels drawn towards God by force of the habit of acquiring this previous birth, and even the seeker of enlightenment of yoga in the form of even-mindedness transcends the fruit of actions performed with some interested motive as laid down in the Vedas.

The journey for transcendence thus begins with the entire set of activities, as is done in this process of waking up. The cosmic energy is full of all potent lives inside the inner center, aligned with the entire body system. The store of energy is under the supervision and control of the Cosmic Mother. The Cosmic Spirit rises through the pathways of sushumna or the vertebral column. It is the channel that ranges from the tail end of the backbone up to the point of junction with the brain. The stimulation occurs with the prana vayu (vital air), drawn within by the art of pranayama. The stimulation reaches muladhara at the end inner point of the vertebral column. Then, only the energy is released by the Divine Mother to sustain the new identity of life.

Thus, the person who became deviated from the path of yoga in the previous life may get the consciousness sharply tuned to God and realize the divine spirit in the best process and attain divine liberation.

Prayatnyat yatamana astu yogi shuddhah kilvishah.
Anenah janma sam siddhoh tatoh yati param gatim. (G.6/45)
The yogi, however, who diligently takes up the practice, attains perfection in this very life with the help of latencies of many baths and being thoroughly purged of sin, forthwith reaches the supreme state.

When the step of visualization starts, the devotee sees a ball of light, made of air only, in a golden colour. This golden ball of light, considered a ball of air now, may proceed upward for the journey of transcendence. Help the process to stimulate with the silent internal chanting: 'Om Bhuoh'; The golden ball of air now grows high. It crosses the boundaries of Muladhara and reaches the level Swadhisthana. The moment this golden ball reaches and attempts to cross Swadhisthana you may feel stimulation in the renal and the factors of sex in it. In fact, the sensual instincts can be easily crossed over with the consistent chanting and sense of God within. The ball of light and air proceeds further to the navel region or belt region. At Manipura, the navel, you have a crossroad.

A yogi is way ahead of others – a noble person who realises divine truth in the way of meditation or any dedicated work, even sustained craving for God.

Tapasvibhyah adhikah yogeh jnanibhyah api adhikah matah.
Karmibhyh cha adhikoh yogi tasmat yogi bhaba Arjunah.   (G. 6/46)
The yogi is superior to the ascetics; he is regarded as superior even to those verging the sacred Lord. The yogi is also superior to those who perform action with some interested motive; therefore, Arjuna, you try to become a yogi in your own abode.

With consistent chanting, you cross it over, and the golden ball of light and air grows up and up with concurrent chanting and remembering God. This now reaches the plexus of *anahata,* which is at the cross-section with the sensory connection to the heart. At this stage, the chanting within changes to the universal prayer of 'Om Namah Shivayo Namah', consecration to Lord Shiva. The spiritual consciousness, as the ball of light and air, now moves to the level of the throat, Vishuddha Plexus. Chanting thus continues along with the thoughts of God within. It is thus heading further upwards.

Anyone who does the rightful practice of meditation with another person as a member of the community of wise people attains realization quicker and sharper.

Yoginam api sarva esham matgatae antah aatmanah.
Shraddhavana bhajatae yohmam sa mae yuktatamoh matah.   (G.6/47)
Of all yogis again, he who devotedly worships me with his mind focused on me is considered to be the best yogi.

With the chanting and thoughts of God continued, the force of realization now crosses the throat region and completes the journey through the vertebral column in the 'Sushumna way'. Thus, with this chanting, it reaches Aajna Chakra. At this level of the forehead or the Aajna Chakra, the chanting within changes to: 'Om Namah Bhagavatae'. This would push the consciousness through the brain up to the physical limit of the top bony cover, the skull. With chanting and God in consciousness, the yogi would push the spiritual ball up further. This ball of air and light would thus find its way further upward to the atmosphere and find its pathway out. There is a spiritual orifice, the Brahma Randhra- a microscopic orifice at a central point of the skull. This makes the way out. The individual consciousness now merges with that of the cosmic.

The yogi now reaches the state of samadhi- oneness with the spiritual identity of creation. Gradually, the person now recognizes the spirit of oneness, yet has a distinct physical identity. The person connects now with God and develops affirmation: *'Tat tvam ausi'* – 'It is you who get revealed through me. You have discovered your spirit in me. You alone exist in this creation'. This empirical self is now his eternal identity in spirit with God who resides within.

10 Material and Spiritual Knowledge

Knowledge and intellect drive our lives. Knowledge of life's activities is learned by an infant gradually from their parents or those who take care. Grooming takes place in that pathway to finally attain workable, winning heights. The modern society is knowledge-driven. Outlook on life and its whereabouts are factors of life in terms of its own rooting and positions in life. The world and this holy nature have arranged a plethora of things for the making of countless numbers of lives in various forms. At the human scale, knowledge is now considered one of the most or the most important aspects of human identity. Resources are also a factor of knowledge now. The other aspect of knowledge is wisdom, the spiritual knowledge. With the spiritual understanding of the broader reality, wisdom seeds are sown in a life, and they grow.

> *Sri Bhagavan ubacha:*
> *Mayae aasaktah manah Partha yogam yunjan mat-aashrayah.*
> *Aushamshayam samagram mam yatha jnasyasi tat shrimuh.*   (G. 7/1)
> Lord Krishna said, Arjuna, this spiritual aspirant who is devoted to me and performs the activities of life based on that receives my endowment in terms of the strength, achievement and glory in the world.

Lord Krishna has given a unique option and input to Arjuna to garner the spiritual knowledge. He has mentioned that Arjuna is to be attracted to him. As he has elaborated by saying that a person is attracted to God in life, the person gets a chance to spread out to the extent of the divine spirit. He suggests that a person be not only attracted to but also develop a kind of addiction to the spirit of God. Spiritual knowledge is the spirit driven by the Divine in the context of the Earth system. The spirit has different orientation and vast spread throughout the span of civilization. Divine spirit helps one to adopt and proceed through the pathways of the spiritual journey and develop the realization of God in the context of the world, such that the truth of divine is present in each and everything, all the material forms of the world and the elemental presence within the abodes of the living entities. Thus, the presence of God is to be discovered by the devotee.

Jnanam tae aham savijnananam idam bakshyama ausheshatah.
Yat jnatva naiha bhuyah anyat jnatavyam na avashishyatae.   (G. 7/2)
I shall unfold to you in its entirety this wisdom, the knowledge of God in absolute, formless God, along with the knowledge of the qualified aspect of God, both the form and without form, having known this, which nothing remains yet to be known in this world.

The knowledge of this spirit is available across the universe. Thus, the Supreme has been relevant to the context of the world. In this way, the entire universe with its causative factors has been very protective of the realities of the world. God has endowed us with all the aspects of life and elements for the same. The aspects of God's revelation spread towards the emergence of the spirit of the same. The divine spirit is such that it contains all the aspects of reality. Knowledge of reality is that it helps in the proper performance and that of the same in the context of the world. It is thus through a process of intuitive perception of the world. It is thus the combination of the material and the perceptive understanding of the work of the world. It is the material content which pertains to the empirical reality of the same. It is the making of civilization that makes the emerging dimensions in different parts of the world. As this pertains to the systems and structures of the creation, this refers to the new reality.

Manushyanam saha shreshu kanchit yatati siddhayae
Yetatam api siddhanam kanchit mam betti tatwatah.   (G. 7/3)
Hardly one among thousands of men strives to realize me, the Supreme, of those striving yogis; again, some attain my realization and know me in reality.

The quest for spiritual learning is actually the quest for God-realization. As Lord Krishna has mentioned to Arjuna, among millions and billions, only a few actually opt for God-realization. Those who opt for God realization are not all serious about it. Again, among the thousands who seriously opt for the realization of God, only a few do really go to the extent of reaching out to the core of the spirit. The core of the spirit, thus, remains apart from the usual locus of people on Earth. The quest is normally tagged to the concerns arising from the individual drivers of life. The drivers of life may have countless ways to live life, thus the living becomes essentially realistic with the spirit of God in just a handful of cases and situations. This pushes the idea of the importance forward in the direction of time. Thus, realization needs to feed the requirement and the inclination of lives lived forward. In the design of things for the world, empirical truth can go hand in hand with the eternal truth. Factors of realization arise in the case of eternal truth. Thus, the aspects of the eternal truth may not be apparently useful but essentially remain vital for the growth in future.

The entire nature, as a part of the creation, sustains life. God has created life in such a way that reciprocity, continuity and homogeneity are maintained in the universe. The cosmic balance is maintained through mutual dependence and an individual's ability to adjust within their scope. The creation, as such, is a unique part that the creator played to maintain a series of continuity among species and elements. The balance is created through interdependence. It is thus highlighted that yama or samyamah, containing and creating balance, is one of the most important aspects. Interdependence is thus made into a fact of life.

> *Bhumih aapoh aunauloh vayuh kham manoh buddhih evacha*
> *Ahamkarah iti iyam mae bhinnah prakritih aushtadhah.*   (G.7/4)
> Art, water, fire, air, ether, mind, reason and also the ego - these constitute my nature divided into eight parts.

As such, nature is ready to create. The soil of the Earth is kept for the benefit of the creatures. Merely tilling the soil does not give rise to a generation of crops. Soil needs to be nurtured for such productive conditions. It is this condition that creates and maintains the productivity based on the input factors in the form of seeds. Seeds make their plants based on the ground condition that makes things available for life. So, when the soil is ready and it's applied with the seeds of paddy, it will give rise to the output of paddy. There are certain groups in the world that campaign claiming that a person becomes a non-killer by being a vegetarian. This is a wrong or misdirected campaign as the seeds of paddy develop paddy plants, which nurture life's itch. It grows when the paddy plant reaches maturity; the paddy is ready now. Harvesting happens now. Harvesting requires the mature paddy to be cut from each of its plants and then put to husking to get rice extracted from the cover. Rice is ultimately the focus of a large number of the human population in the world who consume rice in some cooked form; in many cases, it is the staple item.

> *Aupara iyam itah tuh aunyanam prakritim biddhi mae param.*
> *Jiva bhutam mahabaho yah idam dharyatae jagat.*   (G.7/5)
> This indeed is my lower material nature, the one by which the whole universe is sustained, know it to be my higher nature, the form of the *jiva* and the life principle of my transcendental character.

Now, the paddy plants, after the paddy matures, could give rise to a large community of paddy plants to grow, thereby perpetually. Those who are eating just rice in their pure vegetarian cuisine are also killers of lives. Each paddy plant is in life prior to coming into contact with the human killers who cut them and add to the stream of other things that humans consume at the cost of other lives or through the deprivation of some lives. The way humans procure cow milk is a clear case of deprivation. Cows create milk for the consumption and nurturing of the calf. Collecting cow milk is done through the direct deprivation of the calves. It is this way that all items of human consumption are obtained: through the act of some kind of taking actions contrary to the logical right and interest of another group or entity that is the original recipient of the same. Human society has to depend on this mutual correspondence and the philosophy of interdependence throughout.

> *Etad yonini bhutani sarvani iti upadharayah.*
> *Aham kritsanya jagatah prabhah pralaya tatha.* (G.7/6)
> Arjuna, know that all beings have evolved from this twofold property and that I am the source of the entire creation, and into me again it disappears.

There is a prevailing from a section of psychologists that human beings are 'needing' animals. As such, the pyramid of needs has been created as a doctrine. This is very widely accepted as not only valid but a large number of companies and corporate houses in the world do believe that the human needs, as classified in the form of a pyramid, do fit in the corporate analysis of global markets and societies. Therefore, various human needs, up to the level of self-actualization, can be seen to support urban human tendencies. Kind of market-driven, needs are being pushed forward to make things favourable to the selling and distributing of products. Needs, which are basic requirements, are fulfilled, further giving rise to basic or advanced or added elements of need. The need is pushed down to the condition of greed. Greed arises out of the need for the awaited position of the condition in society. The condition of the work, that he or she has, is the extent of realizing the spell of greed. Greed has roots in the unidentified or unfair position of need. The element of need thus requires to be contained, or else the greed will continue spreading like wildfire. This may trigger disruption in the human system, the society and activities.

The cosmic ecosystem has one of the most basic foundations in mutual connections and interdependence. The plant kingdom generously provides support for the subsistence of the human species. Air that works as the *prana shakti* or the vital energy is continuously getting purified by the plants. Oxygenation of a human person is of utmost importance. One of the most important aspects of the mutual connections is that the plants produce oxygen in abundance and send it into the air. The carbon dioxide content, released by human beings is sent back into the air. Trees are out there to consume the carbon dioxide content of the air. Therefore, it works in two ways: first, it helps sustain human life and provides vital energy. On the other hand, trees also protect by absorbing carbon dioxide.

> *Mattah parataram na anyat kimchit asti Dhananjaya.*
> *Mayae sarvam idam protam sutrae manigana eva.* (G.7/7)
> There is nothing else besides me, Arjuna, like clusters of yarn beads formed by knots on a thread; all this universe is threaded in me.

The act of mutual dependence is maintained in the animal society. Life in the animal society is based on principles of conflict and cooperation. They conflict over the basic necessities of life and cooperate on the issues of sustenance. Spirit of goodness in one segment of lives on the planet is well understood and appreciated by the other segment as well. Each segment of life on Earth has its uniqueness, on one hand, and a generic approach on the other. A unique example of the overall spirit of understanding, cooperation, and mutual act of well-being is given in the Upanishad. It was in the case of a small boy, Satyakama. He hailed from an ordinary part of society, having mother Jabala, as the only parental identity to be furnished if required. Satyakama had developed strong desire to study. That too from a senior and famous sage, Gautama. Sage Gautama and his school of Brahma Vidya, or the study of the streams of God realization. It was, therefore, a difficult task for an ordinary lady, like Jabala, to get her son admitted to the school of sage Gautama. However, she had allowed her son to proceed and explore with his only credential of mentioning the name of his mother. The boy had his journey forward to the teacher. Gautama, the master, had accepted the boy Satyakama as his disciple in school.

Rasoh aham asmi aupsuh kaunteya prabha asmi Shashi surayoh.
Pranabah sarva vedeshu shabdah khae paurusham nrishu. (G.7/8)
Arjuna, I am the sapidity in water and light in the moon and the sun, I am the sacred syllable of 'aum', I am the Vedas, the sound of akshara and the manliness in man.

However, the issues of learning came forward. Sage Gautama identified a very unique and impossible kind of assignment for the student. The given assignment was not only considered impossible, but somewhat risky for life. This again was not a point of resistance to the boy. He was confident that the assignment given by the master must be achievable as the master has to do the task. The task was to take along two hundred and fifty cows and at the same time take care of them. The master had said the student to carry the cows to the forest, take care of the cows and come back only when the number of cows grows to one thousand and not only that, each one will be well in good health. Now the common issue that arises is that of the personal security of the life of the student and the accompanying lives of the cows. It was in the context of the forest, a usual scenario that lions, tigers come forward and eat on the life of this boy and two hundred and fifty accompanying cows. But this did not at all happened.

Punyah gandhoh prithrivyam cha tejah cha asmi bibhaba ausau
Jivanam sarvabhuteshu tapah cha asmi tapasvishu. (G.7/9)
I am the pure order, the subtle principle of the order in the Earth and the brightness in the fire, I am the life in all beings and the austerity in the ascesis.

The actual scenario turned opposite. The strong faith in the boy, Satyakama, had his absolute simplicity made him a different one in the context of the forest and its large number of dangerous animals. Each of this set of dangerous animals could find in the team Satyakama a good potential of palatable easy good. However, the sequence of things was somewhat different. Deadly animals of the forest understood in the simple boy a kind of truth that they should offer respect to. None of those dangerous animals had caused anything bad on Satyakama or his team of cows. Rather, on the other hand, the animals in their own way, had their lessons learnt in life conveyed to him. The animals got sympathetic to the small boy Satyakama. Instead of causing harm to them they started individually sharing with him the message and vibration of God. The trees were also compassionate to Satyakama. They found in him a noble person, therefore took the turn into a disciple or a student of the mother Earth.

Satyakama had earned the compliancy position in nature. All significant elements in the world stood by the truthful and simple person, Satyakama. Here we find even animals also become subdued and friends to an ordinary person. They had been received by the element of nature.

Elements of nature, the trees, herbs, shrubs, animals, all are corded in the garment of things. Thus, the most important part of it was the simplicity, truthfulness, and strong faith. Even the animals, plants can understand, in their own ways, the spirit of noble attributes in life and that of the intrinsic feature of the same at the converse of the universe. The spirit of goodness is not only given respect, but also cooperated and supported. It is this intrinsic value that the universe maintains, and at the same time, comes out with principles of sustainability. The functional principle of our Earth also corresponds to that.

Vijam mam sarba bhutanam biddhi partha sanatanam.
Buddhih buddhimatam asmi tejah tejasvinam aham. (G.7/10)
Arjuna, know me to be the eternal seed of all beings, I am the intellect of the intelligent and glory of the glorious.

The basic pranic energy that is ingrained in the human system is that which makes a thorough maintenance. All lives are endowed with the fundamental energy at their initial budding out in the world. This, as a mechanism, continues to maintain poise in the universe. However, the human mind may, and does, create ripples of turbulence in that poise. This makes the focus of the journey of life different from the desired ones. It is thus a situation that stands for and supports the conditions created by situation and maintained in randomness.

Lord Krishna has mentioned to Arjuna that the valour, energy and power that humans possess is a special gift of God to remedy the ills and evils of the world. It is the gift of God as the energy of the system takes it forward, reaching out to individual elemental positions and thus to maintain the contextual understanding that energy endowed to human beings is required to be of use purposefully. This world thus becomes the guiding principle of the contained energy within.

> *Balam balabatam cha aham kama raga bibarjitam.*
> *Dharmah abiroddhoh bhuteshu kamoh asmi bharatarshabha.* (G.7/11)
> Arjuna, of the mighty and the might, free from the passion and the desire in all beings, I am the desire also, the confuddle desire and not conflicting with the virtue or the spiritual inductions.

Temporary and emotional inclination push towards achieving a certain kind of state, when people would accept the point of view of being carried forward the agenda of conserving by way of restricting the emotional pathways. This actually pushes certain ranges of negative attractions of life and thus actually push down to waste the factors of life that goes away without serving the core purpose. In this process, human society can really elevate its realistic collective understanding of things in nature and ultimately make a better place in this current world. God has mentioned to Arjuna that the energy is created out of the existing setup of this world system. Arjuna was driven by rajas with sattwa guna as the governing principle. Thus, he was following God's path for the well-being of the world.

> *Yae cha eva svattwika bhaba rajasan tamasa cha yae.*
> *Matta eva iti tan biddhi na tu aham teshu tae mayee.* (G.7/12)
> Whatever other entities there are, born of sattwa, the quality of goodness, and those who are born of rajas, the quality of activity, and the tamas, the principles of inertia, know them all as evolved from me alone. In reality, however, neither do I exist in them, nor do they in me.

Human characters do emerge from her or his basic nature. The way one looks at a scenario of the world, the reverse occurs in terms of the world, springing back the same in whatever manner it can. Human conditions have emerged out of human actions and interventions. These actions and interventions always make pathways for those who may be the first runners in establishing the truth on Earth. It is thus a system where each of these persons gets an opportunity to give shape to the visualization. Lord Krishna has mentioned to Arjuna that those who cultivate goodness will have good experiences in life. Each person may have a journey unique in nature, attributes and consequential ends. The one that moves this agenda forward would classify the person based on the driving forces of life that earnestly are in the positions of things, as by an urge strong enough to endure. Being truthfully oriented to God makes the best element in the pattern of living lives on the same principle.

Diversity is one of the key focuses and facts of this world of humans. Human beings collectively maintain three different levels of qualities. This is known as triguna - three qualities. These are sattwa, rajas and tamas. Any combination of attributes that guide and govern human beings in society, and which determines the quality of the person and the dominant feature of that.

> *Tribhih gunamayaeh bhabaih ebhih sarvam idam jagat.*
> *Mohitam na abhijanati mam evyah param abyayam.* (G.7/13)
> The whole of this creation is deluded by these objects evolved from the three modes of prakriti, sattwa, rajas and tamas, and that is why the world fails to recognize me standing apart from this and the imperishable being.

Sattwa is the combination of those attributes which actually directs the forces of life towards unique ways of leading the life. A person of this variety would thus be oriented to set of actions and principles that are good for the entire human society. Sattwa person is truth centric in life. She or he understands that truth is essential to follow and adhere to in life. Sattwa discovers truth in multiple ways. One of the ways that it understands is a pattern that is followed by the Earth system. The nature offers the basics of truth through the way it lives and grows. The nature has the intrinsic principle of coexistence and collective living. One element of the nature maintains its existence and tolerates to a certain extent the existence of the other. Mutual support and acceptance is one of the core values of the nature. This value being visible external in the empirical set up of the world. The factors of this may be commendable truth to search the same set of values within. Within the existence, the biological, psychological and external functional do cooperate to find out the underlying dominant principle of life in the context of the social and external living in the world as a part of the journey in life.

> *Daivi hi esha gunamoyee mama maya Duratyaya.*
> *Mam eva yae prapadyantae mayam etam taranti tae.* (G.7/14)
> For this Divine, most wonderful, the veil, the *maya* of mine, consisting of the three gunas, or the three different types of prakriti, sattwa, rajas and tamas, is extremely difficult to break through. Those, however, who constantly adore me alone are able to cross it.

The sattwa personality thus believes that translating the values of truth in realistic terms in life entails the thoughts and actions to be coordinated accordingly. Tolerance has a specific way of response by trees in the woods. The tree tolerates. It does tolerate to the extent of containing various types of inflicts the world of humans would extend to it. This includes plucking down the leaves unnecessarily. The green leaves plucked mean pain to the tree. Apart from this, in various other ways, the infliction on the trees continues to happen. Essentially, this pattern continues as an inbuilt systemic approach in the journey of life of the trees. It tolerates, sustains and continues to grow. Yet the trees continue to perform their task of giving out for the world.

Na mam dushkritino mudhah prapadyantae narahadhamah.
Mayayah apahrita gyana aasuram bhabam aashritam. (G.7/15)
Those whose wisdom has been carried away by the delusions, the maya, and who are demonistic in nature, such foolish and vile men of evil deeds do not adore me.

As such, the core value being the spirit of tolerance, the spiritual practice continues to give out without having any commercial orientation or expecting anything in return. It gives away its breath, the oxygen. The most critical factor for human life. The tree offers shade to the travelers, protecting them from the possibility of sun strokes. The tree allows the birds and lizards to have their nests on its body and framework. Tree is thus not only offering tolerance as its core value but also stands as one of the most unique examples of giving without expecting anything in return. It is thus the matter of utmost importance that elemental lives in nature to maintain the values in very high esteem and thereby ensure that some amount of learning occurs in life out of that. The degree of elemental learning is a quest in the framework of values in human societies. The learning that a sattwa guna person inculcates is extremely good and healthy for human society. Tolerance is divinity, giving is divinity. The society may follow those values for its betterment. Sattwa guna essentially pivots around that and makes the human society a place of living better than what it is currently in the world.

The sattwa personality maintains life based on a certain set of attributes where she or he does not cause any harm to others, remains friendly and has a helping attitude towards others, and at the same time, does try to find out ways to solve the issues of discord or the problems of the Earth system. Sattwa is the essential master of the three types of human qualities- sattwa, rajas and tamas. Rajas has a good thing inbuilt, which translates to dynamism energy in the work and transactions in the society is which is very essential, which rajas do provide to.

Chaturbidhah bhajantae mam janah sukritinah Arjunah.
Aarto jijnashuh artharthi jnanih cha Bharata barshabha. (G.7/16)
Four types of devotees of noble deeds worship me, Arjuna, the seekers after worldly possessions and the afflicted, the seeker for knowledge and the man of wisdom, O blessed Brahman.

Arjuna was eager to know the fundamentals of human truth. Lord Krishna said, the quest for having wisdom in life is intrinsic to all humans. However, based on the quality of the quest, they are grouped into four different classes. This is, not to be judgmental, but a description of the prevailing context in human society. The four groups are qualitative in their nature. Quantities do vary widely between and among these groups. Groups thus mentioned by Lord Krishna are: *Aarto, Jiggnashu, Artharthi* and *Gnyani*. The first category of the aarto is those who have identified a pressing need for God in their life. They are members of society who, despite their positions, acknowledge that their worthiness for God's touch, grace, or love, or the urgency of their desires, are all ultimately subject to God's wish, grace, and intervention. It is thus the aarto people who may be considered as those who are crying for help, grace or the intervention of God. Usually, these happen in a material sense of the term when the person falls into problems, difficulties, and dangers in life and work.

> *Tesham gyani nitya yuktah ekah bhaktih bishishyatae.*
> *Priyoh hi jnaninoh autyartham ashom sacha mama priyah.* (G.7/17)
> Of these, the best man is the man of wisdom, everlasting, ever establishing me and possessed of exclusive devotion for me. I am extremely dear to the wise and the person who is devoted to me and is extremely dear to me.

However, in most cases, though the 'seeker' is concerned for his personal or identified periphery to get remedies or rescue, there could be other reasons also. A serious pursuer in the journey of life may find the condition almost similar to a person in danger, but with a different objective. They may have urgent questions to obtain answers to, or maybe have some generic questions without solutions. These are the people who keep asking things based on the orientation of mind and the features of the character of the person. It is thus a context where the questions would have two distinct classes. One of these is the empirical pattern of questioning, while the other pertains to the eternal questions. The empirical pattern of questioning is the most widespread in the world. However, there are a very few in number who are really concerned about the external truth and learning the nuances of that as applied in life.

> *Udarah sarboh ebaitac jnayani tuaatma eva mae matam.*
> *Aasthitah sa hi yukta aatma mam eva anuttomam gatim.* (G.7/18)
> Indeed, all these are noble, but the man of wisdom is my very self. Such is my view, for such a devotee has his mind and intellect merged in me and is firmly establishing me along the highest goal.

It is the basic spirit of questions that makes the Lord induced to respond to the same. When it comes to the questions patterned to the urge for realization of God, he himself takes the matter forward to squarely respond to the person's questions in the context of the eternal truth to open its wings in the journey of the divine spirit through the environment of the human spirit. The role of the aspirant has to be pure in intention, without any hidden agenda, for gain of any kind and that of the society to trace back God's preference is to respond to those minds who are pure in hearts and are eager or keen to learn the 'Brahmagnyana'- knowledge of the Supreme in all situation of life. Arjuna had questions about that character. Arjuna had fallen sick in mind due to the impact of worldly factors. His role was to perform war as a supportive instrument of the Supreme. Therefore, questions to Arjuna he even went further to tell Arjuna things which were just understood and not properly spelt out. Arjuna was the only devotee having been blessed with the consciousness of Lord Krishna, even though it was in the context of the war, in the war field. The questions to Arjuna were not only answered but also clarified in clear terms.

Arjuna's position was not just asking questions without any purpose, but was seriously connected with the objective of his being with God. Therefore, whenever he thought of working against or killing the master Dronacharya and grandfather Bhishma, he was bewildered, depressed, stressed and even had lost the mental power to hold the dear weapon Gandiva in hand. The fact stands that he was also frozen in loss of strength and power of decision.

> *Bahunam janmani antae jnanavanah mam prapadyantae.*
> *Basudevah sarvam iti sa mahatma sudurlabhah.* (G.7/19)
> In the very last of all births, an enlightened person worships me, realizing that all this is God, and such a great soul is very rare indeed.

Arjuna was thus an 'aurtarthi' also, meaning he had valid and urgent spiritual reasons to ask and get answers to. These are the combinations of the causative factors leading to the people by Lord Krishna, which have come to the advantage of human society in the form of the *Bhagavad Gita*. *Gita* is the song of God. Lord Krishna himself narrated all the concepts and suggested practices for the practical making of a self towards the fulfilling end of the journey in the pathway of truth. Arjuna, a truthful soul, was very strong in character. During a year, when he had the destined visit to heaven by the grace and advice of Lord Shiva, he was offered a plethora of divinely powerful weapons by different forms of God, each of which was irresistible, and ought to help Arjuna in the war against the criminals.

> *Kameihtaih taih hrita gyanah prapadyantae anya devatah.*
> *Tamtam niyamam aasthayan prakritya niyata svaya.* (G.7/20)
> These, those whose wisdom has been carried away by the various desires being prompted by their own nature, worship their deities, adopting rules and rites and rituals relating to age.

Arjuna was happy receiving all these weapons from different forms of the lords. However, a strange thing happened. Arjuna was approached by one of the *apsaras* to have enjoyment together. An apsara is a woman attractive in every respect, present in the realm of the gods to test the divine character of an aspirant. The art of convincing or even emotionally drenching a person was mastered by the Apsaras. Arjuna was also strongly persuaded. But he could easily decline the call of the enjoyment of flesh. This had led to a curse placed by the apsara on Arjuna, saying that for a period of one year, Arjuna would lose his masculinity and he grouped among a neuter gender. Even then Arjuna did not submit. The strength of character that Arjuna had was actually one of the driving forces behind his being chosen by Lord Krishna as a friend. Since Arjuna's skill and efficiency were topmost, his effectiveness in war and the chance of his victory were tied to the victory of the gods. Lord Krishna offered the recognition of the best among men.

Yo yoh yam yam tanum bhaktah shraddhyah architam ichhyhti.
Tasya tasyah achalam shraddham tam eva bidadhami aham. (G.7/21)
Whatever celestial form of devotee craving for some worldly objects chooses to worship me through reverence, I establish myself in the faith of that particular devotee and in that very form.

Having learned the lessons learnt from Lord Krishna, Arjuna had turned into a person with knowledge and thus acquired wisdom. At the same time, he had turned into a devotee. A devotee is the dearest to God. Arjuna thus got drenched in the advices of the Lord to become a karma yogi, a gnyana yogi, a bhakta and finally he had declared to be dedicated to the Lord by saying *'kaurishyae bachanam tavah'*- meaning 'shall do whatever you tell me to do'. Arjuna thus had gained the spirit of doing nishkama karma or selfless work as a karma yogi, the person who is a dedicated person of work. He became a 'gnayani' or a person with the wisdom of God. Thus, Arjuna had acquired Brahmagnyana, the wisdom of the Supreme. And finally, he could turn himself into a devotee in the truest sense of the term. As a devotee of God, he was destined to obey and follow the path of an earnest devotee. As Lord Krishna gave him the call: *'Manmana bhabah, mad bhakta, mad yaj'*- meaning be turned to me in your mind, be my devotee, expect me in your life and thoughts. Arjuna had full faith in the call of Lord Krishna and followed him fully.

The wisdom in the consciousness of a person is assumed to be a resistant force to the making of a 'bhakta' or a devotee. However, Lord Krishna had persuaded Arjuna to proceed through his life of action. He was destined to do that as the forces of liberation held it as one of the most important objectives of a spiritual self. Arjuna got through the synthesis of yoga. All major aspects of God's connection were in his focus.

Sa taya shraddhyay yukah tasya aaradhanam ihatae.
Labhatae cha tatoh kaman mayivah bihitan hi tan. (G. 7/22)
Endowed with such faith, he worships that particular deity and obtains through that deity, without doubt, his desired enjoyment and verily ordained by me.

Arjuna, with his purity in character and mind, had immense sraddha for Lord Krishna. Sraddha is the act of having faith, respect and love combined.

Arjuna became embodied in that. He had developed deep shraddha for Lord Krishna. This element of shraddha in Arjuna made him strong and keenly caring for the Lord. Arjuna's consciousness confirmed Lord Krishna as a friend in life. However, he never forgot that this friend is an eternal personality. He was fully aware of the fact that Krishna was the ultimate power and the reserve of all truth on Earth and beyond. Lord was thus the friend, the companion, the guide, the person to whom he could make ultimate consecration. It is a surrender with full dedication. His journey in the war had begun with deep depression, and then finally reached the realm of total bliss offered by God in the world. Arjuna was fortunate enough to get a constant series of advice from the Lord, and in all the contexts, he could make his mind open to the call of the Lord, and then realization of God sets in the appropriate sense of the term.

> *Anta battu phalam taesham tat bhabati alpa medhasam.*
> *Devan devajajoh yanti mat bhakto yanti mam api.* (G.7/23)
> The fruit gained by these good people, so I am standing. However, the perishable, the worshippers of gods, attain the gods, whereas my devotees, howsoever they worship me, eventually come to me and me alone.

While talking about the art of karma, Lord Krishna has always mentioned that doing nishkama karma is the ultimate goal. Nishkama karma is very difficult to do. It is accomplishing the work without having concern for the result or outcome of the work. Each work has its own objective or the targets set for it. Lord Krishna narrated to Arjuna, saying that the work that does not carry any element of reward or returns in expectation is the prelude to nishkama karma. The actual condition of this karma is fulfilled when the doer of the karma is fully engrossed in a good karma and receives the joy of doing the karma in the context of the world. Such karma is the fruit of joyful action, and of course, without any thought or calculation in return.

> *Abyaktam byaktim apannam manyantae manaba buddhayoh.*
> *Param Bhama ajanonto mama abyoh ahom anuttamam.* (G. 7/24)
> Not knowing my supreme nature, unsurpassable and undecaying, the ignorant persons regard me, the supreme spirit, beyond reach of mind and senses, the embodiment of truth, knowledge and bliss, to have assumed a finite form towards birth as an ordinary human being.

The source of the things in the accomplished karma may remain unexpressed. It is thus a combination of the visible result and the invisible dimension that contributes to the karma. Nishkama karma is the joyful, devoted work for the world, done with the objective of having reached out to all the corners of the agenda for work and thus bringing in the flowery spiritual scene and smell, raising the karma to a height much superior to any other form of karma in the world. It is the cause of performing and the fulfilment of the cause in the best manner. This leaves examples of such work in the world as worship to God. Real nishkama karma is thus worship of God. Therefore, the doer of this karma shall do it with the earnest reputation and skill to perform, take it up to the level of perfection in life. Nishkama karma is thus not only worship of God, but it carries along direct blessings of God in the context of the world of work and thoughts. Arjuna had focused on doing nishkama karma and dedicated it to God.

God is present in the form, yet he is also formless. He is into all types and identities. He is present in the form of Krishna, the eternal friend of Arjuna. At the same time, he is present as the invisible soul, the atman, residing within the form. The usual and loved place of God to reside is the heart.

Na aham prakashah sarvasyah yogamaya samabritah.
Mudhoh aham na abhijanati lokoh mam ajam abyayam. (G. 7/25)
Bade by my yogamaya or the divine potency, I am not manifest to all. Hence, these ignorant folk fail to recognize me and the unborn, unperishable supreme deity in me, consider me as subject to birth and death.

God is absorbed in the love of the devotee and present within the cave of his heart. He does not just stay like that. He is an eternal companion and friend of the devotee. God's presence is like 'vayu' or air, or like the void 'bhuma'. As if he is nowhere, but he remains everywhere. He remains as aatman within the heart, but at the same time, he remains detached from the existence where seated. A detached self, but remaining within, he fulfils the task of being alone and at the same time, maintains a distance as if he is away at an infinite distance from the self of the devotee. He is thus a witness, sometimes from an intimate position, and sometimes he witnesses from an infinite distance. His being with life may be an involved one. Whenever life is having an active wish and gradually the wish comes full circle towards completion, the Supreme now rushes to him with added urge to be along. It is therefore a factor of the devotee's cause and orientation that makes it happen in life, the association of God in perpetuity.

Vedah ahom samatitani bartamanani cha Arjuna.
Bhabishyai cha bhatani mam tu beda na kah chanah. (G. 7/26)
Arjuna, I know all beings past as well as the present, may even those who are yet to come, but none devoid of faith and devotion knows me.

In the case of Arjuna, the lessons were offered to him directly and through him, to the world as well. It is his call on one hand and the act of surrender to the Lord on the other that had induced the Supreme to get along. Lord Krishna thus conveyed to devotees the message, understood, that cultivation of the spirit within and the call appropriate for, would make God's appearance to him in life in a form and a way that befits the basis and condition of the inner consciousness of the person. Even though God is omnipresent, he is not present to all. Even if he is present to many, he is not present in the same way to them. Therefore, the case of each person is unique. The response of God to each person thus goes in a unique way. It is therefore very important that the willing person cultivates the same. Only the mere cultivation of God does not and cannot yield the realization. It is but the intense urge with strong love that makes it happen.

> *Ichha devesho samah utthenah dandamohena bharatah.*
> *Sarva Bhutani sammoham sargae ganti parantapah.* (G. 7/27)
> O valiant Arjuna, through delusion in the form of pairs of opposites, such as pleasure and pain, etc., born of desire and aversion, all living creatures in this world are falling a prey to the infatuation.

The *Bhagavad Gita* is a huge source of learning how to nurture and develop the spirit of yoga with God. It ultimately focuses on the condition of Arjuna to pass on the elemental lesson to all in the world, such that induction occurs in the mind of those who are actually and truly inclined to God. The fact of a person's being inclined is an art or a state of fact, but the strength of their genuineness in their urge is only revealed through the actions of that life in responding to the call of God. It becomes thus a mix of things on one hand, the urge of the person and on the other, the response of God, Lord Krishna, through a sequence of things, elaborating on these aspects with clarity and detail.

The spiritual journey of a person makes its headway to completion and a full circle, which would make the leading of a new era or that of a new civilization in the human context.

The objective has to be very clear, transparent and direct. A person's objective is the making of her or his physical intellect in life. If the decision is firm and fully supported by the elements of faith with love, devotion and respect, then shraddha occurs in the life of the person. This element of shraddha begets every prospect of progress and achievement.

> *Yesham tu antagatam papam jananan punyakarmanam .*
> *Tae dando moha nih muktua bhajantae mam drishabratah.* (G.7/28)
> But those main virtuous deeds whose sins you have come to an end, being freed from the delusion in the form of pairs of opposites born of attraction and repulsion, worship me with a form resolved in every way.

Spiritual knowledge is direct, like the way material and scientific knowledge is earned. In the case of material and scientific knowledge, the person having earned the knowledge had to pass through direct experimentation in the area of focus and connect the same with the pool of previous knowledge and the connected functional reality that lives across. It is that functional reality which makes things happen in the pathways of rational outcome for the functional and elemental inputs to the system. It is to be further examined and justified in the backdrop of various related components to see the level of response. This is how the objective and the hypothesis are coordinated to examine the various aspects of reality and to have the same felt and extended in the situation put across. Scientific reality requires further testing through hypotheses designed for the future. It is thus the spirit of things which would turn around the task of having the message of the existing findings to compare for the next.

> *Jara maranah mokshayah mam aashritya yatanti yae.*
> *Tae Brahma tad viduh kritsnam cha aukhilam.* (G. 7/29)
> Person having taken refuge in me, strive for deliverance from old age and the dead, know Brahman the absolute, the whole of adhyatma or the spirituality, the total of the lives and the soul, and the entire field of the action or the karma as well as my integral being or the unmanifest and the formless identity of mine, unmanifest divinity dwelling in the heart of all beings as their witness.

Spiritual understanding goes and spreads larger. It is thus visualized as a kind of emerging scenario which has got the nucleus within. There is a structured process. First, you need to have your mind cleansed of impurities of ill thoughts and be focused on the aspects of visualization. Unless the mind purification is not over, nothing can be done further. Mind purification is reliving the bagful of memories stored in *chitta* to get over or empty. Then one has to see that no further content is marching in. The mind is required to be calm, cool, and poised. Once this condition is achieved, the person can now venture to fulfil the urge to complete or proceed further towards completing the process of realization. This condition offers impersonality to all.

> *Sa audhibhutah audhidaivam mam sadhiyajnam chayae bidhu.*
> *Prayana kaleh api cha mam tae viduh yuktah chetasah.* (G. 7/30)
> They who possess a steadfast mind, the clean mind, and a mind and heart with devotion, they witness me, and they who possess such of pure mind, know thus even the hour of death, they too know me alone. And these people have realized not only that realization persists in this life or if any remaining karma is there, their lives continue next in the absence of the remaining karma or when there is no desire remaining, the person is fully freed and the moksha is attained by the person.

Anyone, from any part of the world, and at any point in time, effectively pursuing the mind purification, has to follow the same process. Once this stage as attempted is achieved, the person is now all set for God-realization. Now, at this stage, have an intense thought of God in the way that you wish to go for. This is how you can reach out to your God in the form. When God is expected to reveal himself in form, he does, as he may also reveal his eternal, transcendental identity. This is usually visualized as the divine illumination, the light that comes directly from him, or else you could try his realization as the infinite span of void that exists in the cosmic system. He is omnipotent, omnipresent, and always omniscient. He is always impersonal. Ever in form, he is also impersonal. He is eternal, yet a companion, friend, a mother, a father, or the like on this Earth, and remains forever.

11 The Absolute Revealed

Brahman, the Absolute

Brahman, the Absolute, cannot be properly explained by words. Nor can he be made known to others through formal or informal modes of communication. Whatever the approach to know him, there should be ways to explain. All methods of making Brahman known combined in any way cannot yield the full knowledge of Brahman.

> *Arjuna ubacha:*
> *Kim tat Brahma kim adhyatmam kim karma purushattamah.*
> *Audhibhutam cha kim proktam adhidaivam kim uchyatae.*   (G.8/1)
> Arjuna said, Krishna, I want to know what is the form of that Absolute Supreme Brahman, what is spirituality, the adhyatma, and what is the real karma or the true action. What is called Adhibhuta, or the matter, and what is termed as Adhidaiva or something pertinent to the divinity.

Brahman is satchit ananda in oneself. He is the truth, he is the consciousness, and he is at the same time, the bliss. He is anandamaya. Upon his realisation, everything in this creation becomes known. Once he is known, everything in this cosmos is known. He has embodied all the units of creation, and at the same time, he is the revelation of all creatures, all lives, all elements of matter and all other entities. He is wholesome. He is all in one, and at the same time, he is one in all. He is omnipresent. On his wish, he remains present. He may be present in the entire universe. Again, he is the creative part of the creation. He is all in one, and at the same time, he is immersed in the consciousness of his own creation.

> *Na tat hota purbo agnae yajiyam.Na kavyoh parou ousthi svadhan.*
> *Bisah cha yasya Atithi bhabasi. Sah yajnena balabad devah martan.*
>   (Rig Veda 5th Mandala/3rd Parva/5th Sloka)
> The Supreme reveals himself in the mortal world in such a subtle manner that his presence cannot be understood or recognized by any of the human sense organs. He can be realized through a spiritual meditative

process; he can be perceived as an embodied presence in the sacrificial fire as well.

The Supreme needs to be realized. His realization is vast as the infinite multiplied infinite times. The Supreme is thus involved not only in the creation, but in all aspects of the creation. The Supreme has taken up shape of the living entities. It is the abode of Lord Shiva that offers the seed for the creation. The cosmic nature takes up the abode of the Supreme Mother to hold, nurture and make grow the aspects of life. Thus, each life gets a unique impetus to make things grow out of it. He is intrinsic in his presence in the universe as the gross expand and at the same time, present within the individual or elemental identities as the vital energy of his creation, in particular. The Supreme, thus known in the name and identity of the supreme energy, the supreme soul or paramatma and as God in the creation as well. The Lord is thus the energy and force behind the entire creation. Because of this, he finds a continued responsibility for the world.

Audhijajnyah katham kah autra dehe iha asmin Madhusudana.
Prayan kalae cha katham jneyah ausi niyata aatmabhih. (G.8/2)
I also want to know who the *Adhi Jagnya* is here and how it dwells in the body, and how much you realized that Adhi Jagnya, and what is this condition at the time of a person living the life.

God is the most chosen identity of the Supreme. With this identity, he has to be in touch with the elemental identity with not only with the individual living soul of recognition of a life. His revelation in the world makes the truth of the creation spread out and unfold. With this as the broader reality, the person can be recognized in a different way for the same.

In the process of understanding the Supreme Brahman, one needs to get into the deeper realm of the matter through the subjective method of realization. The facts and factors of such subjective realization depend upon certain factors, such as the extent of faith one has in the process of realization of truth. The other factors such as are the conditions of purity of mind. The position of truth orientation of the person and the focus on the spirit of things that make the way towards the fundamentals of the system and structure of the scenario, and that of further introspection within the system. The system thus yields to a kind of scenario that tries to unfold the dormant and hidden truth within each element of creation in the world.

Sri Bhagaban ubacha:
Aksharam Brahmah param svabhaba audhyatmam .
Bhuto bhabo udbhabo karo bisargah karma samgitah. (G.8/3)
Lord Sri Krishna answered, the supreme indestructible is Brahman, one's own self or the individual soul is called Adhyatma, Adhyatma is the atman which is within, and the spirit which is within is the Vishagya,

and this brings forth the existence of being and during the existence, the karma or the action is protected.

The real position is that the Brahman, the Supreme, takes the form larger than the largest entities and smaller than the smallest ones. The larger entities thus relate to the cosmic revelations, whereas the smaller ones reveal that of the molecular or even further smaller identities. The fundamental issue is that if he is present in the living entities as the soul in life, then how can the same attributes be infused into the fundamental particles? The question is raised by Arjuna about the true identity of the supreme divinity. Lord Krishna gave a narration in response. The narration began with the clear nature of the revelation of the Lord, the Supreme. It was his identity, as mentioned by Lord Krishna, that says that the Supreme has the identity of being undefined. His undefined identity was the most prominent one. The undefined identity had the focus on the formless condition of him. However, this formless condition was just the reflection of the vast and infinite identity that was his initial revelation. In the initial phase, the identity was somewhat deluged in different forms of God. The infinite context and the infinite expanse were thus the definite conditions with respect to the infinite entities created in nature.

The Formless Spirit

Formless is the truly emerging with the vast vacuum or void depicting the finite in the world. The shape of things in the world has its interconnections and interdependencies. The revealed features of collective life forces in the world are the dynamic energy into the lives of the individuals in the world. Each individual thus gets a unique opportunity in life to get along with the dynamism of the wholesome. The Supreme Lord is the first ever entity of God, the great, who reveals to the world. The most important aspect is the potentials for wider spread.

> *Audhibhutam ksharou bhaboh purusha cha audhidaivatam.*
> *Audhi yajnah aham eva cha autra dehae dehabhutam barah.* (G.8/4)
> All perishable objects are Adhibhuta, shining Purusha or the Brahman is Adhidaiva, and this body and you and me where everywhere; myself in the form of God dwells in that, dwelling as an inner witness is the Adhyatma, thus I have the knowledge of all.

This is the basis of intensity that has sustained probing and is the way forward that captures the truth in totality. In order to get hold of this process effectively, the realised truth would be translated into the realities of the person's way forward. Reality is thus connected with the state of acts in the process of things across the forces of the world. The forces of the world are understood through the eyes of the state of material consciousness. This is spread among the states of consciousness. Thus, the impact of things would be classified into the states of: a) Awakened consciousness across the whole of the world of events and happenings; b) The state of dreams- where the external awareness is shut off to pave ways to the factors of surficial mind; and c) Sushupti- the state of semi cognitive awareness.

Aura eva rathanavoh kala Yasmin pratisthitah.
Tam vedyam purusham bedah yatha ma vai mrityu paribyakhya iti.
(Prashana Upanishad 6th Khanda/6th Sloka)
The presence of the Supreme at the centre of human existence, in the cave of the heart as the centre point of the wheel of a chariot, coordinating the dynamism of life from the invisible centre.

The akshara brahma is the perceived and realized aspects of the Supreme. He is the absolute truth- consciousness- bliss, expressed in invisible forms within the entities of the creation and without the revealed presence of him as the force behind all tangible entities; the input thus contains something different within. The elemental presence in the entities thus takes the form of direct energy content, or the inspirational input factor that runs through the vital functions to keep the life purposefully active. Biologically, the flow of adrenaline of life force and the current of inspirational waves inside would combine to create a kind of generic stimulus which would scale up the functional realities of life and activate the power of intuition, creativity and activities involving organs of sense, organs of work, organs of movement, organs of thoughts and organs connecting decisions.

Anta kaalae cha mam eva smaranam uktvah kaulebaram.
Yah prayatih sah mad bhabam yati nah astiautra samshayah.   (G.8/5)
He who departs from the body thinking of me alone even at the time of death attains my state; there is no doubt about it.

The Supreme is beyond all factors of expression. He is the one in everything. Therefore, a life that wishes to relate to the Supreme in any way must create an urge within. The urge could be a call, an amount of dedication or a consecration. When the journey of life comes to an end, the person now has the option to express any desire for continuity in their lives. Thus, the self seated within has to resort to a different or the same way. The usual illusions of life bind the human consciousness to the elements, matter or the factors of life that eventually allow life to experience its test of creation through the projections into the next. The projections thus would connect the person either in terms of the self in revelation, or the elements of the forces of life that might remain dormant in the facts of the life lived so far. It is the human intent that has taken into account the factors of the world and its different types and varieties of cords with other elements in the world. Whenever a person is touched by emotions like greed, desire, jealousy, ego, envy, the impact of these in their life doesn't end so soon as the person may wish.

Yam yam bapi smarana bhabam tyajyanta antae kaulebaram.
Tam tam eva iti kounteya sada tad bhaba bhabitah. (G.8/6)
Arjuna, thinking of whatever entity one leaves the body, the thought that you cultivate at the time of your death reflects in your jivatman, and the person in the transcendental condition attains the same and being ever absorbed in that thought.

At the point of the end of the journey in life, when the vital or the prana leaves life, at that point, it is suggested to have the choice in mind identified in the right manner. The wish that remains as a kind of unfulfilled thing in life makes the prelude to the person's next identity. At this point of leaving life, the jivatman chooses to carry two important elements. First, it chooses to remain in continuity in this creation. If that be so, then the ultimate journey of jivatman shall be tuned to that. Another aspect of this journey is the essence of the life lived. That means that the kind of karma that the life was engrossed in, its thoughts, aspirations, desires, greed, expectations for fulfillment, everything, needs to be settled in life. If it does not, then the balance of these or the remains of this mental debris needs to be nourished. The entire set of these karmas, their related thoughts, and the senses of unfulfillment converge to the content of the samskar in life. Samskar is the qualitative essence of the set of works and all related things in life.

A person engaged in good works, good thoughts, good habits, and good character would finally converge to a good samskar. The mind, if it can transcend the barriers of utter selfishness, would trigger off the facets of noble values in life and samskar.

Divine Spirit

Thus, if a person can pursue the spirit of noble values in life, the same can create a formation of sattwa or goodness and the elemental good attributes in that mind. This impact or effect is enjoyed throughout life. Whenever the same goodness spreads, the person, in most cases and situations, can enjoy the freedom of having his factors of life, also something that can transcend the barriers of the binding forces of illusions of life. The person can develop the agility and the formation that this life is a dedication to God.

Tasmat sarveshu kaleshu mam anusvarah yudhya cha.
Mayee arpitah mano buddhi mam eva asya samshayam. (G.8/7)
And therefore, Arjuna, think of me at all times and fight with your mind absorbed in me, the reasons that set on me and you will doubtless undoubtedly come to me.

Dedication to God in mind induces the factors of devotion, love, respect and then finally, consecration to God. Mind gets reoriented at this level of attainment. The inner consciousness reminds one of the presence of the Supreme in the form of the atman within. The new way of thought like this would thus create a new basis of life. The more your life is oriented to God, the less you are stuck up with the illusory connections with this world. The illusory natures of connections are not felt unless the mind gets oriented to God in the true sense.

> *Aham etat param Brahma veda atah param na austih.*
> I am the Supreme truth-consciousness, present in the creation as it is revealed in the facts of the creation.

The Lord, the Supreme, is sure to be with us. Now the issue is, though he accompanies human beings in every person's life, whether the person accompanies him in the actual sense of the term. Param Brahma Sanatana is ever grateful. Whenever and wherever the glimpses of light from any life come out in the form of the seeking or desiring God's company, he jumps in joy. This creation is a continuity in the experiment to see the sequence of cause-and-effect relations. Samskar reveals the net result of the essence of that cause and effect. In a sense, nothing can be permanently kept beneath the lids and covers. However, people think that she or he has done a lot, and it's now the turn of God to reciprocate. This is a wrong and skewed perception that goes on continually in the realm of the Earth consciousness. Even those who are spiritually oriented do the same.

> *Abhyasa yoga yuktena chetasa na anyagamena.*
> *Paramam purusham divyam yati partha anuchintayan.* (G.8/8)
> Arjuna, he who is with the mind disciplined through Yajna in the form of practice or meditation and thinking or nothing else is constantly engaged in contemplation of God, attains the supremely Divine, the God in the form of Purusha.

Those who are involved in the act of spiritual practices fail to have focus on the core objective in most of the cases. The core objective is what spirituality is for. Spirituality is the art and science which tunes the factors of human consciousness into the divine consciousness. In the process, the human mind tries to influence and finally assert control over that. A devoted approach to God requires uniqueness of the mental faculties. Mental faculties are diverse and have a natural orientation to the things external to the mind. It is the input factor to all good and/or bad aspects of human understanding. On one hand, human understanding runs on its own premise. On the other hand, the imprints of the divine play in the world are filled with or understood by many in many different dimensions. The human spirit understands everything on the human scale. It is the fundamental premise of the dynamism of the world that leads to the fulfillment of a kind of undernourished sense of things in life.

> *Kabim puranam anushasitaram ano aniyamsam anusmarayet.*
> *Sarvasya dhataram auchinta rupam aaditya varnam tamasha*
> *parastad.* (G.8/9)
> Know from me that the person who contemplates on all wise and the timeless and spaceless the person, the supreme entity as a subtle body and the universal sustainer, possessing a form beyond human conception, effulgent like the sun and far beyond the darkness of ignorance.

The pace at which things progress towards attaining autonomy in life and work is the factor that reorients to the fixed and variable aspects of the movement of time. Thus, the elaboration happens in such a way that the fundamentals of human life are pushed to the level of the fundamentals of the Earth system, at the level of human experience and factors tuned to the gross dynamism of the world. It is thus the possible impact of the human system on the inherent wish of each individual. The wish thus gets translated into the facts of the soil or the Earth. The cry of the Earth, the cry of nature and the unexpressed cry of humans combine to be the outcry in the face of the emerging ways of growth and maturity. Spiritual self thus makes it clear and transparent towards the dynamism inherent in the programs and activities. It is thus the unique objective of human society to determine the direction of human life in the factors of the life system. Thus, it is the faces of the system, whereas the dynamic equilibrium thus settlement orientation happen in terms of the new dimension and newly framed spirit in life.

Spiritual Journey

Habits of good thoughts in life beget good actions. Good thoughts need active practice to take forward in life. With the continuous making and processing of those thoughts in life, actions do emerge as the focus at a time when the particularity of thoughts begets the desired action to happen in life. This is what makes for an ongoing spirit of action and things in the life of the person.

> *Prayankaalae manasah achalena bhaktya yuktoh yogabalena cha eva.*
> *Bhrubah madhyae pranam aabeshya Samyak sa tam param*
> *purusham apeiti divyam.* (G.8/10)
> Having, by the power of Yajna, formed the vital energy (hail) between the eyebrows, and at the time of death, if you contemplate on God with a mind fully focused there and with full devotion, you will actually reach the Supreme Divine Purusha, or Me.

The practice of remembering God in life may happen through chanting a mantra and a habit of creating vibrant joy in the process of earning the realization of God. The usual approach to this is the practice of yoga in life.

Yoga is making a connection and continuing with that. The focus of this connection is God. Realizing the spirit of God and the urge to have it in life, forges into certain habits, such as the habit to create things.

Etat hi auksharam Brahma. Etat hi auksharam param.
Etat hi auksharam gnyatva Yah yat ichhyati tasyatat. (Kath.U. 1/2/16)
Om is not just a word, nor a syllable; it connotes the Supreme Brahman. This is transcendental and any one that knows it can fulfil the right expectations of any kind.

Thoughts of God always converge to the good thoughts in the functions and projections of noble attributes in life, particularly when the potential noble attribute is taken up in the process of life. At some points in time, this may give rise to the direct invocation of God in life. This means that his yoga practice first attempts to focus on the mind and create a scenario in which the person would join the stream of life in a way that the mental attributes are tuned to one and focused on the realization of God.

Yat aksharam vedabido badanti bishanti yad yatayo bitaragah.
Yad ichhanto Brahmacharyam charanti tat tae padam samgrahena prabakshmeye. (G.8/11)
I am now going to tell you in brief the supreme goal, God, who is an embodiment of truth, knowledge and beliefs and is the knower of Vedas, knows God as indestructible and who is striving for the realization free from the person's margin to desiring, which celebrates practices of Brahmacharya.

Focused attention, repeated in regular practice, creates a habit in the person. Again, this habit, if taken forward, would contribute to forming certain guiding principles in the character of the person. Regular such practices create ways to emerge out of the Earthly symptoms and some of the very basic and fundamental spirits. This spirit now creates an imprint in life. It continues into having the basics of the realization of the Supreme. Once the process of this spiritual practice is settled, it continues to have an impact on life in accordance. Thus, the process now becomes connected with the unitary focus. Thus, whether the spirit of spiritual awareness continues with the activities that are common in life, it continues and discrete factors of life and its culmination.

Sarvadwarani samyamyh mano Hridaya nirudhyah cha.
Murdhyah aadhayah aatmanah pronam aasthitoh
yogadharanam. (G.8/12)
Having controlled all senses and firmly holding the mind on me in the cave of your heart and then drawing life breath to that hand and thus remaining steadfast in yogic concentration, you attain God's realization.

The process thus would take forward the impacts in life directly. In the process, thus, direct and perceptive views do frame up together with that of the entire contextual diversities of life. Each factor thus corresponds to the factors of the spirit of life. It is thus the inner dimension of the person and his entire life. Here, the habit of the practice of yoga in daily life may lead to the formation of a dynamic profile with the mind. These are the dimensions which converge as the core dynamics. Along with this, the practice of yoga thus permeates into the broader aspect of lives lived. A meditative mind should be constantly cultivating the thoughts of the Divine at each moment of possibility. Therefore, the strength of this makes into the primordial form of energy for human purposes. Thus, it begets the wider dimensions of life but puts the human perspective of existence to find out the useful way forward towards the core spirit of life on Earth.

Spiritual Practice

Among the usual spiritual practices, the mantra – 'Om' plays a very dominant role. This is a root mantra. It has three components - 'au', 'eu', 'mau'. The meanings are this Earth, the world of inner space and the cosmic system, respectively. The idea behind it is to remember that the creation has this extent of facts, and that again means the high involvement of the universal in the facts of the particular.

> *Om iti ekah akshmarah Brahma byaharam mam anusmaren.*
> *Yah prayati tyajanah deham sah yati paramam gatim.* (G.8/13)
> He who leaves the body and senses devotes the uttering of the one indestructible Brahman and utters Aum dwells in me, the absolute form of mine.

God is omnipresent. He is independent of the things or the facts, as it is revealed in the creation by its external revelations and to a certain extent by the intrinsics in the entire play. The power of human understanding is limited and so minuscule compared to the vast span of the same truth, as it is empirical revelations to human knowledge. The issue our sages were confronted with was that the Supreme is present everywhere, but how can one come in contact with his presence in the universe within her or his domain?

> *Aungustha matrah purushah jyoti eva audhumak.*
> *Ishanah bhutah bhabyasha eva ausya sau sah.*
> *Etat vaitat.* (Kath.U.2/1/13)
> The Supreme is smaller than the smallest, when seated within the domain of a human person prefers to remain dormant unless there is a strong urge to make it revealed and vibrant. A devotee would always believe in this.

That is what is being mentioned by Lord Krishna. This same message was in practice and very widely prevalent during the civilization of the Vedic period also. It was central to one's own promise and dedication to the course of the creation or the Creator himself. The Creator thus had revealed through the ways of the creation and made his imprint fully absorbed in the stream of his essential touches to the building of this broader truth. The Supreme needs to be connected in the intrinsic sense. This is the purpose of the mantra in the spiritual realm. Mantra is the bridge through which a human aspirant wants to establish a connection with God in the manner of his revealed facts spread out across. 'Om', as that mantra, is the root of all such mantras that may have a construct on this in further specifics.

> *Ananya chetah satatam yo mam smarati nityashah.*
> *Tashya aham sulabhah Partho nitya yuktasya yoginah.* (G.8/14)
> Lord Krishna says to Arjuna, whosoever always and constantly thinks of him with an undivided mind, to that yogi he is ever absorbed in and easily attainable to him. He continues.

'Om' is thus the central theme of the mantra; a soul can offer to reach out to the realm of the Supreme Consciousness. It is the remembrance of the fact that the Supreme is present everywhere. The power of this mantra is the thin vibration created by the seeker of spiritual realization. Vibration of the mantra is intrinsic to the lives and gets turned into the cosmic system. Om as a mantra is connected with the *aadinadah* or the original tune of the entire cosmic system. The dance of Nataraj Shiva creates the aadinadah in the creation. It is the original tune created in the cosmic system, which is touched upon and connected by the mantra. Mantra connects with the *navipadma* or the naval force of the creation. It has to emanate from the navipadma of the person also. Om, as the root of all such mantras, connects with the different revelations and forms of God. Thus, when the name or any element of the swarup of the Supreme God is remembered or uttered, the vibration arising from the navipadma of the person connects with the direct identity of God in that form and in that state of vibrations.

> *Mam upetya punah janmah duhkhaya aalayam shashvatam.*
> *Na apnu vanti mahatmanah sam siddhim paramam gatah.* (G.8/15)
> Great souls who have attained the highest perfection, having come to me, are no more subject to the world, and which is the abode of sorrow, conceived by nature.

Lord Krishna had reiterated what we now understand as the spirit of mantra. It is thus the guidance of a guru or a master to a disciple or a *sishyah*. The usual scenario can be thought of as that of the system of a monastery or a temple of God, where the master takes up important components of lessons for understanding and practice in life. The mantra thus understood in the right sense of the term makes it evident that it is one of the most important elements of spiritual practice that the person in quest of God can follow and get involved in that for the betterment of the human condition on the Earth.

Again, along with the mantra or apart from that, if a person leaves aside thoughts of any other thing and gets totally engrossed in the thoughts of God, then the person gets blessed with the support or the total care of God. Thus, focused thinking about God is an important element and a strong way forward with the spiritual and intrinsic urge of the person to wish for the attention, grace and vision of God. The Earth system is being fully guided by the considerations of the human scale that are not only oriented to but are overwhelmed by the ideas spiritual to God. It is the intrinsic understanding of life that can really make the world spiritually guided.

Transformations in Life

In the design of God, it is not that lives are only taken care of. But in the true sense of the term, it is considered that the spirit of divine intervention in the world is to reorient the human actions and the pathways of movement to life, that the aspects of divinity which connects with every element of creation are truly those that do touch upon the lives of the humans and others in the world. As such, the factors of life are given a creative thrust.

> *Aa Brahma bhubanah lokah punah aabartinoh hi Arjuna.*
> *Mam upetya tu kounteya purah janma na bidyatae.* (G.8/16)
> Arjuna, all the words from Brahmaloka, what a heavenly, heavenly place, and all the way up and downward to the place of the Earth, and rebirth is the phenomenon, and he says on attaining the realization of God, there will be no rebirth.

The need is to understand earnestly the fact of God having been involved in the functions-activities-revelations and emergence of thoughts, perceptions or the material form of rational understanding. The system of thought that human beings maintain is that of the direct relations between cause and effect. We have assumed that the entire creation is just for whatever is happening in continuity. Time now is the prime focus in that. With the present time being the prime focus, a man lives on existential values.

> *Aushabdam ausparsham aurupam aubyayam.Tatha auras am nityam augandhavat chayat.*
> *Aunadi Aunantam mahatoh param Dhruvam nichayay tat mrityamat pramuchhyatae.* (Katha.U. 1/3/15)
> The supreme self is beyond the reach of sound, touch, abodes, the juice of life, smell, and all attributes. It is infinite, timeless, without beginning or end, and eternal. Knowing this dimension allows the spiritual aspirant to transcend the limits of life and attain immortality.

The values and attributes that drive the existential thoughts are cardinal in the scientific way of looking at lives lived. The scientific view of life is said to be rational in nature. The rationality is based on the empirical understanding of life and the context that supports that understanding. It is material in nature. The material context is often considered as that of a commercial nature. It involves the principles of give and take. Any gesture, any support, any act of well-being, any work done, or any input a person can offer in the context of the world has to be reciprocated either squarely or at a higher degree. It is this, the basic principle, which applies in human relations and in the context of every human aspiration, prayer or any kind of fulfillments in the human design as prayed for.

Sahasra yuga paryantam yat ahah Brahmanoh biduh.
Ratrim yuga sahasram tam tae ahoratro bido janah. (G.8/17)
Those yogis who know from realization of Brahma's day as covering a thousand Maha Yugas, and his night extends to another thousand of great era, know really about the time.

The Supreme is thus expected to contribute things of desire as the offerings done through worship, puja or nibedanam to him in any form. It is thus the human consciousness which acts as the elemental commerce in this relation that a person wishes to establish with God. The Supreme is so spread out in the cosmic existence that its actual impact of being present everywhere gets denied eventually. The universality of the Divine on Earth is thus a matter which requires an elevation from the conditions and spirit of human essence in the larger sense. Human spirit thus requires to be drenched in the spirit of divinity in the context of a particular situation, time frame, area, zones and the elemental consciousness of human existence on Earth. Thus, in order that the Supreme is revealed, you have to meditate.

Abyakta tat byaktayoh sarvah prabhobo antoh aagamae.
Ratra samagamae praliyantae tatra eva abyakta samgnakae. (G.8/18)
All embodied beings originate from the unmanifest, and all coming to the cosmic end of the day, they merge into the same subtle body of Brahman and become unmanifest.

The infinite identity of the Supreme is such that words cannot really express him in their usual manner. Words carry meanings in the human sense of the terms. It cannot transcend the limits and barriers of the human senses in an ordinary context and situation. Thus, the very basis of the expressions and communications in human sense gets mixed with human aspirations and understanding. Whenever a person pursues the spiritual path seriously and eventually attains the meditative state of the mind, the possibility emerges. It becomes possible for a human being in that context that the aspirations are examined in the backdrop of the realities of the world in general and that of the person in particular. It is thus the very basic approach that a person should pursue, where the particular understanding of the person merges with the wholesome consciousness of the cosmic system. It is thus the wholesome which gets the touch of the supreme spirit in a context that has its own factors and specialities of understanding. This is actually the context of realization of God in the context of the world at a definite time and space. The aspirations echoed in the human context are transformed into the items of consecration to God. It is when the divine grace in the form of realization comes into the human context, the understanding for the work of the world and its different empirical facts gets revealed to the person more easily than others.

Manifestation of the Supreme

With this kind of transformation initiated as a process in the human context, the aspirant turns into a devotee of God. A devotee is someone who is in a position to garner love for God. Love for God needs to be ushered in such a way that it is absolutely unidirectional. Love for God should never be associated in any way with any kind of desire or expectation. Whether it is something expected of the world or of something of the kind of eternal, timeless identity, it is to be abandoned.

> *Bhuta gramah sa eva ayam bhutva bhutva praliyatae.*
> *Ratra aagamae abashah patro prabhabati ahah aagamae.* (G.8/19)
> Arjuna, this multitude of things being born again and again is dissolved under the compulsion of nature, and the doctrine of karma is going to shape their existence in the cosmic day and cosmic night.

In the design of the Supreme, everyone is of equal importance and identity. But someone who has developed a little bit of love for God is sure to have secured a special position in the framework of God in this universe and as such would be most specifically garlanded with the blessings for having gradual realization and thus, in a way, to have the universality of God understood in the right sense of the term.

> *Vayuh yatha ekah bhubanam prabistho. Rupam rupam pratirupah babhubah.*
> *Ekah tatha auntah aatmah. Rupam rupam pratirupah*
> *bahih cha.* (Kath.U.2/2/10)
> Like the blowing air, he is present everywhere; he is present in all forms in existence. He is present in all human beings as the inner self. He is present everywhere, even outside.

Thus, the devotee understands the need for faith in the Supreme's universal presence. Faith as such makes the elements of love stronger and more lasting. Faith in God gradually makes the devotee understand that God is omnipresent. As we understand the presence of air everywhere, but the understanding is basically dependent upon the level of involvement in the entire affairs of the world and the impact of the same in the context of an individual. This is sometimes expressed in the context of the current position of the entire world.

> *Parah tasmat tu bhaboha anyoha abyaktyat byakta sanatanah.*
> *Yah sa sarveshu bhuteshu nashyat sun a binashyati.* (G.8/20)
> Far beyond even this unmanifest, there is yet another unmanifest existence, that supreme divine person who does not perish even though everything else perishes.

The Supreme manifests through all creatures. Though his presence remains in such a subtle way that he is never noticed by live in the world. However, the process of Swadhyay makes him reveal the factors of his creation and intends to understand the cause of the same. It is thus a very basic understanding that the presence of the Supreme on Earth is felt by those who would endeavour to have the realization of the Supreme in the context of the world. This world and the presence of other worlds may infuse the ideas of the intrinsics of life in the context of the happenings of the world. The happenings of the world as such would lead to the dismal sequence of things that occur in the world in the right spirit of the factor. It is thus one of the most pertinent matters in the lookout of lives on Earth, having the idea and realization of truth. As such, truth makes an indirect impact on the factors of life and growth. This happens most subtly. In the realm of the divine spirit, it is thus the serious endeavour of the person as an element of divine messages in the contents of expiring indifference.

> *Abyakta hi aksharah iti uktah tam aahuh paramam gatim.*
> *Yam prapyam na nivartantae tat dhamah paramam mamah.* (G.8/21)
> The same unmanifest which has been spoken of as indestructible is also the supreme goal, and that is my supreme abode, attaining which they return not to this mortal world again.

He is expressed and elaborated by many as the rhythm and vibration in the context of the world. Once the realization of the rhythm of God is realized, the outlook about the world changes sharply and forthwith. In the process of earning this realization, the devotee would identify the very essence of the things of life. It is the very essence that works out to be the next best prospects of earning truth in life. The formless existence of the Supreme is like the presence of air. Even air or light from the rays of the sun cannot penetrate every entity or element. It is thus the very basic elemental object and its connection with the factors of life that matters in the whereabouts of the new identity of truth in this world. In the course of doing the empirical world, it is thus observed that any drift in the material context is going to have its share of devoted time and energy into it. As such, the realization is going to be distinctive and squarely differentiated in varied contexts of the world. Thus, the realization of God alone stimulates in the person the good spirit on Earth.

Devotion Driven

Devotion takes time to be grounded in the mind and heart of a person; persistent mental orientation and constant urge are one of the routes to have the initial features of devotion get solidified or grounded firmly. Devotion thus creates its ways through the usual thoughts and propensities of the human mind. Thus, devotion plays an important role in the making of a mental equilibrium. The Divine extends a hand of support to those who have the urge to embrace all the factors of devotion to God. This factor is unique and dedicated love for God.

> *Purushah sa parah Partho bhaktva labhyo ananyah.*
> *Yasya antah sthanih bhutanic yena sarvam idam tatam* (G.8/22)
> Lord says to Arjuna, the eternal unmanifest supreme Godhead, the supreme abode, infinite in expanse, in whom all beings abide, and by whom all things are permitted, is attainable through realization and devotion.

A devotee in the world harbours love for God irrespective of any prevailing conditions. While most human love typically carries an inbuilt element of reciprocity, divine love should not. Here in this world, every element of emotion goes along with the thoughts of reciprocity. Knowingly or unknowingly human love goes along the human relations and transactions in the world with certain kind of desires or expectations from the other side, in most of the cases. However, a true devotee will have consecration and love for God without any kind of expectations from the Divine. In both instances, while pure love exists, it becomes intertwined with the concept of love for God, carrying similar expectations of reciprocation. However, the chord of love among the close ones works in an empirical context.

> *Uttisthitah jaagratah prapya baran nibodhatoh.*
> *Kshurasya dharoh nishita durattaya.Dargam pathah.*
> *Tat kaboyoh vadanti.* (Katho.U.1/3/14)
> Arise, awake to attain the complete wisdom of the atman, the self. Realization of the supreme self requires passage through the pathways that are as sensitive as it is in the case of subtle differences of the cutting line of a knife.

The chords of love and affection are empirical and constrained by the theory of reciprocity. It is bound by time, conditions of mind and the prevailing situations and prospects. In the sense of material terms, these are all very basic to life and are automatic associates of life. Parental love and affection for children are constrained by their satisfaction and fulfilment. Any rupture in that sense of satisfaction and fulfilment may lead to the disruption of the degree and quality of emotions. It is thus constrained by the impacts of time. That is why Lord Krishna calls upon the human sense and consciousness to arise and awake to understand the divine truth.

> *Yatra kale tuh anabrittam aabritim cha eva yoginah.*
> *Prayata yanti tam kalam bakshami Bharatarshabha.* (G.8/23)
> Arjuna, I shall now tell you the time and the path departing when the yogis do not return, and also the time and the path when they return.

In this process, the value and the fulfillment of life depend upon the whereabouts of the living identity. In the pursuit of the realization of truth, the seeker of truth identifies the realistic position of human consciousness in the eternal sense. Thus, when the realization of God starts happening in the individual, the worldview of the person starts changing from its material-human identity to the spiritual-divine identity. The material-human identity would identify all the incidents, happenings, and positions in life as arising just out of the elements of physical situations of the world. The material relations in life and the human response through the human mental orientation happen to be the right material nature of the human mind. The human mind is essentially materialistic in nature. At the same time, when the human mind endorses the consciousness of God in any form, the human mind ascends towards achieving the state of a pure or divine mind.

> *Agnih jyotih ahah shuklah shanamasah uttarayanam.*
> *Tatra Prayata gachhanti Brahma Brahmabido janah.* (G. 8/24)
> Out of the two ways, one is that stationed in effulgent fire, the different forms of God presiding over daylight and bright fortnight, and six months of the northward course of the sun, respectively, proceed along it after death. Yogis who have known the supreme Brahman, being successively led by the Gods, finally reach the Brahman.

Mind turned to God develops the qualities of divinity to respond to the world in the same way that is usual of divine entities. It is thus the divine spirit in man that works and acts as enduring and oriented to the eternal values in the human context. The eternal values are the focus of life that undertakes the quest for God in the context of the world; the work that gets assigned to a person may be classified based on the nature and objective of the work. This objective can be oriented to the purpose of the material context of the world. The other objective of the work would be the work that supports and enhances the cause of divinity on Earth.

Once the mind of a devotee turns towards the divine values, the person gets into that kind of work that helps in attaining devotion and realization of

God on Earth. This kind of work or karma is basically dedicated to the context and objective of karma on one hand and that of the wish or expressed divine intent in the context of the world on the other.

Divine Spirit in Life

Two categories of karma are: *'Kartavya Karma'*, (Dutiful work), and the other is *'Aarabdha Karma'*, (Destined work). Kartavya Karma requires understanding, knowledge and skill of the work assigned by any authority of the world. It comes out of the rule of work in the world from a material, godless perspective. For example, a parent's duty to take care of the child, a student's duty to follow the learning, and a company executive's duty to follow the assigned duty, which is paid for.

> *Dhumoh raatrih tatha Krishna shanmasha dakshinayanam.*
> *Tatra chandramasam jyotih yogi prapya nibartatae.* (G. 8/25)
> The other one is that wherein everything is stationed in the companion course, and is the presiding entity, was smoke, night, darkness, fortnight, and six months, the southward course of the sun, and the yogi taking to this path after death is led by the Gods, one after another, and attaining the lustre of the moon, the fruit of his meritorious deeds in heaven returns to the mortal world.

Apart from the duties in the personal and work space as assigned, the person should consider other dimensions of duty in the personal, family, social, national, environmental and similar other contexts. Duties of one actually serve the other. For example, didn't you have a teacher who came to class properly prepared on the specific topic?

> *Aunoh auniyan mahotoh mahiyan. Aatma ausya jantoh nihitah guhayam.*
> *Tvam aukratuh pashyati bita shokah. Dhatuh prasadyhat mahimanam*
> *Aatman.* (Katho.U. 1/2/20)
> This atman is smaller than the smallest dimension of an atom, larger than the largest dimension of a cosmic body. It remains within the cave of the heart of a person as the jivatman, or the self in life. This atman is above all spells of happiness, sorrow and other impacts in life.

'Aarabdha karma' is endowed when the person is attempting the realization of the Supreme. This does not and cannot be reciprocally oriented. Nishkama karma is the basis of the work for the fulfillment of an objective. Desireless work brings in certain fundamental attributes. Of these, the first is to prioritize the set of actions and the beneficiaries. 'Not me but thou' is one of the fundamentals of the principle. This principle ensures the workflow benefits many broadly and provides sustenance for the individual actor.

Shukla krishnae gati hi etae jagatah shashvatae matae.
Ekayah yati anabrittim annyah abartatae punah. (G. 8/26)
Those two paths to the world, the bright and the dark, are considered to be eternal, proceeding by one of them, one reaches the supreme state from which there is no return, and proceeding by the other, one returns to the mortal plane, being subject to rebirth again and again.

Thus, the proficiency in a particular function is cardinal in the choice of a work profile suited to the person in that function. The performer would strongly pursue this attainment to fit the corporate or organization objective. It is one of the most important dimensions of the destined work that through the process of selfless giving and fully devoted dimensions of work, the person would benefit by way of developing a noble mind that is free from vices of all kinds. The human mind has a natural inclination towards containing desires of varied identities, combinations, clusters and focuses, however, this can be transformed into a pure mind through the process of divinely oriented yoga. Your mind becomes free from the spell of vices and contamination.

Arabdha Karma thus has the basis of its objective. Once the objective gets fulfilled, the effects of Arabdha Karma start getting in. The primacy of divine orientation in life is established in this context. Arabdha Karma is believed to have the original impetus from God in life.

Na aetae sriti Partho janam yogi muhyati kahchana.
Tasmat sarveshu kaaleshu yogayukto bhaba Arjuna. (G. 8/27)
Knowing thus the secret of these two paths, no yogi gets deluded. Therefore, Arjuna, at all times be steadfast in yoga and the forms of equanimity.

The person who has endorsed the wish of God in life should make forward progress in life with the thoughts of divine wish, gradually understanding the course of actions that are of choice by God on Earth. A person having realized the essence of life would devote to the forms and structures of the essential truth in life. She or he will devote to the form of God of choice and likes to have the spirit of divinity in life. The person will continue doing the spiritual practices of meditation in the ways adopted and learnt.

Brahma eva idam sarvam Ishoh rajh rajesharam.
Ananta etad prakasham vishwam auprakasham
Anantam cha. (Self. 28/4/24)
The Supreme in the identity of the Brahman is the creator, owner and possessor of all material wealth of the world and spiritual wealth of the entire creation. His presence in the world is infinite, beyond all dimensions in which it is revealed, as also that which is not revealed.

Deeply immersed in meditation, the person understands that the Lord Supreme is present everywhere and has made his presence as the intrinsic content in the deep, inner realm of the person. The Supreme is present within and puts himself as the leader of life. To a person dedicated to God, he is the force within to guide, control and coordinate in such a way that it leaves the person as the companion in the true sense of the term. It is thus this realization to construes the knowledge of God in life. It is the divine spirit now discovered within that attempts to function as the king and divine guide to lead the person to the right destiny. Thus, the spiritual orientation creates a difference in life.

God Revealed

Not only is the attitude in life different, but a yogi has the power to elevate the material mind from its usual condition of pettiness to the condition of emergence. An elevated mind would consider the spirit of life as the spirit of the eternal in the context of the empirical. It is thus the identity of life as the spiritual person develops the notion and understanding through the process of realization creates the chosen and defined way or the locus of the person's life and set of activities on Earth.

> *Vedeshu yajneshu tapahshu cha eva*
> *Daneshu yat punyaphalam pradistam.*
> *Auti eti tat sarvam idam biditwa*
> *Yogi paramam sthanam upaiti cha aadyam.* (G. 8/28)

The yogi realizing this supreme truth and developing a mind which is steady and full of faith and devotion, transcends all the barriers and reaches the divine domain with the realization of the Vedas and performance of sacrifice, austerities, charities, and devotion to God.

The idea of the Supreme Lord turns into the knowledge of him in the context of the world for a destined period of time on Earth in its own ways. Thus, the spiritual personality would develop the realization that God is present everywhere. Also, the sense develops that God not only remains present within as a kind of invisible entity with inert features. Thus, he remains within but does not reveal his identity in any way unless the person himself is truly oriented towards that. It is an invisible element within, full of potent content, but does not wish to get revealed. However, to a person with a spiritual inclination, his revelations would augment the spirit of God in the spiritual sense of the term. His presence is activated to the person who is truly aspiring for the realization and the touch of God in life. Thus, the life of the person is activated differently. This life develops the primacy of God even into the spirit.

> *Divyo hi aumurtyoh Purusha sarva bahya Abhyantarah hi aujah.*
> *Apranah hi aumanah shubhrah hi aksharayat*
> *parat parah.* (Mundak.U. 2/1/2)

That transcendental form of the Divine is not revealed; still, he is present within and without. He is eternal – without birth and death; he is not in any living cell with which this formless form is revealed to the world of activities.

The Supreme decides to be in the intrinsic association of persons busy in the spiritual practices in life. The practitioner who does the spiritual practice in life attains the boon in life in terms of the spiritual pursuit in the cause of the world or the cause of spirituality in life. The person gets the automatic support and cooperation from God. It is thus the total amount of devotion to God that works as the devotee of God. He is out there to support and serve the spiritual pursuit in the context of the world. It is the spiritual consciousness that matters in this analysis. The expressed empirical consciousness of the world thus attempts to correct the true spirit of life by way of discovering the divine spirit in life. This creation is the result of the wish of God in the form of its spread.

Tatah param Brahma param brihantam
Yathah nikayam sarvo bhuteshu guhrham.
Viswasya ekam paribeshthi taram
Isham tvam gnyatvaaumrita bhabanti. (Sveta.U. 3/7)

That transcendental identity of divinity is beyond the scope of the world. It is, above all, different types of material identity. Residing within the cave of heart of everyone. The spirit of this realization is also essential for the total wisdom of the scenario and the endowed presence of the formless in the context of the world.

In the process of a spiritual journey through the life of a person, the realization of God makes inroads into the stream of thoughts and lives on Earth. For a transformative life, the divine spirit plays a cardinal role in terms of driving the human spirit towards elevating to the divine spirit in life. The transformation that works across the span of life works out to be the active factor of life that works smoothly and works as the focus of life, driven by the factors of good attributes of life. It is thus the new horizons identified in life that work across life.

Vedah aaham etam Purushah mahantam. Aaditya varnam tamasa parastad.
Tvam eva biditva auti mrityum eti. Na anya panthah bidyatae auyanayah. (Steva.U. 3/8)

The realized self of a sage, having earned the wisdom of God, mentions with self-affirmation that he or she has realized the supreme in his illumined form like the shining Sun with highest brightness – he is self-revealing; knowing him positrons a person on the right track. Knowing him makes him transcend the barriers of life. Knowing him is the only way to overcome mortal limits – no other option remains in life.

Through the spiritual practice, whenever the realization occurs, the spiritual orientation of life develops in the process. The spiritual form of life attempts to make a way through the thoughts and practices of life. The thoughts and practices are imperative to the ideas in life. Through this process, the spiritual person develops the affirmation of God in life and thus develops the belief in the self that would enhance certain attributes that infuse confidence in the process of life. It is a context in which the Absolute gets revealed through realization of the spirit in life.

12 Raaj Yoga – The King of all Yogas

The God Connect of the Leader of the World

Realization of the true spirit of God happens with the practice of inner yoga. Cultivation of the spiritual principles in life is constantly to be in the realm of the overall spiritual climate within the person. This way of getting into the realm of connecting with God requires deep diving within the factors of inner consciousness. Lord Krishna says the essentiality and unique position of this yoga is one of the most conspicuous and has the basis of a strong scientific spirit. This is also one of the most secret functions and approaches in the stream of spiritual realization.

> *Idam tu tae guhzyatamam prabakshami anusuyabae.*
> *Jnanam vijnanam sahitam yat jnaatah mokshasae ashuvyat.* (G. 9/1)

Arjuna, who are devoid of copying the spirit, I shall now unfold the most sacred knowledge of Nirguna Brahma or the transcendental form of God, along with the knowledge of the manifest of divinity divine in the form, which you shall be free from all evils of worldly existence on understanding.

This stream of knowledge encompasses the empirical sciences and the cosmic science of empirical and eternal truth. **The primary condition for the realization of this yoga is that the mind of the aspirant be free from the stresses of doubts, ill feelings, ill motives and evil tendencies, if any.** The mind that is free from the impacts and impositions of vices contributes to the growth and well-being of people on Earth. Thus, knowledge becomes comprehensive and fulfilling when it is founded on the context of the pure mind. Pure mind is free from the emotional inflicts and negativities of the person. A pure mind can only grasp the pure consciousness and thereby understand the uniqueness of the poor personality. Lord Krishna has termed Arjuna as a person with a pure mind, free from the usual impurities of anger, greed, gluttony, envy, jealousy and falsehood. Hence, he is the right recipient of the knowledge of the supreme truth.

> *Raaj vidya raaj guhzyam pabitram idam uttamam.*
> *Pratyaksham avagamam dharmam susukham kartum abyayam.* (G. 9/2)

This knowledge of both the transcendental being and the being in the form is a sovereign one; It's a sovereign science, it's a sovereign secret, it's supremely holy and most excellent, directly enjoyable and if someone understands this, they get the virtue and it's very easy to practice and once someone practices, they will become imperishable.

The special knowledge of spirituality is actually at the top of the pool of all knowledge in the world. It is the profound knowledge of the material world and, at the same time, that of the spiritual world that collectively contributes to the pool of holistic knowledge. For gaining insights into the material world, the rational parameters from a material point of view are important. However, for the spiritual world, through the process of deeper understanding and final realization of the inner dimensions, the truth in eternity gets spread across human existence, as also the entire world and the cosmos, to take care of the entire creation of things and reach the heart of the wholesome truth. Arjuna, being a person with purity of mind and intent, was considered by the Lord as the best-suited person to receive and possess the total knowledge in sequence. This is the wisdom of the divine.

Aushraddaddanah purusha dharmasya asya parantapa.
Auprapya mam nibartahtae mrityu samsara bartani. (G. 9/3)
Arjuna, people having no faith in this dharma or these attributes failing to reach me continue to revolve in the path of the world of birth and death.

People in general who have failed to develop respect for God and faith in God, fail to understand the cosmic spirit in its right perspective. Lord Krishna tells Arjuna that the intrinsic and special knowledge, rather, the elemental wisdom that accrues in the devotees, remains far away from what is expected of. Shraddha, or respect based on faith and love, is fundamental in the design of the things of the Lord in the context of the creation. It all depends on the mental orientation, attitude, faith, and honesty of the purpose in life of the person aspiring to set a target in life. Gradual attainment of a mind that is free from vices of all kinds and, on the other hand, inclined to God, would be blessed to have the understanding of the factors of wisdom in life and devote to the spirit of God.

A special piece of advice was given by Lord Krishna to Arjuna. The entire creation, in its totality, belongs to God. He is not the creator alone. But he maintains things created in a way that begets the worth of the creation through the fulfillment of its purpose. In his urge to create and maintain, the Lord has made it clear that the entire creation belongs to him in all respects. His presence is inherently woven into creation, thus ensuring its continuity.

Maya tatam idam sarvam jagat abyakta murtina.
Mat sthani sarva bhutani na cha aham teshu abasthitam. (G. 9/4)

The whole of this universe is permeated by me and is unmanifest divinity like this water, and all beings rest on this idea within me; therefore, really speaking, I am not present in them.

Continuity in life is maintained through the infusion of the purposeful urge of the creation in its objective. God's appearance on Earth has always been oriented to a specific purpose, usually for the protection of the eternal truth and the truthful lives on Earth. Purpose, at its core, is what God envisioned at the outset of creation. In its continuity of purposeful involvement God has always delivered the key strength and the energy that makes the purpose operational. In the domain of God, the purpose in general, stands as the righteousness of life. Righteousness is the establishment of those values in life that help the world to follow the path of and the orientation to the purposeful existence that takes care of the individual acts and the collective acts in the world. Righteousness is established on one hand with the existence of sattwa-guna, and on the other hand, to see the transformation of other categories of attributes into sattwa-guna. A truthful personality and orientation in life foster the qualities of sattwa in an individual. Attributes that are inclined to the godly existence in life and attributes that take care of the same in a manner where the person feels the urge to change. Through the process of transformation, the attributes of rajas and tamas can be transformed into those of sattwa in the context of the world. This is again variant to time as it appears the personal qualities are unchangeable; the conceptual change is needed to transform.

Na cha mat sthani bhutani pashya mae yogam aeishvaram.
Bhuta bhrit na cha bhutastha mama aatma bhuta bhabanah. (G. 9/5)
All these beings abide not in me, but behold the wonderful power of my divine yoga, though the sustainer and creator of beings, myself in reality, dwells not in those beings.

When God descends on Earth in a human abode, he maintains a scheme of things to make things right on Earth. Sattwa is practised and cultivated in thoughts first, so that the spirit of the same is transmitted to the world of actions. Sattwa stimulates truthfulness in thoughts, habits, characters, and actions of all kinds. Certain basic attributes are representative of sattwa, such as integrity, honesty, and poise of mind. Cooperation and others are among similar other attributes that make a sattwa character. In the design of things for the world, sattwa thus makes things righteous in their approaches, and that makes it workable in the context of life. The world as it is created possesses the potential of all kinds; it is thus the usual place where things change and progress in the light of life. This is also dependent upon the time frame for the life and its progress through the usual pathways of life.

Yatha aakasha sthito nityam vayuh sarvatrago mahan.
Tatha Sarvani Bhutani mat sthani iti upadharayah. (G. 9/6)

Just as the free air in the sky, which is moving everywhere, being born of ether and ever remains in the infinite zone, likewise know that all things that have originated from me also abide with me.

God is omnipresent and thus his presence can be experienced in all corners and places of the world. His presence can be experienced in the context of the world at any place and in any context. Each moment is a moment of God, each point and part of the world is the point and part where the world can experience its prerogative what so ever. It is thus the perspective of God and that of the realistic aspect of the world. Thus, God connects with the world in his prerogative to move forward in the span of life. In a move to have things of the world in the right perspective, the world thus makes things smooth and easy for the empirical to assertion of the system to make things happen such that the mutual perspective of the world is fulfilled. God's perspective makes it happen in a way that removes all obstacles to the truthful existence of the Lord for the revelation of truth on Earth. Thus, the fundamentals of the instincts of life are revealed to the world in its new perspectives of love for God.

During periods when Earth's well-being is prioritized, the quality of life and living significantly influence the circumstances and conditions of existence. Whatever good things that life may aspire for, things that are the providers of perspective to the world, human progress in life occurs in the human context alone. Good and bad are associated with human actions either knowingly or unknowingly. A spiritual aspirant needs to be adaptive to good and exclude bad from life.

Sarva bhutani kounteya prakritam yanti mamekam.
Kalpa kshayae punah tani kalpadou bisrijami aham.   (G. 9/7)
Arjuna, during the final dissolution of all things, enters my holy nature and the prime cause of this creation, and I send them once again.

Human thoughts and aspirations thus attempt to make a distinct identity by being sometimes a sattwa personality and at other points of time, getting time-pressured influences that make life oriented to certain values, which are otherwise non-recommendable. Anger, gluttony, biological desire, untruth, greed and so on are some of those which are collectively the spirits of demons. These are sometimes the right depictions and sometimes not, even though the facts of life are to be sustainable. Anger for the world appears on two diverse parameters. Anger acts on the mind to make it obsessed with the causative issues for anger. The degree of obsession depends upon the degree or the depth of action related to anger. It is the perspective in the world that suffers a change because of the impact and implications of anger. Anger in thoughts only, but not expressed in the spirit of things, as its reactions are just the type of anger and the changes of anger in some specific context. Tamas people develop anger in mind, cultivate that within. This erodes the conditions of health and mind of the tamas persons. Similar things happen with other similar negative emotions in life.

> *Prakritim savam abastavya bisrijami punah punah.*
> *Bhuta gramam imam kritsnam abasham prakritaeh bashat.* (G. 9/8)
> Yielding my nature, I release again and again according to their respective karmas or the quality of action, all this multitude of being subject to the influence in their nature.

The universe has its own dynamics of movement as created by God. The cosmic nature under the impact of which individuals live or different kinds of formations to exist is guided and driven by the divine in the context of a series of happenings across which the entities and lives thrive. Lord Krishna tells Arjuna that lives are under the illusory satisfactions in the state of things or the identities of their existence in particular. It is this identity that works in the form of an independent and autonomous being. Behind all independent and autonomous existences lies the deep core of the being, the supreme spirit in its nuclear form. It is the direct focus of God where each life has a boon to reap in and at the same time diverting personalized emotions that would seek the unit of life, a kind of energy and strength, choice, preferences, taste, and others impact the overall life of the world. Under the process of realisation, at times, this dimension controls the growth of man.

> *Na Chamamtani karmani nibodhnanti Dhananjaya.*
> *Udasina eva udasinovad asaktam tasum karmasu.* (G. 9/9)
> Arjuna, those actions, however, do not bind me unattached as I am to those actions myself, standing apart as it were.

Strictly speaking, God plays a very pivotal role as an idea or a flow of viewpoints to the guides in a realistic way. Every creature wants to retain its creative concern across its own position and identity. It would be great if the focus of the unit of life turns to God. Thus, whenever a human person stands on the brink of a river, with uncertainty, she or he fails to effectively coordinate with all subtly. This, as a phenomenon, wanted one approach, unified in nature and that of the idea of an Indian sage. As a sage lives the life of an ordinary man, mixes with and gets involved. Finally, the person's initial identity changes to a new person with a transformation and then continues in the lives of these few individuals. Truth of God, if maintained properly by the power of nature, it offers a new life. They remove the barriers to actual emergence work that connects with God at this level. Emergence is the gradual awakening of divine wisdom in a person.

Lord Krishna declares that he is the *adhyakshma* of the creation. The entire creation, including the world of humans, is the result of nature making it under the guidance, support and coordination of the Lord. Just like the cultivator of a land connects the seed of the desired product with the soil under the appropriate conditions, he is also there in this entire creation, connecting the units of lives with that of the soil. In the human system, he connects the potential seeds with the nature of life.

> *Maya adhyakshenah prakritih suyatae sacharacharam.*
> *Hetuna anena kounteya jagat paribartatae.* (G. 9/10)
> Arjuna, with me presiding, the nature brings forth the whole creation, constituting both sentient and insentient beings. It is due to this cause that the wheel of samskara is going round.

In the design of the Lord, it is clear that the human world is poised to have the real potential for life to grow into its pinnacle, in order to take care of the creation. God sows the seed of consciousness in the material content of nature to get infused into the potentials of life. A plant takes on its life in the context of nature. Similarly, the care of different forms of life on Earth and that of different categories and forms of life provides abundant energy for the creative potential in life. There occurs the connection with different varieties of form in the life of its continuity of existence. These lives, along with the varieties of their functions in the world, the set of actions that they undertake, and the journeys demonstrate the two-story mind in the context of thoughts and tools of growth, of life, progress, which is evident by the virtues behind the back.

> *Abajananti mam mudha manushim tanum aashritam.*
> *Param bhabam aujanantah mama Bhuta mahesharam.* (G. 9/11)
> Not knowing my supreme nature, the ignorant think low of me, the overlord of the entire creation, who has assumed the human form, and I try to make them understand through my presence that they don't understand me in the human form.

In this perspective, the nature of the cosmos comes down to the nature of individual entities. When matter and spirit are made to combine, it results in a living entity. The determining factor is the nature of the prakriti of the person. When we talk about prakriti in general, we mean the externalities of the person, which involve external revelations of the person's activities and behaviour. But prakriti involves the inner dimensions also. Prakriti has two segments: (a) Inner Prakriti and (b) Outer Prakriti. Inner Prakriti includes the mind and consciousness of the person, whereas the Outer Prakriti is tangible and visible.

God on Earth, in human abode, has a certain purpose to fulfil. It is the basic understanding of the divine spirit that makes the realization happen in a way to understand the nuances of the divine habits of the divine. Lord Krishna says that his appearance on Earth is understood by the realized people as having descended from the Divine abode on this earth with a purpose.

> *Moghah aasha mogha karmano moghajnana bichetah,*
> *Rakshasim aasurim cha eva prakritim mohinim shritah.* (G. 9/12)
> Those bewildered persons with vain hopes, futile actions and fruitless knowledge are possessed of a plundered, demonical and elusive nature.

Lord, the Supreme, expresses his eternal identity. He laments, saying that humans in the world consider him one among them. The external forms having similarity in many aspects with human forms make a person perceive the God on Earth as one of their kind. But the presence of God on Earth is actually out of compassion for all living beings. Since his appearance in the human abode, he has taken up the purpose of establishing an order on the Earth based on the principles of dharma or righteousness. It is the Supreme who, in the passage of life, begets the most difficult and important aspect of rightful living. He maintains the equilibrium or balance in the cosmic system. Whenever the balance or equilibrium is destroyed, the cause is created for his presence, and thus he descends. Thus, evil forces try to have the system study in such a way that it forms a balance. It rather has other objectives of the address and a proper disciplined approach of making the forces of empirical existence in the realistic sense and identity, if any.

When a person identifies the relation between the empirical material self and the causative eternal self, the journey in life of the person takes a different shape. The person identifies the scopes and limits of life on one hand and understands the possibilities and prospects of life on the other. God descends in human abode to make a point for understanding of the humans that each person has a source of immense power within. If a person can cultivate that power in the best possible way, it would be the best translation of the concept of divinity in life. Divine presence on Earth is mostly purposeful. The basic purpose of divine emergence centres around the well-being of the creation. Each race, and for that matter, each element in the creation has its own and collective objectives in life.

There are certain inherent tendencies in each creature. Some of these are pertinent and supportive to human society in various aspects of life, while there are others additionally contributing to human lives. God is for everyone. He is known as 'Lokanam Ishvaram'- he is the God of all human beings. In the realm of God, those who are general people have their duties performed in accordance with the intrinsic objective of life. Somewhat objective, this is very much vibrant in the context of the current state of things happening in the world. In this context, it is pertinent that in order to have the right choice in life, the mental orientation of the person needs to be made to converse with the spirit of divinity. This spirit is to be realized in the context of the emerging truth of the world. Lokanam Ishvaram is what it means to be the message for the masses. It is the essence of spiritual realization that the spirit of the Divine is present in the embodied personality of every person. Whatever be the factors of living, life may get connected to the divine spirit in its own way to trace back to the realm of usual material factors of life. The factors essential for the usual living of a person are related to the required context of the human person. It is, as such, the attempt of the person who intends to contain the impacts of the thoughts that reorients itself towards the happenings of the world. The attitudes that are pertinent to the context of material satisfaction make the world turn to the objective of life on Earth in its own ways. However, it requires thorough involvement of the mind, heart, and brain so much that the usual orientation by the person it fulfils much of the person's urge to fulfil the underlying objective of life. Once the inner realization is complete, it becomes easier for the person in the world to have God-realization.

Lord Krishna tells Arjuna that the great souls are those who maintain the divine attributes of being truthful in life in all situations, have the attribute of character of noteworthy goodness and have honest habits with self-control and mental habits. These are the noble souls who have realized the spirit of divinity.

Mahatmanah astu mam Partho daivim prakritim aashritah.
Bhajanti ananya manoso jnatva bhutadim abyam. (G. 9/13)
On the other hand, Arjuna, great souls who are imbued with the divine nature, knowing me as the prime source of all being and the imperishable eternal, worship me constantly with one-pointedness of mind.

With the spirit of divinity inbuilt in the character of a noble person, the ways in life, used to maintain habits of work and thoughts, are unique in their approaches. These people understand that the difference between the materialistic and selfish view of life and that of noble, selfless approaches in life stands apart from the other categories of life. The noble soul can be in a position to realize the spirit of God and the presence of divine elements in life. It applies to the kind of thoughts the person undertakes and the set of actions initiated in the context of the world; they should be turned to the noble spirit and oriented to the divine actions. Faith in God is developed in the mind of this person, and he or she understands that every bit of action in life is but the culminating point of the thoughts. The person understands that God's intent has made this creation out of its hatches. At this point, the person develops a kind of orientation that makes a continuity of realization within the deeper realms of the truth in assertion.

Satatam kirtayontoh mam yatantah cha drishabratah.
Namasyantah cha mam bhaktah nityayuktah upasatae. (G. 9/14)
Devoted in my consciousness with chanting constantly and bowing again and again to me, those devotees of firm resolve and the firm resolve and the strong faith ever united with me through meditation, worship me with a single-minded devotion.

When the faith gets instilled in the personality of a person, realization of the Divine occurs in continuity. The person evolves her or his own ways of worshipping the Supreme in such a way and manner that attempts to make things happen in the rightful ways of accomplishments in life. The person has to maintain the mental equilibrium and poise to make things happen in the right manner. This personality, as it is turned to the spirit of the Divine, maintains truthful habits and accepts those dimensions in life that are supportive in real terms to the world of work and habits. Inner dedications to God continue with the spirit of godly realization in the life of the person. Chanting the name of God and remembering the spirit of God within are a few such indications that continuously create a touch with the Divine and maintain the same. This person, being turned to the spirit of God, maintains deep spirituality in life and work.

Jnana yajgena anyae apicha jajanto mam upasatae.
Ekatvena prithaktvena bahudha viswatomukham. (G. 9/15)
Others who follow the path of wisdom through sacrifice may take themselves to me through their offerings of knowledge, worshipping me in their own ways and themselves, while still others worship me in my universal form, cosmic form and transcendental form, taking me as unmanifest in diverse celestial forms.

A devotee who is firm in her or his mind in believing God would focus on the spirit of God, realized and accepted in life. Always being in tune with the spirit of God is possible through continuous chanting of the sweet name of God in the context of life and work in the world. It is a functional and operational factor in the life of the devotee. Underlying this concept is creating elements of devotion within. This talks about the path of devotion towards attaining God-realization in life.

There could be another set of people who know and understand the art of knowledge. Knowledge of God in life is crucial to understand the impact and purpose of this creation and also to know the real purpose of getting revealed. In his design of things, the Lord wishes to have the experience of living human form. In the context of changing dynamics of the world of work and the stream of lives God in human abode acts as autonomous spirit of divine influence on the individuals and societies in the world. This empirical understanding in life can be considered sometimes as that of the most truly lived empirical basis.

In the world of spirituality, truth needs to be discovered from the vast resource of knowledge and experience of the passage of time and the change of time with respect to life through the patterns of life in this way, the known and positive aim, the sense of being is one of the most important realistic views of life in an empirical sense. In this path of knowledge, the aspirant would be in the process of understanding God in his external formless revelation in a way that remains true throughout the ages.

Aham kratuh aham jagnah svadhah aham aushadham.
Mantra aham ajamah aham agnih aham hutam. (G. 9/16)
I am the Vedic ritual, I am the sacrifice, I am the offering, I am the departed, I am the harvest, I am the food grains, I am the sacred formula, I am the clarified butter, I am the sacred fire, and I am verily the act of offering oblation into the fire.

In this revelation, the Lord unfolds partly his magnificent presence in the context of worldly actions and affairs. The Lord himself represents all the possible rituals of the world for humans targeted towards the Supreme. Rituals that are prescribed or suggested in the Vedas and other scriptures of the Vedic or post-Vedic period are all included in the scheme of things of God on Earth. Dedication or worship is always aimed at offering faith, love and devotion to God. As Lord Krishna mentions to Arjuna, the dedication, faith and love for God is the context which Lord invocates to. Lord Krishna advises to have focus on the spirit of God in the context and background of the world. It is this that is made into the context of human relations in the world. It is that God himself is present in the world, not limited and confined within the boundaries of God's spiritual presence in the context of the actions of the world. His presence remains as a matter of continued presence and thereby trying to rescue the mind from material context.

Pita haham asya jagata mata dhatah pitamahah.
Vedyam pabitram om karah Rik Sam Yajuh eva cha. (G. 9/17)
I am the sustainer and ruler of this universe, its father, mother and grandfather, the one worth knowledge, one mind and the purified, the sacred syllable 'Om' and the three Vedas, Rig, Jaju and Saam have arisen from me.

The Lord identifies himself as the spiritual element present in the life of man on Earth. It is the world that needs the affirmation from the Lord about his being omnipresent to all. God on earth with his purposeful presence still continues to remain omnipresent in the intrinsic of every human individual. Though he remains very tiny, unnoticeable, yet his conscious presence, once realised, transforms the person from that of a worldly personality to a divine-oriented personality. In the world, the relations that prevail within societies or families are important to understand and accept in the human transactions in the context of the world as such; thus, the Lord identifies himself as the intrinsic self within all types of human relations. As such, he declares that he is present in all as the father and, at the same time, as the mother. Thus, the Lord can be conceived of in the manner and ways humans identify their dear ones in all situations.

Gatih Bharta prabhu sakshih nibasah sharanam suhrid.
Prabhavah pralayah sthanam nidhanam vijam abyayam. (G. 9/18)

I am the supreme goal, supporter, the Lord, witness, abode, refuge, all where we shall seek no return, origin, end, resting place, stone house to which all things belong and imperishable seed.

The Lord explains further to Arjuna that he is the goal of life in the short term as also in the longer term of life. He is the Supreme of all forces and maintains the continuation of the world in the sense of making it happen through the thoughts and actions of the world. The thoughts and actions thus make it happen in a way that takes care of the facts and prospects of the world.

Lord Krishna explains to Arjuna that the intrinsic truth of his presence in the world is that he is the goal of creations. He is the one who protects everyone. He who makes the consciousness of the person exist. He maintains his position as the master. He is the embodied entity that presents the world in a way that makes the human world blessed with the faith that God is present in the world as the creator- protector- maintainer and culmination of all stages of the world. It is thus the most effective and vibrant concept that the Lord is present in all the situations and outcomes of the world, as something dominated humans temporarily.

The Lord stands as the destiny of the new world, where the human intent would be to have the realization of the Lord. It is the prevailing condition of a person that proves to be important when the devotee finds in the mind the potential which would make the person inclined to the spirit of God on Earth, with his presence in the world, the spirit of goodness and that of divinity. With the revelation of the intrinsic factors of life, humans should get into the dynamics of the world in this context and scenario that involves the Divine spirit for the benefit of humans.

Tapani iha aham varsham aham nihgriham aham utsrijami aham cha.
Amritam cha eva mrituh cha sat asat cha aham Arjuna. (G. 9/19)
I radiate heat as the Sun and hold back as well as the fourth showers. Arjuna, I am immortality as well as death, even so I am being and non-being both at the same time.

When an understanding person grasps the facts of the world's existence alongside the Lord's constant presence, they embody a kind-hearted nature, intrinsically connected to the essence of life itself. It is thus the facts of life that make things happen. The survival and growth of humans are most pressing with the pure intent converging to the spiritual content of the world. God offers the energy and the heat to accept the world as the living dynamism. The dynamism absorbs the energy gifted by God and at the same time, he is heat, he is all the cold, he is the waterfall, the rain from the sky and the clouds. The presence of God on Earth fulfils the spirits of the same in the context of the world. The Lord is thus present in the world at a time when the entire basis is confirmed.

Trei vidya mam somapah putapapa
    Yajgeih ishtah sargati prarthayantae.
Tae punyah masa aadya surendralokae
    Ashananti divyan divi devbhogan. (G. 9/20)
Those who perform actions with some interested motive as laid down in the three Vedas and drink the juice of realization have defeated sin, worshipping me through sacrifices, seek access to heaven, attaining the paradise as a result of their virtuous deeds, they enjoy the celestial pleasure in God, God's realization in heaven.

Eternal truth has been revealed by the three Vedas- the Rig Vedas, the Saam Vedas, and the Yaju Vedas. It is thus the basis of human actions and the works that situations other than those which are products of human intents, aspirations, and the factors of goodness. It is this factor of goodness that makes the world a new place to allow the growth and sustenance of goodness as the factor of life that focuses on the prospects of being drenched in the factors of truth and the spirit of goodness. It is thus a new basis of the renewed life that the world makes its way based on divine truth in the life of humans. The realistic truth exists within the world, and this truth is also directly experienced.

Tae tam bhuktva svargalokam vishalam
    Kshinae punyae martyalokam bishanti.
Evam trayih dharmam anuprapanya
    Gatah aagatam kamah akama labhantae. (G. 9/21)
Having enjoyed the extensive heaven world, they return to this world of mortals on the stock of their merits, which is exhausted, thus devoted to the rituals with interest and motive recommended by the three Vedas.

The human factor in the context of the divine world is the basis that attracts factors of transformation in a way that helps establish the divine truth. The Lord thus projects that the truth of the world merges with the total and complete realm of truth that would help in the process of the transformation. It is the basis of the would-be new life and the contextual basis of the eternal truth as applied to the facts of the world. The new life through the process of transformation would be surfaced in a way to sensitize the intrinsic factors of life. Rig Veda attempts to make the invocation of God on the prevailing flow of life. It recommends the wisdom garnered in the context of life and the journey of humans in this world. Whatever work has been undertaken so far paves the way to have more. Wisdom is the total knowledge and experience of God. The wisdom of Brahman is Brahman himself.

The factors of work that are talked about in the world primarily focus on the spirit of things that support the cause of the progression of eternal truth in the world. Wisdom of Brahman makes way to the moksha or the final liberation from the cords of the material impediments in all situations.

> *Ananyah chintayantah mam yae jana pari upasateh.*
> *Tesham nitya aviyuktanam yogakshemam bahami aham.* (G. 9/22)
> The devotees, however, who solely love me, constantly think of me and worship me in a disinterested spirit, to those ever united in thought with me, I bring full security and personally look after their own needs.

However, Lord Krishna narrates the factors that help the human spirit to be drenched in the impressive factors of the world of habits and that of characters. The truth realized through the understanding and realizing the spirit of the Divine, adopting the same in the intrinsics of life, requires deep love and devotion to God. It is the very basis of these material factors that makes the spiritual journey. When the aspirant is fully engrossed in God and leaves aside all material and other thoughts and all senses, and converses with God, the person gets divine support, protection and companionship in life.

> *Yaeh api anyayah devata bhakta yajantae shradhayah annitah.*
> *Taeh api mam eva kounteya yajanti bidhipurbakam.* (G. 9/23)
> Arjuna, even those devotees who are endowed with faith worship other gods with the same interested motive, worship me alone, though with a mistaken approach.

For a devotee, the process of attaining a realisation of God is not that subtle or easy to accomplish. Factors of God-realization primarily depend upon the task of having the mind purified. The meditative route talks about various dimensions of the meditative cycle. Through a long-drawn and repetitive method, the Divine can have the same recognised as an endeavour serious and sincere enough to accomplish. Cleansing the mind of its emotional, behavioural and characteristic impurities requires the vigour of yogic practices. The most profound method, as mentioned by sage Patanjali, has different steps called limbs. A sincere passage through all such steps helps the devotee or yogi identify these steps as the steps of achieving God-realization. However, as assured by Lord Krishna, the path of devotion and surrender to the lotus feet of God immediately gets the divine realisation and support.

> *Aham hi sarva yajna nam bhoktah cha prabhu eva cha.*
> *Na tu mam abijananti tatwena atah chavanti tae.* (G. 9/24)
> For I am the enjoyer and also the Lord of all sacrifices, but they do not know me in reality, and those who do not know me in reality, they fall.

As the context arises for Lord Krishna to gradually reveal his intrinsic identity. As he guides Arjuna through different categories, it becomes imperative that one of the most important points is the desire-free mind and that he induces the particular and thus life renders continuous services to benefit the devotee in his or her. This makes the initiative of the class. At the end of everything, in God's realm, to comprehend in the right frame of interest for human society. Vedic society, as such, works for the world can be accomplished in a desire-free world. Faith in God and his magnanimity would instil the sacred activities paced together to create a homogeneous process of God realization.

> *Yanti devabrata devan pitrin yantih pitribratah.*
> *Bhutani yanti bhutejya yanti mat yajinah api mam.* (G. 9/25)
> Those who worship any form of God, those who are votaries of names, reach the names, those who adore the spirits, reach the spirit and those who worship me, they come to me alone.

Worshipping God in any form of choice ultimately connects with the process of realization. Once the realization of God sets in through any of the methods that provide the very core of faith, it ultimately reaches out to the cause of dedication. Gradually, the scenario becomes realised, understanding the spirit of God on Earth of the element. Lord Krishna assures of even direct realization once the person has gathered in a way that acts as the bridge between the difficulty of any soul and the heights of realization. The devotee is now endowed with the basis of the creation as it has been visualized as a world of the very fit and convenient. In the care of devotion, the critical point in all is the supporters remain committed to have faith. Even the basis of devotion in the mind may be the world. Thus, the creation becomes full with support throughout.

Lord Krishna says that in his design of things, everyone is equal. Whatever the external identity from the point of view of the world, in the eyes of God, all enjoy the same position. It is the goodness of devotion that makes man dear to him.

> *Patram pushpam phalam yoh mae bhakti prayachhati.*
> *Tat aham bhakta upahritam aushnami prayati aatmanah.* (G. 9/26)
> Whosoever offers me with love a leaf, a flower, a fruit, water, I appear in person before the disinterested devotee of a sinless mind and delightfully partake of that article offered by him with love.

Whether a person offers some flower petals, whether it is from a rich person or a poor person, does not create any difference. The Lord is satisfied with the offerings of a leaf, a flower, or just the words of devotion. No number of glorious things or valued products is going to add to the notice of God for the devotee. It is just the oneness of mind dedicated to the spirit of God that makes the causative elements and factors of the world. Concentrated on the spirit of God in a way that makes it happen in such a way that the aspirant develops a mind cleansed of all negative emotions of mind. At the micro and personal level, the individual may find ways ahead with a twin focus. On one hand, it is the focus of the person towards the fundamentals of truth on Earth, and on the other, it is the cause of the entire creation to thrive that needs to be understood. Once this is understood, the seeker would give it a try to have the inclination towards realising the essence of truth as it gets revealed for the benefit and welfare of people.

> *Yat karoshi yat asnoshi yat juhosi dadasi yat.*
> *Yat Tapasya ausi kounteya tat kurushva mat arpanam.* (G. 9/27)
> Arjuna, whatever you do, whatever you eat, whatever you offer, whatever oblation you do, is sacred fire, whatever you bestow as a gift, whatever you do as an action, you do that with the way of penance and offer that to me.

Oneness of the aspirant's mind is one of the essential requirements of God to interact in the world. A special message to Arjuna, as mentioned by Lord Krishna, is the urge of God for humans to have a destined and dedicated consciousness. Lord Krishna emphasizes focusing on the inner contents and dedicating all thoughts and actions to God. Lord Krishna offers to the world that whatever work anyone undertakes needs to be dedicated to God. It is also urged by him that devotees dedicate their spiritual practice.

> *Shuvah ashubhan phalei evam mokshasaekarma bandhaeih.*
> *Sannyasa yoga yukta aatma bimuktoh mam apeishyasi.* (G. 9/28)
> With your mind thus established in me, this is the yoga of renunciation, you will be freed from the bounds of karma or the action in the form of good and evil consequences and freed from them, you will attain me.

Once the mental orientation to dedicate occurs in the context of work of the world, the spiritual practices, the conflicts, the acts of giving or the meditations for God, all these are performed or visualized in the world by the aspirant's God realization. It is thus very pertinent that God is also in form to attain the dedicated devotion, and that is why the spirit of God is understood and spread in the realm of human understanding and realization. The act of dedication to God would bring in the blessings of the Divine for human emergence.

> *Samah aham sarvabhuteshu na mae deshyah asti na priyah.*
> *Yae bhajanti tu mam bhaktya mayee tae teshu cha apyaham.* (G. 9/29)
> I am equally present in all beings; therefore, there is none hateful or especially dear to me; however, those who devotedly worship me, abide in me, and I too stand revealed to them.

The Lord tells Arjuna to be devoted and dedicated to God. The work, the thought, the food, the puja or sacrificial activities, any kind of austerity or the work of life and even personally inclined categories of work are endowed to God in the sense, the mental and conscious orientation of the aspirant. In the act of doing so, the devotee would be free from the cycle of work and the outcome of that work. It is in this context that the devotee is urged to be dedicated in mind. Dedication in spirit and actions is true devotion.

> *Aupi chet suduracharo bhajatae mam ananya bhak*
> *Sadhuh eva sa mantabyah Samyak byabasitoh hi sah.* (G. 9/30)
> Even if the vicious sinner worships me with exclusive devotion, he should be recognised with the same and has rightly resolved.

The attitude and mind of the person are important in the spiritual world. It is not the economic standard or the social position of the person; it is not even the identity of clan, creed, culture, nation or any singular or collective identity that sounds important, it is but the purity of mind and intent and eager love for God that makes an aspirant dear to him.

The person dedicated in spirit and empirical existence to God sustains himself. She or he does not connect in any way to the path of further decline and destruction in any way. Whenever someone has accepted God, the impact of negative emotions, like, greed, anger, gluttony, envy etc. are balanced by the positive and Divine ones.

> *Kshipram bhabati dharmatma shashvantim shantim nihgachhanti.*
> *Kounteya pratijanehi na mae bhaktah pranashyatih.* (G. 9/31)
> Speedily he becomes virtuous and attains lasting peace, know it for certain, Arjuna, that my devotee never suffers a fall.

Even if the person has indulged in something wrong in life for any reason or is caught in some situational constraint, at times, it may happen that the person faces a genuine crisis. The nature of the crisis may vary. It could be personal matters related to living, health, esteem or even very basic amenities of life; or it could be that all of a sudden it happened in some way, accidentally or in any situation, a person who has devotion to God does not finally get constrained by it. A person devoted to God remains always under the godly umbrella cover. This umbrella cover is always full of blessings. Even the evil results of bad karma do not affect the person if he or she has come under the cover of God's ambience. God in mind, truly placed, puts the person to the realm of a free condition, wherein the nails of evil reaction of the world, if any, bounce back to the source external only.

> *Mam hi Partho byapaashritya yah api suh papayonoyah.*
> *Striyoh Vaisya sudra tatha tae cha api yanti param gatih.* (G. 9/32)
> Arjuna, women, person with vices and those who belong to negative categories of attributes, corrupt personal character and types in nature,

as well as those who are impious or barred, whoever they may be, if they take refuge in me, they too attain the supreme goal.

God's grace is always available for everyone. Whether the person is apparently known as good or bad does not matter to the realm of God. It is the element of devotion that matters most in the design of God on Earth. Devotion breeds the touch of God in the life of the devotee. Devotion needs to be pure in nature. Pure devotion is one where reciprocity is not called for. The person may seek God for some solutions to problems, some fulfilment of desires and for some other reason. But there could be very few cases of devotion where the reasons for orientation to God are for the cause of devotion and love alone. In this case, the devotee tries to truly understand the spirit of devotion and breeds enormous love for God, for which the devotee does not have any expectation that anyone with any identity may have.

Kim punah brahmanah punya bhaktaa rajoyah tatha.
Anityam asukham lokam imam prapya bhajasva mam. (G. 9/33)
How much more than if the holy persons of the royal sense devoted to me, therefore having obtained this joyless and tensioned human life, constantly worshipping me, they get my realization heavily.

If someone develops that kind of devotion, he or she becomes not only dear to God, but turns into the person of God in the true sense of the term. It is thus the solemn call that God makes in the context of the world to become a person seeking the divine in life. This is not in the sense and motive of gaining personal satisfaction, but with the view to have the realization of God on one hand, and to transform life so that it even equates to or transcends the consciousness of a sage king in life. A sage king maintains the role of a king who does not work for herself or himself, rather is dedicated to the cause of the people.

Manmana bhabo mad bhaktoh mad yaji mam namaskuru.
Mam eva eishyasi yukteih eva aatmanam mat parayanah. (G. 9/34)
Fix your mind on me, be devoted to me, worship me and make obscene to me, thus uniting yourself to me and entirely depend on me, you shall come to me and I will always be by your side to liberate you from all bondages.

Sages are dedicated to God. They usually live a life that centres all thoughts and activities around that of God. God remains at the core of the consciousness of a sage. It is thus the sage personality in a person that makes him oriented to God. And if this sage personality involves the thoughts and actions of a selfish person, the entire set of attributes of the sage personality is lost. However, added to it, the kinghood in the sage personality makes the person a complete devotee. A complete devotee is inclined to have the spirit of God in all situations and all contexts. Lord Krishna has made the final call to Arjuna, urging him to become like that. He mentions and urges having the mind consecrated to him without any other distractions. He urges humans to become his devotee and the constant seeker of God in a way and in the context of the world. The person is urged to feel the heart and soul with devotion to God, and at the same time, to get thoroughly drenched in the spirit of God. With this, the devotee turns into the dearest person of God on Earth in the context of the human and material world. The spiritual aspirant thus earns devotion and realization of God in human life.

13 God Revealed

God in creation urges us to be Godly

The world of humans, animals, trees and life on the bed of soil, water or in the air has the touch of God in terms of its life and growth. Life is, thus, a gift of the supreme energy and supreme power, providing vital energy to it. It is the essential element of all living entities in the context of the entire creation. Creation remains vibrant with each element contributing to it in harmony and joy.

> *Sri Bhagavan ubacha:*
> *Bhuyah eva mahabaho shrinu mae paramam vachah.*
> *Yat tae iham priyamanayah bakshyame hita kamaya.* (G. 10/1)
> Sri Bhagavan said to Arjuna, Listen, I am going to tell you the supreme words as you like to hear. These are so dear to me, listen carefully.

Lord Krishna tells Arjuna about the relevance and purpose of creation, and at the same time, to focus on the spirit of divinity that is connected with the spirit of individual segments of the creation. The fact that God is present in each of the living element is noticed in the fabric of things in a way that factors the divine energy into its most viable option of the context into its patch of being known in its revealed identity, where the factors of the understanding God would be most rigorously put across in the supportive dimension of it happening in the world. This knowledge is thus conspicuous in the creation.

> *Na mae biduh sursganah prabhabam na maharshayah.*
> *Aaham aadihi devonam maharshinan cha sarvashah.* (G.10/2)
> Neither the gods nor great sages know this secret fully, the secret of my birth, the secret of my doing and the prime cause remain secret to the seers for a long.

Some of the forms of gods and the great sages do not have the idea of God's real identity with respect to the creation. The knowledge gets revealed in the mind and consciousness of these immortal souls from the point of their respective emergence in life. Experiential knowledge is that of an ultimate one earned through practical realization or a direct way of understanding, while in the world. It is thus the factual exposition of the position of a life in the world concerning that of the universal truth as revealed in the world. It is thus the most profound revelation of cosmic truth in life.

> *Yah mam ajam cha anadim cha betti loka maheshvaram.*
> *Asammudhah sa martyeshu sarvapapaeih pramuchyatae.* (G. 10/3)
> He who knows me in reality as eternal, without any beginning and end, as the supreme lord of the universe, he, undiluted among men, is first of all sins.

Lord Krishna continues to say that a person having realization of God, that his presence on Earth is the embodied appearance of him, in a context that easily reveals the worth of a human in the context of the world. Those who have earned divine wisdom in the process have garnered the same. It is thus a basic fact and, for that matter, the fundamentals of the creation. The urge a single seeker may have is that of the ultimate realization of the spirit in a way that prefers some aspects of revealed truth over others. This fact was conveyed to the world of many and urged upon to take in life the actual process of taking truth forward.

> *Buddhih jnanam asammohah kshama satyam damah shamah.*
> *Sukham duhkham bhabah abhabam bhayam abhayam eva*
> *cha.* (G. 10/4)
> The right reason and right knowledge, right understanding, forbearance, diversity, control over the senses and mind, and joy and sorrow, evolution and dissolution, fear and fearlessness, these are all. Preferred to understand and to have the realization.

Many attributes in human society are meant for a partial moment or a specific period of life. Thus, for the moment, the factors of knowledge are stipulated in the context of the wholesome spirit as revealed to the wisdom and realization of many in the backdrop of all and sundry happenings of the living society. Each person creates destiny through karma or action in life. Karma or the orientation of life is experienced by the person in their own thought, and the inclination of the mind. The law of association works well in this context. The person associating with the divine thoughts, divine talks, divine works and divine spirit in personal orientation will always be, in a way, turned to the content of the same and get impacted by the same spirit in terms of imbibing the ideal that would gradually always strengthen the influence of the associate in life. Thus, on the other hand, constant touch and orientation towards animals in any way would impact life, making it visibly touched by the person. The person thinking of God, chanting the mantra of God, offering service to any form of God with great love and devotion and based on faith, makes way for divine life.

Karma orients life in a positive direction towards creating the right destiny for the person. Destiny is primarily the creation of most cases, the activating orientation towards the goodness of the person towards God. Qualities of goodness extend the message of being with God. Sattwa guna in a personality wins the *Daivi Guna*, the attributes adoring the personality of divinity. Equality, considering all as part of the same; all the possessions of goodness and truth are eternally divine.

Ahimsa samata tushtih tapoh danam yashah ayashah.
Bhabanti bhaba bhutanam matta eva prithak bidhah. (G. 10/5)
Equanimity in all situations, non-violence, contentment, austerity, charity, fame, equality of mind, compassion, all these are divine attributes of creatures, all these emanate from me alone.

Lord Krishna tells Arjuna about the attributes that would make the world a better place. Among the divine attributes, Lord Krishna includes some specific ones that would make the character of the seeker towards divinity. Right reason and right knowledge are very important in the realm of God. God-realization means that every thought or action should stem from reasons imbued with goodness and divinity. In this case, a clean understanding of truth in life is possible with the right kind of reasoning and understanding. The prelude to this is the proper control over the mind, having made the mind free from desire, greed, jealousy, passionate mix with the material joy and involvement in selfish orientations. Fearlessness, equanimity, austerity, contentment, non-violence, truthfulness, trust, integrity, all these divine attributes make the spiritual aspirant come and remain close to God in life.

Maharshayah sapta purvae chattvarae manabah tatha.
Mat bhabah manasah jata yah esham lokoh imah prajah. (G. 10/6)
The 7 great seers are born of me, and their elders are also born of me.
The 7 great seers are Marichi, Angira, Atri, Pulasta, Krutu, and Vasishta.

Lord Krishna elaborates, saying that the seven great seers and sages were the torchbearers of the divine truth, and there were the four others who were even before the saptarshis. These seven great sages are immortal. They have survived through the ages and remain in the sky as constant sources of illumination. The sages are: Marichi, Angira, Autri, Pulastha, Pulaha and Vashistha. Atri had guided Sri Raam on the pathways of divine life. Pulastha, Pulaha and Angira were involved in guiding the sages of generations to guide the people in society towards the pathways of truth in life and work. Marichi and Kratu were silent inspirations to the spiritual seekers over the ages. Great sage Maharshi Vashistha had pioneered and guided the leading sages.

Etam bibhutim yogam cha mam yoh betti tatvatah.
Sahah abikampena yogena yujyatae na atra samshayah. (G. 10/7)

He who knows in reality the supreme divine glory and the power of mind, gains eternal bliss in life and attains devotion.

Lord Krishna has also confirmed and then emphasized the role of the saptarshis as mentioned as the eternal features of truth. The divine context in the creation is created out of the spread of truth in the world. This would ultimately be in the context of the world and as such is involved in the act and run of the world. The pages of human existence through the turns of the human races, called *kalpa,* pass through certain flows of value that are essential for the turning around of the core orientation of lives. Anyone who understands God's revelation through the various facets of life also comprehends that God's realization on Earth and the spread of truth occur through this understanding.

> *Aham sarvasya prabhabah mattah sarvam prabartatae.*
> *Iti mattva bhajantae mam budhah bhaba samannitah.* (G. 10/8)
> I am the source of all creation, and everything in the world moves with me, and knowing me makes a person wise and creates devotion, develops devotion in the person.

This great *bibhuti,* or the demonstrative revelations of the presence of God in the context of the world, is the driving force for establishing truth in life. God intends to spread the eternal message to the world of humans. The supreme divine message wants the world of humanity to foster the truth of God. God used to create the eternal truth in a new form to create a new reality. God holds the entire creation with love. The seven great seers are the constant inspiration.

> *Marichih, Angira, Autri, Pulastha, Pulaha, Kratuh, Vashishtha iti*
> *Saptatae manasha nirmita hi tae.*
> *Etae vedabidae mukhya veda Acharya cha kalpitah.*
> *Pravritti Prakriti nirman cha eva Prajapatyae cha kalpitah.*
> (Mahabharatam, Shanti Purva, 340/69-70)
> Marichi, Angira, Autri, Pulastha, Pulaha, Kratuh, Vashishtha – these seven great sages are masters of the Vedic wisdom. These wise sages have contributed to the making of ideal characters, personalities and the ideal context in the world for a truthful personality and making of a truthful sequence of lives.

The seven great sages who are there in the *saptarshi mandal* of the super sky. These immortal souls are the great stars of the divine illumination. God is the source of this great storehouse of light in the universe. The wheel of creation revolves through the periods of the solar and lunar movements. The run of the wheel of time revolves across the phenomena and incidents of the world.

The seven great sages have collectively guided and coordinated the factors of empirical truth. God's intent has been transmitted through the actions of the human world as expressed through the souls who are the guiding spirits of the world. This guiding spirit has been the sensitizer of goodness and divine truth in the world. The great Saptarshi sages not only guided humanity's progress but also spread the words of God to conquer darkness and reveal the world's truth.

> *Mat chittah mat gata prana bodhayantah parashparam.*
> *Kathayantah cha mam nityam tushyanti cha ramanti cha.* (G. 10/9)
> With the mind fixed on me and their life surrendered to me, ever resting and enlightening another by glories, my devotees will remain always contented in delight.

When the mind of the spiritual aspirant is focused on God, then she or he understands the power and scope of the truth in the world of creation. This creation has the essence of the total revelation of the divine truth and has the intent to remove all patches of darkness from the stream of truth in the creation. This creation, therefore, proceeds towards a higher degree of illumination than usually perceived in the human world. Mind fixed on God and the inner urge to dedicate consciousness to God is thus the ultimate way to get into the spirit of the Divine in the creation. Thus, the creation has all aspects of the truth of transcendence as applied to human conditions. It is thus the flow of cosmic vibration that makes life divine and transcendent.

> *Tesham satatayuktanam bhajatam pritipurbakam.*
> *Dadami buddhiyogam tam yena mam upayanti tae.* (G. 10/10)
> On those ever united through devotion with me and worshipping me with love, I confer that yoga of wisdom by which they come to me.

The union with the soul of the devotee occurs in consciousness. It occurs in such a way that the spirit begets its position of acceptance in the living soul and gradually helps it to get transformed. It is thus the clear and specific dimension of the human world that every spiritual aspirant pays attention to the cause of creation and turns the focus to the creator. The loving and faithful devotees are expected to get drenched in the art and content of divine love, and be favoured by God. Those who constantly devote their mind and focus of life to God are blessed by God. These dedicated personalities thus proceed to have the acceptance of their spirit by God, the Eternal. Lord Krishna promises to be with them.

> *Tesham eva anukampa artham aham ajnanajam tamah.*
> *Nashayami aatma bhabastha jnana dipena bhasvata.* (G. 10/11)
> In order to shower my grace on them, I reside in their heart and remove the darkness which they are born of and the ignorance is replaced by wisdom.

When a mind gets completely concentrated and focused on an object, it can gain penetrating knowledge of the object. Lord Krishna elaborates to Arjuna, saying that a mind focused on him is poised enough to earn the divine light in the thoughts and works of the world. If the mind is totally dedicated in its conscious endeavour to have love and devotion for God and, at the same time, is devoted to the cause of the Divine on Earth, God himself extends, supports, guides and provides the required inputs of knowledge so that the person attains realization of God. The Lord infuses into the mind of the devotee the knowledge and helps her or him to get connected.

> *Arjuna ubacha:*
> *Param Brahma param dham pabitram parama bhaban.*
> *Purusham sashwatam divyam adidebavam ajam bibhum.* (G. 10/12)
> Arjuna says, I understand that you are the transcendent, eternal, supreme abode, the greatest purifier, and all those greatest people and the divine purusha, they all worship you as the supreme god.

Lord Krishna again affirms his promise of being with the person who develops love, faith and devotion for God. On the other hand, if any roadblock or resistance appears to receive profuse energy for realization, any darkness that has stayed would be driven by the Divine, who will act as a facilitator in support of the seeker of realization. It continues to receive the unique feature of the devotee, and becomes the centre of it. Lord Krishna says the eternal spirit of his being resides in the cave of the heart of the devotee. As a matter of fact, all light of wisdom is contained here within, and the inner realization takes place. Requital scenario turns golden and illumined with the process of devotion. The devotee has the power not only in the carton of personal devotion, but God that guides in this world make the devotee divine.

By virtue of being in the company of Lord Sri Krishna and the spirit of divinity, as explained by the Lord to Arjuna, a strong sense of understanding of the Divine came into the mind of the devotee. Arjuna said to Krishna, 'You are the supreme Brahman, you are the ultimate destiny, you are always the pure and spread across the spirit of purity on Earth'. He says, having achieved the divine consciousness, he understood the Lord as the cause behind the creation. The Lord himself has taken the abode of the sages of great wisdom like Ashitah, Devolah, Vaisah, Naradah and the other great personalities of the world.

> *Aahu tvam rishayah sarvae Debarshi Naradah tatha.*
> *Asitoh Devalo vyasah svayam cha eva brabishi mae.* (G. 10/13)
> I consider you as unborn and all-pervading like the sages Narada, Sages Ashita, Devala and Vyasa; all those are actually your worshippers.

Whoever is in the world spreading the thoughts and actions of goodness from any dimension is in the spirit of divinity. God has nurtured the thoughts in a way that has been discovered as having forwarded the good thoughts and goodness to the entire creation. These great sages are vibrant with the discoveries of truth at their respective end. The spirit of God is present in all the good aspects of the world. Sages have not only earned the realization of God on their own, but the entire universe turns to the cosmic vibration on receiving the wisdom and truth of God. As such, the creation continues with the intrinsic *chhanda* infused in the flow of the truth in different phases. The sages would thus embody the spirit of God in the normal spell of life, to the extent possible.

> *Sarvam etad ritam manyae yat mam badasi Keshava.*
> *Na hi tae Bhagavana byaktim biduh devah na danabah.* (G. 10/14)
> Krishna, I believe as true in all that you tell me, Lord, neither demons nor gods are aware of your unmanifest.

The truth of creation is constrained by that of time, space and entities. The limits of truth are thus revelations of the empirical realities. It is such that at the moment of making the thought or getting into the act is a moment of temporal truth. As such, that period of having the realization of truth seems to be the realizable truth. The organs of senses do experience this truth of the moment or the situation as the only revelation or truth. Transcendence is experiencing the truth beyond the tangible, visible dimensions of reality. The reality is thus revealed in the understanding of the empirical truth. Time and space of context now is the reality or the real-life truth from an empirical point of view. God is revealed throughout the phases of truth for now and the truth is eternal. It is the realizable aspect of truth being empirical that is usually something shadowed by truth.

> *Svayam eva aatmana aatmanam betthu tvam purusha uttomam.*
> *Bhuta bhavanah Bhuteshadevadeva jayatptae.* (G.10/15)
> Oh creator of beings, oh ruler of creatures, god of gods, the lord of the universe, oh supreme purusha, you alone know what you are and you are yourself.

Eternal truth thus goes beyond the boundary of time and space. God turns himself into the all-profound and invisible form that creates a span of continuity from time now unto time eternal, and the infinite span that permeates all barriers and obstacles. God takes the form of life or a material object that stands the test of time. Thus, the essential component of realization works out to be the sole provider of truth. The provider of truth relates to the new dimension of the realization of truth. God remains in the inner domain of the entity, thus relating to the working of the aspects of divinity. It is the primacy of God's spirit that offers divine touch to the empirical lives and the core of the material being.

Vayaktum arhasya ausheshana divya hi aatma bibhutayah.
Yabhih bibhutihbhi lokanam iman tvam byapya tishasi. (G. 10/16)
Indeed, you alone can describe in full your divine glories, whereas when you pervade all these worlds.

Arjuna could realize that the wide and diverse revelations of God are only partially understood in usual human consciousness. However, his elaboration upon the diverse forms of his appearance is the conclusive one. As such, Arjuna appeals to Lord Krishna to be sympathetic to his urge to know about the Lord's diverse and unique revelations in the world. Thus, the oneness and diversity simultaneously get revealed to Arjuna in the interest of spreading the divine knowledge to the world. The entire living nature and the grounded non-living material objects all receive the same flow of energy from God. Thus, in the light of this attainment, the seeker would then initiate a journey towards attaining self-learning to realize the vast oceanic form of infinite entities. Arjuna now realizes the power of the Divine in the context of creation. With the huge energy and strength, Lord Krishna mentions that his process of reckoning is his intense creation. Thus, with the understanding of the reality being a part of the eternal process, the Lord would motivate the disciple with the task of creating inner power to augment the gap of things prevailing and to discuss the works of the world as an extension of the wish of God to make the world a better place. Historically, the single aspect of consciousness, the process, the energy, contextual endowment are all proposed.

Katham bidyam aham yogin tvam sada parichintayanah.
Keshu keshu cha bhabeshu chintayah ausi Bhagavan maya. (G. 10/17)
You are the master of yoga and through that continuous meditation, shall I know you and in what particular forms, oh lord, that I understand you, you to be meditated upon, please tell me.

Arjuna had developed a genuine quest for the right way of realizing God. He made a few points in the form of questions. Arjuna was eager to know what the ways are that a devotee may follow to have the right kind of realization. It was considered one of the primary methods to determine if unwavering devotion to God would result in the unveiling of divine understanding for the devotee. Thoughts of a kind may continue as a kind of flow from within, and a different pattern of thought may cause interruptions in this process. The interruptions may tend to push the divine thought towards the material domain of smallness. Smallness does make its way into the inner faith, and the devotee deviates. That is why God has mentioned to be in constant touch with the spirit of God in some way or the other.

Vistarena aatmano yogam bibhutim cha janardanam.
Bhuyah kathayah triptih hi shrinvanto naasti mae amritam. (G.10/18)

Krishna, tell me once more in detail your power of yoga and your glory, for I know no satiety in bearing your nectar-like words.

Arjuna went on further to understand whether further advice from the Lord would be more helpful to him to understand the true spirit in the facts of life. This made Arjuna to request Lord Krishna to have the true ways that would be lust for him. Thoughts of God on one hand and doing different sacrificial worships or any other means could be the best and most suitable in the case of Arjuna. This was now a serious issue that Arjuna was curious to pursue and get proper guidance or suggestions for the same. Having the final way out, Arjuna took the position of a serious devotee and thus wanted the Lord to speak further and offer a clear direction.

Sri Bhagavan ubacha:
Hantya tae kathayishyami divya hi aatma bibhutayah.
Pradhanyatah kurushreshtha na asti antah bistarasyah mae. (G. 10/19)
Sri Krishna said to Arjuna, Now I shall tell you, my conspicuous divine glories, there is no limit to my magnitude indeed.

Impressed by the sincerity of Arjuna, Lord Krishna opened up to explain to him the infinite ways of God's revelation to the human world. God's revelation isn't limited to the period of living creatures, but rather continues through the ongoing nature of beings formed by human activities within the world. When God himself mentions this in explicit terms, it is a total mention. In the real sense of the term, God's revelations have to be understood in the context of the world and in terms of human conditions. Human conditions do vary with respect to the static things. It changes with the dynamism generated within.

Aham aatma gurdakeshah sarva Bhuta aashaya sthitah.
Aham aadih cha madhyacha bhutanam antah evacha. (G. 10/20)
Arjuna, I am the universal self-seated in the hearts of all beings, so I alone am the beginning, the middle and the end of all beings.

Lord Sri Krishna mentions in the beginning about his presence in the cave of the heart of individuals. The Supreme is present in the cave of the heart of every individual as the atman in the living form. The onset of creation and its continuation would be maintained in a way that remains away from the empirical identity of forms of human existence. Lord is not only the cause of the creation, but at the same time, when that comes to an end, it's also through the absorption of the presence of Lord in the context of the world. It is thus his embodied presence that he remains present throughout the pathways and passage of time over the current of events and incidents happening in the world. A world of humans is a world with the presence of God. However, God's presence here is in the form of the entities in the world with an inbuilt spirit of God.

The whole universe is a manifestation of God. All objects comprised therein are generally the manifestation of the glory of God on Earth. The glories of God are thus spread throughout the world of the creation. The story and majesty of God are spread out in all aspects and directions in the creation. With reference to the most prominent divine consciousness, the creation continues.

Aadityanam aham vishnuh Jyotishanam Ravih Angshumana.
Marichi Marutam asmi Nakshatranam aham sashi. (G. 10/21)
I am the Vishnu among the twelve suns of Aditya, the radiant sun among the luminaries, I am the glowing Marukhs, I am the stars and planets.

It is the most conspicuous element of the creation which represents the governing and guiding objects. It is the luminous objects of the cosmic system. The cosmic power is revealed through the various forms of the creation. It is thus the visible element of the creation that gets into the world of work and obtains the matching recognition of the spirit of God. It is thus the specific manifestation of God and has taken the form of the divine objects. Thus, Lord Krishna mentions that he is Aditi himself. However, he is revealed in the form of Vishnu. He is manifested through the radiant Sun. In the abode of the Sun, he spreads the cosmic energy through radiant illumination. He offers the life-sustaining energy through the Sun.

Vedanam sam vedah asmi Devanam asmi Basavah.
Indriyanam manah cha asmi Bhutanam asmi chetanah. (G. 10/22)
Among the Vedas, I am the Samveda, among the gods, I am Indra, among the organs of perception, I am the senses, I am the mind, and I am the consciousness of a living being.

He is also the glow in the sky, as the billions of luminaries, but especially among the stars in the sky. But his manifestation is soothing and smooth, a representative shining light, especially in the form of the moon. Lord has also expressed his identity as the element of truth that prevails in the world. The supreme truth is identified as the Vedas. He is the truth of the Vedas. Among the four Vedas are the expositions of different types of truth in different ways. The Lord identifies himself with the spirit of the Saam Veda. The Sam Veda is the source of truth that identifies devotion as the principal way of God-realization. In the Saam Veda, the central thought gets revealed in the view as 'Tvat Tvam Ausi'- meaning that flow of devotion is yours; you are identified with the devotee.

Rudranam shankarah asmi cha bittaesho yaksha rahshasam.
Basunam pavakah cha asmi meruh shikharinam aham. (G. 10/23)

Among the eleven Rudras, I am Shiva, among the Yakshas, I am Rakshasa, among the gods of vices, I am Kubera, among the eight Vashus, I am the God of fire, and among the mantles, I am Meru.

Among the four Vedas, he identifies himself as the supreme truth that recognizes the relation between God and his devotee. Gradually, the height is attained when a devotee realizes her or his identity as the inseparable entity with themselves. He identifies himself as having in possession the power of destruction. He declares to be in identity with the yakshas or rakshas. He is the Kubera among all these forms, having thus identified with the material world as well. Lord Krishna says that he represents the Meru Parvatah or the Polar Mountain. He contains and nurtures the climatic balance in the living world.

Purodhasam cha mukhyam mam biddhi Partha Brihaspatim.
Senaninam aham skandah sarasam asi sagarah. (G. 10/24)
Among the priests, Arjuna, I am the sage Brihaspati, among warrior chiefs, I am Kartikeya, and I am the reservoir of water, I am the ocean.

Lord Krishna says he is also the guide of wisdom and spiritual personalities. He is a great repository of the world. Among the guiding teachers, he is Brihaspati. He is a part of the knowledge process. In the profile of Brihaspati, he takes up the role of a teacher. Brihaspati is the master of the godly entities and the abode of the gods. Brihaspati infuses the knowledge that opens as the flow of the lives of goodness in the context of the world. He is the teacher and priest in the form of the gods. Lord Sri Krishna identifies himself as the master of masters, and he is blessed with the wishes of the creations of the world. It is thus the material world turned into the basis of the world. As it happens, the world is the abode of the world in the form of the wisdom-centric souls of the human world supported by the gods. It is the realistic idea of the human world that masters of wisdom would continue to support the creation with its own aspect of the revealed truth.

Among the wise persons offering the spread of wisdom in the world of humans. Lord identifies himself as the sage offering teaching to the world of learners. He considers Vrigu as the sage who bears the torch of wisdom of the world and spreads the truth of the Vedas among the aspirants of truth. Bhrigu is the teacher who used to spread the message of God in various forms and the transcendence.

Maharshinam Bhriguh aham gitam asmi ekam auksharam.
Yajnanam japah yajnayoh asmi sthabaranam himalayah. (G. 10/25)
Among the great seers, I am Bhigu, I am the words, I am the sacred words, Om, among the sacrifices, I am the japa, and among the immovables, I am the Himalayas.

The great sages of the world are those who have served the truth of the world as supported by the world of humans; thus, the Lord would identify himself as one of the great sages. Bhrigu, as the teacher among them, would offer the message of God in the context of the spread of creation. The supreme truth that identifies with human selves as the power that transcends the boundary of time, as the effective personality endowed with supernatural power. The truth is not at all bounded by the limits of time, space and the elements of personalities. It is thus the effective power that governs as the driving force, and the fragments of truth that make it to the resurgence of divinity in the world.

Ashvathah sarva brikshanam Devarshinam cha Naradah.
Gandharbanam chitrarathan siddhanam kapilo munih. (G. 10/26)
Among the trees, I am the Ashwata, among the celestial sages, I am Narada, Gandharvas, and Chitravatara, among the Siddhas, I am the Kapila.

Among the mountains, the Lord puts himself in the identity of the polar mountain, the Meru. Similarly, among the trees, he identifies himself as the other form of the banyan tree. It is the fig tree with the scientific name *Ficus religiosa*. It is the tree which is termed the medical holy tree. The fig tree is the ruler of the trees in the forest. Lord Krishna declared himself the king of trees. According to the study of Ayurveda, the *ficus religiosa* is beneficial from a medical point of view. Its leaves, fruits and barks are all good for the lives of all creatures, offering the benefits of the trees in human life.

Ashvanam Uchhei shravanam biddhi mam amrita udbhavam.
Aeiravatam gajendranam Narayanan cha nara adhipatim. (G. 10/27)
Among the horses, no need to be the celestial horse, I am the *ucheishrabha* among the mighty elephants, Aeirabata, I am among the elephants, among the men, the King.

The fig tree is a provider of natural cure to different ailments in the human body, particularly like purifying blood containing phlegm, wind and bile, removing burning feel in the body out of nervous disorder or the endocrine imbalance, dropsy, vomiting, want of appetite, poisoning cough, hiccup, remittent fever, bruise in the heart, disease of the nose, dry spreading itches, worms, leprosy, sore on the skin, a burn and so on. All these are supported and remedied by using different parts of the fig tree.

Aayudhanam aham bajram dhenunam asmi kamadhuk.
Prajanan cha asmi kandarpah sarpanam asmi Basukih. (G. 10/28)
Among weapons, I am the thunderbolt, among the cows, I am the celestial cow, Kamdhenu, I am the genetic passion, I am the lease of proclamation, among serpents, I am Vasuki.

The Vedic sages used to prefer sitting beneath the fig tree for meditation for a long duration. The air and the environment around created by the fig tree are different from those in other places. Beneath the fig tree, even standing or sitting itself makes a lot of difference. It helps humans to breathe better, works on the skin, leaves, root, green branches, flowers, fruits and overall, the quality of air created by a big fig tree around it. It is the effect of this tree and its organs that helps the person a lot. Lord Krishna identifies himself with this tree and, in turn, offers the welfare role for the elements of creation. It is thus a very special revealed entity of the creation which provides the creative curative and supportive force for the well-being of humans in the world.

Among the horses, the Lord identifies himself as the 'Vccaihshrava', the celestial horse that used to serve the gods. And among the elephants, he is the Gajendra or the king of elephants, serving the world. Gajendra is also the Airavata, the king of elephants serving the king of the Vedas, Indra. Among men, he is identified with the king of the world and the king of kings.

> *Anantah cha asmi naganam Barunah yadasam aham.*
> *Pitrinam Aryamah cha asmi yamah samyatanam aham.* (G. 10/29)
> Among Nagas, special serpents, I am the serpent god, Ananta, and I am Varuna, the lord of water, among the names, I am Aryama, among the rulers, I am Yama, among the culminations.

The horse king Vccaihshrava was identified as the horse power of divinity at the point of the Samudra Manthan, the churning of the ocean. The Supreme makes everything special about it. In all realms and segments of life, God is revealed in the pinnacle, and he makes the qualities of lives and entities very special by virtue of attempting perfection for it. Whenever it attains perfection, the factors reach greatness. It's the best element of any segment. Among weapons, he is the thunderbolt of Indra; among the cows, he is the celestial cow, the Kamdhenu, and among the serpents, he is the Vasuki, the king of the serpents. He is manifested through the best lives and the best among the entities. Lord is the pivotal identity of any of the segments of life on Earth.

> *Prahladah cha asmi daityanam kalah kalayatam aham.*
> *Mriganam cha Mrigendra aham bainateyah cha Pakshinam.* (G. 10/30)
> Among the demons, I am the great devotee, Prahlad; among the reckons, I am the shrine; among the quadruplets, I am the lion; among the animals, among the birds, I am Garuda.

Among the creatures of the water world, he is the Ananta Nag. He is the essential entity in the form of gods and always in relation to the activities of the world. He resembles the form of Yama among the rulers and Aryama among the 'pitri' selves. Among the sacred cows, he is present more in the entity of the Kamdhenu, the provider of plenty. He takes the rule of the continuity of races through Kandarpah. He is present through all the forces of the gods. He is thus embodied in the spirit of goodness in all. Among different forms of God, he is the Lord of all good thoughts and good deeds. He is present in all entities in an invisible form to provide goodness. Among the world of demons, he is Prahlad, a great devotee.

Pavanah pavatam asmi Ramah shastra bhutanam aham.
Rishanam makarah cha asmi shrotasam asmi Jahnavi (G. 10/31)
Among the fast movers, I am the wind; among the warriors, I am Sri Rama; among the fishes, I am the alligator; among the rivers, I am the Ganga.

Among the demons, Prahlad is godly. A great devotee himself, though born of a demon king, Prahlad was an ardent devotee of God and finally could spread the goodness of thoughts in the form of practising and spreading devotion. As such, God gets revealed through him. Lord says he represents time and keeps pace with the rhythm of life. Among the deer, he is the king deer. Among four-footed, the king lion. Among flying beings or birds, he is the Garuda, the divine bird flying fastest.

Sarganam aadih antaho cha madhyam cha eva aha Arjuna.
Adhyatma vidyanam badah Prabatamaa ham. (G. 10/32)
Arjuna, I am the beginning, middle, and end of creation of all knowledge, I am the knowledge of the soul, I am the knowledge of everything, I am all the resonant.]

Lord Krishna mentions that he is the form and the shakti of Pavan among the swift movers. He is the Supreme present in elemental form as the element of consciousness. He is the atman. As wind and air, he maintains life with the right kind of support for the lives on Earth. The wind makes the inauguration cling. It serves the act of purification and helps lives to sustain. The plant kingdom, animal kingdom, and human world all depend on the right mix and flow to maintain things in their respective forms and ways.

Lord Krishna mentions his idea and reckons the fact of his presence in the atmosphere at different levels of its presence. Lord himself is embodied in the lower middle and upper atmosphere in the context of the void. Lord remains present at the time now in all creatures. He was there amid the creatures from each of the lives.

Lord explains his presence and perpetuation. Therefore, his presence understands the work and the promise of God. When it comes to learn and teaching, the act of communication is not on to verbal exposition. He resembles the first letter of the alphabet. He is therefore known as 'Akshara Brahma'. This concept begins with the letter 'A' and represents the continuous flow of knowledge cultivated through wisdom.

Aksharanam aukaroh asmi dvindoh samasikah asya cha.
Asham eva akshayah kaalo dhata aham vishvatoh mukhah. (G. 10/33)
Among the sounds presented by various letters, I am 'au', the first alphabet, different kinds of compounds, I am the grammar, and the cumulative compound, I am the endless time, and I am the streamer of all, my face is revealed to all sides.

I am the first letter of any language among all the letters composed in the words of the language; among the compound words I am that with the meaning of salutation; I am the Supreme abode containing the flow of time from its origin and I do preserve this creation over the infinite span of time and maintain the uniqueness of each element within the framework of the eternal time. Universally, the factors of the universality process the particularly going through a stage. I am the dispenser with faces being omnipresent.

Mrityuh sarbaharah cha aham udbhavah cha bhabishyatam.
Kirtih srivak cha narinam smriti medhah dhritih kshamah. (G. 10/34)
I am the all-destroying great emulators of all origin, and shall be born of femininities. Among all, I am the woman as Kirti Sri, Vak, Smriti, Medha, Dhriti, Kshama.

It is the linguistic grammar that recognises the Aukarah as the first initiation. 'Aukaroi vai sarvah vakah-' the *Aeiteriya Aranyaka* mentions this. There are four compounds according to the Sanskrit grammar. These are the compounds agreed upon according to the linguistic aphorisms of Sanskrit. Four different compounds are: (a) Avyayibhaba, (b) Tatpurusa, (c) Bahubrihi and (d) Dvandva. Avyayibhaba is important in terms of the content driven by the essence of the content. Lord Krishna says that the spell of the extinction of the end of one era or lives brings in the spell of the others. He is the embodied new life and at the same time the end of lives through the culmination of Karma.

Brihad sam batha samnam Gayatri chhandasam aham.
Masanam marga shirshoh cha ritunam kusum aakarah. (G. 10/35)
Likewise, among shrutis that can be sung, I am Vrihat Sama, among the Vedic hymns, I am the famous Gayatri, I am the 12 months, I am the Hindu calendar, I am the Margashishya, I am the spring season, among all seasons.

Lord also says that all the feminine and motherly qualities of life that is representative of the Lord in the context of the world. He represents Kirti, Sri, Vak, Smriti, Medha, Dhriti and Kshama. He represents the mother form of glory, prosperity, speech, intelligence, steadfastness, tolerance and forbearance. God himself talks about the profoundness of the qualities, the collective song of the 'Udgeet' of the Sam Veda that creates a chhanda in the mind of the devotees. It is the chhanda or the vibration of the Gayatri Mantra that actually elevates the materially conscious mind to the spiritual realm, which eases the thoughts of God.

> *Dyutam chhalayatam asmi tejah tejashvinam aham.*
> *Jayoh asmi byabasayah asmi sattwam sattwabatam aham.* (G. 10/36)
> I am gambling among deceitful practices, I am the glory among glorious, I am the victory of the victorious, I am resolved to the salute, I am the goodness of the good.

So, when the spiritual awakening occurs in the life of the devotee, it is the primordial spiritual elegance of the devotee that attempts to make things happen. Whatever the best course of things the devotee may think of is the basis of god's stepping into the world of thoughts and words. The Lord has expressed that he remains with the devotee's awareness. Even when a person is engaged in a profession that is different from the logical awareness and ways of thinking of ordinary persons, the sincerity of purpose in the functional approach and honesty in discharging duties make the task of the spiritually oriented person very simple. Otherwise, a simple transaction in the context of the world would make the scheme of things very different from that of the pattern of most of us. God is present in all living things and objects. He is equal to all good, bad or the mid-category of lives. Through his presence, he inspires all to either turn to goodness or enhance its goodness. A deceitful envoy may feel his presence glorious within the core of the glory, the victory of the victorious and the goodness of the good in the world.

Lord Krishna identifies his presence among the clans of Vrishnis or the particular clan of Kshatriyas, the warrior class. he places his role identified with Krishna among the sages. He identifies the role and profile of Vyasa: Sage Vyasa, with his enormous contribution to the world of truth through the unfolding of the core truth of divinity. Among the clan of Pandavas, he identifies that of the profile and form of Arjuna and among the poets as Ushana, a poet for his Wisdom poems.

> *Brishninam vasudevah cha asmi Pandavanam Dhananjayah.*
> *Mununam api aham vyasah kabinam ushanah kabih asmi.* (G. 10/37)
> I am Krishna among the brahmins, I am Arjuna among the sons of Manu, I am Vyasa among the sages, I am Shukracharya among the wise people.

The primordial source of wisdom and knowledge resides in the identity and revealed form of Lord Shiva, the Lord of lords. The first vision of the Supreme Mother manifests in the form of Mother Uma, Haimavati. She had revealed her identity to the lives of the world. Indra had the chance to have the vision of the Supreme Mother Durga in the form of Uma Haimavati in the upper sky. However, this vision was possible even for Indra, the king of gods, only when he could thoroughly set aside ego and develop a mind of faith, dedication, and love for the supreme god. He was the forebearer of the truth of the Supreme God's revelation to the world that he has taken direct support of the elements of the world. God is thus revealed through the ages and the recurring spirit of wisdom for the creation.

> *Dandah damayatam asmi nitih asmi jigivatam.*
> *Mounam cha eva asmi gahthanam jnanam jnanavatam aham.* (G. 10/38)
> I am the subduing power of the rulers, I am the righteousness of those who seek to conquer, I am of all things to be kept secret, I am the custodian of the form of the essence, I am the wisdom of the wise.

The rulers of the world have always loved the principles of rule. In this context, the ruler would thus be returning to the principles of good rules. The ruler shall turn into a benevolent person and shall extend the spirit of goodness. It is the spirit of goodness of God that spreads into the areas across the world to make it a better place in the world. As the divine ruler would have the rule with righteous principles, Danda or the law of control would turn into the principle of the human world, spreading the spirit of divinity.

> *Yat cha api sarva bhutanam bijam tat aham Arjuna.*
> *Na tat asti bina yat syan maya bhutam characharam.* (G. 10/39)
> Arjuna, I am even that who is the seed of all man, for there is no creature, moving or unmoving, who exists without meaning, and without me.

The Lord is the intrinsic seed of all seeds present in the world. He is the invisible content in the seed of seeds with the blessed attribute of the world. He is the core truth of all forms of truth in the world. He is the focus of the holistic truth to turn it into the spirit of perpetual truth. Life then turns into the life of a divine entity who lives by the principles of righteousness always.

> *Na tae asti mama divyanam bibhutinam parantapah.*
> *Esha tu uddeshatah proktoh bibhutae bistarah maya.* (G. 10/40)
> Arjuna, there is no limit to my divine manifestation; it is only a brief description by me of the extent of my glory.

The elaboration of the glories of God is really infinite. As he mentions that God's manifestation in different forms and abodes is infinite. He has mentioned only a few among that infinite span of things. Thus, each element of glory that is possessed by a person is, in a way, the revelation of God in its own way. The presence of God in the lives of individuals is the total presence at the core of the heart of individuals. Every living being, every creature, thus makes it to the core of the character of the person. The mind of the individual makes a difference in it through imposing the spirit of the lives of the creatures in the creation.

Yad yat Bibhuti mat sattavam srimad urjitam eva bah.
Tatto devabo gaccha tvam mama tejah amsha sambhavam. (G. 10/41)
Every such being as is glorious, brilliant and powerful knows that to be a part of the manifestation of my glory and my presence in the world.

Lord Krishna finally reveals to Arjuna that wherever a good attribute or somewhat goodness is found, God in his design of things would reveal through that life. As the atman, he is present in all his presence is unique and the same everywhere. He is present in all living all together, thus the presence of the divine in life as the real essence of the truth in the world of creation. It is the divine truth that involves the intrinsic goodness of God in the world.

Athava bahuni etani kim jnatena tava Arjuna.
Vishtavya aham idam kritshnam ekamshena sthitah jagat. (G. 10/42)
What will you gain by knowing all these in detail, Arjuna? It is sufficient to say that I rule this entire universe by reflection of my yogic powers.

The creation is the contribution of the essential grace of God to the souls that have come in touch with the empirical soul of individuals in the world. However, a person who is fully convergent with the divine truth and has thus attained true devotion attains the realization. Lord Krishna finally declares:

'*Narah tvam ausi durdharsha Hari Narayanah hi aham. Kaalae lokam imam Prapti*
Nara Narayana aavritah. Anantah Partha mattva tvam tat aashryoh tvam tathaeva cha.
Nah abayarah antarah shakyam veditum Bharatarshav.'
(Mahabh. Vana pras. XII. (46-47)
God is present here in the form of the god incarnate. He is the god embraced human personality. God is present in the abode of man; he is present in a form and is supported by the greatest warier. He has embraced the entire creation and rescued the human society from the clutches of the unrighteous elements.

Lord says, "O Arjuna, you are always indomitable, none can defeat you. You are the divine man and I am Narayana myself. At one point of time, we descended as Nara Sage and Narayana Sage. So you are none other than me and I am no other entity than you. Oh best of Bharat clan, know for certain that no one can discriminate between you and me. Tvat Tvam Ausi".

14 Man Sees God

Empirical in the Infinite Cosmic Ocean of Transcendence

Choice in Life

The cosmic dance of Nataraj Shiva has put in motion the ticking of time in the empirical world of the living creatures. Our world of humans is a part of that cosmic dance of the Supreme over the spread of the facts of the flow of lives on Earth and the flow of time to initiate the intrinsic cause of all transactions: seeding, dynamism, blossoming, fruits of actions and maintaining the flow of the thoughts-perceptions-emotions-realizations and the intrinsics of lives. Every beat of rhythm that the entire super cosmic system partakes in is the factor initiating the cause of life and discovering the purpose of this creation. An eternal question that had vibrated through the lives of the Vedic sages from the dawn of civilization was 'why this life and the world?', 'What are the intrinsic relations between lives on Earth through the pathways of creation?', 'What is the right cause to initiate and take life forward?', 'What should be the final objective and orientation of lives lived?' and many more such fundamental questions in life. The sages of the Vedic civilization shaped human destiny by identifying the cause of life and guiding it along a divine path. The wish of God for the fulfilment and the journey of the creation is understood through the meditative process of realization and many other ways. The Vedic mind was inclined to achieve the realization of God in his macro-existence of as such the micro-existence and the subtle are the eternal spirit fused in the empirical aspect of truth that makes its presence in the lives on Earth. Realization, as a process, occurs through a meditative way but the chance to have God in the life in the empirical context is always subject to the gift of God. It is through his grace that one can think of coming to the close spirit of God. God is omnipresent. He makes his way from the position of an ordinary life to that of a special one. The speciality is earned by the intrinsic orientation of the person. The intrinsic orientation that a person has is important from the perspective of things of the world. It is thus the essence of every inherent orientation and approach that makes life develop a sharp inclination to its making. A touch of God in life allows and pushes life to become more inward-seeking than otherwise.

God is an outsider to a non-believer and a constant companion to a believer. The story of Narada in his early childhood is important to keep in mind. As the scriptures mention, Narada, a boy of less than ten years of age, had lost his mother. The boy and his mother used to live in a forested area together. His mother used to work in households and monasteries for a livelihood. One night, it so happened that his mother was bitten by a venomous snake and died from poisoning. When she was on the verge of breathing last, she had mentioned to Narada that his maternal uncle is always present and will be available to support whenever he is called urgently. Narada realized his mother was gone, prompting him to immediately seek his dear maternal uncle rather than wait. The boy then went out, crying aloud in his search. Soon, he met his uncle, but by then, he was unconscious from exhaustion. To his delight and relief, when he gained consciousness, Narada found his maternal uncle holding his hand, helping him stand up and go on in his life, urging him to initiate a life of surrender to God. The situation was such that Narada started realizing that this way of life. With the charms of assuming the position of a devotee, he consecrated before the maternal uncle. However, the uncle had his bid to give farewell. When he was about to go off, Narada, the boy, asked him about the next chance to meet. To this, the uncle pointed at the fig tree and said, through his own endeavours of meditation, spiritual practices, God's vision would again be with him after thousands of lives, as many as the number of leaves of the fig tree. Alternatively, if he gets elements of true love for God in his life, then the grace of God will be present as a constant flow of good things, like a waterfall carrying the message of God in life, in continuity. Narada said, in turn, that the other ways of reaching God, like meditation and spiritual practices, are not known to him. He had no knowledge about the practices of spirituality. However, he believes what his mother had said to him is true, and he would follow that way in life. He held a firm belief in the existence of his maternal uncle. Also, he believed strongly that the maternal uncle was not only a momentary presence, but whenever he needed his support and visualization of him, his uncle would be there.

Realisation

Arjuna had that rare mix of fortune in life, which culminated in being in the constant company of God. As Arjuna was briefed by Lord Sri Krishna about the different dimensions of spiritual practices, he could develop a mind oriented to the spirit of God. Arjuna had initially allowed his worldly mind to remain sensitive to the cause of the world, and be involved himself in the emotional pulls of usual human considerations. Arjuna, here, represents the human sentiment in an ordinary manner. However, the ordinary state of reflections and impacts on the mind is remedied through the process of spiritual instructions, as Lord Krishna had offered to give. Arjuna's journey in spiritual learning had passed through several ways of God-connect or yoga. In the beginning, the spell of depression was countered through the conveying of eternal knowledge of the inner self under the generic title of sankhya yoga or the eternal knowledge of the supreme self, as he prefers to remain unattached, indifferent and concerned about the matrices of life. The ultimate truth of life is expressed thereby. The depression is the state of a deluged mind that is overwhelmed by the foremost factors and facts of existence. It is thus the faith in the words of the mother that impacts life and makes it vibrant in the cause of spiritual attainment in life. The spiritual attainment has been the focus of the empirical life, and has the truth in existence for the living souls in the world. The eternal teaching through sankhya concludes on the immortality of the soul. The true identity of the soul is that in the early phase of living, and that continues to unfold through the spell and process of realization. Emotions, attachments, possession, and a sense of owing in life continue to be futile. Such things are named as God's eternal companions. However, the truth is actually the eternal existence of divinity present in all things, as the very spirit of life. Right action is that which, when viewed through the lens of life's greater vision, contributes optimal energy and factors. However, it is work performed as a righteous duty, free from selfish calculations, that truly shapes a person's life. Selfish work dedicated to a divine cause is the right sense of the term. Lord Krishna explains the different forms of yoga. The jnana yoga refers to the God connect through the ways of wisdom. The wisdom of God is the ultimate wisdom in the context of the living world. It is thus the position of things in the creation that concludes in tune with that of God's spirit to be in the process of understanding the same in life. Realization occurs throughout the process in different forms. Sannyasa yoga or the God connect through the process of renunciation and ascesis. Through the process of purity of mind and systemic process of giving up or selfless activities go for winning realization of God in life. Dhyana yoga, jnana yoga, vijnana yoga, akshara brahma yoga and raaj yoga are among the different ways of God realization which truly prepares the mind of the aspirant to have any other way of life than oriented to God. God helps in understanding the true spirit of life. In order to compare the focus of the situations in the context of the world of thoughts and action it is thus the most important aspect is to inculcate the spirit of God within.

Human Orientation

Man with God now reaches the highest point of the knowledge shared. Lord Krishna has so far taught Arjuna the methods of different yoga, or the God connect, to reach the supreme height of realization of God by men. Some of the areas of yoga or the God connect are of extreme importance to God as well as men on Earth.

> *Arjuna ubacha:*
> *Mat anugrahayaya param guhyam adhyatmam samgnitam.*
> *Yat tvayo uktvam bachana tena moham ayam bigato mamah.* (G. 11/1)

Arjuna said, I convey my sincere regards to you for the most profound words of spiritual wisdom that you have spoken out of your kindness to me. This delusion of mine has entirely disappeared.

Arjuna became happy after Lord Sri Krishna narrated to him the most profound spiritual wisdom, the divine glory of the Lord in terms of his own revelation about his unique identity of him in the world. Arjuna was overwhelmed by the wide and diverse forms undertaken by the Lord. He was most taken up with the lives and forms. He became concerned that the eternal spirit of God is the application of divinely attributes in the life of those who have realized the truth of Brahman, the Supreme, through the process of their spiritual journey. The delusion through depression that had cropped in the mind of Arjuna disappeared through the impact of the yoga of God's revelation. Arjuna now had renewed love and praise for God. It had reinstalled faith and full respect for the Lord, having understood that he is the Supreme on Earth.

Bhaba apayoh hi bhutanam shrutou bistarasah maya.
Tatvah Kamala patraksha mahatma api cha abyam. (G. 11/2)
For Krishna, I have heard from you in detail an account of the evolution and dissolution of being, also your immortal glory.

Arjuna has opened up his mind, expressing to Lord Krishna that the cause of the entire creation was something that alone had the entire strength, energy and perpetuation for the creation. Arjuna had understood that the Lord, the Supreme, is not only the creator but, at the same time, full of care, concern, love and compassion for the creation. He maintains the creation and does not interfere in the process and journey of his creation. A structured and universal principle, as spelt out in the yoga of action, Lord Krishna has explained the principle as that of the governing principle of the level of karma or action.

Evam etad yatha aahuh tvam aatmanam parameshvarah.
Drashtum ichhami tae rupam aeishvaryam purushottamam. (G. 11/3)
Lord, you are precisely what you declare yourself to be, but I long to see your divine form, possessed of wisdom, glory, energy, strength, valour, effulgence, O the Supreme Soul and the Supreme Being. May I have your vision, Krishna?

Arjuna had expressed his realization of Lord Krishna as the Supreme in whom rest all energies, all power, all strength, all knowledge and power, glory of all kinds and effulgence, valour of being the Purushottama, the supreme being. He believed that it was the essence of all these attributes together. Arjuna had developed truth for himself and the world as well. Though he had also shown the impact of this vision of the cosmic identity of God, Arjuna now had the courage and power to fight the war. But he was curious to know further about the Lord on Earth.

> *Manyaese yadi tat ichchhkyam mauya drashtum iti prabhu.*
> *Yogeshvarah tatoh mae tvam darshayah aatmam avyomah.* (G. 11/4)
> Krishna, if you think that it can be seen by me, then O Lord of Yoga, reveal to me your imperishable form.

Having developed such strength of mind, Arjuna now approaches Lord Krishna to be merciful to him and reveal God's cosmic presence. He requested Lord Krishna, mentioning the real cosmic identity. This identity is the revelation of the Lord. It can be explained only by him and no one else. On the other hand, he was very curiously interested in having the direct vision of God's own reality vis-a-vis the creation from the onset of it, through the journey of life and existence.

> *Sri Bhagavan ubacha:*
> *Pashyah mae Partha Rupani shataha shatah sahasrashah.*
> *Nanabidhani divyani nana varnah aakritanih cha.* (G. 11/5)
> Lord Sri Krishna says, Arjuna, behold, presently my manifold, multifarious divine forms of various periods and shapes and their hundreds and thousands, you can see me now.

Now, Lord Krishna formally opens strongly with his conveying of the spirit of divinity in the creation. He begins by saying that he is present in the elemental identity of his creations, past, present, and future. Lord Krishna, on seeing this, may hear the cosmic phase. Lord Krishna had said that millions, billions and trillions of human and other forms and creatures, and the universe in a way would be seen in the new phase of the creation. Arjuna would now perceive elements of vision previously unseen and unknown to anyone, for he would be equipped with Krishna's cosmic presence.

Lord Krishna now invites the attention of Arjuna to his continued presence of the spirit of the Divine among the cosmic luminous objects. He is the light of the heavens. He is the light of life, and at the same time, he represents the universal spirit and the cosmic energy. The godly dimensions present in the universe are revealed in a sequence of things that are connected.

> *Pashyah Aadityan Basunah Rudranih Aashvinih Marutauh tatha.*
> *Bahuni audrishtah purbani pashyah aashcharyanih Bharatah.* (G. 11/6)
> Behold in me, Arjuna, the twelve sons of Aditi, the eight Vashus, eleven Rudras, two Ashinikumars and the forty-nine Maruts, and witness all the more wonderful forms never seen and known before.

Lord Krishna says to Arjuna, the creation has offered various types and identities of lives in the continuity and flow of the eternal existence in the form of different sets of creations. It is all at the same flow of the eternal time through the period now, which Arjuna might observe in the Divine. The presence of things in the realm of the empirical factors of the world, in such a situation, gets into the process of life in the world of things. It is thus the spirit of the cosmic force that upholds the features of uniqueness of lives. It is the fundamentals of the flow of life that work in the process of worldly transactions. The identity of each cosmic element in the world, the gods residing in heaven and the actions of the world were the principal aspects of life in the current of affairs.

> *Ihah ekasthaham jagat kritsnam pashyahaadya sacharacharam.*
> *Mamah dachae Gudakeshah yat anyahad drashtum ichchhasi.* (G. 11/7)
> Arjuna, witness, as concentrated within this body of mine, the entire creation consisting of both the animate and inanimate beings and whatever else you desire to see.

Lord Krishna explains that the form of the Supreme is universal in this context and contains all different varieties of lives and the material objects of the world. It is thus the effective use of the realistic process which supports the consciousness spread across the entire set of things in the world. The entire creation is contained in the broad infinite extent of the form of God, the Purushottama, the supreme reality. Arjuna receives the boon of the realization that all different forms are infused into the same form, which appears human. It is thus the way of visualizing the ultimate truth that brings into life the empirical reality in the context of the flow of human consciousness.

Vision Gifted

> *Na tu mam shakyasae drashtum aunena eva sva Chakshushah*
> *Divyam dadami tae chakshuh pashyah mae yogah ishvaram.* (G. 11/8)
> But surely you cannot see me with these human eyes of yours, therefore I bow straight to you, the divine eye. With this now you can behold, you can see my divine power of yoga.

Concentrated within the body and the revealed form of the Lord, it is thus the embodied presence of the Lord that creates things to make a difference in the realm of the usual flow of life. A variety of lives, good or bad, is the essence of the flow of lives within the spirit of divinity. A wide range of the infinite number of forms that exist in the world work as the fundamentals of the lives or events of the universe. Cosmic forms do not only comprise the illumined objects like the Sun, the Moon, stars and other important bodies of the world. It includes all lives in essence. Each one forms a part of the supreme truth.

> *Sanjay ubacha:*
> *Evam uktvah tatoh rajan maha yoga Ishvaram Harih.*
> *Darshayamasah Parthayoh paramam rupam Ishvaram.* (G. 11/9)

Sanjaya says, My Lord, having spoken thus, Sri Krishna, the supreme master of yoga, forthwith revealed to Arjuna his supremely transcendental divine form.

In the design of God, the factors that have actually grown in the realm work as the basic pillar of the truth of life. The infinite and vast ocean of the revealed world becomes the spirit of divinity in the form of life in the world. It is thus the introductory mention of the Lord's infinite expansion of truth. This was an imperative to show a glimpse of the entire contents of the universe, which Lord Krishna explained to Arjuna.

> *Auneka baktra nayanam auneka audbhutam darshanam.*
> *Aunekah divya aabharanam Divyo aunekah divya udyata*
> *aayudham.* (G. 11/10)

Arjuna saw the supreme form of God, possessing many mouths, eyes, presenting many a wonderful sight, it is clad in many divine ornaments, yielding many affluent divine weapons.

Sanjaya thus started explaining further what exactly had formed the basics of the larger truth of the universe. In the series of descriptions, Lord Krishna started off by mentioning that Purushottama had the identity of the sum total and much more, as understood and witnessed in the entire cosmic creation. This has never been seen by anyone before, and that of the Supreme in the form of the eternal divinity in the lives of all individuals, in essence, in the abode of the God, the Supreme.

The Divine is the creator of all wealth and resources. He is the creator and owner of all the wealth of the world. But he is not involved in enjoying the possession of any of it. Anyone, perhaps, gets dressed up with the resources and wealth of the world at God's will.

> *Divyo maalyah ambaram adharam divyo gandhah aunulepanam.*
> *Sarva aashcharyamayam divam Anantam visvotomukham.* (G. 11/11)

Wearing divine garlands and crows, and seated all over the divine sandal-paths and all the wonders of the infinite and having faces of all sides.

The view of the Divine, which is adorned by the humans, is that when all the goodness, all the beauties of the world, are added to the form of God made visible to Arjuna. Arjuna eventually saw the unique form of God dressed in all the most precious ornaments of the world. In the cosmic body and identity of God, an infinite number of luminous objects are ordinarily visible by humans in ordinary vision. His forms that are especially known, one each as unique, to the devotees and had appeared together in one place when Arjuna, with the power of divinely gifted eyes of vision, saw the cosmic revelation of the Lord. It was blessed with the effulgence of the universe that gets revealed at a specific time.

Divi surya sahashrasyah bhaveda yugapad utthitah.
Yadih bhah sadrishih sah syad bhasyah tasyah mahatmanah. (G. 11/12)
If there be thousands of thousands of suns bursting forth all at once in the sky, even that would hardly be like the splendour of the mighty Lord.

Sanjay continued to brief the scenario to his king, Dhritarashtra. He had the boon from God of having developed distant vision, and also the power to hear every beat of sound from somewhere far away by a huge length of space and distance. He was narrating to King Dhritarashtra the incidents and explaining the scenario to the king. Sanjay had such a televisionary power that he could obtain all minute details of the target scene. It was the scenario of the Mahabharata war at the battlefield of Kurukshetra. Lord Krishna was telling Arjuna the words of divine wisdom in this context of the war. After having shared with Arjuna the conceptual basis of true spiritual wisdom, Lord Krishna had developed a very special vision of his cosmic form.

Tatra ekastham jagat kritsnam prabibhaktam auneketha.
Aupashyat tat deva devasya sharirae Pandavah tatha. (G. 11/13)
Arjuna had visualized that in the cosmic abode of the Lord all kinds of human relations in his earlier lineage, the different forms of Gods and other creations of the world were present in their respective forms.

Arjuna was fortunate in getting to see the identity of God in the context of the creation. As such, he was trying to garner the truth of the creation as the gift of God to the world of humans. It was the compassionate view of the Lord that he had considered the request and prayer of Arjuna to reveal his overall cosmic reality. Lord Krishna had revealed this to Arjuna. First time in the history and records of spirituality in the world, the devotee was blessed with the direct vision of the overall cosmic reality to a devotee and he himself explained the same.

Tatah sa vishmaya aabishtoh hrishtaromah Dhananjayah.
Pranamya shirasa Devam kritanjalih bhashatah. (G. 11/14)
Then Arjuna, full of wonder and with the hair standing on and, reverentially bowed his head to the divine Lord and with joined palms said this thing, thus worship.

Sanjay described the Lord's revelation as a luminous brightness so intense that even thousands of suns combined couldn't match its brilliance, truly ascending to a new level upon witnessing the power of the Lord's illumined presence. Arjuna thus witnessed the power and strength of the Divine. He experienced, with all his sensory organs, the consolidated presence of the entire cosmic creation in one place. He also experienced that whatever could be thought of, and again, anything beyond thoughts or cognitive understanding, was exposed in the Lord.

Wisdom Flows

> *Arjuna ubacha:*
> *Pashyami Devah aham tava deva dehae*
> *Savam tatha bhutah bishesha samgan.*
> *Brahmanam Isham kamala aasanashtham*
> *Rishim cha sarva anuragang cha divyam.* (G. 11/15)
> Arjuna said, Lord, I behold within your body all gods and hosts of different beings. Rama, throned on his lotus feet, Shiva and Rishis and the celestial serpents.

Arjuna presents his respect and prayer with folded hands and starts describing what he was witnessing. Arjuna mentioned to Lord Krishna that he was viewing all the forms of God in the form of Lord Krishna. He faced that the Supreme was in his form, being thoroughly absorbed in the parts of the Lord in the context of the world. In other words, all possible expositions of his trillions of elemental creations were combined in the void or space. The wonderful and majestic sight of the Lord was full of the wonderful creations of his will to make the world divine.

Arjuna goes on describing what he was witnessing; this revelation of the Lord, the billions, trillions of faces, mouths, heads, arms, legs, eyes, and ears had been with him in the context of these visions.

> *Aunekah eva bahuh udarah baktra netram*
> *Pashyami tvam sarvatoh ananta rupam*
> *Na antaham na madhyam na punah tava aadim*
> *Pashyami viswarupah.* (G. 11/16)
> O Lord of the universe, I see you endowed with numerous arms, various mouths and eyes and having innumerable forms extended to all sides. O Lord, manifested as you are in the form of the universe, I see now that you are beings, not the middle, not the end itself.

Arjuna saw in this exposition of the Lord that the manifestation continues in the areas of all living creative forces and of the elements of the universe. The formations of all the creatures of the world, and known to be the all-pervading forces, were also present in the form of the Lord. Having revealed the innumerable forms of the creation, he was the fortunate being in the form of a human scale in the world of creation to have the spirit in one place as a consolidated revelation of the Divine in the context of the world. Arjuna understood the fundamental power of the divine self in terms of his being eternal, infinite, timeless and omnipresent.

Kiritinam gadinam chakrinang cha
Tejah raashim sarvatoh diptimayam antam.
Pashyami tvam duh nirikshmayam samastad
Dipti aunala aurka dyutim prameyaam. (G. 11/17)

I see you endowed with diamonds, diadems, mesh, discursive muscles, splendour growing all around, having the brilliance of blazing fire of the sun, hard to gaze at and immeasurable in all directions.

The cosmic vision viewed by Arjuna was not only pleasant but vast in the power of the entire space. The brilliance he embodies provides him with one of the most comprehensive ways to spread the message, as he truly understands the revealed reality. The Sun, the Moon and the entire range of stars not only offer illumination but also remain as the infinite ocean of light and energy. Living creatures reveal the power of illumination and the energy of the Supreme Divine. The Lord carries him down from the place of the divine force on Earth. Arjuna was not only overwhelmed but had developed a full, concentrated view of God.

Tvam auksharam paramam veditavyam
Tvam ausya viswashasya param nidhana.
Tvam avyaha shashawata dharma goptah
Sanatanah tvam purusho matoh mae. (G. 11/18)

You are the supreme, indestructible, worthy of being known. You are the ultimate refuge of the universe. You are again the protector of the useless, this righteousness. I consider you to be an eternal and imperishable being.

Now, Arjuna folded his hands to offer pranam to Lord Krishna in the way the sages of the Vedas with God-realization used to do. He thought of the pure and supreme truth in God and tried to explore the prospective truth to get further revealed. He started explaining and uttering the words of the mantra to offer his consecration to God. Arjuna said, 'You are the indestructible, the supreme truth. You need to be realized and known first. He said of God as the ultimate refuse of the world'. He continues mentioning that God is the protector of everyone. He is the protector of the truthful cultures, traditions, and religions.

Na aadih Madhya antam ananta viryam
Ananta vahum Shashi Suraya netram.
Pashyami tvam dipta hutashanah bakram
Svatejasa viswam idam tapah antam. (G. 11/19)

I see you without beginning, middle and end, possessing unlimited prowess and endowed with numberless arms and having the moon, the sun of your eyes and blazing fire of your own mouth and scorching the universe, your radiance.

Arjuna mentions lord Sri Krishna being the *abyay sanatan*, the immutable cosmic being and the eternal provider of truth in life in the world, in the ways that it was the essence of empirical truth in the world. It is the dedication that is the true spirit of the eternal divinity of God.

> *Dyaba prithibyo idam antaram hi vyaptam tvayahi ekena dishascha sarvah*
> *Drishtva iha adbhutam rupam tava ugram tava idam*
> *Lokah trayam prabyathitam mahatamanah.* (G. 11/20)
> The interspace between heaven and Earth and all quarters of the entire field by you alone seeing all these transcendental true forms of yours, your soul, of the universe, all the three worlds, I feel greatly alone.

Arjuna understands the timeless existence in the abode of God. He is truly the continuation of the happenings, and he is the origin, the middle, the true existence. He is also the culmination of all creation. He reveals his eyes as the sun or the moon. His mouth is the one which reveals the words in the world, sweetest of all; again, that mouth devours the erotic and the wrongs.

In the context of the war of the victory of life of those who have the power of the world have all to concede to the factors of the universe and finally get deluged in the flow of life and the flow of the time eternal. All warriors of life have the ultimate destiny of converging to the void of creation.

> *Aumi hi tvam surasamghah vishantih*
> *Kaechit bhitah panjalayah grinavantih*
> *Svashtih tuh iti uktvah maharshih siddha samghah*
> *Stubantih tvam stutibhih pushkalabhih.* (G. 11/21)
> Hosts of gods are entering you and some of them palms joined at you and they are worshipping you, recounting your names and glorious multitudes of the great sages and the attendants and the spiritually attained wisdom people, wise people and let there be peace and it's all extolling you by silent hymns.

Arjuna visualized the cause, continuation and culmination of lives across the span of the universe. In the creation of the Lord, every element in existence shall find its destiny in the cosmic centre of creation. The entire cosmos, being at the wish of God, having been created, finds its own way towards the pathways of individual destiny. In this quest for individual destiny, the ways towards finally reaching out to the ocean of God's truth of the wheeling of life. Each person, in her or his ways and progression in life, creates the destined and redefined focus in the subsequent part of the factors of life. Those who have realized the essence of divine truth in life get to understand the eternal divinity in creation.

Rudrah aadityaa basavoh yae cha Sadhya
Vishvae cha ashvinoh marutoh cha ushmapah cha.
Gandharva yakshma aasurah siddha sangha
Bikshmantae tvam vismitah cha eva sarvae. (G. 11/22)

The 11 yudhis, 12 adityas, 8 vashishthas and sadhakas and the Ashwini Kumaras and 49 Marut, as well as the names of multitudes of Gandharvas, Yakshas, Ashuras, Siddhas, also Vishwapurus, all these gaze upon you in amazement.

Since God has opened up his cosmic infinite form before his chosen devotee Arjuna by the grace of Mahakal, the great creator of time, everything is tuned to the entire space of the cosmic vital. Through the space of the cosmic vital, the entire scenario is now in the scope of spiritual realization of the sages, the entire creation and different plateaus of creation, from each of which the spiritual quest was being fulfilled with this revelation of the Lord. One devotee, Arjuna, was instrumental in having that unfoldment. Arjuna was instrumental in getting the graceful view of the Lord for the world.

Rupam mahat tae bahu baktra netram
Mahabaho bahu baahuh upadam
Bauhu udaram bauhudrangstra karalam
Drishtva lokah pravyathitah tatha aham. (G. 11/23)

Lord, seeing these splendours of your dreadful form and your possessing numerous mouths and eyes, innumerable infinities and uniforms on the organs of the thing, you look so vast, so infinitely vast that I am terror-stricken and it appears terrible.

However, as the Lord had revealed his proper understanding, he was exposed to the spawn of the world. It is thus a phenomenon initiated at the battleground of Kurukshetra as a part of the war of the Mahabharata; his unique and magnanimous form had opened up as a marvel of the creation. Arjuna now sees that Lord Krishna, the single person, is essentially infinite and vast. Arjuna sees billions and trillions of faces, heads, eyes, and ears in Lord Krishna.

Navah sprisham diptam auneka varnam
Vyattva ananam dipta vishala netram
Drishtva hi tvam prabyathita antah aatman
Dhritim na bindami shamam cha vishnoh. (G. 11/24)

Lord, seeing your form reaching the heavens, a thousand multicoloured bodies having their mouths wide open and possessing large flaming eyes, I become frightened and have lost control and find no peace.

Such a magnanimous view, which is infinite times infinite, meaning indeterminate, now opens up infinite dimensions in a physical sense. It revealed to all sages and realized souls of the world as something that breeds fear, and the creation, with all its possessions, comes to know the limits of individual lives and the real infinity that the Lord has bestowed upon them.

> *Drangshtva karalani cha tae mukhani*
> *Drishteva kalah analah sannivani*
> *Dishon a jaanae na labhae cha sharmoh*
> *Prasidoh deveshah jagat nivasah.* (G. 11/25)
>
> Seeing your faces frightful on the front of their abyssal teeth and blazing like the fire of the time of universal destruction, I am utterly bewildered and find no peace. Therefore, have mercy on me, O Lord of the entire creation of the whole of the universe, please have mercy on me.

Arjuna also became a little scared of such an infinite expanse of Lord Krishna, being otherwise used to knowing him as a friend. Arjuna now gets down to offering interactions to Lord Krishna, but as a devotee chosen for the specific purpose of viewing the infinite and eternal cosmic form of the Lord. His billions and trillions of organic forms were actually gifted to his creation to have their own form and actions to live the chosen and cherished life in the universe. Arjuna, the chosen devotee, visualized that.

Arjuna saw the unique condition in the field of war: everyone who had sided with the demonic force of the Kauravas was seen to be having their individual destiny of getting annihilated, and the end of each is converging to the infinite.

> *Aumi cha tvam Dhritarashtrasya putrah*
> *Sarve sahah eva avanipal samghaeh.*
> *Vishmah Dronah sutaputrah tatha ausou cha*
> *Saha asmadiyoih api yodha mukheyih.* (G. 11/26)
>
> All the sons of Dhritarashtra, with a host of two kings, are entering you, Bhishma, Drona and others, Karna.

All the major warriors who have stood against the righteous forces have preordained end to their lives and were finally finished into the void by the Lord himself. The major warriors like Bhishma, Drona, Karna and others all have the feeling and conviction that each of them was a great warrior and undefeated. The king of wrongdoers, Duryadhana, harboured the misguided belief that his formidable power, bolstered by many great war leaders, guaranteed the Kauravas' victory in the war due to their obvious collective strength. It was the basic conviction of king of the Kaurava forces.

> *Vaktrani tae tvaramana vishanti*
> *Drangshta karalani bhayanakani.*
> *Kaechit vilagnah dashan antareshu*
> *Samdrishyantae churniteih uttama augneih.* (G. 11/27)

The principal warriors on the sides as well after rushing head-on into your fearful mouth and looking all over the terrible account of their awesome teeth, some seem stuck up in the gaps between your teeth and their heads that rush.

The vision of sages, has been depicted in the Vedas, as those which are the ultimate truth of this creation. Wisdom is generated with the realization of the supreme truth, as has been opened by Lord Krishna before his chosen devotee Arjuna. When the devotee achieves the realization of God at that moment, the truth of the Divine starts slowly being revealed to him through the process of spiritual practice, when the person attains the condition of samadhi. It is perceived that the selfish calculations of the wrongdoers were much misconceived. Lord Krishna had offered the vision to Arjuna, where it was visible that all these forces were destined to face the end of their lives through terrible processes of death on the field of the war. It was such that they had the personal notion about themselves being perpetually alive and continuing to dominate the forces of honesty.

Yatha nadinam bahavo ambubegah.
Samudram eva abhimukhah dravanti,
Tatha tava aumi naraloka bira
Vishanti vaktrani avivijjalanti. (G. 11/28)
As the mighty extremes of the universe rush towards the sea alone, so do you, so do those warriors of the immortal world enter your flaming mouth.

Arjuna realized that as all the major rivers of the world finally meet their individual destinies of getting connected to the oceans; similarly the lives of infinite number of the creatures are destined to have the end individually or collectively with the finish of the kind of karma that each of them individually or collectively have performed or are in the process of performing. Rivers have their names and individual identities when they remain in the identity of a river, but they lose their identity at the end of their tenured karma and get merged in the vastness of the ocean. The vast and infinite ocean of life thus contains all life forces.

Yatha pradiptam jvalantanm patangh
Vishanti nashayao sammriddha begah.
Tatha eva nashayao vishanti lokah
Tatha api vaktrani sammriddha begah. (G. 11/29)
As mouths rush with great speed into the blazing fire and extinction out of infatuation, even so, all these people are with great rapidity entering your mouths to meet their doom.

The doctrine of karma says, 'as you sow, so shall you reap'. Thus, when the time comes for the culminating assessment, it is the rule of Mahakal,

250 *Rama Prosad Banerjee*

the lord of time and all creations, Lord Shiva sets the principle of reciprocal attainment. Lives thus lived attain the respective return on the works and thoughts maintained in life. The end is pleasant for those who have maintained pathways of goodness. However, those who have sided with wrongdoing will face consequences as inevitable as insects rushing into a fire.

> *Lelihayasae grasamanah samastad*
> *Lokan samagran badanei jaladbhih.*
> *Tejahbhi aapuryah jagat samagraham*
> *Bhasanta ugrah pratipantih vishnou.* (G. 11/30)
> Swallowing through your mouth, blazing all mouths, all through people on all sides, you are breaking your mouths, your lips, O Lord Vishnu, your terrible ways are now devouring the whole universe with their fierce glow and all scorching heat.

The fire accumulates to absorb and engulf in totality the forces of goodness on Earth. The vital power and strength in life then turn around to destroy. It is the vital energy of an infinite number of creatures who get deluged in the ocean of the burning rays of the cosmos to culminate in ashes. However, the writers once made it such that its own source of energy goes back to the world of living souls, providing immense inspiration to live on the pathways of the writer's souls. They are maintained in their memories of noble actions throughout the subsequent phases of living. In a way, Lord Krishna is inducing the living world through Arjuna to maintain righteous principles in life and develop devotion to God in the world.

In the process of attaining realization of God, the devotee finally prays to God for his gracious support so that the end of the domain of realization is reached. In the process, the devotee makes a kind of immersion in the flow of the spirit of life on Earth. Thus, the process concerns the behaviour, character, attitude to life and final fabric of life lived.

> *Aakhayahi mae ko bhaba anugraha rupo*
> *Namah astu devabarah prasidoh.*
> *Vijnatum ichhami bhantim adyam*
> *Na hi prajanami tava pravrittvam.* (G. 11/31)
> Tell me who you are with a form so terrible and my obeisance to you, O best of the gods who be kind to me, I wish to know you, the primaeval being in particular, for I know not you in a real sense. Lord Sri Krishna says.

This vibrant quest in Arjuna's consciousness makes him a representative figure among all participants, uniquely positioned to effectively nurture the growth of the divine spirit within to its logical culmination. In the action and flow of actions, the guiding metric occurs from the focus of the spirit, and thus it is the essence of the orientation of the devotee's mind that would be inclined to the focus, and the essential identity behind the revealed identity of the Supreme. Arjuna has just seen the cosmic span of the form of God in the context of the world. Now he is in a position to understand the deeper paradigm of the divine spirit. Thus, Arjuna is urging God to find the ways to receive the full span of truth.

> *Sri Bhagavan ubacha:*
> *Kaloh asmi lokah kshmaikrit prabriddhoh.*
> *Lokan samahartum ihah pravrittoh.*
> *Ritach api tvam na bhabishyanti sarvae.*
> *Yae na avasthitah pratyanikeshu yodhan.* (G. 11/32)
> I am mighty Kala, I am the time spirit, the destroyer of the world, I am out of the exterminate, these people, even without you, all these warriors are buried in the enemy's camp, must die, they will die of their own karma.

Arjuna made an earnest appeal to Lord Krishna for the full revelation of truth in the interest of realization. Even though he had the love and fortune to have witnessed the cosmic identity of God, Arjuna had a strong urge to hear from the Lord. Being satisfied with the expressed intent of Arjuna, Lord Krishna said of him as the Supreme embodied to perform the act of culmination, also when it turns up in a human form. He expressed that the creation would come to an end of its own culmination. Even if Arjuna does not participate in the war, all the heroes of evil would be annihilated.

> *Tasmat tvam uttishtha yasho labhashva*
> *Jitva shatrun bhukshv rajyam samriddhvam.*
> *Mayeivatae nihatah purvam eva*
> *Nimittvam matram bhavah savyasachin.* (G. 11/33)
> Therefore, do you arise, win glory, conquering fools, enjoy effluent kingdom and the warriors stand already slain by me, and you only are the instruments, Arjuna.

Lord Krishna gave the call of awakening to Arjuna. He said to Arjuna that waging the war himself and achieving victory in that is not only the right choice but also good for earning the fame of victory in war. Lord Krishna mentions that it is a cause of the universal creation that the good and right ultimately win. However, it's not that those kinds of acts depend on individual persons alone to take forward as her or his cause in life.

> *Dronah cha Bhishmah cha Jayadjratah cha*
> *Karnam tathahi anya api yodha biram*
> *Mauyah hastan tvam jahi ma byathisthah*
> *Yudhyasva jetasi raunae saptnanah.* (G. 11/34)
> Do you kill Drona, Bhishma, Jayadrath, Karna and others brave warriors who stand already killed by me, fear not, fight, and you will surely conquer the enemies in the world.

Lord Krishna now specifically takes the names of major and prominent heroes of the evil forces. He mentions that Bhishma, Drona, Karna, Asvatthama and many others who have sided with or supported the wrongdoer king would all be finished. However, Arjuna's act of doing the Lord's work would make him a great and noble hero in perpetuity for generations.

Sanjay ubacha:
Etat shrutva bachanam keshavasya
Kritanjali vepamanah kiritih.
Namaskritva bhuyah ebaha krishna
Sagadgadam bhitabhitah pranamyah. (G. 11/35)

Sanjay said, fearing these words of Bhagavan Keshava, Arjuna, trembling, about to bow his head and folded hands and bowing again and again, extreme terror spoke to Sri Krishna in a choked voice.

Hearing these final words from the Lord, Arjuna became frightened. He offered his pranam, the consecration that makes him dedicate his wisdom, self and the entire identity as a human being. Arjuna now had the prayer offered to Lord Krishna in his totality. As the Lord has said, everything in this world has been preordained, and Arjuna is just the symbol of the entity having done that and thereby will earn the blessings of God.

Arjuna mentioned to Lord Krishna that the world is attracted to the magnanimity of God's presence in the world. The human society realizes him as the God, expressing the attributes of the Divine through his revealed focus to beautify the world.

Arjuna ubacha:
Sthanae Hrishikesha tava prakirtityah.
Jagat Prahrishyati aunurajyatae cha,
Rakshamsi bhitani disho dravanti.
Sarvae namasyanti cha siddhasangah. (G. 11/36)

Arjuna said, Lord, where the universe is exhausted in the field with love and chanting your names, Bhaktas and Gauri, terrified Rakshasas are fleeing in all directions, and all these also Siddhas are going to you.

The sages get the obvious realization of God. When Arjuna was having the vision of the cosmic identity of God, the sages who were of the same period and those having the eternal existence, all had the opportunity to witness the expressed identity of God through their respective pathways of realization. They were all individually offering pranam to God and welcoming the grace of God to their chosen devotees. On the other hand, the demonic people by seeing this terrible scenario exposed by God, got extremely scared. In a simultaneous phenomenon, the holy souls would be pleased and be blessed.

Kasmat cha tae na namaeron mahatman
Gariyasae Brahmanoh api aadikatrae
Ananta devesha Jagat nivashah
Tvam auksharam sad asad tat param yat. (G. 11/37)

O great soul, why should they not know you, you who are the originator of Supreme Truthy, the greatest of the great, O Infinite Lord of Celestials, O abode of the universe, you are that which is existent, shat, you are that which is non-existing, you are also that which is beyond indestructible.

Arjuna had uttered the words of worship to Lord Krishna. At this point, he became conversant with the set of things in this creation where the presence of the Divine was identified in the heart. Arjuna realized that revelation of God is inherent in the facts of life. Lord Krishna's cosmic revelations were a particular force and inspiring energy, immersing thoughts and actions into the facts of incidents and the flow of functions.

Tvam aadi devah purushah puranan
Tvam asya viswasya param nidhanam
Vettwasi vedam cha param cha dhamah.
Tvayah tatam vishvam ananta rupam. (G. 11/38)

You are the primordial, most ancient person, you are the ultimate resort of this universe, you are both the knower and knowable, the highest abode, it is you who pervade the universe, O infinite, assuming endless forms.

Arjuna offers puja or offerings to the Lord by expressing the most respectful dedication to him. He says of the Lord as the creator of the world, as the primordial godly form of life. Arjuna offers prayer to Lord Krishna by saying that He is the primordial form of the Gods, the Divine in the form of humans, the classical form within which the entire creation rests and the ultimate goal and destiny of all lives, as revealed through the infinite and vast form as visualized. Thus, those who have not visualized the forms of life and their infinite existence, stay muted to the sweet blessings of the Lord.

Vayuh Yamah Agnih Varunah Sashankah
Prajapatih tvam Prapitamahah cha.
Namoh namastae astu sahastrakritavah
Punah cha bhuyoh api namoh namastae. (G. 11/39)

You are air in God and Yama, the God of death, Agni, the God of fire, Shramun God, the God of water, Brahman, the God of creation and father of Brahman himself, you are a thousand times, salutations, repeated salutations to you once again, once again.

The Lord's infinite revelation includes the entire spectrum of truth. The eternal now shows everything in the components of inner and outer. The inner journey of the spiritual experience is the concept and practice of the creation. Here, the individual soul understands God's universality. He is like air. He gets spread to keep a connection with the entire creation. He reaches into all elements of the living world.

> *Namah purastad atha prishthatah astae*
> *Namah astu tae sarvatah eva sarva*
> *Ananta virya amita vikramah tvam*
> *Sarvam sama aapnoti tatoh ausi sarvah.* (G. 11/40)
> O Lord of infinite progress of salutations to you from the front and from behind, O soul of all souls, obeisance to you, my gratitude to you, my pranam to you, that you who possess infinite might forbid all, therefore you are all.

Arjuna has got the visualization of the Lord as infinite and vast and as such offers pranam to the Lord, expressing that the later is the creator and is in possession of infinite energy and has spread across the entire creation in the cosmic system.

> *Sakhetih matva prasabham yat uktvam*
> *Hae Krishna hae Yadav hae sakhaeti*
> *Ajanata mahimanam tava idam*
> *Maya pramadat pranayena bapi.* (G. 11/41)
> The way I have importantly, importunately called out either through intimacy or thoughtlessly, oh Krishna, oh Yadava, hey comrade, hey friend, so on, unaware of the greatness of yours, thinking only of a friend of which you are, O Achyuta, the infinite, infallible, have been cited by me while at play, posting, sitting at all these, I have considered you as my equal for all that, O immeasurable, O the Lord, I crave forgiveness from you, you forgive me for that.

Arjuna now realizes that the infinite, total truth is embodied by Lord Krishna. He knows now that Arjuna has the privilege of making him understand that even though he has these revelations, of act as a new dimension of him. He still remains positive and affirmative in nature. Arjuna, the supreme devotee of Lord Krishna now has founded the process of the creation of all and have blessings for all.

15 Consecration through Devotion

Arjuna attains the Divine Spirit and Power of Devotion

The attainments in life are basically contributions through the actions and thoughts towards a set of actions. While the actions of the world have causes behind them, leading to the actions, it may so happen at times that the action is causeless.

> *Yat cha eva biharah sajyah aasanah bhojanaeshu*
> *Yat cha eva avahasa artham asatkritah ausi*
> *Ekah authaba tat samakshmam*
> *Tat kshmayaei tvam auprameyam.* (G. 11/42)

O Krishna, always like a common friend of mine and dear to me, In all situations of normal interactions as a friend, I have not understood you and considered you as very ordinary. Please pardon me for that. Please pardon me for my ignorance and lack of understanding, lack of realization of yours.

Human power of thinking is mostly constrained by the conditions and situations around. However, ultimately, the intervention of will power or the power of the spirit can make a proper turnaround in the dynamics of things and the karma initiated. Perceptions at the human scale can make the Divine intents stop for some time. It is the problem of understanding the true dynamics of eternal truth in the context of the transactions at the empirical level. Arjuna had witnessed the vast identity of the Lord in ultimate terms. Until that moment, Arjuna was habituated to know and address Krishna as his friend and a well-wisher.

> *Pitah ausi lokasya characharasya*
> *Tvam asya Pujyash cha guruh garian*
> *Na tvat samaha astih na avyahdhikah kutoha anya.*
> *Lokah traya api aupratim prabhaba.* (G. 11/43)

You are the father of this moving and unmoving creation and the greatest teacher worthy of adoration, O Lord. Incomparable might is there in you, realisation, in the three worlds, and none else can even be equal to you.

Relations, in the worldly sense of the term, and that in the cosmic, divine sense are not the same. The worldly relations have been designed, and thus, they operate on the principles of mutual understanding, a shared basis of existence and the nuances of the world. In this transaction, the basis of the same includes aspects of belongingness, care and duty-based nurturing. Thus, the role of a father is considered to be to take care, provide support, and stand by as a protection in the events of the required nurturing for his offspring.

Tasmat pranamya pranidhyaya kayam
Prasadayae tvam ausi Ishavam idyam
Piteva putramsya sakheva sakhyum
Priyah priyayah ausi deva sodhum. (G. 11/44)

Lord, prostrating my body and at your feet and bowing low, I seek to propitiate you. I am the ruler of all the worthy and all the priests. It behoves me to bear with me, even father bears with his son, a friend with his friend, husband with her beloved spouse.

Arjuna realizes that the person he'd previously thought of only as a friend is, in fact, the supreme embodiment of God on Earth. Arjuna also understands that God's appearance on Earth is always for a cause. It is important to identify the cause of the appearance of the Supreme on Earth in the form and abode of Lord Krishna. Realising this as the essence of truth, Arjuna now bows before him. This act consecrates a devotee to God. Therefore, it's crucial that genuine devotion accompanies this act of consecration.

Audrishtapurvam Hrishitoh asmi drishtva
Bhayena cha prabyathitam manoh mae.
Tat eva mae darshayah deva rupam
Prasidah devah jagat nivasah. (G. 11/45)

Having seen your cosmic forms of the world and those never seen before, I feel transported with joy, yet tormented by fear. Pray, reveal to me the divine form, the form of your peace, the form of your transcendence and the abode of the universe. Be gracious to me.

Arjuna prays before the Lord at this stage that his mistakes, arrogance or any kind of wrong behaviour, including disobedience, be pardoned in the spirit of a father endorsing the similar mistakes made by his children. Arjuna begets the mercy of the Divine and continues with the usual normal behaviour. Arjuna, now, does consecration from the core of his heart.

Kiritinam gadinam chakahastam
Ichchami tvam rupam drashtum tatha eva
Tenah eva rupenah chalur bhujenah
Sahastrabahu bhaba viswa murtae. (G. 11/46)

I wish to see you adorned in the same way as the radiant man had, and I wish to see your cosmic form of pleasing form of a pleasing person and graceful form of a graceful person.

Arjuna understands the magnanimity and infinitely vast spread of God among all creatures of this universe. Thus, even when he is constrained by the actions on the battlefield, Arjuna declares that he understands the infinite design and plans in the context of the world. The Supreme in the form of the Lord is as close a friend to Arjuna as he was, but with a difference. Understanding the true spirit of the Lord is not easy. Simplicity, purity and true devotion that exists in the intrinsic understanding of Arjuna had made this happen.

With the devotional consecration of Arjuna to Lord Krishna, the ambience was turned conducive to the revelation by God. It is in this context that the Lord now opens up, with his remarks to his devotee.

Sri Bhagavan ubacha:
Maya prasannena tava Arjunah idam
Rupam param darshitam aatmayogam
Tejomayam vishwam ananta aadyam
Yat mae tvat anyena na drishtapurvam. (G. 11/47)
Lord Sri Krishna said, Arjuna, pleased with you, I have shown you through my power of yoga the supreme effulgent primal infinite cosmic form which was never seen before by anyone other than you.

Lord Krishna is now very pleased with his devotee, and the scenario is favourable. On one hand, the person is expected to be a true devotee, and thus, the divine message is now open for the revelation to the world. It is the context of getting the personality ready in body, mind and soul to just put into the pathways of the true revelation of the Lord, sitting and working in front of him. The Lord is clear in his choice and elaboration, speaking to the world in the spirit of things. The form of Krishna, thus revealed until now, is the wider identity, the larger and broader expression of what he stands for. He is responsible for the entire creation. His responsibility extends beyond just the material and empirical; it encompasses a holistic approach.

Na vedah yajnenenoh adhyaneno na danci
Na cha kriyah bhi na tapoh abhiruchacih.
Evam rupah shakya aham nrilokali
Drashtum tad anyena kuru prabirah. (G. 11/48)
Arjuna, in this mortal world, I cannot be seen in this form by anyone other than you, either through the study of the Vedas or by rituals or again through the gifts and actions of austerity.

The transcendental form of the Lord is again that which is common in the universe from any point of view. However, Arjuna's conviction has, by now, grown to the light of the Divine. It is because of that divine illumination, it reaches the senses of those who are not only ready to receive the same, but are in a position to be devotees who have attained the height of being the spirit of the noble elements. Arjuna, through his way of understanding the process of the world, now gets revealed in his total spirit. This is why Arjuna sees the spectrum of creations leading to annihilation at the end. Lord Krishna says that devotion is the way of realisation:

> *Ma tae byatha ma cha bimuda bhava*
> *Drashtva rupam ghoram mama idam*
> *Vyapetibhi pritamanah punah tvam*
> *Tat eva mae rupam idam prapashyah.* (G. 11/49)
> Seeing such a dreadful form of mine, if this does not put out and perplexed with fearlessness, a tranquil mind, behold once again, I am the same poor form of mine, and disgust, mess and all these things.

This revelation that begins here starts with the infinite and vast expanse of the Lord in the spectrum of the facts of the world. One aspect of creation thus becomes clear: it encompasses the facts of creation, maintenance, and ultimately, destruction within its entire spectrum. The most important aspect of this is to understand the process which the Lord, in his design of things, understand the spirit behind the scenario so.

> *Sanjay ubacha:*
> *Yti Arjunah vasudevah tatha ukthvah*
> *Sah ekam rupam darshayamasa bhuyah.*
> *Ashvasayamasa cha bhitam enam*
> *Bhutva punah soumyah eva soumyam eva purbamah aatmah.* (G. 11/50)
> Sanjay said, Having spoken thus, Arjuna, Lord Vasudeva, again revealed to him the same way was in poor form, pleasing form, assuming a general form, the high soul, Krishna, considered the frightened Lord Arjuna.

At this point in the scenario, Sanjay, the observer, got back to his act of description. Sanjay is narrating the entire episode to King Dhritarashtra. It is a kind of running commentary and explanation in realistic, on-time description, sharing all conditions. Sanjay could see from a distance as he continued narrating. He heard the conversation between Arjuna and Lord Krishna's words, which included grooming a devotee through a series of steps.

> *Arjuna ubacha:*
> *Drishtaeva idam maanusham rupam tam soumyam Janardanah.*
> *Idanim asmi sambrittah sachetah prakritim gatah.* (G.11/51)
> Arjuna said, Krishna, seeing the gentle human form of yours, I have regained my composure and my own self again, regained to my consciousness.

Thus, in the beginning, Krishna had mentioned the eternal identity of every life. In every life, there is a descent of God. The only important point here is that the intrinsic reality of eternal truth lying within is not revealed to God. Thus, the wisdom required the sharing of the position and true identity of the Lord. The eternal spirit is present within as the idea of the empirical, having access to the eternal and being possessed of the same supreme self with the identity of jivatman. This jivatman is the other form of armatmam in the context of God's creation. Thus, sitting within the person's heart, the jivatman observes the functions of the person in life.

The forms and abodes of the world that are noticed and observed in the empirical eyes of human beings are the ones that are externally visible and, in most cases, are the apparent reality of the material revelation. This apparent reality is considered the only reality by human beings. Reality talks about truth. Human empirical truth is the apparent reality.

> Sri Bhagavan ubacha:
> Sudarsham idam rupam drishtavanasi yat mamah.
> Devah aupyasya rupasya nityam darshana aakamkshinah.   (G. 11/52)
> Lord Sri Krishna said, The form of mine with four arms, which you have just seen, is exceedingly difficult to perceive. Even the gods are always eager to behold this form.

This has been narrated in appropriate terms by Lord Krishna that the apparent reality as such would reveal the ultimate position of reality when the world of humans conforms to the expected dimensions of the spiritual reality. Arjuna was in the context of the war. His role was to fight against the wrongdoers through the war of righteousness and offer a good life to the people with goodness. However, this was the context in which Lord Krishna had opened up the world's horizon, thereby considering the special purpose of God's presence on Earth. The objective was to annihilate evildoers and their associates, and in turn, establish the rule of dharma, or righteousness. The aspects and concerns for righteousness thus make it a kind of induced agenda for the noble warrior to consider the waging of war not on a personal scale of choice or preferences. It is, however, having the same on an objective scale, and thus taking part in the war.

> Na aham vedaeh na tapasa nadanena nacha ejjayah.
> Shakya evam bidhah drashtum vanasi mam yatha.   (G. 11/53)
> Neither by study of the Vedas, nor by penance, nor again by charity, nor even by rituals, can I be seen in this form as you have seen me just now.

Arjuna's participation in this war thus makes him a warrior-devotee, where the war is initiated and performed to establish dharma or righteous principles on Earth. In the process, the good and noble-hearted people are those who are just at the helm and in custody of those who have the agenda to establish truth and divinity in the world. To prepare Arjuna for that fully, Lord Krishna focused on the devotee's true identity. This is because the devotee now understands that the role of a human in this flow of events and transactions, God's role has been to give a shape to the entire set of activities and emphasize that the mind of the warrior should be free from the impacts of any kind of impurities. Thus, he took Arjuna to the shore of the noble river of the flow of lives to make him understand that the cause shall sustain even when the person is unable to or refrains from the war.

Bhaktya tu ananyah shakya aham evam bideha Arjuna.
Jnatum drashtum cha tattvena prabestum cha parantapah.   (G. 11/54)
Arjuna said, The devotee is exclusively and constantly devoted to you, as just earlier, adored you as possessed of forms and attributes, and neither adored the knowledge and bliss certified of these two types of worshippers, who were the best knowers of yoga.

Lord Krishna explained to Arjuna that his role was to participate in the war, as cause drives to the end point, and destiny had already ensured the final defeat of the evildoers' entire forces. Even if the noble warrior fail to do the work to abolish the wrongdoers, the entire range of the evil forces would lead to the end of their existence and thus, the work that he is expected to be into is to follow the path scaled by the Lord and bring into focus and establish the example in the world, that crimes get paid through the loss and end of the lives in the world. Thus, Lord Krishna had mentioned to Arjuna that he would be doing certain things that are done already.

Mat karma krit mat paramo mat bhaktah samga varjitah.
Neih beirah sarva bhuteshu yah sha mam eti Pandavah.   (G. 11/55)
Arjuna, the person who is engaged in the works dedicated to me and cultivates devotion for me, always remains within the divine consciousness of mine, is not in enmity with anyone, having an outlook of friendship to everybody and devoid of desires, is most dear to me.

The work of the Lord on Earth is thus to see that the dharma of the spirit of righteousness is re-established in the form that should act as the pioneer and the stalwart example for the world. It is thus the event which requires a proper understanding of the ways mentioned in the world beforehand. So, it is the best and the most important action of life that would be the work assigned by God. As such, in this journey, the devotee needs to develop complete faith in terms of the actions bestowed upon. The Lord doesn't interfere with the war; rather, it is the pure mind, pure character, and faith in selfless work—all for the benefit of the world—that guide its course. Through the vision of the cosmic form of God, Arjuna came to the final understanding of the ultimate goal. Arjuna realizes that he was not exactly doing the war; rather, he was developing the life of a true sage-devotee in Arjuna and thereby, getting him induced to do the duty as intended by Lord Krishna for him to perform with dedication.

The ways of worshipping and trying to realise God are known among many. One of these categories of people considers that God takes the form of a known kind and thus he can be approached as a personified entity with all the qualities and attributes of the Supreme. It is thus the god in human form who plays a role in human history for the benefit of the human world, and as such, the impacts of this in the flow of human journey and the formations of the human spirit through a process of corrections and redefinition of the mental environment of the person.

> *Arjuna ubacha:*
> *Evam satatayuktah yae bhaktah tvam pariupasatae.*
> *Yae cha api aksharam abyaktam tesham kae yoga vid uttamah.* (G. 12/1)
> Arjuna asked Lord Krishna about his decision on the superiority of being totally devoted and continuously engaged in spiritual actions, leaving aside all works or maintaining a normal and usual living of life and developing a love for God.

The other stream of thought about God is thus transcendental, omnipotent, omnipresent, omniscient and eternal. He is indestructible. The Supreme cannot be located and identified in forms; thus, he cannot be cut apart by weapons, he cannot be burnt, he cannot be washed off by the flow of water, he cannot be blown off by air. God is unborn and does not have any terminal point of identity. He wants to remain in everything. In the lives of creatures, he remains in some way. In the lives of human persons, he remains the god of everything in such a subtle and minute manner that he remains away from human understanding in most cases. These two broad views remain valid.

> *Sri Bhagavan ubacha:*
> *Mayih aaveshya manoh yae mam nityayuktva upasatae.*
> *Shraddhayah parayah upetah astae mae yuktatama matah.* (G. 12/2)
> Lord said, I consider them to be the best of yogis, who were endowed with the supreme faith and were united through steadfast devotion to me and worshipped me with their full mind concentrated on me.

Arjuna was curious to know from Lord Krishna, among these varieties of thoughts as maintained in the world, which intent remains ingrained in. Arjuna specifically asked Lord Krishna which of the two paths of human understanding He recommended as superior for worshipping God or attaining spiritual perfection by creating a path of further realization through individual meditative initiative in the context of the world. The Lord responded to Arjuna by mentioning that an aspirant who has in her or his possession unquestioned ultimate faith in God, or in another way, the person who, with a pure mind, purity of intent and dedicated love, along with true devotion, is very dear to him. Thus, the spirit of realization would get impacted by the thought to initiate the urge to have love for God becomes dear to him.

Yae tuh auksharam aunirdeshyam abyaktam pari upasatae.
Sarvatragam auchintam cha kutastham auchalam dhruvam. (G. 12/3)
Those, however, who, fully controlling all their senses and even-minded towards all, have devoted to me the welfare of all beings.

The transcendental revelations of God are in the form of the idea, concept and wisdom of the Supreme. The factors of realisation lie everywhere. The factors of wisdom also lie everywhere. God, the transcendental, offers his cosmic presence to the world of things in such a way that it is a matter of perception from the intrinsics of lives to assimilate and form the idea of the realization of God in the context of the world. As an example, to get a clearer perception, consider that air is spread everywhere. Even the minutest form allows air to penetrate, thereby connecting its inner content with everything outside. Universality of the Supreme thus connects everyone and everything.

Sam niyamya indriya gramam sarvatra samabuddhyayh.
Tae prapnuvanti maam eva sarvabhutae ratah. (G. 12/4)
Constantly adored as their very self and the unthinkable, omnipresent, imperishable, indefinite, eternal, immovable, unmanifest and the changeless, supreme, they too come to me.

The human organic system runs on the overall coordination of the mind. The mind is mostly driven by human consciousness. It is thus the coordination initiated by individual consciousness that drives the mind to perform organic activities, as also does the act of connecting with society and the world. Functional requirements of the mind thus effectively connect with the fundamentals of the internal organic orientation of the person or that of the external functionalities that drive the system towards cosmic level congruence. God has designed his creations in this manner to take care of their needs.

Kleshah audhik tarah tesham abyaktah aasakta chetasam.
Abyaktah hi gati duhkham dehavat bhi aubyapatae. (G. 12/5)
Of course, the strain is greater for those who have their mind attached to the unmanifest, for oneness with the unmanifest is attained with difficulty by those who are centered in the body and embodied.

While human action works as an indicator in the pathways of journey in the world, it is the quality of the work that is established through the functioning of the human organic system, in general, and the mind that is ideally the determinant of the quality of the person. The rational view of the work is that the orientation of the mind is the outcome of a person's internal dimensions and the mind. Thus, the mind remains and works as the indicator and the driver of all human actions. When the mind drives the activities on empirical parameters and sense, it has to accomplish that through the dynamics of the organic involvement and the power of human actions. However, when the same is done on a god connection in mind, a part of or the whole of the result of the action is endowed to the cosmic system and the chosen form of God.

God becomes a choice in life when an individual's personality becomes egoless. When this occurs, a significant portion of their work transcends worldly limitations, making many previously impossible tasks easy to accomplish.

> *Yae tu sarvani karmani mayee samnasya mat parah.*
> *Ananyana eva yogen mam dhyayanta upasatae.*   (G. 12/6)
> On the other hand, those depending exclusively on me, surrendering all actions to me, worship me and meditating upon me with a single mind of devotion are better off.

Oriented to God are the thoughts of God cultivated within in such a way that the work performed by the person does not remain a personal matter. It is rather something that is connected with the world and thus, with the dynamics and functioning in such a way that the work performed contributes to the dynamics of the world. The human mind usually looks for the benefits to the person first, and then it is poised to contribute to the cause or the growth of the broader system. The vibrant dynamic, when it plays as a tool for personal resurgence, can thus have a direct positive impact on the immediate next larger entity, and that could be the organization the person has decided to work for. In the process of this, the role and factors of the human mind are taken out of the barriers.

> *Tesham aham samuddharta mrithu samsara sagarat.*
> *Bhabami na chirat partha mayee aaveshitah chetasam.*   (G. 12/7)
> Those Arjuna, I swiftly deliver form of the ocean of birth and death and their mind being fixed on me.

When the mind cultivates dedication to God, it has to work in such a pattern that the doer is destined to do the works in a manner that would certainly be tuned to the cosmic system in the positive sense of the term. The direct connection with God happens through yoga. It is the connection that would inspire the doer to undertake work in the best spirit. No amount of personal seeking is present in this dimension. Work thus becomes the connection between the doer and God. The doer thus gets connected with the Divine; it is a general connection between them on a specific function, but as the spread of action-specific connection of the doer with the Divine gets widely spread out in the process, the framework of the mind requires some sort of understanding that continues ever. It turns the person into the personality of divine qualities through the association with God.

> *Mayee eva manah aadhatsvah mayee buddhim nibeshayah.*
> *Nivasishyasi mayee eva auta urdham na samshayah.* (G. 12/8)
> Therefore, fix your mind on me and establish your intellect in me alone. Thereafter, you will abide solely in me, and therefore, there is no doubt about it.

A mind oriented toward God is inherently eager to immerse itself in the ocean of divine consciousness, which holds infinite possibilities. One of such possibilities is to be engrossed in God and to set the process of life and actions in such a way that the cosmic vitals and construe the individual mentals in accordance. A person not only initiates and does an action but actually makes it in such a way that the world and the cosmic system see many providences through that work for a sustainable and universal nature. Thus, when we find that the work of that doer is on, all are served.

> *Autha chittam samadhatum na shaksoshi mayee sthiram.*
> *Avyasa yogenah tatoh ichhah aaptum mam Dhananjayah.* (G. 12/9)
> If you cannot straightly fix the mind on me, Arjuna, then seek to attain me through your yoga of repeated practice.

Human urge is always towards benefiting from every bit of action of the doer, offering puja in the form of her or him to locate the new functions of human action in continuation with the eagerness to offer the work as service to the cosmic system. It is, as such, the essence of work that is noted in the context of the world and to serve the world. Thus, the factor's victory in life is, on one hand, to garner the spirit of work and be in the system of work with the details and dynamics, on the other. In order to have the same accomplished, the work must be performed in the highest possible quality.

> *Avyasae api asamartham ausi mat karma paramoh bhabah.*
> *Mat artham api karmani kurvan siddhim auvapsyasi.* (G. 12/10)
> If you are unequal, even to the pursuit of such practice, be intent on working for me. You shall attain perfection in the form of realization, even performing actions for my sake.

The mental habit made through varied spread and dynamics of the work is one of the most important aspects of the universality that connects one element of work with the other. Whenever the same is initiated, an invisible message goes around to embrace the world. Messages of the world thus get the invisible connection in the mind to provide the message of the spirit of work everywhere. It turns into God's paradise when all such paradigms of the world converge to offer a specific message and input that the entities across the globe get similar vibrations. Minds thus receive an input of inspiration from their core spirit, which is the inner consciousness. It is the fundamental aspect of organic functioning in the context of the world of events and the world of thoughts-ideas-dreams combined.

The entire cosmic system is run and driven by the fundamental universal principle of cause and effect. The quality and pattern of effect are usually determined by the quality of the action accomplished. However, the action is again driven by the spirit and quality of thought underlying the action. Any deterministic position of the action thus requires thoughts that are tuned to the actions.

> *Autha etad api aushaktah ausi kartum mat yogam aashritah.*
> *Sarva karma phala tyagam tatoh kuru yat aatmavan.* (G. 12/11)
> If, taking recourse to the yoga of my realization, you are unable even to do this, then subduing your mind and intellect instead of relinquishing the fruit of all actions.

One's mind turns into that of a devotee when faith in the Supreme in any way develops in the mind. Faith in the formless, transcendental and eternal identity of God connects with the understanding of the Supreme being present in everything and everywhere, in every moment of the passage of time. It is thus the same faith that makes an understanding of cosmic endowment in life in the context of the gradual emergence of nature and the creation to tune into the truly harmonized thoughts of the world. It is the fundamental spirit of God's creation to keep his touch alive in all entities- living or material. In its way of moving forward, the natural system has developed an interdependence, a set of things that are embedded in the creation all over.

> *Shreyam hi jnanam avyasad jnanad dhyanam bishishyatae.*
> *Dhyanat karmaphala tyagat shantih anantaram.* (G. 12/12)
> Knowledge is better than practice without discernment. Meditation on God is superior to knowledge, and renunciation of the fruits of action is even superior to meditation. The peace immediately follows the renunciation.

The entire creation has the universality of the same roots of wisdom prevailing upon the lives to make happen the creation in its own way. The eternal in empirical form thus may appear disconnected, but it would have a connection in one form or the other. Within the purview of this known world, these endowments of air and light are the cords of universality being present everywhere. This is such that it's available to everyone immediately, whether they want it or not. The requirement of faith and wisdom is thus this belief that all over, the streaming of light and air is a unique gift of God.

Adveshtha sarvabhutanam maitryad karunah eva cha.
rmama nirahamkarah sama duhkhah sukhah kshami. (G. 12/13)
He who is free from the malice towards all beings, friendly and compassionate, and free from the feeling of ego, I am mine, balanced in joy and sorrow, forgiven by nature, ever centered and mentally united in me.

Knowing that the elements of cosmic connections are gifts of God is the basic wisdom in the system. This wisdom is known as spiritual or divine wisdom. Wisdom is God-centric. We need to understand the spirit of wisdom as a gift of God. The vision of Lord Krishna, as also his descriptions and utterances to Arjuna, reveals the fact of his having created and maintained this entire world with the objective of creating the revealed goodness of life within and without. This is the independence of life as gifts from the supreme spirit in creation.

Santushtah satatam yogi yat aatma drirhanischayah.
Mayee arpitah manoh buddhih yah mad bhakah sa mae
priyah. (G. 12/14)
He who has subdued his mind, senses, and body, and is free from all the six enemies of the senses, and resolves to surrender to me and have strong faith in me, the devotee of mine is dear to me.

The mind that gets a sense of this realization is the realized mind. The realized mind, in a way, makes God evident for the lives in the flow of time, on one hand and the pull of time, on the other. Each creature has to contribute to the flow of creation. In this flow of time, in eternity, the individual creature does the same function of creating something for the time to come. It could be in the form of some good words, good thoughts, or thoughts tuned to the natural process.

Yasmat na udvijatae lokae lokanna udvijatae cha yah.
Harsha amarshah bhayoh udbegahei muktoh yah sa
chamae priyah. (G. 12/15)
He who is not a source of annoyance and he who follows the creatures, he who returns to feed the beasts and feed the creatures, who are free from delight and envy, perturbation and fear, is dear to me.

However, in their own way, individual creatures develop a tendency that shows independence in the functioning and life of the creatures. It is their own footprint that every creature wishes to leave behind as a mark of its own contribution to the cosmic system. Thus, faith in a creature, in most of the cases, is the faith that boils down to personal acclaim. Thus, even devotees who have been into the process of divine realization fail to understand and differentiate between the right and the wrong, mistakenly choosing the wrong in the understanding of the right. Historically, God has been truly denied in most cases.

Individuals may understand the cosmic reality in three different ways. These are the understanding of the world of existence, as God himself has made the world understand in his own unique way. The creation has been depicted in three different ways through three worlds of depictions. These are known as *Rupa Loka, Rasa Loka* and *Bhaba Loka* or the world of forms, the world of the liquids (water) and the world of thoughts (or realizations). The visible human world is a part of the Rupa Loka. This is the revelation of the divine truth through forms, structures and material contents.

> *Anapekshah suchih dakshah udasinoh gata byathah.*
> *Sarva aarambha parityagi yah mad bhaktah sa mae priyah.* (G. 12/16)
> He who expects nothing, who is both internal and external, pure, is wise and impartial, and has risen above all distractions, and has renounced the feeling of worship and undertaking, such a devotee of mine is dear to me.

Understanding of truth in the Rupa Loka is important and direct. This is the existence that is caught through vision and is understood through the visible, audible and tangible existence. Through the organs of sense and knowledge, the world of forms and structures is understood clearly. The entire range of understanding is bound by the boundary conditions of space, time and context. It is the way that depictions have occurred before human knowledge, and as such, humans have experiences of the Rupa Loka forthwith. However, the Rupa Loka can be revealed more clearly to human observation when one goes beyond the externally perceived or merely visible dimension and penetrates the organics to understand the psychosomatic dimension of a person. This is essentially the organism's inner dimension that connects with the mental framework to drive the mind.

> *Yoh nah hrishyati nah dweshti nah shochati nah kamkshati.*
> *Shuva ashubha parityagi bhaktimanah yah sa mae priyah.* (G. 12/17)
> He who neither rejoices, nor hates, nor grieves, nor desires, who renounces both good and evil actions, and is full of devotion, is dear to me.

Knowing the presence of the source of mind within would draw the attention of a person from the superficial to the inner aspects. However, a total personality is the combined expression of the Rupa Loka and Rasa Loka; that means the externally visible dimension of the human framework gives an idea about the person. Inner dimension is revealed through the impact of her or his psychological framework on the total entity. The psychological framework is understood in the first place through the behaviour of the person. The psychological aspect reveals behaviour which is again variant to the conditions of time, space and the situations around, having impacts.

> *Sama shatrou cha mitrae cha tatha maanah apamaanoh.*
> *Shitou ushnou sukhah duhkhaeshu samah samga bibarjitah.* (G. 12/18)
> He who is alike to friends and foes, as well as to honour and ignominy, he who is alike in heat and cold, pleasure and pain, and other contrary experiences, free from attachment, is dear to me.

The revelation of God having been present in the entire creation induces the understanding that not only is the creation his, but also he has taken the task of maintaining the goodness of this entire creation. The wholesome truth or complete reality cannot be realized without the physical and mental environment of the person. Thus, the person needs to explore another dimension of her or his inner reality. This is the spiritual dimension. In the spiritual dimension, the intrinsic truth of the same is both observed and realized. The spiritual dimension is truly understood through the extent of realization of the person. This realization is that of God in creation. God, the supreme truth, is the creator, and a spiritual mind would always try to have a connection with the supreme truth to get it embedded within.

> *Tulya nindah stutih mounih santusthau yena kenochit.*
> *Aniketah sthirmatih bhaktiman mae Priya narah.* (G. 12/19)
> He who takes praise in fruits alike, he in given contemplation, and is contented with any means of subsistence, whatever entertaining, no sense of ownership, and attachment in respect to the dwelling place, is full of devotion to me. That person in a stable mind is dear to me.

Realization occurs in a mind that is in poise and does not rest on the factors of the world in any way. The mind needs to be *'nirmoha'* or free from delusions. The mind connected with the external world acts as a variety of matter. However, the material orientation of the mind is revealed from its clinging to the world's empirical identity, on the factors of orientation that try to contain the functioning of the mind.

> *Yeh tu dharma amritam idam yatha uktam parih upasatae.*
> *Shraddha dana mat parama bhaktah asteya ativa mae priyah.* (G. 12/20)
> Those devotees, however, who partake in a disinterested way this nectar of pious wisdom set forth, endowed with faith and solely devoted to me, they are extremely dear to me.

It is thus the fundamental spirit of the person that gets revealed once the person attempts to have a spiritual realization. Spiritual realization is the act of the person to explore the connection with the Supreme. The Supreme resides in every element and everything and gets slowly, gradually revealed when the person makes her or his mind truly cut off from the factors of the world. This is *'Aunapeksha'*, or not being dependent on others, or based on the actions or sensitizations by others. In this condition of the mind, the aspirant or devotee needs to refresh her or his mind through the pathways of a dedicated soul having a strong aspiration for God.

It is in this context that the mind acts as free and with the intrinsic input of the basics or the fundamentals in a manner that acts as a cleanser of mental impurities involved in the paradigm of the God-seeker. Thus, *'mukta-maun'* or the independent mind works as if it is born fresh from God and carries along and forward the qualities of purity.

> *Arjuna ubacha:*
> *Prakritim purushah eva kshetram kshetrajnam eva cha.*
> *Etad veditum ichhami jnanam cha Keshav.* (G. 13/1)
> Lord Sri Krishna said, the body, Arjuna, is found at the field, and those who know it, it is in the north of the field, Kshetra and Kshetragya, by the sages, they are singing the truth about God.

By the intrinsic quality, one should consider that the independent mind is expected to have developed the core of mind that doesn't fall prey to the desires, primitive attributes, like those that pull down to the lowest of the choice in terms of the aspiration of life in such a manner that those which are bestowed with a golden mind. This is that state of mind which understands the various dimensions of life. The mind gets involved in the process of the world. The visible factor the person carries or focuses the same for life on Earth. Therefore, it is required to understand the real dimension of truth in life, and thus, the role of spirituality could be known through differentiating Purusha from Prakriti.

> *Idam shariram kounteyah kshetram abhidhiyatae.*
> *Etad yoh vetti tvam prahuh kshetrajna iti tat vidah.* (G. 13/2)
> Know myself to be the Kshetragya or the individual soul, and the Kshetra of the field, Arjuna, and is the knowledge of the field, is in me, the matter with its evolution is contained in the spirit, that's what is the wisdom.

The fact of existence is classified between the wholesome truth of the Supreme and the derived truth from the Supreme, called the Prakriti. Prakriti is feminine, motherly. It has the power, strength to conserve as well as to multiply. Prakriti makes the structure and the form functional in the world. It has the essential power to augment, nurture and lead to its culmination, the seeds of the future. Thus, the Prakriti contains and creates nature. In the ordinary sense of the term, it is the broader nature. Prakriti offers the food required to sustain. It allows people to experience the joy of living.

> *Kshetragnam cha api mam viddhi sarva kshetraeshu bharatah.*
> *Kshetra kshetragnayo jnanam yat tat gnanam matam mamah.* (G. 13/3)
> What that field, knowledge of the field and the field, the modifications in that, the cause and effect have arisen, and the changes occur because of the intervention of the action.

Prakriti is the endowed creation of the Lord. It is the forerunner energy in motion that makes the world interact, communicate, collaborate, and in the end, act on the experience. It is thus the framework of the universal feature of God where the Supreme takes up the abode of the mother and allows the movements of life on Earth. Prakriti is also advisory, in addition. It is the nature that helps in the transactions of lives on Earth and at the same time, adds new inputs to lives, allowing lives to experience their own joy and happiness in a realistic way and at a real point in time.

> *Tat kshetram yat cha yadrik cha yat bikari yatah cha yat.*
> *Sa cha yoh yat prabhavah cha tat samasena mae shrinuh.* (G. 13/4)
> The truth about this abode and the truth about the knowledge of the field have been expounded for years in many ways, again it has been separately stated in different mantras of the Vedas and consummated texts and the Brahma Sutras.

Prakriti draws the power and inspiration from the Purusha. Purusha is the *Param Purusha* or the Supreme Personality. Identifying the supreme self and the original creator of the entire creation, it has been said that the entire universe has only one and the same origin. The god of gods, Lord Shiva, in his supreme abode of transcendence and formless consciousness, has seeded the entire creation for the Supreme to take it forward.

> *Rishivih bahudhah gitam chhandobhih bibidhei prithak.*
> *Brahma sutra padei cha eva hetum etat bibidha nischitei.* (G. 13/5)
> The five elements, the ego, the intellect, the unmanifest, the ten organs and the mind, these five objects of sense, they all control, they all arise out of it.

The entire design of creation is in this way the existence of God and the Supreme Mother in the form of the Prakriti or nature. Thus, Prakriti has to be revealed in various ways. The Cosmic Prakriti or the Cosmic Nature, the Jagat Prakriti or the nature of the world and the Jiva Prakriti or the nature of a creature, are revealed through the actions and the consequential conditions of the same in the world of humans. Jiva Prakriti, or the nature of the human is the combination of the inner and the outer, or the internal and the external attributes of the nature. The real aspect of this cosmic nature is to create and maintain the elements of the cosmic system in a sequence of its survival in a way that would make things happen most feasibly. The creation is nurtured and maintained until its logical end. However, the most preferred process is the continuity of the system. Continuity in the cosmic system would be clearly established through a balance between the series of creation and that of its annihilation at the appropriate point of time. Thus, the large-sized cosmic bodies also would find annihilation in terms of their vitality and existence in realistic terms. The knowledge of modern space science about the death of stars and finally getting into the black holes to absorb the rays of light from all around in the flow of time and space echoes this view. It is to create symmetry between all ends; Prakriti does the maintenance.

> *Mahabhutani Ahamkarah buddhih abyaktam eva cha.*
> *Indriyani dashah ekah cha pancha cha indriyah gocharah.* (G. 13/6)
> Also, desire, aversion, pleasure, pain, physical body, consciousness, formlessness, is thus the field, and evolves briefly stated.

The cosmic nature has a wide impact on the lives and processes of the world. Broader balance is established through the awakening of all entities that exist everywhere and at the same time; to get the inner world properly understood within individuals. Rupa Loka and Rasa Loka, as they are present in the cosmic system, make up that as it takes into account the biological process within individuals. The human biological process is a combination of Rupa Loka, Rasa Loka and the Bhaba Loka. It is the spirit in a human being that makes the process. The spirit drives the mind towards things of the world. It is the spirit that takes care of the psychosomatic paradigm of human life.

> *Ichhah dweshah sukham duhkham samghata Chetana dhritih.*
> *Etad kshetram samasenah savikaram udahritam.* (G. 13/7)
> Absence of right freedom and from hypocrisy, non-balance, forbearance, self-righteousness, peace and mind, etc., devote of service, preceptor, internal and external purity and statefulness of the mind, control of the mind, mind and senses, all these are a part of that.

Human dimensions are essentially narrowed down by the constraints of time, place and everything around. However, the Inner Prakriti or the Jiva Prakriti determines the character and behaviour of the person. The Jiva Prakriti has an inbuilt inheritance that governs the facts of life, on one hand, and on the other, inspires life to go beyond the human scale and try to reach out to the divine scale in life. The transition from human to divine in life is a transition that may surely be termed as a transformation. This transformation occurs when the forces of life are coordinated together to behave and act in a manner that attempts to make life get tuned to the divine qualities of life. As and when the divine qualities are adopted, that is changed to a new one in life.

Amanitvam adambhitvam ahimsah kshantih aarjavam.
Acharyah upasanam shoucham stheiryam aatma binigrahah. (G. 13/8)
Dispassion towards the objects of enjoyment of this world and the next, also absence of egotism, pondering again and again on the pain and abuse, inherent in birth, death and old age.

It is in this context that man behaves so differently that sometimes it becomes difficult to understand that they are humans. Man, at this stage of transformation, becomes more or less godlike in spirit and the facts of life. Then truthfulness, honesty, integrity, sincerity, cooperation, caring, compassion and the like become obvious associates of life. Selfish tendencies and personal ego, which are associated with human characters, get out of their own nature and start embracing the world as their own place. Everyone in this world has someone so dear, so close kin in the true sense of the term. A person turns into an individual without selfishness and personal ego and becomes selfless in their approach to life.

Indriyartheshu vairagyam ahamkarah eva cha
Janma mritya jarah byadhi duhkhah dosha anudarshanam. (G. 13/9)
Absence of attachment and the feeling of close bonding in respect of son, wife, home, etc., and a constant sense of equality of the mind, both unfavourable and favourable circumstances, are also a part of this knowledge.

The person now realises the presence of God within and thinks that the presence can be further enumerated when the new abode of the fundamentals of the person has the golden mind that embraces everyone as so dear to him and takes care in accordance. Inner organs coordinate to fulfil the dream of life. That apart, the mind becomes so much engrossed and absorbed that the world to him or her turns into a place and a point of joy. For the moment and bliss in life is experienced by him. Bliss makes a sense of unity and oneness on Earth.

Aashaktih anavishanghah putra darah grihadishu.
Nityam cha sama chittvam ista anistam upapattishu. (G. 13/10)
Unflinching devotion to me through the exclusive attachment, living in secluded and holy places and finding my enjoyment in the company of worldly people is one of the ways to unrealise me.

Given that blissful realization, the human world turns inward. The inner domain of the person thus initiates, maintains and takes up the whole as the inspiration of life. Lord Krishna, while answering the question raised by Arjuna, said, the entire cosmic order is a set of such continuity in the qualities of life and urged humanity to consider each other as close persons. This means that the world, when viewed through the eyes of noble personalities, reveals that human life can be lived in a godly manner, thereby eliminating all negative attributes and emotions from humanity within the cosmos.

Prakriti and Purusha are both the revelations of the same Absolute and the integral truth on Earth. The Absolute is revealed through everything in life; a person's thoughts, words, and deeds are simply its phenomenal manifestations. In the identity of the Prakriti, the supreme truth takes the abode of Mother to bless the Earth.

Mayee cha ananya yogena bhaktih abyavicharinih.
Vibikta desha sevitvam cha jana samsadih. (G. 13/11)
Constancy of self-knowledge and seeing God as the object of true knowledge, all this is declared as knowledge, and what is contrary to this is ignorance.

Mother God is the blissful and graceful face of God. When the Divine finds the person transforming from the mere human form to the transformed person with the divine qualities or *daivi guna*, the person turns dear to God and begets divine grace without even seeking the same. This qualitative transformation becomes an impediment to those who aspire to become the companion of God on his journey through the creation. This is, at times, as undertaken by him, a physical journey being present in human abode and other contexts, a spiritual journey through the Bhaba Loka of human existence and thus, to take care of the process of divine intent to see the light of the day in their proper perspective. When the understanding takes a proper shape, it covers the dimensions of existence in reality and in the appropriate sense of the term.

Adhyatma gnyana nitya tvam tattwa gnanartha darshanam
Etad gnanam iti proktam gnanam yad atah anyatha. (G. 13/12)
I shall speak to you at length about which ought to be known and knowing which attains the supreme bliss, the supreme Brahman who is the Lord of all the Lords.

This body is a sum of various material ingredients. Each individual cell reveals its material nature. Cells of blood, the bones, muscle, skin or the nervous connect all have their own physical and chemical properties. It is when they are exposed to chemical transformations, they tend to behave in a way that would be transformative to each of these categories. In the human world as such, these are made to make the journey higher than just the human domain. Journey in life takes a new and elevated shape, with superior attributes undertaken.

Gneyam yat tat prabakshami yad gnatvah amritam ashnutae.
Anadimat param Brahmah na sat tat uchayatae. (G. 13/13)
It has hands and feet of all sides, eyes, heads, mouths, directions and ears all around, stands pervading in all universes.

A decision within a human system is needed as to what should be the chosen way of life and what is to be avoided therefrom. In this act of decision making, human choice determines the shape of things to happen in the process of living life. It is thus the orientation of mind and, before that, the quality of spirit driven by the human consciousness. Lord Krishna makes it very explicit and clear to Arjuna, saying that the matter of the intrinsic relation between the human consciousness and the Divine is the spiritual science of the abode and the lord or the owner of the abodes. This is the gift of God, as has been endowed with an abode that takes about the journey of life and the chosen course of actions and expectations through this life.

Sarvato pani padam tat sarvato aukshi shiroh mukham.
Sarvato shrutimat lokae sarvam aabritya tishthati. (G. 13/14)
Though perceived in all senses and objects, it is speaking in the word of all senses, and among us it is the sustainer of all; nonetheless, though attribute-less, it is the enjoyer of all these attributes of goodness.

The kshetra must understand the *kshetrajna*. Kshetra is understood through the process of self-introspection. Ask yourself, 'Who am I?'; when someone attempts to get the question answered, they get the ways to reach somewhat clarity of the supreme truth. It is thus the moment kshetra is understood that a dimension of life force opens up, which attempts to make the process simple and direct the focus towards the wholesome truth that has been the foundation of the cosmic design on the human world.

Sarva indriya gunah aabhasam sarvo indriya bibarjitam.
Ashaktam sarba bhutah cha eva nirgunam gunabhaktri cha. (G. 13/15)
It exists without and within all beings and constitutes moving and unmoving things of the creation, and by reason of its subtlety, it is incomprehensible and it is close at hand and stands afar too, knowing this makes a person wise.

With the good intent of absorbing divine qualities within, the aspirant turns into a devotee. With devotion thus ingrained in human personality, the person wins sattwa-guna or divine qualities. The person is now engrossed with the noble attributes of life and proceeds towards sharing the same with the world, thus within her or him, there happens a transformation, reorienting the focus of life to God in a manner that makes life divine. For a person whose ultimate goal is to consecrate, obtain, and offer their conscious self to God, love and devotion become the autonomous guiding principles.

16 Divine Personality

Making of a Personality that promotes Equality, Fraternity and Liberty

Arjuna had always been on the path of his chosen work, endowed with the power to learn, grasp, rediscover, develop, transform and develop all required skills to be the best. Arjuna had been additionally fortunate in having the grace of physical company of God on Earth in a realistic sense. He was a unique blend of extreme action with all the factors and attributes of devotion within. Being a great warrior, it was the easiest task for Arjuna to face any kind of combination of enemies. Arjuna had proved the fact of being the most powerful and superior to the sum total and combinations of the warriors of his opposite camp, the enemies. The entire enemy force, including all the war leaders, proved to be fewer when compared.

> *Bahih antah cha bhutanam aucharam charam eva cha.*
> *Sukshumatvat tat bigjeyam duratham cha auntikae cha tat.* (G. 13/16)
> Though integral like space in its undivided aspect, it appears divided, the Supreme Divine in its non-formed condition, as it were, is present in all animate and inanimate beings, and that when the Supreme takes a form, the only object worth knowing is that He is the sustainer of all created and also preserver of all created.

When Arjuna, in disguise, was helping the prince of the Virat kingdom, he had an opportunity to demonstrate his power in war. At that moment, he rendered all attacking generals and soldiers senseless on the battlefield. This allowed Arjuna to easily kill King Duryadhana and all his powerful, famous generals, who had all become incapacitated. Arjuna had spared them all. He let everyone come back to their senses and then fly away to save their lives. This is because he also wanted to maintain ethics in war.

> *Abibhaktam cha bhutaeshu bibhaktam iva cha sthitam.*
> *Bhutabhartri cha tat gjeyam grasishnu prabhabishnu cha.* (G. 13/17)
> The Supreme Brahman is said to be the light of all lights, entirely beyond the illusions, and God is the knowledge itself, worth knowing and worth

attaining through the real wisdom and realization, and it is particularly abiding in all hearts and all creatures.

The Lord is a constant friend to Arjuna. He is always accompanying the devotee. He mentions that a dear devotee is one who expects nothing, who is both internally and externally pure, is wise and impartial, and has risen above all distractions, and who renounces the ego or the sense of being the doer and claiming things for his own, and remains dear to him. The Lord calls upon Arjuna to fix his mind on God and any kind of thought that would make the person get attached to him, in the way he has urged everyone to be oriented to God.

Jyatisham api tat Jyotisham tamasah param uchyatae.
Gjyanam gjeyam gjana gamyam hridi sarvasya audhishthitam. (G. 13/18)
The truth of the Kshetra and the knowledge, as well as the object, are worth knowing. Kshetra is the place, the seed-bed, that is God; it has been briefly discussed, and the entire Kshetra or the place is God himself. Knowing this in reality, he becomes the person, God's devotee, and enters into God's transcendental being.

Human habit is to gather and maintain joy when she or he has achieved the desired things in the world in a way which satisfies their expectations. Here, Lord Krishna suggests becoming a true devotee by bestowing oneself upon God. This means the devotee should always seek factors connected with the intrinsic system, thereby finding the intrinsic elements to connect with God.

Iti kshetram tatha gjanam gjeyam cha uktam samasatah.
Mat bhaktah etat vigjayay mat bhabayah upapadyatae.   (G. 13/19)
Two things, Prakriti and Purusha, or the nature and the Supreme Godhead, this is beginningless and endless, and Arjuna, you must know that all modifications, such as lies, dislikes, etc., of all objects constituted with the three gunas, as born of the nature or Prakriti.

It is assumed that a devotee shall never nurture evil will in life, and try to accept in life and adopt those attributes which are otherwise a distant hope for the devotee. When a person turns into a true devotee, she or he find the world as a place that bears a touch of God. It is a kind of permanent touch that the devotee would identify elements of divine touch in everything in the world. Thus, the devotee develops a kind of blessed position in life, having got whatever is available in life. A devotee considers life's possessions and attainments as blessings of God in life.

Prakritim purusha cha eva viddhi aunadi ubhou api.
Vikaram cha gunanam cha viddhi prakriti sambhaban.   (G. 13/20)

Prakriti or the nature is said to be responsible for bringing forth the evolutes and the instruments, while the individual soul is declared to be the cause of experiences of joy and sorrow.

The concept of 'me' being the master of things is not the kind of mind that the devotee would develop. If the devotee widens the focus of consciousness in the context of the world, he or she would certainly identify the world as a place where a large number of such personalities would prevail. A devotee would dwell upon the objects and the subjects of the world, as that would imply the factors of reality to be the deciding factors for the perception as such. When the mind of the devotee gets absorbed in God, she or he turns into God's own person with the thought and as when the forces of distractions, attempts, divergence, the devotee with strong faith in God would defeat those negatives easily.

Devotion to God redesigns the course of life. To this person, the transactions and interactions in life reveal the oneness of the mind. The person remains the same in situations that might be opposite to each other. Thus, this position is empirical oneness.

Karya-karana kautritvae hetuh prakritih uchyatae.
Purushah sukha dukhyanam bhoktritvae hetuh uchhayatae. (G. 13/21)
Only the Purusha or the Supreme Soul, in association with the nature or Prakriti experiences the objects of the nature of the three gunas evolved from the nature or Prakriti, and it is attachment with these gunas or the nature that is responsible for the birth of this soul and embodied form in good and evil forms.

In the event of attaining the empirical oneness, the devotee responds to opposing inputs to the sentiments as that of the same in ultimate analysis. Thus, any kind of praise does not sway the person. On another critical note, the person also responds neutrally to the stimulus. It is thus this position that yields a lot of curiosities from the world of society, such that the curious other mind would understand the equal position of the devotee mind in situations that are conflicting or opposing to each other. The devotee aspires to keep the mind fixed on God in the sense that it enjoys the searching of a conscious condition and thus the conscious behaviour with the fundamental faith that he or she is just a minute component of God, having the inspiration, potential and spirit.

Purushah prakritisthau hi bhungtae prakritijaana gunan.
Karanam guna samgoh asya sat asat yoni janmasyah. (G. 13/22)
The spirit dwelling in the body is the same as the Supreme. He has been spoken of as the witness and the true guide, the sustainer, experiencer as the embodied soul, and overlord and absolute as well.

These are things which would make the system of the world much congruent to the factors of life and thereby make it such that the devotee as a person remains calm and poised in mind with the basic understanding of what the Lord has gifted to the devotee. When one attains that amount of strong faith in God, remains unshaken in the faith and transacts on all scores in the world with the same set of chosen contexts or unforeseen contexts in life. A devotee may obtain the realization of the universality of God. This would mean the devotee's own realization that God is present everywhere and in everyone as well. Thus, the devotee would respond to every person as it occurs in the mind, equally responsive to all.

> *Upadrashtha aunumanta cha bhartah bhokta Maheshvarah.*
> *Param aapnoti cha api uktah dehehasmin purushah parah.* (G. 13/23)
> He who thus knows the spirit or the Supreme Being and the nature of the Supreme Being when he or she takes the form together with the gunas, even though performing his or her duties in every day, is not reborn again.

While Lord Krishna was expressing the 'Kshetra' and 'Khetrajna'. The most important components of the same were the context and the person in the context to find out whether to be concurrent or automatic. 'Kshetrajna' is one who understands the object of realization to be God himself, knowing that the Lord himself is the master of all knowledge. So, the said factor of the conditions, attainments and mechanism of living in the same purposeful way. The world expects God's resources. A human person possesses these as just a custodian.

> *Yah evam vetti purusham prakritim cha gunaeih saha.*
> *Sarvatha bartamanoh api na sa bhuyoh avijayatae.* (G. 13/24)
> Some of the meditations behold the Supreme Spirit in the heart and keep their consciousness refined and the sharp intellect. Otherwise, realization of the Supreme through the yoga of knowledge and others through the yoga of action, karma yoga, makes the person understand the true being and the truth behind the existence.

Prakriti of a human person is the combination of the inner and the outer of the person in a true and realistic sense. Thus, the devotee understands the reality behind prakriti being the extended set of the qualities that the creation is exposed as. The true nature of this creation is the spread-out form of the Supreme Mother. The cosmic prakriti is God as the mother, and on the other hand, the individual human prakriti is that of the person having almost a similar functional basis within.

> *Dhyanena aatmani pashyantih kah chit aatmah na aatmanah.*
> *Aunyae samkhena yogena karma yogenah cha auparae.* (G. 13/25)

Persons with an ill motive, however, not knowing through meditation even as they heard from others that those who are the knowers of truth, even they who are thus devoted to what they have heard, are able to cross the ocean of mountains, existence in the shape of deep.

Lord Krishna narrated to Arjuna the diverse methods and ways to earn the revelation of the Supreme on Earth. The way of meditation or dhyana is one when the devotee collects all senses within and, assuming the presence of God in an invisible, infinitesimally small dimension, tries to have a vision of the same in the form of flame or light. This could be the chosen material form of God on Earth. Having the realization of his identity, as such, the devotee would attain the riches of *Viveka-Vairagya-Bhakta*. These are the states of the consciousness in the person that would make the mind and intellect competent to differentiate things of godly orientation and the same of empirical worldly orientation. This is essentially differentiating between truth and untruth. Whereas, truth is something of experiencing, perceiving, and realizing, the untruth appears through the flow of attributes in the identity of a person. Thus, truth is denoted by the factors of the tangible, visible, rational description on one hand and the perceived, experienced, and realized on the other, in any context or at any point in time.

Viveka is not only the power of discrimination, but the context of the flow of life as well. A person with awakened consciousness, the spirit of things which a human person in this context would make, is oriented to the contextual basis of things and thus would make it happen in a way that the intrinsics are taken into total consideration for accomplishing things on Earth.

Aunyae tu evam aujanantah shrutvah hi aunyebha upasatae.
Taeh api cha autitarantih eva mrityuh shruti parayanah. (G. 13/26)
Arjuna, whatsoever being animate or inanimate is born, know that it is enumerated from the union of the matter or the place and Kshetrajna or the spirit. It is a combination of the matter and the spirit that makes things happen.

The other set of attributes of Kshetrajna refers to vairagya in life. This is the methodical approach to be above all kinds of passions in life. Passion for something makes the person cling to the contextual reality of that and hold a fragment of the same in the flow of life. Vairagya means becoming gradually neutral to the happenings of the world as a kind of gesture and commitment to the cosmic spirit in such a way that the person is above the ground reality in terms of being a part of it. And on top of that, the person would cultivate the scheme of things in life that are directly oriented to God in the true sense of the term. Vairagya makes the person work intensely but not get involved; so, the selfishness is missing here.

Yavat sanjayatae kim chit sattvam sthabarajanghanam.
Kshetra kshetragjyam samyogat tat viddhi Bharatarshabhah. (G. 13/27)
He alone truly sees who sees the Supreme Lord in imperishable and abiding equally in all perishable objects and beings, and animate and inanimate.

Devotion or bhakti is the real vehicle in life to establish communion with God. Thus, the agenda of doing many works in the world gets bruised by the factors of devotion. At times, it so happens that the act of devotion could be carried out directly or indirectly. Direct devotion is the first-hand understanding leading to realization. Once the realization is earned, it continues to have an impact. It is the personal preparation through the Sama-Dama-Shraddha-Titiksha-Sacrifice: these are internal poise containing senses, sense of inner gratitude, tolerance and the urge to dedicate to a cause. It is the context of divine expectation and a segment or the whole of realization that creates a self-giving spirit in a person.

Samam sarveshu bhutaeshu tisthatam parama Iswaram.
Binashyatshu aubinashyatam yah pashyati sah pashyati. (G. 13/28)
By seeing the Supreme Divine equally present in all, the person does not kill the self by himself and thereby attains the supreme state.

Oneness of context and the understanding of similar situations invite the good soul for the functional clarity to achieve the realization of God in the passage and continuation of life. It is mentioned that self-giving as a spirit develops in the being of the person when it acts as the face and the focus of the issues life tends to confront. This act ultimately focuses on the entire issue, maintaining the mind's orientation towards achieving a specific dimension of involvement in the world, while simultaneously determining the functional identity of the person's role.

Sama pashyan hi sarvatra samah abasthitam Ishvaram.
Na shivantih aatmanam aatma tatoh yati paramgati. (G. 13/29)
And he who sees that all actions are performed in every way by nature, prakriti and the self as well as non-doer, he alone truly sees.

With the realization, as such, the person with immediate understanding of the cause of things in life would make the situation far away from the locus of life. Realization of God is essentially realizing truth in life and developing the practices in life in order to have the truth unfold in life, with a view to having the value in life of the realization to achieve total truth in the function in tune with that spirit. Only complete faith indicative of shraddha may lead to realization of the Supreme.

Prakritvya hi eva cha karmani kriyamanani sarabashah.
Yah pashyati tatha aatmanam aukartaram sah pashyetai. (G. 13/30)

The moment a person perceives the diversified existence of the Supreme as rooted in one supreme spirit and the Spirit in fourth and all beings and the same, that every moment the person attains the truth and consciousness of the supreme being, and the person is now capable enough to have the final liberation.

When the person develops the mind to consecrate, it is the hope built in the person that may be get in the person the act and do things in the context of the happenings in the world. As such, it begets superior calls to be ingrained in the life of the person in all contexts. The devotee is now fully convinced of the role of the spirit in shaping life in a way that makes the journey of life very smooth. At this stage of having developed faith in the spirit, and thus begets the truth of eternity to contain the sense of vision, touch and grace of God. Anything that connects God with the world has the power to present the whole truth.

Lord Krishna tells Arjuna that the entire creation, with the animate and inanimate, or any other identity it is the union of the Kshetra and Kshetrajna that has made it happen and whatever is there in the context of the world is an invariable combined outcome of the Kshetra and Kshetrajna. The quest for truth in this creation is the urge to be permanent, overcoming 'vinasha' or annihilation in the flow of time.

> *Yada bhuta prithak bhavam ekastham aunupashyateh.*
> *Tatoh eva cha vistaram Brahma sampadytae tathah.* (G. 13/31)
> Arjuna, being without the beginning and without attributes, this indestructible Supreme Transcendental Being, though dwelling in the body, in fact, does nothing but gets contaminated.

A realized person, as has been explained by Lord Krishna to Arjuna, is one who has constant endeavour to look for the truth in the Earthly reality and another set of things that are expected in the act of living a truthful life that is oriented to God in all contexts. The flow of time makes the empirical life perishable in the environment of the Earth system. The soul that resides within does not perish. The soul continues with its existence; it carries along the experiences of living a long flow of life in the context and paradigm of the Earth system and for human beings, at large.

> *Aunaditvyat nirgunatvyat paramatmam ayam abyamah.*
> *Sharirasthah api Kounteya na karoti na lipyatae.* (G. 13/32)
> As all-pervading ether is not tainted by reason and its subtlety, though permeating the body, the self is not affected by the attributes of the body due to its subtle character.

Realization of the Supreme could happen through seeing him or receiving any glimpse of Truth, His existence in the chosen form. Whatever method one uses to realize it, it's the extreme urge that facilitates the unfoldment of truth in its own unique way. Arjuna was conspicuous in receiving the quintessence of the divine truth in human form. Thus, truth would be revealed to the devotee in such a way that the essence of realization as a supplement would remain with the intrinsic of the person.

> *Yatha sarvagatam soukshmayat aakasham nah upalipyatae.*
> *Sarvatra upasthitoh daehae tatha aatmah nah upalipyatae.* (G. 13/33)
> Arjuna, as the one Sun illuminates this entire universe, so the atman, the Supreme, seated within every individual, illumines the whole kshetra or the field.

When such a devotee realizes God and attains the magnanimity of getting an elevated position in the world, having developed the power of meditation. The action in the world should be coordinated in such a way that it remains harmless to others, on one hand, and contributes to the growth and spread of goodness in life, on the other. Life is a continuity in the realisation of the absolute, and may take a long way to attain that. Thus, it's poised to understand the divine truth.

> *Yatha prakashayatae ekah kritsnam lokam enam Rabem.*
> *Kshetram kshetrih tatha kritsanam prakashyati bharata.* (G. 13/34)
> He who does perceive with the eye of wisdom the difference between the field and the knower of the field.

Upon seeing the eternal form of God, Purushottama Lord Krishna explains to Arjuna that to perceive God with total faith and complete understanding of truth means that all factors of growth in life now become inherent to the person, bestowing them with what is called 'ekasya prapyam', or a destined component. It is thus the focus of the life of a devotee to see the touch and a fragment of the diaspora of life.

> *Kshetra kshetragjyah evam auntaram gjanah chakshushah.*
> *Bhuta Prakritim moksham cha yae viduh yantih tae parama.* (G. 13/35)
> The phenomenon of liberation from nature, with her evolution, reaches the supreme eternal spirit through the realization of Brahman.

The realization stimulates wisdom within. Those who perceive wisdom of being able to have the penetrative element of consciousness, Kshetra and Kshetrajna would create appropriate focus in the world to unfold them to proceed through the stream of life in a manner that justifies the things of life with truthfulness and God-orientation. As Lord Krishna had said to Arjuna, explaining that the void and Akaash- the space, remain within everything, he is also present within every entity and thus omnipresent in the creation. He is that one sun that illumines the entire universe, removing all darkness and revitalizing the spirit in the form of illumination in the world of humans and the entire set of animate or inanimate.

The cultivation of wisdom in a person, which first started in a systematic and rigorous way during the Vedic age, was very important to invoke the spirit within and thereby draw inspiration towards having the same spirit applied in life in the context of work and living in the world, and therefore apply the wisdom in life.

> *Sri Bhagavan ubacha:*
> *Param bhuyah prabakshyamih gjananam gjanah uttamam.*
> *Yat gjvtah munayah saravae param siddhim autoh gatah.* (G. 14/1)
> Sri Bhagavan said, I shall now tell the supreme wisdom, share with you the best of all kinds of wisdom, and the wisdom which the sages have all acquired with the highest perfection, and thus they have got themselves liberated from the bondages.

Lord Krishna now tells Arjuna that the same quintessential spirit needs to be inculcated in life in the context of the flow of things in the world. Wisdom in normative condition is something that would be best known and recognized when it comes to human context in the form of the input energy and inspiration to the person who wants to follow and have wisdom play a role in life. This is why the Lord has mentioned this as the most superior among all types of knowledge. Once the factors of Kshetra and Kshetrajna are understood clearly, the factors of human prakriti or that of the total personality of a human being, in the context of the run of things in human life. He suggests that by knowing this through their meditation, the sages have achieved godly lives.

> *Idam gjanam upashritya mamah sa dharmam aagatah.*
> *Sargaeh api nah upajayantae pralayae na byathantih cha.* (G. 14/2)
> Those who, by practising this wisdom, have entered into my cosmic being are never born again, and they get the flavour of cosmic devotion and get associated with my cosmic presence.

The wisdom of God was spelled out in eloquent terms with full clarity by the sages of the Vedas during the ancient period around fifteen thousand years ago. However, the depiction of Lord Krishna in elaborate terms to Arjuna makes it revealed again during the Mahabharata period towards end of the Vedic era. Arjuna, being the most important person to carry out the agenda and the task of the Lord, having now descended on Earth, his life requires to be blended with the intrinsic wisdom in the form of functional presence and inculcate in the personalities while doing the duty and accomplishing the tenets of application of that wisdom as the knowledge of life.

Manaah yonih mahat Brahmah tasmin garbham dadhami ahom.
Sambhavah sarva bhutanam tatoh bhabati Bharatah.   (G. 14/3)
My primordial nature, or the nature in origin, is a great Brahman, and I am the creator. I put the seed in the process of creation, and all beings, all matter and non-material living beings are my creation.

The process of life stems from cosmic wisdom, just as a seed is to the factors of creation, with divine Prakriti driving it forward. This has been mentioned in clear terms in the Chandi (the great work depicting the victory of the Supreme Mother over the demonic forces) by the sages of wisdom that the primordial mother and the god of all gods, Mahadev-Lord Shiva, is the source of this creation. It says, *'Jagato jananyei jagat ekah pitrae'*. The supreme mother is the mother of all creation, and Lord Shiva himself, with the power of his divine wish, makes the creation happen throughout. This, in essence, is the meaning of the process and factors of creation on Earth.

Sarva yonishu kounteyah murtayah sambhabanti yah.
Tasam Brahma mahat yonih aham vijah pradahah pitah.   (G. 14/4)
Of all embodied beings that appear in all the species of various kinds, the natures are the revealed form of this world, and that should be considered as a mother, and I contribute the basic living seed to that.

The varieties of forms of life, termed as the species, are the essence of the original inputs to the creation. It is the divine intent to create that has made the creations happen. Therefore, the infinite number of lives have been out of the same origin, being allowed to be processed through the factors of lives at the respective forms and standards of lives. It is thus the most important and noticeable factor that whatever form of life has been there on Earth has a connection in terms of getting its origin from God.

Sattvam rajah tamah iti gunah prakriti sambhabah.
Nibadhanti mahabahoh daehae dehinam abayayam.   (G. 14/5)
Sattwa, rajas and tamas, these are the three gunas born of nature, and these are percolated down to the individual souls, and the imperishable soul in the jivatman also carries this.

Human personalities have always varied based on the qualities that shaped their lives. As has been mentioned earlier, three major types of human characters are depicted through the concepts of sattwa, rajas and tamas. The Lord attempts to project a world free from the dominance of rajas and tamas and establishes that of the sattwa. It is thus the quest in life and the usual pattern of response through the kinds of inputs showing and reflecting behaviour that makes the person involved in the formation of things. The usual types and patterns can make it oriented to a particular and desired mix or combination of things in life. As such, this is clearly conducive to the formation, as knowing each attribute in detail and trying to combine them is beneficial for life.

The world has a mix of varied qualities in human society. Whereas all have some relevance, the dominance of sattwa will create a better society in the human world. This human society and the system are actually comprised of people of different types, having different combinations of these qualities in their variety of forms and differences in the objectives of life. Thus, the classifications are not only for a usual, informal act of things, but are required.

Tatra Sattvam nirmalatvat prakashak manamayam.
Sukha samgenah badhnati gjanasamgena cha aunagha. (G. 14/6)
Of this, sattwa is truthful, and it is illuminating, it is flawless, it binds through the divine attachments, and happiness and knowledge are inbuilt in it.

Lives are construed, in the usual sense of the term, across all these qualities. However, the factors of life that are good to cherish and are good for human society are to be cultivated in the charted way or in a manner that begets the divine. Lord Krishna tells Arjuna that these three gunas, sattwa, rajas and tamas, are required to be carefully noticed and determine the dominant set of attributes in the realm of things for the objective of getting the best set of things in life and then develop that combination in the personalities to fetch the best required and then construe the paradigm of chosen characters from the set of available combinations. Lord Krishna describes that the quality of sattwa is absolutely pure. It is the illumined aspect of any character. It also spreads illuminations to the world.

Rajoh ragatmakam biddhi trishna aasamga sama udbhabam.
Tat nibadhnyatih Kounteya karmasamgena dehinam. (G. 14/7)
The other quality is rajas, which is actually a passion, attachments, and it binds through attachments in the actions, and the force of the actions.

The rajas carries with it a set of actions based on passions. A rajas person is born of desires and attachments of material objects in life. Rajas is mostly aggressive in actions with arrogance in nature. Thus, the person tries to find the drivers of life in the form of having dynamism nurtured towards the fulfilment of the eternal desire of the person in terms of achieving the objectives of life and grabbing things in accordance. The rajas person has been identified with the hunger for personal attainment, possessions and fulfilment on one hand and making of the thirst for the nourishment of the soul in the process of its journey.

Tamah tuh augjyanajam biddhi mohanam sarvadehinam.
Pramada aalasya nidrahabhih tat nibadhnati Bharata. (G. 14/8)

The third one is the tamas, and is the deluder of all those things that look upon as their own selves. It brings in utter selfishness through ignorance, and becomes sloth, sleepy, and error-stricken.

The tamas person thinks that this body, the biological instincts of the individual, is the ultimate objective in life. Tamas represents the inertia and thus the cognitive faculty of life gets dominated by the personality that makes all elements of the world converge to the personal satisfaction and the sense of individual attainment in life. It is thus the most important dimension of life which boils down to the dominance from within and without some negative factors.

Sattvam sukhae samjayatih rajah karmani Bharata.
Gjyanam aabritya tuh tamah pramadae sanjoya atyuta. (G. 14/9)
Sattwa draws the happiness eternal, rajas is pushed to action, while tamas is the indolence, and it puts a person to error and invites sloth in life.

The quality of sattwa gets a person into the bliss of life. It is the kind of sukha or happiness that makes life most vibrant in terms of its attainable things. Sattwa guna provides happiness in life in the context of the world. Though apart from the lowness of enjoyment. It is thus most important to have the fundamentals of life identified, and thus the good qualities like the factors of truth, cooperation, self-giving, tolerance, and joy in others' achievements are the attributes focusing on the perspectives next to the horizon and within.

Rajah tamah cha abhibhuyah sattvam bhabati Bharata.
Rajah sattvam tamah cha eva tamah sattvam rajah tatha. (G. 14/10)
Overpowering rajas, tamas, sattwa prevails, overpowering sattwa and tamas, rajas prevails, even so, overpowering sattwa and rajas, tamas sometimes prevails.

Sattwa provides all goodness in life, and life is lived in the context of the things of life. It is that factor in life that makes the inroads to the goodness of life and activity. Rajas has the power to collate the sattwa and tamas in life. Sattwa is, by nature, soft, docile, polite, with purity of mind within, whereas rajas is that of the profoundness of the same in the context of the world of things and world of activities. Rajas has the power of dynamism, which should be a mix in all phases of life, and it puts across the aspects of life that are conducive to and contributing to the effects of nature in rajas. This is a factor that makes the prominence of rajas as a quality in the context to overcome any barrier to thrive. Rajas is thus considered a good match for sattwa for its elements of goodness to spread, as sattwa would be focused on the factors of achievements in life. However, other aspects of rajas need to be contained within to factor the best output and perform the best in life.

The knowledge about these three gunas in life is an important parameter that attempts to reshape the flow of things in the world. As such, the human spirit, if recognized in that manner, takes into the system that it has to abide by the norms of human understanding that it takes to the system that is thoroughly dependent upon the functioning of the world.

Sarvadwareshu deheha asmen prakasha upajayatae.
Gjnanam yada tada vidya adi bridhham sattvam iti uchyatae. (G. 14/11)
When light and discernment dawn in this body, as well as in the mind and senses, then one should know the Sattwa is predominant.

A combination of the attributes that effectively make it into the factors of life, as it is in the factors of the material aspects of life. The organs of this entity are actually driven by the effects and the factors of life that eventually make it into the factors of life. The organs, each of which is driven by the factors of life that beget the ground realities for affecting the basics and fundamentals of life. Thus, each organ has its own way of functioning and attracting the connect of the mind to focus on the way. A factor of this kind that works on the principle of sattwa is actually, at times, a transformative journey. The orientation of truth and goodness in life would make the human living such that sattwa domination works for the effective turning of the orientation of functioning by the organizations in focus. Sattwa reorients to truthfulness.

Lobhah prabrittih aarambhah karmanam aashamah sprihah.
Rajasih etani jayantae bibriddhae Bharatarshabhah. (G. 14/12)
With the predominance of rajas, the greedy activity, unattained actions, with interest in motive and egotism, restlessness, and the thirst for enjoyment.

In the process of living, human tendency at times converges to the factors of desires of various kinds. Desires are common in human personality, but when the desire solidifies, gets concentrated in its own form, the chances are very high that desire turns into elemental greed. Desires of widespread nature may converge to the congruent factor of greed for variety, where desire is the most prominent in its happening. Desire being so prominent would thus make inroads into the pathway that is apart from the basics of elements in life, and thus desire turns into the factors of greed in human life.

Auprakashoh iha pravrittih cha pramado moha eva cha.
Tamasi etani jayantae bibriddhae kurunandanah. (G. 14/13)
With the growth of tamas, Arjuna, the mind and senses are disinclined to perform one's obligatory duties, and they cause errors out of ignorance.

The tamas-driven person does not follow the chain of things leading to goodness in life and the world. A tamas person remains unfaithful in works and deeds. And thus, this slow pace of doing may lead to somewhat avoidance of the dutiful works of the person. It is thus the quality of the person that proves very negative in the gamut of things. The person thus makes it ideally plausible to the extent of being responsive to their own personal interest and thus denies the factual presence of the demands or expectations of him or her to discharge work at a higher rate or of a superior quality. A tamas person is indolent, insincere and insensitive to things.

> *Yadah Sattvae prabriddhae tu pralayam yati dehabhrit.*
> *Tat uttama vidyam lokan aumalan pratipadyatae.* (G. 14/14)
> When a man dies during the preponderance of sattwa, he obtains the strongest eternal body in heaven, and that's the highest attainable form.

Greed in the sattwa personality and that in rajas has a difference. The person with rajas would initiate the pathways to fulfil the greed in their own way and enjoy the factors of greed. Whereas the tamas person would be driven by greed, be mentally obsessed and develop a passion to fulfil the greed. The idea, thought, and mental mechanism dominating a person's own psyche is tamasic greed. And on the other hand, when the actions are initiated to fulfil the hunger of greed, it then becomes the factor of rajas in life. Rajas is that factor that makes a person win the world on the issues of greed. The consequential end of the person of rajas and the tamas is to obtain a lesser and ridiculing life after the current one comes to an end.

> *Rajasi pralayam gautvah karma samgishu jayatae.*
> *Tatha pralinah tamasih mudhah yonishu jayatae.* (G. 14/15)
> Dying when rajas predominates, he is born among those attached to action. Even so, the man who has expired during the preponderance of tamas is born into the species of senseless creatures such as insects and bees.

The sattwa person would have illumination in life. The illumination is that of the truth-consciousness-bliss factors in life and that of the spirit of the same, revealed through the precious positioning of the factors which would otherwise make the journey of life something of the eternal bliss in the human context. The tamas, the mind is caught by factors of indolence. With these factors of indolence, the person would find a focus in life and refrain from accomplishing the factors in such a way that would turn the focus of the world to something where the intervention of the person becomes important and thus takes it forward to achieve the dutiful purpose and search for its end point and the goals.

The acts of tamas and rajas in the ultimate analysis lead to bigot sorrows in life. It could be either a perpetual experience of sorrow or a momentary one. The momentary one could be into the facts of human providence, where the darkness in life is eradicated. This is the eradication in terms of the features of the future of life. The future of that total perpetual elaboration of the same in the context of life.

Karmanah sukritasyah aahuh sattvikam nirmalam phalam.
Rajasah tuh phalam duhkhyam ajnanam tamasah phalam. (G. 14/16)
The reward of a righteous act is sattwa, thoughtless and in the form of happiness. Wisdom, which has got the divine touch, sorrow is declared to be the fruit of rajas, and ignorance is declared as the fruit of tamas.

The righteous action leads to sattwika. The sattwika is faultless in the form of happiness, wisdom and not at all met with the person. The person thus acts with a focus on life here. Sorrow finds a distant separation from this act of life. What is the purpose of life's progress in the act of things in life? Sorrow is accrued through the pathways of rajas and tamas in life. They, together, are very strong anchors of ego and selfishness in life. It is thus the factors that are tuned to the purposeful experiencing in the passage of the actions in life. The rajas and tamas lead to the blend of a person who would further make the purpose of life more articulated towards the rooted aspects of ego and selfishness.

Sattvyat samjayasae gjnanam rajasoh lobha eva cha.
Pramado mohah tamasou bhabati agjnamae eva cha. (G. 14/17)
Wisdom follows from sattwa, greed is the outcome of rajas, and error and stupidity, ignorance is something, and there are many others like indolence, sloth; these are the results of tamas.

The rajas-driven enjoyment of life converges to the dark and negative realm where an individual makes a total resurgence of things that are conducive to the realm of and the factors of positive impacts in life. The rajas actions are thus calculated and then structured in a way to the factors of initiating the new dimension and a focus in life that attempts to make a clear choice of accomplishing things in the form of a power driving the desired objects to fulfil the targets in life in the best possible manner.

Urdwam gachchhanti sattvasthvam madhyae tishthani Rajasah.
Jagnanya gunasya vrittvabtha audho gachchhanti Tamasah. (G. 14/18)
Those who abide by the quality of sattwa, when their ways are upwards, while those who are rajasic disposition stay in the middle, the tamasic go to the lower world, and they always remain in the lower.

It is thus the fundamentals of the scenario of the world that attempts a new blend in the character to build a chosen destiny, the persons in focus and thus the embodied personality hold back their own and possessed attributes to achieve their ends in the world. Thus, the impact of rajas and tamas together or separately into the factors that either of these or together it bring up the factors of the world, which drives to the fulfilment of the person in their own way, though that cultivates and promotes darkness.

> *Na anyam gunebhyam kartaram yah drastha aunupashyati.*
> *Gunebhyah cha param vetti mat bhabam soha adhigachchhati.*(G. 14/19)
> When that fear perceives no agent other than the three gunas, it realizes me, and that is the condition when someone has to overcome and rise above the limits of all or the spirit of all the gunas and go beyond that to understand the divinity.

Wisdom is garnered through the process of sattwa. Sattwa spreads a positive vibe, and it elaborates upon the quality of positive things. The positive aspects of these are those that are actually possessed in life by the forces and the factors of truth and sustainability in life, and thereby to take the forces of goodness ahead. It is that force of goodness which could rise above the individual barrier and get into the focus of life, living in the spread of things.

> *Gunani etani autitya trinah dehih deha sam udbhavan.*
> *Janma mrityu jarah dukhya baihmuktah hi aumritam*
> *ashnutae.*   (G. 14/20)
> Having transcended the ever-ceaseless three gunas which have caused the body and feet from birth and death, old age and kinds of sorrow, the embodied soul attains supreme release.

The three gunas, sattwa, rajas and tamas, identify the elements of character of a personality and thereby choose the dimension in life that actually focuses on the perspectives of the actions and possibilities of creating goodness in society. The factors of goodness would imply the light of the divinity. It is just that in the factors that bring in the aspects of the world, where role of a person is important. The combination of the sattwa and the dynamism of rajas that makes the true spirit of a personality, and at the same time, to put across the light of the divine for emergence and bring in positive factors in life and illumination for all.

It has been declared by the Lord that when the devotee understands the spirit of this classification through different combinations of the three gunas, she or he understands the purposeful orientation of the entire thing and thus makes effective inroads into the space between the goodness and the bad elements in life. Neither of the three gunas nor any combination of the attributes of these three is going to have any inroad into the realisation of the Supreme in the real sense of the term. However, the factors are averted if the person attempts to realise the goodness of the spirit going beyond the boundaries in a way that makes it tune to the factors of goodness in life and work. These factors of goodness are just the forward movement of individual consciousness as a mark of the divinity, as Lord Krishna mentions the supreme spirit stands entirely beyond the gunas.

Arjuna ubacha:
Keih keih lingach trinah gunani etana autitah bhabati pravoh.
Kim aacharah katham cha etanah trinah gunantitah
autibartatae. (G. 14/21)
Arjuna said, What are the marks of him who is rising above the three gunas, and what is his conduct and how to rise above these three gunas?

The sages state that the supreme spirit reveals itself in various forms and identities. However, Lord Shiva, the Lord of Lords, depicts the Supreme in a human abode, allowing for the unveiling of the Supreme as a minute and invisible illumination in the core of the heart. This grants life a feeling of the Supreme Goddess, though not a direct touch. It is the fundamentals of life that focus on the Divine embedded in the chosen souls. It is the fundamentals of living. The basic objective of the Lord is to sensitize the aspiration of a life that adopts goodness as the principle of living and tries to have lives lived on the basis of the sattwa attributes, with dynamism added to it. The basics of these are the distance and effort one is from the basic objectives of life. It is the fundamental spirit that comes down to the stream of thought and activity in the midst of the flow of things in life. Even if the mind of the person changes towards goodness to sattwa, the divine attributes remain far off.

Sri Bhagavan ubacha:
Prakasham cha prabrittim cha moham eva cha Pandavah.
Na dweshthi sam prabrittani na nibrittanih kankshati. (G. 14/22)
Lord Krishna said, He who abhors no light and activity or even stupor when prevalent nor longs for them when they have ceased.

Arjuna was curious to understand what happens to the person who has been able to transcend all three qualities and has been able to rise above the barriers of the flow of life. If a person can transcend life's limiting delusions, the question then becomes: what impact does such a transformative focus have on their life when those delusions are overcome? Lord Krishna tells Arjuna that the lack of sattwa in a personality loses the illumination and power of light of the life.

Udasinonbat aasinou gunaiyoh na bichalyatae.
Gunah vartanytah iti evam yah eva autitisthati na ingatae. (G. 14/23)
He who sits like one unconcerned is not disturbed by the gunas and knowing that these qualities of these three varieties are there, but it remains, establishing identity with God and has a divine devotion and enjoys that state.

Dullness and indolence are the twin factors of darkness, as induced by the factors of rajas and tamas in life. It is thus the response of God that says wisdom, tranquillity and joy are impediments to the elements of darkness and friends to sattwa. These are truly ingrained in the person, having fully understood and adopted the pathways of Divine Light as perceived and really understood in the end. The role of the Divine in this process is to remain indifferent. However, in the case when the Divine is explicit in his role as a factor of the world, He may choose to interfere and adopt a way to extend supportive help to the person. Thus, it happens that the person needs to seek the light of the Divine in life to illumine the aspects of mind-thought-consciousness. and thereby to elevate the seeker from the domain of the darkness in life to the illumined pathway that paves the way to realization. In cases of the spirit being compassionate, the devotee finds it easier to have the process of transformation in place, and thus it occurs physically.

God mentions the ultimate chosen condition that needs to be achieved in this realm. As such, the person needs to attain the condition of oneness or that of equality is the ultimate condition of life. Lord says he who is ever established in the self, when the person genuinely feels the happiness and sorrow in the same light, the darts of Earth and that of gold material are considered the same, with hardly any or no differentiation between them. This is established as the position of oneness.

> *Sama sukha duhkhah svasthah samaloshtashna kanchanah.*
> *Tulyah priyah aupriyoh dhiroh tulya nindah aatma*
> *samsthutih.* (G. 14/24)

He who is ever established in the self and takes pain and pressure like rivers cloud and hour, rivers, cloud of Earth and stone, the piece of gold, equally in value, is possessed of wisdom, accepts the present, pleasant as well as the unpleasant in the same spirit, is the person who is rising above that.

As the Lord establishes the conditions of equality, it can be understood through the fact of life when it mentions the attained condition of mental and spiritual state of oneness. The person now hardly sees anything bad or dirty that would trouble him or her. On the other hand, she or he would find the same kind of indifference in mind to the amusements of the precious gold. Thus, a lump made out of mud and dirt, on one hand, as a precious material on the other hand, is considered the same by the person. When both appreciable and non-acceptable impacts on the human system evoke the same genuine response, a person achieves a state of non-discriminative oneness. This is the condition that Lord Krishna suggests to Arjuna to have in reality. This would be the oneness that is the prelude to God-realization. Now, when the person is on the lanes of that oneness, of that in life, the connection with the other is thus established. God comes into purview when he is sought here.

Maan aupamaneyoh tulyah mitra aurih tulyah pakshayoh.
Sarvarambha parityagi gunatitah sa uchyatae. (G. 14/25)
He who is indifferent and ignominious, his life was a frame as well as that of an enemy, but when he knows the sense of worship when undertaken, he is said to have risen above the gunas.

Lord Krishna mentions to Arjuna once again the problems of good attributes for a good life on earth and recommends the cultivation of those good attributes in life in all kinds of human actions. This person shall feel one in the case of honour and ignominy in life. When honours are bestowed, life feels complete. On the other hand, when ignominy is also there to experience, the response that is autonomous from within matters a lot to the person. An autonomous response being the same and equal would make the person focus on the divinity and not on the personal attainments that would take the person through all their conflicting and mutually opposing scenarios in life. This equality of response is all.

Mam cha yah abyabhicharina bhaktiyogena sevatae.
Sa gunan samatitah etan Brahmabhuyayo kalpatae. (G. 14/26)
He who constantly worships the Divine and me through the yogas of devotion and meditation always, he is in a position to get liberated from the three gunas.

Lord Krishna suggests that the impact of the gunas in life directly shapes the objectives of human lives, serving as their perpetual associates. The oneness, if attained, is the condition to focus on the spirit of God in life. This leads to the attainment of divine wisdom in life. However, wisdom does not come with the touch of the spirit of God. Wisdom creates the basis of understanding the transcendental, formless and eternal being in the form of truth. Wisdom paves the way to develop shraddha and love for God.

Brahmano hi pratisthay aham amritasya abyahsya cha.
Shashvatah cha asya dharmasya sukhei ekantikashya cha. (G. 14/27)
I am the basic and infinite supreme God, I am the immutable, the immortal, as also the eternal, the virtuousness, I am the absolute bliss, I am sat, I am chit, I am *ananda*, I am *satchitananda*.

Lord Krishna now mentions that he himself represents the supreme truth and that they are tuned to God, to the person who wishes to have proper orientation and realization of God in life. This realization is based on the attainment of the oneness in life that works for the orientation to God. As in this case, Lord Krishna focuses on oneness in spirit, the realization of formless, omnipresent, omniscient, eternal, formless is having that wisdom to understand truth within and that of the vast oneness of all creatures and the remaining elements of creation as the factors of the same truth on Earth. As such, the personal God with form is achievable in both the spirit of him and through deep devotion supported by love for him. It is the love for him in the ultimate sense of the term that begets the vision, touch and company of God on Earth, causing victory, poise and liberation of the devotee.

17 Divine Attributes

Human attributes conducive to sustainability – Success and Self-Fulfillment in Life and Works

Godly qualities in life are unusual in the world of humans. Only a few among millions possess godly qualities in life. In the common setting in the human world, godly qualities have hardly any takers because of the lack of adequate supporting factors for living godly lives. Because of living a godly life, apparent and immediately noticeable benefits are so minimal that it averts the focus of most. Not only that, some people immediately respond with examples from around them where following godly attributes seemingly led to an immediate loss of opportunity. These are some impediments to godly living.

> *Sri Bhagavan ubacha:*
> *Urdhah mulah aubakah shakham aswatham prahuh abyayam.*
> *Chhandangsi yasya parnani yah tvam vedah sa vedabit.* (G. 15/1)

Lord Krishna said, showing a peepal tree, that Arjuna know that this entire creation is like this peepal tree, which is imperishable and is a long term, and is from time immemorial, it is very difficult to measure the period of and life of this peepal tree, so know that the supreme being is like that, I am like that, and its branches, leaves, trunk, everything are reflected through the scriptures, Vedas being the basic fundamental trunk of that.

God on Earth is the focussed revelation of the Supreme in the human context. It is his love for his own set of creations that he, externally, chooses to take up different types of forms and abodes in the world. The infinite eternal is formless. He is the flow and continuity of the eternal resources and has the urge to carry forward the essence of truth created by him only. The entire universe, the known, unknown, perceived, beyond perception limits and what abouts in the flow of lives and matter that knowing him becomes altogether a different and a difficult matter to achieve.

> *Audhah cha urdhvam cha prasritah ausya shakha*
> *Guna prabriddhah vishayaprabalah.*
> *Audhah cha mulani aunusantatani karma aunubandhani*
> *manushya lokae.* (G. 15/2)

Fed by the three gunas or three different types of attributes, having sense objects for their tender leaves, the branches of these trees, shape different orders, colours of creation, and they take different forms, but the root remains same, it is there spread in the human body and human creation, all regions, higher and lower, are included in that.

Thus, in order to make Arjuna have an easy and direct understanding, Lord Krishna came up with a metaphor to explain how the Supreme is present in the world in the context of the flow of lives and presence of the material process of evolution. As such, it is in the paradigm of spirituality that the presence of God in the world is through, and then realised as a massive fig tree. A fig tree or a Banyan tree usually provides shelter to a large number of lives of birds, small creatures and even used to resist climatic onslaughts, to the sages in meditations.

Na rupam ausyah iha tatha upalabhyatae
Na auhtyoh na cha dinah cha sampratishtha
Aushvatham enam subirhurham mulam ashanga shastrena dhrirena chhittvah. (G. 15/3)
The nature of this tree of creation does not, on a mature thought, turn out what is represented to be, for it has neither beginning nor end, even stability, therefore cutting down the peepal tree, which is most formidably rooted in the form of the world, with the formidable axis dispassion.

The example of the fig tree is such that it is inverted, that is, made upside down. Its long and short roots have connected with the cosmic system, and the branches with leaves are widely spread across human existence. So, the branches and the billions, trillions of leaves exist in the form of the creatures-the human being, each with its uniqueness, also having a wide diversity in between. It's like an inverted fig tree of infinite dimension, where the factors of life are found at its lowest points, branching out like leaves.

Tatoh padam tvat parimargityavyam
Yasmin gatah na nibartantih bhuyah.
Tvam eva cha audyam purusham prapadyae yatah pravrittih prasrita puranih. (G. 15/4)
Man should diligently seek the supreme state, the Godhead, and the Supreme residing in that, would actually be blissful to the person, who tries to understand the primordial and the celestial existence of the God himself, and understands that he is the root of everything, he is the seed of everything, he is beginningless and endless.

Essentially, it means that the entire world with all creations is assumed to be like the leaves of the infinite Banyan or fig tree, containing the varieties as well as equality among all in this creation. The tree draws its strength and vitality from the world of gods and transmits the same through its trunk, which is also infinite in its dimensions. This is the tree of life. Here, each individual life, considered a leaf, is tuned and connected with the new system where the understanding develops and grows of the connection with God directly.

> *Nirmana mohah jita sangadoshah*
> *Audhyatma nitya binivritta kamah.*
> *Dvandaeih bimuktah sukha dukhah sangaei*
> *Gachhantah mudhah padam abyam tvat.* (G. 15/5)
> The people who have understood and realized the Supreme Divine in different forms, they are the people of wisdom, and they don't have any delusions in the life, and any attachments in anything, any cravings for anything, and doing that, the opposites, between the opposites, they come to the neutrality, and they are completely immune to the qualities and attractions by the qualities.

The roots of this inverted tree of creation are ingrained in the vast cosmic existence of God. He is so gracious as to provide this connection with the idea, thought, and feeling that God is directly taking care of creation. This makes the creation competent to aspire for his connection in life. It has been mentioned by Lord Krishna that the entire creation is in direct touch with God, but the creation hardly takes a look at that. Even if few people look into it, the factors of vital force reveal into the fathoms of life. The tree is the spectrum of the creation, containing the elements of life in it and thus having the focus of the god connect in life so that in this creation, the factors of God connect would be understood from an empirical perspective and really realised from the eternal perspectives of the flow of lives.

People having the urge to know the Divine would try to get the realisation in their own ways. Lord Krishna suggests to Arjuna that the urge to realise God is the best option to have God in mind and develop devotion for him.

> *Na tat bhasayatae suryah na shashankoh na pabakah.*
> *Yat gatvoh na nibartantae tat dhamah paramam mamah.* (G. 15/6)
> Neither the sun nor the moon, nor anything else, the sun cannot reveal him, the moon cannot, the fire cannot, the stars cannot, and this small fire flame of a candle, how can it see him, it's only his grace which can make a person visible.

The human condition is such that each person has her or his own personal priorities. These priorities are those which are really for the person only. Hardly does it contribute to wholesome perspectives. It is thus the human condition that needs to be addressed properly. In the process, the perceptive dimension of what people find as a factor of existence. It is a context that requires to be looked into, as it has been observed that those who are into the practice of meditation in life, are better in having the realisation of God in life. Devotion has been considered the best way. Lord Krishna has suggested that Arjuna follow the same. However, a set of practices is essential to be true to that.

> *Mam eva aungshoh jivalokae jivabhutah sanatanah.*
> *Manah shahthani indriyani prakriti sthani karshatih.* (G. 15/7)
> The jivatman, the self within the individual body, is a particle of the Supreme Divine, and it has the same nature as the Supreme, and it resides with the same nature.

Different organs in the human system have different perspectives. Thus, each organ has its own functions and demands. As Lord Krishna has trained Arjuna through the process of the three gunas, he has elaborated, saying that the gunas have their identified attributes. The three gunas collectively can describe the habits and character of each person. Whereas the habits and characters are described and analysed, the three gunas can have mobility or the transformative dimension from one to the other. The transformative dimension is having initiated a journey from one stage to reach the other. Thus, it can be said that a tamas, if willing, may turn into rajas, and then into sattwa.

> *Shariram yat aapnoti eva yat cha utkramat ishvarah.*
> *Grihitvaei etani samyati bayuh gandhan eva nih aashyat.* (G. 15/8)
> As the wind flows throughout, and it is put on, it continues, like you know, if one place shuts the windows for the wind, it goes to the other place, and it leaves one place and gets into the other place, similarly, the self transcends one existence and gets into the separate existence.

The ideal combination, as Lord Krishna has narrated to Arjuna, is sattwa having the impetus of the rajas of dynamism. Thus, the dynamism of rajas added to the general attributes of sattwa makes the combination that has the best empirical formation. However, as Lord Krishna suggests that God realisation is not a prerogative of any of the gunas. It is not tamas-rajas or sattwa or any combination of these that could foster the journey of consciousness for having God realisation. Lord Krishna, however, categorically explains the role of devotion and love for God towards having the deeper realisation and to get into the realm of the Divine in life.

> *Shrotram chakshmum sparsham cha rasanam ghranam evah cha.*
> *Audhisthayao manah eva cha bishayan anu upasebatae.* (G. 15/9)
> It is the small self, or the self within the living person, while associated with the senses of the body and existence, it carries certain elements of

the existence for creating the next and fulfilling the unfulfilled desire of the person for the future.

A set of regular practices of spiritual activities leads to the gradual development of the orientation of the person's mind and thus consciousness. It is thus the direct approach, irrespective of the conditions found in the analysis, that has been the orientation to identify the impediments. Thus, any restrictive force that it detects can be avoided through resorting to the different dimensions. Thus, these factors would make the objects of such analysis the primary focus of the devotee. The devotee now tries the direct way to God. She or he achieves this through the opening of opportunities in life to be in touch with God. Thus, it allows a forward move for the same.

Utkramantam sthitam baapi bhunjanam ba gunanvi tam.
Bimudhah na aunupashyanti pshyantih gjnachakshushah. (G. 15/10)
The ignorant, those who have not cultivated the wisdom of God, don't understand the blessed existence of him in this human world, and therefore they are driven away by the senses, and the senses are constructed across the three different types, the sattwa, rajas, and tamas.

The organs have their own pull factors. For example, the sensory organs would expect the vitalising through the rise of senses. On the other hand, the organs of action would expect the mind to coordinate in a way that leads to the control of things. Mind having the power to control can truly make headways into the factors where the power of mind is just connected with the realms of goodness on Earth, identifying the factors of goodness and applying the same. it is thus a factor that effectively happens in the life of a person. It is, therefore, noted here that the grace or the Divine may be spontaneous. It is dependent upon the initiative and urge of doing that in a manner that proves not only acceptable but attractive to God. Thus, Arjuna would spend his focus on the priority of having realisation first and then having God's design in the world understood. Once the intent of God in the world is understood, the way forward is to proceed in the process. Any specific agenda that comes forward can be addressed from the right perspective in life. As Lord Krishna suggests, the entire situation now converges to the intent of the devotee to serve God in the way as is expected of her or him.

Tuned to the spirit of God, the devotee now wants to find out the ways to achieve the focus so that divine intent is better understood and better served. God is not tuned to the devotee, but the devotee is tuned to God. It is the spirit of divinity that would certainly draw focus to the core of his intent. The intent being that God realisation would bring focus to the possibilities.

Yatah auntah yoginah enam cha pashyanti aatmani abasthitam.
Yatah auntah api aukritah aatmanah na enam pashyanti
chetasah. (G. 15/11)

Striving here, those who are perceiving, those who are trying to perceive the realization of God, they realize through their self-initiative, and the self-initiative is always supported and handled by the Divine, and the person who carries in his or her heart in a purified condition, the person has got the ability to realize the supreme Brahman.

When a devotee is truly tuned to God, then she or he would try to have the touch of God, word of God, view of God and ultimately, the vision of God in the way of her or his choice. It is thus a factor that would take the spirit of devotion to the point of its functional attainment. The devotee now thinks of God as an entity and allows her or his auditory system to hear the words of God. Words of God are the exposition of truth in this world. The devotee wants to have an experience of the sum-total of the human interactions at their respective levels, which would just get into the realm of divinity and inspire the person to be and remain in the horizons of the same divinity. It is in this context that the divine element is opened.

Yat aaditya gatam taejoh jagat udbhasayatae aukhilam.
Yat chandram ausi yat cha augnouh tat tejoh biddhi mam
ekam. (G. 15/12)
As the light of the sun, which illumines the entire world, similarly, the moon also shines, similarly, the fire also shines, and all these lights are all signs of the Divine.

Words of the Divine are those that make their way into the factors of life on Earth. A true devotee would draw delight from hearing the words of God. It was a moment of delight for Arjuna to have heard God in human form speaking. Lord Krishna, the Lord Supreme, having descended on Earth, had the intent and destined duty to defeat or annihilate the evil forces and establish the profound superiority of the Divine on Earth. It is the function of God to always be in touch with the chosen devotee, Arjuna. Thus, the factors that would make the scenario tuned to the system would be the right way towards it.

Gam aavishya cha Bhutani dharayam ojoh shah.
Pushnamih cha auishadhih sabah somo bhuttvah rasah
aatarakah. (G. 15/13)
The permeating soil, so I support the creatures by vital energy and becoming of nectar in the moon, I nourish the plants, God himself is nourishing in the soil.

Some great devotees yearned to understand the unique match between Arjuna and Krishna, specifically why Arjuna was considered such a competent counterpart to Krishna. Lord Krishna, after all, found it convenient that the very purpose of his earthly incarnation, as is widely known, was to protect the virtuous and, simultaneously, to vanquish evil from the Earth. God is the master of the entire creation. Therefore, to protect oneself from the bad forces in the Earth system ultimately comes down to him as an element of duty. Divine intervention does not occur frequently. It does not happen overnight.

> *Aham vaishvanarah bhuttva praninam deham aashritam.*
> *Pranah-apanah-samanah yuktah pachami aunnyam chatur*
> *bidham.* (G. 15/14)
> Taking the form of fire, or vishvana, I am lost in the body, I maintain the energy, or the vital energy of the body, and the vital energy takes it forward, the life forward, and that's how life exists, written by five.

This, as a fact, has also been followed in the Mahabharata. The bad and cruel forces of the world are those which make an impact on the minds of the masters of the world. The atrocity on Draupadi was really one of the causative factors towards the divine resurgence in the lives and activities of the world. Apart from this single action, there were other things like the attempt to kill the entire family of the Pandavas by burning them alive, and that's another reason here.

> *Sarvasyah aham cha hridih sat nibishtoh.*
> *Mattoh smritih gjnam aupohanam cha.*
> *Vedei cha sarvae aham eva vedyah*
> *Vedantakrit veda videvah cha aham.* (G. 15/15)
> It is I who remains seated in the hearts of all creatures as the inner controller, I am there within the existence as the memory of the knowledge of that, if it is understood and realized by the person, the re-creation, or the re-creative facility of the person is then energized in the person, and the Vedas would reveal that to realization.

Whereas the atrocities on the good people are considered, on the other hand, how is the goodness of them also measured? Adequate goodness would imply that the goodness gets clubbed with or is based on the noble attributes. A deep analysis reveals that goodness, to meet the standard of righteousness, implies it's fundamentally comprised of righteous attributes and factors. Lord Krishna observes that these principles of goodness, based on righteousness, are truly ingrained in the Pandavas in general, and Arjuna in particular. The strength of goodness would thus be the way to the factors of the analysis. Lord Krishna makes the straight way to reach the object.

For Krishna, Arjuna is the choice, as Arjuna alone has been fortunate in having all the required learning and training to develop. And thus, the attainment of Arjuna was unique, Krishna needed to have a person with noble character, good orientation of mind and the ultimate qualities of being honest, sincere, diligent, duty oriented, integrity in character and dedication.

> *Dvabimou purushah lokae ksharah cha aukshrah eva cha.*
> *Ksharoh sarvani bhutani kutasthah auksharah uchgatae.* (G. 15/16)
> There are two forms of mine in existence, one is my eternal and transcendental form, the other is my empirical form; the entire human existence is the empirical form of mine.

Arjuna did not have the selfish intent of gaining things for his enjoyment and gain. Even when he had won the war or the competition or any test of life, he had always endowed that to the larger community. Arjuna had the highest level of sensitivity to character. Since the factors of life push to a situation of war, Arjuna was neutral to all situations. Arjuna was given an access to visit the place of the Gods for some reason. At this point the Apsaras (the beauties of the heavenly place who test the power of celibacy a person's entering that place) had approached Arjuna for the same purpose but got denied thoroughly by Arjuna. He was brought to the same test of sensual control by the internal system within that place.

> *Uttamah purushah tuh aunyah paramatmah iti aahritah.*
> *Yoh lokatrayam aabishya bibhartah abyoh Ishvarah.* (G. 15/17)
> Yet the supreme person is in others, those who have encompassed all the three worlds, are first to be, and maintains all, and has been spoken of as the imperishable Lord and the Supreme Spirit.

Arjuna was not scared. Rather, he had a determination across his character. Arjuna, with his very strong foundation in the divine spirit, had to endure the wrath of the Apsara, who cursed him for refusing her company. Although the gods of heaven were pleased with Arjuna, they couldn't reverse the Apsara's curse or change her decree. In a way, this was part of Arjuna's charted destiny, and the one year of lost masculinity was also a necessary part of it.

> *Yasmat ksharam autitah aham auksharat cha api uttamah.*
> *Autoh aushmih lokae vede cha grathitah purusha uttamah.* (G.15/18)
> Since I am wholly beyond the perishable world and no matter of Kshetras, I am superior even to the imperishable and to the individual self, and therefore, he is always eternal, and God is always available in every element and every constituent of the world.

The entire episode of the Mahabharata is the pathway through work and concerns for the good. Arjuna was tuned to the war. The opponents were also very powerful and strong. So a person who would be expected to defeat all, and therefore, he should have all the super powerful divine weapons and learning. This is what was imparted to Arjuna. The ultimate destructive weapons gifted by the gods were all essential in the process, and they were to be those applied in the war in the appropriate situations.

Yoh mam eva sam mudhah janati purushah uttamam.
Sah sarva bidah bhajati mam sarbabhabena Bharatah.   (G. 15/19)
Lord Krishna addresses Arjuna, says that the wise men are those who realize his Divine and supreme person, and he constantly worships him, and therefore Arjuna, you worship me and understand me, through that you can understand everything.

Thus, Arjuna had that power of character, skill to learn, power and knowledge to apply and on top of everything, the knowledge and wisdom about the cause and effect of the paradigms of using super destructive tools and weapons in the context of the war. Thus, he was the one with the ideal combination of ethical perspectives of the actions, consequences of the actions, art and science of the domain of action and on top of everything, the winning power.

Iti guhjyatamam shashtram idam uktam mauyah aunaghah.
Etad buddha buddhiman syat krita krita sha cha Bharat.   (G. 15/20)
Arjuna, this most esoteric teaching has been thus imparted to you by me. Grasping it in his hands, a man becomes truly wise, and his mission in life is accomplished.

Thus, Arjuna became the right match for Lord Krishna and hence was a choice for friendship in the world. Arjuna's profound dedication brought him God's grace. Beyond that, he had complete faith, full surrender, and a deep, strong love for God. This made Arjuna a dear friend of God, instrumental in his divine plan. The basis of perspective is selfless dedication endowed with the factors of love and respect. Arjuna was the best fit to become a true friend and a partner in accomplishment.

God is omnipresent. He is omniscient and universal. Still, it is not easy to have the vision and realisation of God. Lord Krishna has mentioned to Arjuna that the essential component of God realisation is the making of character. It is the essential component that once the person is competent to have the vision of God gets a set of qualities befitting to become holy in life. The competence is achieved through making of character. He says Arjuna that this competence needs to be acquired by the person in the process.

Sri Bhagavan ubacha:
Abhyam sattvah samshuddih gjnanah yoga byabasthitih.
Danam damah cha jyogjnah cha svadhyayah tapah aarjavam. (G. 16/1)
The absolute fearlessness, perfection, purity of mind, constant fixing of yoga and meditation for the self-realization and study and teaching of the Vedas, sacrifice, hardship and simplicity is what the daivi guna or the first variety of the divine equalities.

It was with the intention of teaching Arjuna this very concept that Lord Krishna explained: Purushottama is God's invisible yet factual presence, a presence neither felt nor understood by anyone unless specific conditionalities are fulfilled. The factors of these conditions are gradually embedded in the automatic process of becoming a true devotee of God. Thus, when those chosen attributes are in place, there develops an easy and direct communication between the devotee and God. In the design of God, these direct connections are actually supported by the power of God's grace, and he holds the hands of the devotee in all situations. The priority in life, if set to have the realisation-touch-vision-companion of God, the true devotee obtains that.

> *Ahimsah satyam aukradhah tyagah shantih upeishunam.*
> *Dayah bhuteshu auloluptvam mardabam hrih auchapalam.* (G. 16/2)
> Non-violence, words and deeds, truthfulness and the softness in speech, non-doership, quietude of mind, abstaining from slander, compassion towards others and containing the senses and the mindless, doesn't disturb others or cause any kind of difficulty or problem to others.

Broad classifications of human attributes have been done by Lord Krishna. He has mentioned a certain set of qualities as those of daivi guna and a certain other set of qualities as the *aasuric guna*. These are the divine and demonic attributes, respectively. The divine qualities are similar to sattwa guna to a great extent, with some differences in the emphasis and focus. Whereas the aasuric gunas are a mix of the rajo guna and the tamo guna in the context of human society, the divine and demonic qualities both can be nurtured and developed in life through a process of cultivation and spiritual performance.

> *Tejah kshamah dhritih shoucham audrohoh na autimanatah.*
> *Bhabanti sampadam deivam avijatasya Bharatah.* (G. 16/3)
> Sublimity, forbearance, fortitude, extraordinary purity, purity of mind, bearing enmity to none, absence of self-esteem, and these are the qualities of the divine person.

Lord Krishna mentions about twenty-six qualities that are highlighted are just the representative qualities and not exclusive. He says abhoy-*sattwa* orientation- the cultivation of *jnana yoga* – *devam* – *daman* – *jagjnya* – *swadhyah* – *tapas* – *aarjabam* – *aheinshah* – *satya* – *aukrodhah* – *tyagah* – *shanti* – *dayan* – *autoluptam* – *mardabam* – *hrih* – *auchapalam* – *tejah* – *kshamah* – *dhritah* – *shoucham* – *audrohah* – *na autimanasa* – these are twenty-six attributes considered divinely qualities. Simple explanations of these are fearlessness – sattwa orientation – wisdom seeking – giving – containment of senses – sacrifice – self realisation – meditation – simplicity – non injury to others - truthfulness.

Dambhoh darpoh aubhimanah cha krodhah parushyam eva cha.
Augjnanam cha aubhijatasyah Partho sapadam aasurim. (G. 16/4)
Hypocrisy, arrogance, pride, anger, hardship, ignorance, these are the marks too, which are the attributes of a demonic person.

Not getting influenced by anger - giving up – peace – merciful – poise – not involved in others' matter - energetic – merciful – balance of intrinsic power – cleanliness of inside and outside – clam mind – controlled ego are the attributes that effectively contribute to the making of divinely personality. A combination or a mix of these are ideal in the flow of life. Thus lord Krishna mentions to Arjuna to adopt these qualities in life thereby to make the personality in the category of the Divine.

Daibi sampadah bimokshayah nibandhayoh aasurih mata.
Ma shuchah sampadam daivim aubhijatasya ausi Pandavah. (G. 16/5)
The divine endowment has been recognized as conducive to liberation and the demonic has conducive to bondage.

The demonic attributes are destructive in nature. It destroys the potential of a person, destroys the harmony in society or in a larger system. These are the operative dimensions of those attributes that make a person aware of them. The objective is to avoid or eliminate these negative qualities from one's life. The highlighted attributes—such as arrogance, personal pride, selfish concerns, anger, jealousy, and ignorance—are representative of those that influence individuals. By transforming these aspects within themselves, people can be saved, leading to the realization of a better world. Thus, in the focus of things, the performance becomes conducive to society and thus becomes an element of goodness in human society. The recommendation to Arjuna is to adopt daivi guna in life.

In the human domain, both sets of attributes are available in abundance. Desire-anger-greed- ego-attachment-jealousy are the six major attributes that obstruct the flow of goodness in life. Therefore, these are considered the direct enemies of having the spirit of divinity in life. *Sharha ripuh* or six enemies are disturbing to a spiritual aspirant.

Dvoui bhutah svargaei lokeha ausmen deiva aasurah eva cha.
Deveih bistarashah proktah aasuram Partha mae shrunuh. (G. 16/6)
There are only two types of men in the world: one has a divine nature, the other one is having a demonic disposition. Of these two, the opposing one of divine nature, we have mentioned, and now we are going to discuss those who are of demonic nature.

Lord Krishna has suggested that Arjuna to adopt the divine qualities in life as well as in war. When in a war field, doing the dutiful work in the context of the Mahabharata, Arjuna is advised to prevent any way of the creeping of the demonic attributes and in place of it to follow the divine qualities in the process of the war. Though he has been facing enemies in war, it was advised by Lord Krishna that even in the context of the war, it is difficult for a person to stop anger and hatred towards the enemies. Yet, in this case, Lord Krishna suggests that Arjuna do so. Therefore, in the war between the righteous and the unrighteous, the terrible state of the war could be seen as the place and context where anger and arrogance come out automatically. However, Arjuna had refrained from that unless terrible provocations were in place.

> *Prabrittim cha nibrittim cha jauna na biduh aasurah.*
> *Na shacham na aupi cha aacharoh na satyam*
> *taeshum vidyatae.* (G.16/7)
> Men possessing a demonic disposition know not what is right, what is wrong, cannot discriminate and consider the untruth as truth.

This is why Arjuna did the war in the sense of doing an endowed duty. He was endowed with the duty to serve God by going to the war. Arjuna had, however, severe provocations in the middle of it. The provocation was to give a proper answer to the horrific scenario of a very young man, Abhimanyu. The son of Arjuna was encircled by many great warriors of the enemy, and violating the principle of one-to-one war, Abhimanyu was encircled by seven leading commanders of the enemy. This thoroughly unjustified act of the enemies had actually incited anger in Arjuna.

> *Ausatyam pratistham tae jagat aahuh aunishvaram.*
> *Aupasparam rasah sambhutam kim aunyat kama heitukam.* (G. 16/8)
> Men possessing the demonic disposition say that the world is without any foundation, they don't believe in God, and they decry God and they are fallen in grief of greed and lust, that's how the dream tells us.

The killing of Abhimanyu in the most unjustified way had fueled the power of involvement by Arjuna. Even though he had the determination tofight in a disillusioned manner, this single and brutal act, unjustified as per the norms of the one-to-one war, turned around the context of the war. Deviations from the set principles started occurring in this context, and thus, the very essence of goodness was deviated from. Arjuna had struck to the goodness of things, but now onwards, war turns victory into of loss of life. Thus, the very purpose of a dutiful war had somewhat departed.

> *Etam dristim austyabhgam naushta aatmano aulpa buddhayah.*
> *Prabhabanti ugra karmanih kshayah jagatah auhitah.* (G. 16/9)
> Clinging to this falsehood and ignorance, they think that they are good, but they invite their destruction, terrible ways, when time comes.

Sri Krishna suggests that the divine qualities are the ways to make personalities have peace, poise, happiness and peace in life. Whether it is for the individual or a group, the contextual analysis, in a way, should lead to the adoption, continuation and elaboration upon the basis of that condition. On the other hand, the adoption of the demonic attributes leads to the fragmentation of the contents of potentiality and power of the person. For any society, organization, it happens that the practice of daivi guna offers the blissful and best outcome in life.

Kamam aashrityah dushparam dambha mana mada aunnitah.
Mohat grihitvayad asadgrohan prabartantae aushuchibratah. (G. 16/10)
Cherishing insatiable desire for the false doctrine through ignorance, these men are impure in conduct in this world, hypocrisy, pride and arrogance.

Cherishing insatiable desires and holding false doctrines born of ignorance, some people in society behave improperly. These individuals, marked by hypocrisy, false pride, and arrogance, sometimes adhere to consistently self-serving methods to achieve their selfish desires. Their ignorance often leads most of them to become addicted to life's attributes that run counter to the path of God. Falsehood is the way most live on, believing truth to be present in falsehood. Arrogance makes up in the lives of these people in such a situation that it to the core of life. In the core of life, it is the orientation of human consciousness that shapes the attributes of the character as it prevails in the world. The longing for something, if it is entertained in life, leads to the factors of a character and those of a mind. Oriented to God, this mind is thus an inspiring sun which could make it divinely vibrant.

Until the person is devoted to the cares of the passion, until the end of the tenure of life, it turns to be mending in the flow of life. The desire was such an intrinsic potential that once it is nurtured the life would be devoted to the principle of living in the continuity of togetherness of existence in life. The qualities in life are those of practice and that in the event of thoughtful creations, get into the factors of the world based on the fundamental attributes. The combination of attributes that are beneficial to the world are those that create no harm to others. Work initiated by the person thus gets tuned to the context of neutrality and those, on the other hand, thoughtful contributions to the facts of the world in such a way that enlightens.

Chintam auparimeyam cha Pralayantam upashritam.
Kama upobhogena param aetat biditva nischitah. (G. 16/11)
Giving themselves up to innumerable fears and they invite only destruction and death for themselves and beating in the sensuous enjoyments only.

While a work or a series of works is based on the preconceived thoughts of a person, sometimes because of the factors drawn from hidden desires, it makes the work accomplished in the context that is given, as a kind of barrier or as a supportive one in the context of the world. These may have thoughts which get added to the context of the person. Thoughts are likely to arise in the process of the work as well. When the person is into the work, the first internal factor that may come up is the intrinsic desire of the person in a context which may not have existed then. The person is now in a better position to discharge the work induced by the vectors of the currently aligned thoughts. The guiding direction comes from the positions of things around. An idea may thus come up, having the fundamentals of the work in a series of things which would make the world a better place compared to others. Thus, the lowness in life, if any, would breed outputs which are low in themselves.

> *Aashapashah shateiva baddhah kama krodhah parayanah.*
> *Iihantae kama bhogartham anyaenah aurthah sanchayan.* (G. 16/12)
> Held in bondage by hundreds of ties of expectations, only giving themselves up to lust and hunger, these types of dramas, and unfair means.

Certain set of attributes that are really harmful and destructive are those that would certainly either help the person to move forward or retard in any context in the world. It is, however, advised in general that the factors would be having somewhat commonality with respect to the factors of the world. It is thus obvious for the smooth functioning of the system of nature and that of the individual. In a way, thoughts are the revealed identity of the person in a given context and at a particular point in time. Good thoughts of sattwa variety would thus breed in good rewards and returns from the world of actions. Accordingly, if a thought is contaminated by the spirits of the world of darts, it would be the opposite.

> *Idam audya maya labdham idam prapsyae mano ratham.*
> *Idam austhi idam aupi mae bhabisyati punardhanam.* (G. 16/13)
> They say to themselves, mass has been secured today, they don't go for realization, they want to get everything done with ease.

The world as such is a comparison with the varieties of the intrinsics. Hidden desires, if any, would thus not remain hidden. Rather, it comes out as a mix with the characters of the person. The agenda which have been thoughtfully desired may thus prove that of a skewed one. As the empirical agenda gets mixed up with the design thoughts and thus becomes the one which turns out to be truly intrinsic, mixed, extrinsic, combining both into the totality called holistic. This holistic approach would thus have one element of the hidden instincts and the other is the boundary factors, together conditioning into the parameters that contribute to the growth and survival.

> *Ausou mayah hatah shatruh hanishae cha auparana api.*
> *Isvarah ayam aham bhogi siddhoh auyam balavanah sukhi.* (G. 16/14)

That enemy has been slain by me and these are the people who invite their own destruction.

Destiny has everything of this creation settled for. However, it is the initiative, vigour, strength and factors of creation, contribution that make into the power to recreate and have a new set of destiny in place. With the sattwa factors in life, the person can make a change in the orientation of life and thereby a factual drift in the context. With the context having drifted somewhere, the result of the action now makes a dramatic change into the void in presence to fill it with a new set of destiny in the world of humans in any context and situation.

Aadhyau aubhijanaban ausmih kah aunyah austhi sadrishou maya
Yakshmae daashyami modishyae iti augjna bimohitah. (G. 16/15)
They have got pride and they think that they will become wealthy, they try to become wealthy, they become blind with their own resources and they don't give a bit of that because they are always trying to possess things, these are the demonic qualities.

When life turns to the Divine on Earth or the form of the divine chosen or the infinite, indeterminate and omniscient, life becomes in a position to garner a pool of energy that has been gifted or that which is garnered within. Cultivation of the goodness thus makes it to the set of divine spirits on Earth that gradually gets on to the existing factors of work as the additions to what has already been garnered in the world. It is thus the initiative that a human person can take to make life more vibrant and workable in the context of the things on Earth, and as a part of the entire cosmic system. The world of actions thus makes a headway into the world of thoughts. The dynamics of the gunas in life means a process of transformation. It happens from the state of tamas through that of rajas, and then gradually having the same transforms to sattwa. With sattwa in place in life, the person now has characteristic poise and that of goodness as a gift to the world.

Factors of dispersion are in abundance in the world. Nature is full of things of attraction. Nature has all the elements in abundance to attract the focus and attention of people. The focus may be beauty, then the person looks around the world to find the objects of beauty.

Auneka chitta bibhranta moha jala samabritah.
Prasaktvah kama bhogaeshuh patantih narakah aushu chouh. (G. 16/16)
Thus blinded by ignorance and enveloped in the image of delusion and addicted to enjoyment sensations, sensuous pleasures, their minds are bewildered by numerous thoughts and these people invite their own destruction.

Abundant sources of beauty are created in the world. It is the essential factor of life that makes the life and existence of the world full of beauty. It is thus the factor which attracts the external senses of a person to look into the factors of beauty. However, beauty is a natural concept. Every piece of this creation, including the living and material objects, has beauty that is inherent. Beauty as an attribute has a variable notion. Certain categories of human forms thus make up to create beauty. Trees produce flowers to position them with beauty. Thus, it appears that in his creation, God has added to the factors present that of beauty as a psychological factor. Thus, every eye cannot experience the same beauty.

Aatma sambha bitah stabdhah dhana- manah-madan aunnvitah.
Jajayantae nama Jagnjnenah tae dambhae nana bidhi
purvakam. (G. 16/17)
Intoxicated by wealth and honour, they are self-conceited and these people are actually dangerous to the world, therefore, I don't allow them to win ultimately.

The beauty of nature is inbuilt in it. Flowers arrange themselves in such a way that the beauty is revealed to the eyes of all. It is the existential beauty. By virtue of their presence and blossoming on trees or plants, in a context, the world of those places does get filled in with factors of beauty. In the ultimate sense of the term, thus the exhibited beauty remains variant in and through appearance to people. It is an appearance on Earth as a surficial factor and parameter of beauty. The other parameter of beauty is the internal one. It is said that the human mind makes and breaks the beauty in life.

Ahamkaram balam darpam kaamam krodham cha samsthitah.
Maam aatma param deheshu pradvishayantah
aubhyasuyakah. (G. 16/18)
Given over the egotism, brute force, arrogance, lust and anger, these demonic people try to kill the divine forces.

The individual ego makes a person think great of her or his. The ego stands as a barrier to the Godly vision and the holistic way of thinking of a person. It is advised by Lord Krishna to Arjuna to set aside the individual ego and to look for the presence of atman within. If atman is in focus, then the person understands that she or he is not the leader of her or his life; instead, God is. God remains within the small cave of the heart of the person in an invisible form. Identifying him is actually a factor of consciousness. Individual consciousness, through realization comes to understand this in life.

Tena aham dvishatah kruran samsareshu naradhaman.
Kshipyami aushuvan aasuresh eva yonishu eva. (G. 16/19)

These haters, sinful and cruel, vaguest among men, I crush them again and again, I crush them always.

Thus, the divine intervention in life occurs when the person pays attention to the divine within and acknowledges the fact of his presence throughout. God is thus an autonomous resident in the heart of the person. He stays within, maybe as an invisible force, and thus is not attracted to the factors of the mind but considers those aspects of the mind where the divine call has given momentum to the functioning or the consciousness. Human consciousness is now drenched with the factors of divinity as an opportunity to have divine intervention in life.

Aasurim yonim aapanna mudhra janmani janmani.
Maam auprapyah eva kounteyah tatoh yah auntah
audhaman gatim. (G. 16/20)
Falling to reach me, failing to reach me, Arjuna, these stupid persons are born life after life in their demonic wombs and they verify to sink to lower planes even.

The types of births that create a person low in mind and nature push the ways further down. Unless it creates an urge to transform, nothing good and noble in nature. Good and noble are obvious presents to all lives, but unless a person gets into that with an intense urge, she or he cannot have that at all. It is such that a baby, whenever it cries, gets the touch of the mother. However, unless it cries, it doesn't get those factors in practice. Intense urge is that which can bring down the grace of God for a transformation. However, certain factors are there which make a person believe in the dark as light, black as white, wrong as right. Thus, these factors are only in place when the factors are really, in a way, credible and autonomous. With the human intent getting vibrant, the human intent is thus set to the factors of transformation. It is possible only when she or he sets aside personal ego.

Lord Krishna had mentioned to Arjuna the various pathways to making a life full of divine qualities. In the selection of attributes, he had asserted the need to have sattwa orientation in life. However, rajas and tamas may be the associated factors that are present in the world in large numbers. It is thus the potential attributes that are oriented in the formation of lives. And thus, when they were made to happen like the true and vibrant position, that would make it real.

Tribidham narakasya idam dvaram nashanam aatmanah.
Kamah krodhah tatha lobhah tasmat etat trayam tyajyet. (G. 16/21)
Desire, anger and greed, these people are the gates to bring them downfall, you know, when they are captured by these three, they can never come out of it, and they invite their destruction.

The realistic turn in life is thus the basis of the spirit in a dormant form. The spirit inherits from the ancestors and thus has the broad objective of getting into the factors of life that focus on the spirit of things in life. However, Lord Krishna says of three important parameters and attributes that act as the factors to pull down the overall character of the person from its position in the particular pattern of the character of a person. Three important factors are Desire, Anger and Greed. Desire-Anger-Greed are the three factors that lead to the gradual downslide of the person. Overall position of the context is one of complex situations of becoming gradually demonic in the identity of the person in the world.

Eteeh bimuktah kounteyah tamo dwaroih trivih narah.
Aacharati aatmanah shreyah tatoh yati param gatim. (G. 16/22)
Freed from these three gates of hell, man works on his own salvation and thereby attains the Supreme God.

Desire plays a pivotal role in the making of the final formative character of an individual, and in turn, it makes the behaviour of a group of people. Desire has a penetrative dimension. Desire makes the person a lot of things driven is the maker of a selfish paradigm. It is that the prospective pattern of the character's desire is thus an important parameter that the proper way to proceed in such a way that of the public level, to that of destructive parameter, now that it takes into account different courses of life which could be done in the context of the things of the world.

Yah shastrah bidhim utsrijyah bartatae kama katarah.
Na sa siddhim eva aapnoti na sukham na param gatim. (G. 16/23)
Having cast aside the injunctions of those preachers, he too has his own arbitrary way according to his own all suited, a person never gets the perfection and never earns the enduring peace of mind.

As Lord Krishna mentions that desire anger and greed are those qualities of life that do not get exposed to the inputs of the world Anger is also another factor which erodes the potential services to the mankind about the attribute like anger Lord Krishna had narrated before a sequence of progression in life Anger begets the condition of mind when it becomes touched down by the anger. Anger leads to the creation of delusion in life.

Tasmat shastram pramanam tae karya aukarya byabasthitou.
Gjnatva shastra bidhano uktam karma kartum arhasi. (G. 16/24)
Therefore the Vedas alone are your guide and follow that and follow the divine path and the divine scriptures.

Anger brings in delusion. It brings in the condition of mind that leads to the formation of the condition of loss of memory. When memory is lost, it creates a situation in when the intellect is blurred. Intellect makes the progression of life. Intellect drives the functioning of the person. Intellect drives the focus of life and the world. It is the factors of the world that make the world of work as active. It is the pattern of intellect that makes the pattern of work and ultimately creates the factors of work in life. The intellect thus makes it so smooth a function that, without the pressure of intellect in life, the factors of life get lost as the impact of the loss of intellect.

Arjuna ubacha:
Yae shastra bidhim utsrijyam jajantae shraddhaya anvitah.
Tae sham Nishtha tu ka krishna sattvam aaho Rajoh tamoh. (G. 17/1)
Arjuna said, those who are endowed with the faith, worship of God other disregarding the injunctions of those preachers, what do they stand, Krishna?

Anger then puts into the scenario that makes it happen in the parameters that make the lives go smooth. Anger generates delusion, delusion leads to the loss of intellect, and that happens through the loss of memory. Memory loss is a situation that is aimed at making of the situation in that context. If finally, intellect is shattered, the person then leads to a situation that attempts to reach the terminal end of losing the anchors of life. It is the situation of having the identity of a person. Desire, anger, and greed are the trio factors of the normal flow of life that have arisen because of ignorance. This ignorance is again a factor that has only one way out to make life hybrid in the world of work. This is a factor that continuously makes the pattern of turnaround in life. This turnaround is possible only through the kindling of the factors of life within the system. Life that understands the importance of divinity within holds the key to the illuminations in life for all in the world.

The three impediments to illusions are desire, anger, and greed. Once a person is freed from these factors, the person is endowed with the positive qualities in life through inspiration for getting inclined to develop the good qualities of life. It is thus the illumination that has made it happen in life that is tuned to the goodness in life.

Sri Bhagavan ubacha:
Tribidha bhabati shraddhva dehinam sa svabhajah.
Sattviki Rajasi cha eva Tamasi cha iti tam shrunuh (G.17/2)
Sri Bhagavan said, These are the people with the innate faith of men, Atrika and sattwika, rajasika and tamasika, I am going to tell that.

Divine endowment in life turns out to be the selective availability of goodness. Faith is the cardinal parameter in the making of a good life. It is the best factor in life that holds for the gradual making of it. Now those who follow the parameters of goodness in life are making the life of a devotee. The lives of devotees are those on the basis of faith and added to that factor, it is only the factor of goodness that acts as a paramount importance in the attributes of a particular type in the world. It is thus the makeover of things in life that leads to the total avoidance of the winds of the world of generic types. Thus, the fortunate souls are those who are good-hearted and try to have the passions of looking into the added qualities of goodness.

> *Sattvah aunurupah sarvasya shraddha bhabati Bharata.*
> *Shraddhamayah ayam purushou yoh yat shraddhah sa eva sah.* (G.17/3)
> The faith of all the men conforms to their mental disposition, Arjuna, faith constitutes a man, whatever the nature of his faith, readily he must exist in the same way.

It is the set of sattwa qualities that are the essence of the lives of the devotees that the basis of it in the process of attaining the realization of God, realization of the spirit of the Divine through the spread of the factors of goodness. It is the basis of the goodness that actually attracts the notion of the divine spirit in a way that makes it into the holistic goodness for life. This goodness is empirical, but it turns into eternal with the divine inspiration in life. This divine inspiration is thus invited to have the spirit of God within. Thus, devotion to God needs to be seen as to what is the essential spirit of the same in a way that contributes to the essence of the spirit of the Divine. In a way, this leads to a variety of types.

> *Yajantae sattvika devan yakshah rakshamsi Rajasah.*
> *Pretan Bhuta ganam cha aunyae jajantae tamasha janah.* (G.17/4)
> Men of sattwika disposition worship the Gods and radheshika temperament, worship the demigods and demons, while others of tamasika disposition worship the spirits of the dead and cause.

Lord Krishna now suggests to Arjuna that the devotion that one may garner has three different types. Thus, devotion is of three varieties – the sattwa devotion, the rajas devotion and the tamas devotion in life. It depends on the variety of the person that induces in her or his fundamental attributes in life. Thus, the basis of life is the faith that has been ingrained in her or him. It is thus the sattwa quality in life that makes it the basis of the factors of personal attributes of the person. People with divine qualities are the basic factor that finally makes an inroad into the fundamentals. Thus, the message of life turns around to become the message of life of a godly person.

> *Aushastra bihitam ghoram tapyantae yae tapah janah.*
> *Dambhah ahamkarah samyuktah kama raga bilambitah.* (G.17/5)
> Men who practice severe penance and austerity, take all sanction by the scriptures and who have love for God, are devoid of egotism, and they have no attachment and power.

If faith has a proper root in the consciousness of a person, it makes it to the core of our understanding to the basis of the functions of life. It is good habits and good character that breed good behaviour. It is thus the basis of the divine life that makes it into basic and fundamental view of becoming 'sattwa bhakta'. The sattwa bhakta, or the devotee with the positive and truthful limits in life, is thus related to the factor of life making a new horizon that makes it the basis of the functioning of a devotee.

Karshayantah sharirastham Bhuta gramam chetasah.
Mam cha autah sharirastham taan biddhi ausuran nischayan. (G.17/6)
And who are there with the elements constituting the body as well as the touch me, the supreme spirit dwelling in their heart, no, those senses of people are there, who don't understand me, who don't accept me, they are demonic in nature.

Those who impose restrictions imposed by themselves on the habits, qualities of different types make inroads into the basis of life. It is thus one of the bases of things in life that lead to the fundamentals of our new objects of life. The new objects would thus make their way into the factors of usual metrics of life. It is thus the quest for the fundamentals of divinity that makes it the basis of happenings in life. In the material context, the same three types as classifications based on sattwa, rajas and tamas are applied to food, characters, choices, tastes and preferences in life. Divine attributes thus make it to the realization of God. It is that factor of life which works as a better fit for life on Earth.

18 Moksha: The Liberation

Defeating the negative forces for Victory and Emergence in Life and Works

Processes of thought are intrinsic to a person. As the person maintains her or his thoughts in life, work takes shape therefrom. Noble thoughts are the definite preludes to the set of noble works in life. If a person wants to have the spiritual way of life, somehow it forms a shape such a way that spiritual inspiration seeds in and gradually pushes the forces of noble thoughts and spirits from within to surface in life, and that seed may ultimately lead to the realisation of God within. The realisation as such is not just a factor of the cultivation of good thoughts for a noble spirit, but the process of thoughts with a noble spirit facilitates the realisation better.

Aaharah tu api sarvasya tribidhoh bhabati priyah.
Yagjnyah tapah tatha danam taesham bhedam imam
shrinuh. (G. 17/7)
Lord Krishna explains that just as individuals vary in their inner disposition (guna), so too do their preferences and practices. He categorizes food, sacrifice, penance, and charity into three distinct types, each aligning with a specific inner disposition. These types are described in detail to illustrate how different actions and choices reflect and reinforce an individual's inherent nature or guna.

The type of character a person maintains and nurtures in life is important from the point of view of developing a culture of good thoughts and being able to garner and nurture good thoughts for winning a noble purpose in life. Thoughts do arise from the basic intent and the intrinsic consciousness of a person. It is thus the very basic trends in character and the basic oreintations. Thus, in a way, the properties of sattwa guna may act as a set of facilitators in the life of people to either live a life of materialistic domain or to be into the spiritual domain through cultivation and practices of the sattwa guna in life. It is thus that Lord Krishna has guided Arjuna on the importance of the three gunas – the sattwa, rajas and tamas. He mentions the influence of the principles of the three gunas in the backdrop of the flow of lives on Earth. Thus, food shall have three gunas oriented in the life of people and work.

Aayuh sattvah baloh aarogya sukha priti bibardhanah.
Rasyah snigdhah sthirah hridya aaharah sattvikah priyah. (G. 17/8)
Foods which promote longevity, intelligence, vigour, health, happiness and cheerfulness and which are juicy, succulent, substantial and naturally agreeable are liked by men of sattwika in nature.

Here is the basic identity of things that lead to the desired destiny in the world. Destiny as such is the result of a total living. Anyone having the intent to have God realisation in life would thus be the definite achievable for those who are thus inclined to God. With an inclination toward God, a person will have less focus on and attraction to material and worldly enjoyments. This mental orientation will prevent attraction to superficial goodness. Thus, a spiritual person would draw goodness from factors that are pleasing to the sense organs, moving beyond externally attractive factors and the boundaries of sensual joy in life.

Katuh aumlya labanah auti ushnah tiktva rukshah bidahinah.
Aaharah rajasasya ishthah duhkha shokah aamayah pradah. (G. 17/9)
Foods which are bitter, sour, salty, over-hot, pungent, dry, burning and which cause suffering, grief, sickness are dear to the rajasikas.

While choosing her or his food thus the person would take with graceful mind those elements of it that are soothing to the senses. Items of food that help in ease of internal assimilation are good for keeping mind relatively undisturbed. It is the way of soft and aligned good items cooked with a higher than normal level of absorption are good for spiritual life. Thus Lord Krishna mentions to Arjuna that it is the choice of food that plays an important role in making the mind used to and having the process of realisation on the skies of the assimilated factors. Pungent, acidic rich with spices in the process of making food creates certain amount of toxicity in the food such consumed and thus may create difficulty in the ease of digestions.

Yata yamam gata rasam putih paryushitan cha yat.
Uchchhitam api cha aumedham bhojanam tamasa priyam. (G. 17/10)
Foods which are ill-cooked and not fully ripe, insipid, but retreat, stale and polluted and which is impure too, is dear to men who are tamasikas in disposition.

Even natural items like fruits, vegetables and the ingredients of any kind of raw material in nature, if fresh are good for consumption and get digested and assimilated in the best possible way. Lord Krishna suggests to Arjuna that whenever things of the plant or vegetative origin are taken to see that these are fresh and not contaminated, nor fermented in any way. It is thus the pure, the fresh, that are good to consume. Thus in the paradigm of realisation the divine oriented mind would consume the fresh and pure. Sanjay liked all these.

> *Auphala kamkshibhi yagjnaei bidhi dishtah yah eijyatae.*
> *Yahshtavyam eva iti manah samadhayao sa sattvikih.* (G. 17/11)
> The sacrifice which is offered as ordered by scriptural injunctions by men who expect no return and who believe that such sacrifices must be performed is sattwika in character.

Sanjay had narrated right in the middle of the war of the Mahabharata the sequence of thoughts and advices by Lord Krishna and thus it is all about the powers of spirituality which would ultimately shape the character and behaviour of the person in a manner that would be the most suitable for a healthy mind to grow and remain. As such this healthy mind is actually the one that would in a way make the personality oriented to God, on one hand it is oriented to God and on the other the attitude to work undertaken gets drifted to the core of the same. Mental poise and calmness on a perpetual scale is what is achieved and thus the most important condition of getting realization works in this context in life. It begets a situation called God in life. Though God is always with the lives on Earth, its presence is that of the most important parameter in life. As always it is known as before that as the messenger of God in life prophets have in life thus makes the world a better place and the better qualities of people on Earth.

The three toxic poison for life are the desire, anger and greed. However all these three arise from the fundamental problem of ego and the envy of a person. *Ahamkara* or high ego is something that is considered as one of the most important parameters in human life that not only restricts the flow of goodness in the human society in all sense of the term. Human society needs people who are docile, amiable and are inclined to each other. This emotional bonding has been a prerogative to create a sense of deeper understanding of human being. Extreme form of ego remains as the root cause of evils in human life and societies.

> *Aubhi sandhvayoh tu phalam dambha artham aupi cha eva yat.*
> *Eijyatae Bharata shreshtha tam yagjnam biddhi Rajasam.* (G. 17/12)
> That sacrifice, however, which is performed for the sake of more mere show or even with an eye to the sprue, no, it falls for Rajasika Arjuna.

Anger is one of the most important killers of the noble qualities and goodness in human context. It is as such required to be seen, identified and taken care of. Lord Krishna says Arjuna that whenever a person is caught by anger the memories of good things, subtle and noble parameter of life, the conscience all get blurred for the period that anger persists in the mind of the person. Memory is one of the most important factors of survival in a human context. With the loss of memory the person has the distractions from the continuity of the empirical emotions in life the person is further constraint in the path of the journey in life. The scientific civilization cannot progress without the support of things in continuity. Pythagoras to Einstein, each step of scientific invention and discovery has a continuity with the previous. If the continuity were lost the idea of the fundamental particles as it is now would not have emerged. Impact of sound and light in the making and running of human societies would thus lead to a blank. If Faraday and Maxwell or Cavendish were not in the continuity of thoughts modern day electronics and semi conductors would not come.

> *Bidhihinam shritam aunnam mantra hinam au dakshinam.*
> *Shraddha birohitam yagjnam tamasam parichakshatae.* (G. 17/13)
> Sacrifice which is not in conformity with scriptural injunctions, in which no food is offered and no sacrificial feasts are paid, which is without sacred charkit of hues and devoid of faith, is a tamasika sacrifice.

Continuity of thoughts and connectivity of patterns is one of the most important parameters in the emergence of scientific thoughts. The idea that particles could be having only energy as content without the contents of mass could not be carried forward. Acharya Satyendra Nath Basu had identified the concept and developed the model that it was possible to think of situation where a contentless or apparently void situation having some energy content had a long impact for the development of the set of particles. Boson and the emergence of the view photon being a particle of light, the wave function of De-Broglie got finally converged into the wave-particle duality having identified the role of energy quanta and mass-less particles. Similarly the technologies of now bank on those that were developed and fine tuned in the previous century.

> *Devadwija guru prajnana pujanam shoucham aarjavam.*
> *Brahnacharyam ahimsah cha shariram tapah uchyatae.* (G. 17/14)
> Worships of God and brahmanas, one's teacher, elders, great souls, purity, straightforwardness, continence and non-violence, these are called the penance of the body.

Memory plays an important role thus in the life and works of people on Earth. Anger is therefore an important and dangerous killer of good thoughts and spirits in life. Loss of memory is arisen from the condition of a deluged mind. This is why the impact of anger on creation of delusion needs to be taken care of. At the outset of it, the course and cause and effect of such anger needs to be corrected and thus envisioned in the beginning of it. It is thus the care human mind needs to be careful of in that mind remains cool and calm and any kind of turbulence is to be carefully avoided and in the process, it should have the spirit and the culture of sattwa values within so that the elements that are poised to be otherwise round need to be either avoided or faced off to contain the same in life. If that is done the intellect remains fresh and vibrant.

Aunudbega karam vakyam satyam priya hitam cha yat.
Swadhayah abhyasanam cha eva bak mayam tapah uchyatae. (G. 17/15)
Words which cause no annoyance to others and are truthful, agreeable and wholesome, as well as steady through the study of the Vedas, and it remains steady through the scriptures, practice of repetition of divine nature, these are known as the austerity of speech.

Lord Krishna has suggested Arjuna to do the war as an intrinsic duty to his God. At the same time, the process of maintaining poise within needs to be maintained. Yoga in the form of king or principal of all yoga called raja yoga was thus mentioned by Lord Krishna to his dear disciple Arjuna. While doing that, the mental form of the person would be contained. The crazy desire of a person is a constant enemy that keeps the elements of turbulence vibrant within and thus mind gets its peace to calm down. The Yoga would thus make a person thoroughly disconnected from the factors of depression and causes of stressful situations affecting human mind. It is thus the context created through meditation that sense of satisfaction develops. This makes the mind free from all senses of deprivations and thus a free mind is attained through which the person would experience not only satisfaction but joy in life.

Manoh prasadah soumyatvam mounam aatma binigraham.
Bhaba samshuddhi iti etat tapoh maanasa uchyatae. (G. 17/16)
Carefulness of mind, placidity, having contemplation of God, control of the mind and perfect purity of inner feelings, all these are called austerity of the mind.

In the process of the meditative initiatives for God realization, it is expected that the mind would be free from all different kinds of bondages and be tuned to the cause of the supreme having done this creation with his divine purpose in mind. Oriented to God, the human mind should be cheerful and maintain its poise through placidity. This mind shall acquire the power to contemplate upon the behaviour of a godly personality. Thus, the mind of the spiritual seeker would be focused on God and be tuned to the conditions of love for God in a way that suits the life mostly. This mind is free from morbidities like dejection and fear, anxiety and grief, agony and perturbation etc. and on top of these shall be full of illumination and vivacity to remain and become cheerful always. Negative attributes like jealousy, envy, vindictiveness, ruthlessness, arrogance, ferocity etc. create ripples of mind and make it turbulent.

A turbulent mind fails to fix on the consciousness of God. Cool and calm mind with the sense of joy and devoid of any desire is the one that can have the capacity to concentrate on and thereby can proceed in the line of the spiritual attainment. You have the basis of devotion ingrained. A controlled mind gets freed from the impacts of the worldly emotions and illusioned condition of the mind. Illusion can push out any negative attribute gets controlled or they go off from the mind. This helps the mind to become equipoised -steadily one in all situations. Mind turns around and develops a calm and condition of poise.

> *Shraddhvayah parayah taptam tapoh tat tribidham naraih.*
> *Auphalakamkshabhih yuktaeih sattvikam parichakshatae.* (G. 17/17)
> This threefold penance performed with supreme faith by yogis expecting no return is called sattwika.

Purity of mind is attained in a context which gets over from all kinds of negative emotions, expectations and desires. Thus, the mind which is no way is a seeker of anything to fulfil the eternal habits of responding to the most positive way of living in this. Thus, devotee would be tuned to the seeking of God. As Lord Krishna has suggested Arjuna that it is the usual living culture that makes an impact on the person deep inside the regularity of interactions with the calm and cool mind now may thus concentrated once it the cheerfulness to it may be principal impact it had a difference in the mind. Complete absence of the things that afflict the body and mind such as coldness, jealousy, arrogance, envy, anger, sloth, indolence all should be removed.

> *Satkarah maanah pujah artham tapoh dambhena cha eva yat.*
> *Kriyatae tat iha proktam rajasam chalam dhrubam.* (G. 17/18)
> The penance which is performed for the sake of revised non-honour and adoration, as well as for any other selfish gain, which in all sincerity is by way of ostentation and yields an uncertain and momentary fruit, has been spoken here of rajasika.

Faith acts as the total adherent to the spirit of goodness in life. Faith in God induces the overall consecration and dedication in the form of the goodness of life. Faith begets elemental love for God and, in return, creates elements of love for the people on Earth and everywhere. It is as such the dominant fabric of the human society that brings in satisfaction to the minds of people. It is thus the reversal from the desire of results accrued from the actions initiated. Thus, the main focus of the mental orientation is such that every bit of support is drawn from the cosmic presence. Mental approaches in the cosmic system is the inclusion of the factors and elements of material or objective reality as revealed in the world.

Commensurate with the noble qualities the application of sattwa guna in life stands materially important in the world. Faith brings in the flow of the quality of lives and the parameters are the essential attributes and the penance in a spiritual life. Faith has the focus of the contributory parameters and factors essential for best way of making the goodness in life that may happen. It is thus the factors in the flow of good qualities which make the fundamentals of good life. Goodness is an automatic flow and an associate of a sattwa life and thus brings in a flow of that.

Mudha grahena aatmano yat pirhaya kriyatae tapah.
Parasya utsadhanan artham ba tat tamasa udahritam. (G. 17/19)
Austerity which is practiced through partiality and accompanied by self-mortification or is intended to harm others, such austerity has been called tamasika.

Penance is not an essential element in the human context for the realization of God. It is renunciation in life exercised through the formation of the mind as such. The mind is thus the main vehicle that may contribute to the direct realization of God. However, there are certain approaches by some people who do the penance, making the fact of doing penance known to others to garner some kind of appreciation. This is some kind of act which deviates from the principle of sattwa, and thus it is another variety of the set of attributes that deviates very widely from that of the truthfulness.

Databyam iti yat danam diyatae iha anupakarinae.
Daeshae kaale cha patrae cha tat danam sattwikam smritam. (G. 17/20)
Gift which is bestowed with a sense of duty on one from whom no return is expected is appropriate time and place to a deserving person, that gift has been declared as swatika.

If perversity and self-mortification takes the centre stage of individual character, it makes austerity and penance falling into the category of tamas. Tamas-focused austerity is thus the basis of the lowness in life. Any good work that is carried by the drive of the selfish interest, and sometimes attempted by perversion, goes against the interest of goodness in the society. Maintaining the goodness in life in a manner that elevates one's own mind from the forces that bind the minds of persons in society through cords of concern and love. Tamasic actions become prone to the darkness within. If a person carries in mind the pull factors for darkness, sattwa remains farther away than even the thought of. Sattwa breeds the illumination to make life blessed.

However, in the act of giving remains the scope to get up to the spirit of sattwa, a gift that is bestowed with a sense of duty on the part of the giver. It is that attribute in the context of the giver, and thus it becomes so much glow. Sattwa breeds in the mind of these people in any context, in any way.

Yat tu prati upakarartham phalam uddeshya ba punah.
Diyatae cha pariklishtam tat danam rajasam smritam. (G. 17/21)
Gift which is bestowed by grinding the Gajip spirit with the object and getting a service in return in the hope of obtaining a reward is called rajasika.

Spirit of goodness demands that the person has to operate things in the world in a way that makes things oriented to do good to human beings is always constrained by the conditions around. One can overcome the impacts of the prevailing conditions by doing the acts which are by virtue of their maintaining certain set of attributes that are tuned to the spirit of God and are tuned to God-realization. It is thus the prevailing factors that are tuned to the intrinsics of life in a context that the endowments are based on the truth and goodness of life in the world. Need of a person fulfilled through the gifts of another person is the matching correlation through one person's good wishes for the other. It is that important aspect in the life of a person that helps to bestow a person with the same of other. It is thus the facts of life that needs to be coordinated for good of all.

> *Aadesh kaalae yat danam patrebhyah cha diyatae.*
> *Ausamaskritam aubaginatam tat tamasam udahritam.* (G. 17/22)
> Gift which is made without good grace and goodness is absent, it is being full spirit and out of time and place, and undeserving person, a person is said to be tamasika.

Sattwa is revealed through the acts and thoughts of a person. Anybody who is in need of something is to be filled in by a good person with good wishes and intents. In this case, the person is the Patra or the person who is the correct recipient of the gift visualized for. This gift is something that works as a noble endowment in the given circumstance in the world. It is thus the given context of the living endowments and the gifts. This is thus meeting the hunger and thirst and thus the meeting and fulfilling of that is one such is in need of certain things. It is thus the effective elemental sattwa that acts as the right element for giving at a given time and place. Thus, the very best option is to give unto the person or the group of people that are the elements external to the system in a context.

> *Om tat sad iti nirdesho brahmanoh tribidhah smritah.*
> *Brahmanoh tena vedam cha yagjnash cha bihita purah.* (G. 17/23)
> Om, Tat and Sat: this has been declared as a three-fold application of the Absolute, who is truth, consciousness and bliss, by that the brahmanas and the Vedas as well as the sacrifices were created at the cosmic dawn.

Giving cannot be something with elements of commerce in mind. Giving cannot be return-seeking. Returns in the context is something that is something which is the next level of objectives and that of the contextual transaction in life. It is usually advocated to gratify one's level best to those who deserve that most in life. Service to God is the most auspicious one. Service to God is possible when there is somewhat perceptive idea or an element of faith or at least some kind of understanding about the goodness. This is possible when the price of the service is understood. It is that what is about the facts of the world about the proper realization of God.

Tasmat om iti udahritya yagjnya danah tapah kriyah.
Prabartantae bidhano uktvah satatam brahmah vadinam. (G. 17/24)
Therefore acts of sacrifice, charity and hostility as enjoyed by sacred perceptions are always commenced with the noble persons given to the recitation of Vedic chants with the invocation of the divine name Om.

Lord Sri Raam had his observation about his great devotee Sri Hanuman that none among the Hanumans and others in life have been able to render services to God as it was rendered by Sri Hanuman. Sri Hanuman was so unique in the understanding of the mind of God, he never needed to talk about the required things of God's intent in the context of the world. God in history or on the facts of the literature of divine play comes on Earth in order to fulfill the intent of doing some fundamental good things for the transformation of society on Earth. It is thus the coordinating endeavour that God's role in the world is fulfilled.

Tat iti anabhisandhyay phalam yagjnah tapah kriyah.
Dan kriyah cha bibidhah kriyantae Mokshakankhibhih. (G. 17/25)
With the idea that all things belong to God, who is denoted by the appellation of thought, acts of sacrifice and hostility, as well as acts of charity of various kinds, are performed by the seekers of blessedness, expecting no return for them.

Service rendered to God in terms of material objects in the world is what could be considered as very subtle and most of the places an insignificant one. It is thus the most important element of service that which makes somewhat delighting thing to the world, but it may prove to be less delighting to God. However, the factors that makes the divine delightful in the context of the world, it is thus most important to understand that the factors are those, the most of the things that needs to be focused on to render the solutions that are available to take it ahead of the concern for the world. The service rendered to God in the form is the essential approach needed to delight God on Earth in a way that makes a thorough approach at the initials of the presence of God on Earth. Service provided as such needs to be totally free from the impacts of any desire or any mix of the human ego in any way.

Om Tat Sat, once uttered, it invokes the spirit of God within. The absolute is expressed through Om. It connects the creative and driving energy to the factors of life in a way that acts as the energy input to take it forward for maintaining the life and activity of the people on Earth. Om is the input of the person, acoustics that brings in the potency for facilitating the forces of material orientation that make good the factors of life by orienting lives towards God.

Sadbhavae sadhu bhavae cha sat iti etat prayujyatae.
Prashastae karamani tatha sat shabdah partha yujyatae. (G. 17/26)

The name of God as Sat means the truthfulness is employed in the sense that truth and goodness are inbuilt in him and he is the source of all truth and all goodness, and the word Sat is the praiseworthy action of God. Lord Krishna says this to Arjuna.

Om is uttered to connect with the divine consciousness in the context of the world. It is thus the factors of elemental devotion and meditation that would bring in the impact in life to fit in for the acts of austerity and charity. Sacrifice should occur as an automatic revelation of the factors of ascendance and at the same time to bring in the goodness of life in a way that binds the factors of life in the way recognizing the supreme being present in life and works to fit in the elements of the material world and at the same time it is that energy inputs of the good elements. Thus, it is thought of the Divine intent to make the world Divinely and as such to initiate the purpose of making a transformative journey unto that.

Yagjnaeh tapasi daanae cha sthitih sat iti cha uchyatae.
Karma cha eva tat arthiyoh sat iti eva aubhidhiyatae.   (G. 17/27)
Steadfastness in sacrifice, hostility and charity is likewise spoken of as Sat and action for the sake of God is verily termed as Sat.

The Supreme creates, maintains and puts across the factors of life in the context of things happening in the world. It is such that Tat Sat is the inclusive idea of all. He is the creator and at the same time he represents the world of things in the context of the world of human lives. The divine truth as revealed in the utterance of Om. Tat is that he is all and all are in him. He is present as all over, as the intrinsic essence of the spirit of life and thus he begets the elements of the factors of life in the context of the world of actions, in the factors of the life of each human person and thus the elements as such is the essence in the context as such to understand the spirit of equality in the context of the world. It is thus the effective total reality that is reflected in the lives of the individuals are contextual.

Aushraddhyaya hutam dattam tapah taptam kritah cha yat.
Asat iti uchyatae partha na cha tat pretyah noh iha.   (G. 17/28)
Oblation which is offered, a gift given, an austerity practiced and whatever good deed is performed, if it is without faith, it is all termed as not, that is, asat, therefore it is of no avail and here and hereafter.

The idea that goodness and sattwa is thus the gift of the divine in the event a person considers God as the focus of life. Realisation of the divine points at the context of the world. Truth of the world in the form of empirical identities are understood through the organs of senses. These are elements of truth that are essential inputs for the understanding of the essential reality of the world. In a way, Om Tat Sat refers to the intrinsic understanding thus revealed to make the point that the visible, tangible truth of the world is the creation of the divine in a context of his intent to create. Beyond this, the non-revealed one is also the contents of the greater truth that aims at the factual understanding through revelations in consciousness and thus the one that attempts to bring into the understanding of the world that every life, each element of matter and life is but the revealed identity of God.

> *Arjuna ubacha:*
> *Sannasasyah Mahabahoe tattvam ichchhami veditum.*
> *Tyagasya cha hrishikesha prithak keshinishudan.* (G. 18/01)
> Arjuna said, O Krishna, you are the supreme, and you are the supreme energy. I wish to know clearly the truth of sannyasa and tyaga.

Sacrifice-austerity-charity are the elements of character that pertain to the 'Sat' or the truth-consciousness of the Supreme. An oblation, a gift given, an austerity practised and whatever good deed one performs without faith it becomes something called 'Asat'. When faith is reinstated in person, it may not be the right perspective in a way that happens to be the remedy for transcendence. Noble things done without faith is fruitless that is why they are considered Asat. The value of action that is good and deterministic is that the urge to use sacrifice through sustained practice.

> *Kamyanam karmanam nyasam sannyasam kaboih viduh.*
> *Sarba karma phalam tyagam prahu tyagam bichakshanah.* (G. 18/02)
> Lord Krishna said, some sages understand Sannyas as giving up all actions motivated by desire, and others, discerning thinkers, declare that tyaga consists of relinquishing the fruit of all actions.

Faith is essential in the making of a spiritual character. A character groomed in good values is rightly positioned to initiate the transcendence of qualities, thus forming an affirmative and welfare-providing character. Hence, human character is the basis for a person's attaining divine realization. A right character drives a person towards maintaining good habits. A good person initiates good works and then takes them forward towards a good end and thus making it a chosen action in the process of living life and maintaining goodness in attitude in life and works. Thus, the element of the focus in life makes it a good orientation in life in the spell of things in life and works in the world.

The lasting freedom in life is the capacity of the character towards the spirit of the divine in life. The spirit of divine, realised properly, pertains to the true orientation in life. Bondage in life comes from within. The focus of life on desire gets reengineered by the impact of things and issues of life. As it is the case the spirit of goodness and faith in God gradually creates the focus and intent to have the primacy of intent and focus on God. God in consciousness is the liberation.

Tyajyam dosha eva bat iti eke karma prahuh manishinah.
Yagjnya danah tapah karma natyajyam iti cha auparae. (G. 18/03)
Some wise men declare that all actions contain a measure of evil and are therefore worth giving up, while others say that acts of sacrifice, charity, and penance cannot be given up.

Liberation in the ultimate sense is that which is termed as moksha. It pertains to the holistic attainment. Life gets oriented to God in the way of having intrinsic faith in God. This leads to the sensitization of the spirit of divine attributes in life. The supramental transformation in life occurs with the devotion and thus the person initiates the journey within. The team of people in the process of living life in the best way to maintain the same is to be the person's same approach in lives.

Sat Karma or good action, Sat Chinta or good thoughts, or the set of attributes, would make many such spiritual activities dedicated to God. In a way love for God with faith creates the path of liberation.

Nischaya shrunu mae tatrah tyagae Bharatasattvam.
Tyagoh hi purusha bayghrah tribidhah sam prakirtitah. (G. 18/04)
Between sannyasa and tyaga, the conclusion of mine is renunciation. Renunciation is the ultimate essence of tyaga. Renunciation can be of three kinds, sattwika, rajasika and tamasika.

Arjuna was curious to know the nature of true renunciation and its proper process. The essential attributes of sannayasa was in point of understanding by him. Whether Karma or action needs to be abandoned or not was a matter of concern and proper understanding. In the process of doing the spiritual practice by a seeker what are the realistic attributes that makes effective headway to the factors of thought and action. Thoughts may be contaminated in a context that breeds forth action. Thus actions which pertain to the purity is an action in the context of the flow of works in the world. As Lord Krishna elaborates – the actions of giving, sacrifice or renunciation can be made to fit in the objective of the person.

Yagjnah danah tapah karmah na tyajyam karyam eva tat.
Yogjnah danam tapah cha eva pavanani manishinam. (G. 18/05)
Acts of sacrifice, charity, and penance are not worth giving up. They must be performed. For sacrifice, charity and penance, these are the preservers of the world.

It is the orientation of the mind with respect to the work is ordinarily resides lots of expectations. At times, these expectations are driven by the forces of animal habit in nature. Arrogance, anger and greed sometimes capture the mind in a way that determines the nature of the personality. Desire is an overarching element as a driving force in the mind. Covered by these desires by the impact of the external factors makes it happen in the best way.

> *Etani api tu karmani samgam tyaktva phalani cha.*
> *Kartvyanih iti mae partha nischitam matam uttamam.* (G. 18/06)

Hence, the acts of sacrifice, charity and penance, all these acts are the duty of human beings and must be performed without attachment and expectation of reward in return.

As Lord Krishna suggests to Arjuna, the acts of sacrifice, charity and penance in life. This would basically get into the fundamentals of any life. Lord Krishna declares that the acts of giving should be the true with the flow of the cosmic truth in the world. In order that the world continues to give priority to the good actions supported by the spirit of life, Arjuna wants to be the torch bearer of truth in the life of the person in it.

> *Niyatasya tu sannyasah karmanoh no upapadyatae.*
> *Mohat tasya parityagah tamasah parikirtitatah.* (G. 18/07)

Certain acts should be avoided, and the acts which are avoidable acts, the acts are with desire, motivated by desire, have no doubt, they should be given up and abandoned. Such abandonment is out of ignorance, has been declared as tamasika.

The power of the character comes while nurtured. The creatures may develop the doer in a sequential manner along very particular way of continuing of the stream of lives. Attachments could be of different types. It is something that breeds in factors of realisation in life gets influenced in the wide variety of context. One of these is the direct attachment to work whereas the other one is the eagerness and greed that makes doer profusely attached to it. Acts that are motivated or guided by the desire are required to support work but bending it towards an improper end in the stream of actions. Renunciation practised with the aim to have love for God is deterministic and leads to God realisation.

A person who considers work troublesome and abandons it because it feels external to them acts as a rajasic individual. Allotted duties or inherently good tasks should be accepted as a series of actions that bring the best outcome for any work situation or interaction. Interaction thus becomes oriented toward actions that yield goodness and welfare for all.

> *Duhkhyam iti eva yat karma kayah kleshah bhayat tyajyet.*
> *Sa kritva rajasam tyagam na eva tyaga phalam labhet.* (G. 18/08)

Should anyone give up the duties for fear of physical strain, thinking that all action is merely the nature of discomfort, practicing such rajasika form of renunciation, they cease and they try to keep the fruits of it.

Karma of any kind may be performed by anyone in the society. It is thus the diversity of approaches that induce the person towards achieving the ends in a given context or even a context created by the person. It is such a situation that the person may get into dimensions of human emergence at all times. Thus the work undertaken by a person begets its best outcome in the event of its best performance through the work. It is in the context of spiritual practice to attain the realisation that somewhat care is needed to maintain certain amount of discipline in the habit of food intake, called 'Aaharshuddhi'. Traditional method of spiritual practice refers to developing a system that would be good for spiritual attainment. Thus Lord Krishna has spoken to Arjuna by saying that external purification and material purification of the biological system would get the mind of the aspirant reach a point of sattwa.

Karyam iti eva yat karma niyatam kriyatae iha Arjuna.
Samgaum tyaktva phalam cha eva tyaga phalam labhayet. (G. 18/09)
Prescribed duty which is performed simply because it has to be performed, giving up attachment and fruit, that alone has been recognized as sattwika.

With the ways of the purification thus known the devotee may like to have it in the process that enters into the process of understanding of the same at a time when the same is caused into the factors of spirituality in a manner that affects the entire process in a sequence of things or events which prove to be working for the process of realisation. In this context when the acts of purifications are done properly, the essence of it is made to have the dimensions of spiritual practices that are true to the perspectives of the situations that are apart from the focussed intent or the aspirant for realisation of the supreme in context of the world.

Na dweshthi kushalam karma kushalae na anusajjatae.
Tyagi sattwa samabishtou medhabi chhit na samshayah. (G. 18/10)
He who neither hates action but does the action to bring the lasting happiness and he does it without any attachment and this is conducive to blessedness and he gets the goodness of the world and devotion of mind.

The classification based on fundamental classification is actually principles of the actions of the same as it is the elemental aspect of the fundamental tenets of life of human personalities. As such, the issue of differential character comes in. Thus, the work would be in a way that creates a different pathway for having realisation of God. As such, every aspirant would fall in the same line of action to embrace the truth of eternity as applied to the contextual reality.

Na hi dehabhruta shakyam tyaktvam karmani ausheshatah.
Yah tuh karma phalatyagi sa tyagi itti avidhiyatae. (G. 18/11)

Since all actions cannot be given up in their entirety by anyone possessing a body, he alone who renounces the fruit of actions can be called a man of renunciation.

Duties of a person in the context of the world have been identified as those of the greater humanity and the world. The basis of a duty orientation is the goodness of the character. A person with a sense of duty in mind can have a culture of work that is oriented to goodness in life. Sattwa orientation can transform the work in a way that attempts to be engaged in the flow of work always and qualify the work and its context as something that makes a transformation in the work context and the dynamics of work. Thus with the new dimensions in the work and its flow, the world of action takes a new look in the perspective of the world to win the fortune.

Anishtam ishtam mishraya cha tribidham karmano phalam.
Bhabati autya tyaginam pretyah na tu sannyasinam kahchit. (G. 18/12)
Agreeable, disagreeable and mixed. Threefold indeed are the fruits that accrue thereafter at the actions of the unrenouncing, but there is none whatsoever of those who are renounced.

It is the work connect with the spirit of divine that is the strength of the work and the connection with the potential prospects of the context of the situation as it is the basis of the progression of the forces of vitality. Karma yoga is that context when a noble mind connects with the world of work and thus makes a headway into the process of transformation. Work gets the status of better quality, better outcome and at the best perspective. It is thus the proper bent of the orientation of work. The Karma has to be performed in the manner that creates the continuity of purpose. This is known as the niyatah karma which creates a continuity on the pathways of time. The art of work of 'karmashu koushalam' in the sattwa way is recommended.

Karmayoga offers a perspective distinct from that of conventional work situations. A sattwa orientation in life facilitates a new approach to the flow of work, making it effective through elemental awareness of the work's fruits in all contexts. Sattwa gunas, or a truthful personality, are the context of the world; they embody the spirit of creating wonders.

Pancha imani mahabaho karanani nibodha mae.
Samkhae kritantae proktani siddhayae sarva karmanam (G. 18/13)
In the branch of learning known as sankhya, which prescribes means for neutralizing all actions, five factors have been identified as contributory to the accomplishment of action. I want to tell this now to Arjuna.

Some of the terms in the world are those that affect elemental consciousness and that of the essence of the same spirit in a way that would make this world a superior place. At a time, the basis of the work would prove to be oriented to the work only. It is thus the very basic understanding of work that now pointer to new work. The new work is for attaining the spread of the fruits of the work, but not getting into any expectation of the person doing the work. Work accomplished without any expectation or the work being made to happen in a way that not only fulfils the core objective but also makes it workable from all dimensions.

Audhisthanam tatha kartah karanam cha prithak bidham.
Bibidhan cha prithak cheshta daivam cha evatra panchamam. (G. 18/14)
The five factors towards the accomplishing the actions, they are the body and the doer, organs of different kinds and the different functions of many different kinds and the fifth is daiva, destiny, which is there from the transcendental.

In the modern context, it is expected that there should be fewer impositions or no impositions of either goodness or fitness into the stream of work. Works are done through classified approaches and segmentations. Acts performed by a person begets the results matching with. It is the quality-type and pattern of the work that makes it a way in the context of the work. At times, the work performed may bring in heavenly bliss. It may make the person land on a bed of roses to enjoy life in all possible ways. However, there could be other situations where the person may be pushed into the context of misery in life.

Sharerah vak manobhi arshat karma prarabhatae narah.
Nyayam ba biparitam ba panchaiti tasya hi etabah. (G. 18/15)
This daiva, the contributory causes whatever actions, right or wrong, man performs with the mind, space and body.

Whether it is the condition of heavenly bliss or that of sorrow in life, the situation can leave the person to reverse it. A person with a neutral mind can create a position of equidistance in the profile of work with mental neutrality. A neutral mind is independent. A neutral mind can maintain its variability impacts. A mind that varies in the context of work can be made to work in the actual field of action. Certain types of works, thus, may be treated as those which have the potential outcomes that are acceptable in practice or agreeable in theory. It is thus the best method of action that puts sattwa.

Tatra evam sauti kartamam atmanam kevalam tuh yah.
pashyati kritavah buddhitayah buddhitu annya durmatih. (G. 18/16)
Notwithstanding this, however, he who, having an impure mind, regards the absolute, taintless self alone as the doer, then the pervasive understanding does not view or write.

Sattwa, as the driving pattern of character, makes an orientation of mind that attempts to get into the factors of such activities in a way that fulfils the broader perspective for the welfare of the world. This welfare is the resultant aspiration of society and humanity. Thus sattwa attribute would infuse a certain set of qualities in the human character, which creates the bent of mind for offering quality work to fulfil the work agenda and at the same time, without any selfish calculation in the work.

> *Yasya na ahamkrito bhabo buddhih yasya na lipyatae.*
> *Hatah api sa iman lokan na hanti na nibadhyatae.* (G. 18/17)
> He whose mind is free from the sense of doership and whose reason is not affected by the attractions of the worldly and activities of the worldly nature, does not really kill, even having killed all those people, nor does any sin accrue to him.

Selfish calculations in the work creates desires, maybe sometimes these, as it progress further, may involve any kind of negative emotions in the workplace to have the fruits of the work for a short term gain. This is likely to invite happiness in the short term. This happiness may be the fruits of immediate achievement, victory or the acts of pleasure. Each one of these may lead to the disruptive prospect of the person in the scenario, thus highlighted.

It is thus the whereabouts of the basic structure of work that is important but more important is to understand the mechanism through which factors of these good attributes have their own in the horizon of good works for the wellbeing of the society of the world.

The actions thus may create diverse possibilities. Karma leads to Karma yoga when each element of Karma is associated with God in some way.

> *Jnanam jneyam parigjnatae tribidha karma chodana.*
> *Karmanam karma karta iti tribidhahi karma samgrahah.* (G. 18/18)
> The knower, knowledge and the object of knowledge, these three motivate the action and even so, the doer, organ, and activity, these are the three constituents of the action.

This refers to the principle of God realisation. It is thus attributed to the set of actions done or undertaken in the context of the world. The person may do it for certain perspectives, and thus it is the basic variation that is induced from one particular karma to another of a different variety. A karma performed based on own decision and for the primacy of personalised idea or thought makes the work more of the variety of the needs of the situation. The responsibility of the doer is now a higher degree of dependence on the doer increase.

> *Jnanam karma cha karta cha tridhaiva gunabhedatah.*
> *Prouchachatae guna samkhanae yatha aboshrinnutae.* (G. 18/19)

In the branch of knowledge dealing with these attributes of the gunas, of the modes of prakriti, the knowledge of the action as well as the doer, has been declared as the three kinds according to the gunas and attributes. I am going to tell them now.

However, if the doer does the work of the person could be based on the basis of understanding and thus it connects back to the work in the best possible way. Since the person as the doer does not have any role in the decisions, in most of the cases, actions prove to be of a lesser degree of involvement and the outcome becomes less rewarding to the world. The hazards or resistances to the work may thus be something that has the power to stop or put obvious inclinations or force of skewness.

Sarba bhuteshu yeneno ekam bhabam avyayam ikshatae.
Aubibhakam bibhakteshu tat gjnam biddih swattivikam. (G. 18/20)
That by which man perceives impenetrable divine existence and undivided and equally present in all individual beings, know that knowledge to be sattwika.

The 'Prarabddna' or destined work is something that is drawn from the series of actions drawn from the core of the carried forward essence. Prarabddha karma is construed on the basis of the essence of the works in a life. If the essence of it is oriented to God, then the person is logically alienated from the spell of work and the factors of the set of actions. It is thus effectively the parameters which make the doer inclined to the divine spirit. Prarabddha karma may connect the person to the divine spirit in a sharper and easier way than most others.

Prithak tvena tu yat gjnam nana bhabena prithak bidhan.
Bettih sarveshu bhuteshu tat gjnanam biddhi rajasam. (G. 18/21)
The knowledge by which man cognizes many existences of various kinds from one another in all beings. It is to be known that knowledge is rajasika.

Prarabddha chinta or the endowed thoughts, may bring forth the thoughts of doing things divine nature. These persons will turn sattwa guni or with truthful characters. these are the people who would think of God always and initiate the works that are helpful to God realisation. Thus, the divine spirit in man and the direct emphasis on the elemental goodness would make the bright inclusion of divine activities in life. It is thus the spiritual endeavour that brings in realisation of God.

Yat tu kritsnasubat ekasmin karyae saktam aheitukam.
Autah twad artha bat aulpanch vad tat tamasam udahritam. (G. 18/22)

Again, that knowledge which is clinging to one body and as if it were the whole and which is irrational, has no real grasp of truth and is trivial, has been declared as tamashika.

God himself is present among all creatures. For that matter, every human being has the prospect and potential to address the divine in the flow of life through activities. Actions undertaken on the basis of the faith in God and his universal presence would be drenched in the spirit of God and thus make a headway into the factors of the permanence of divine connection. The belief that God exists in all and his spirit is present in every living entity causes the final understanding of nishkama karma – this entails that the lives are all embraced by God and thus the world is a place that takes the form of work as dedicated to God and essentially tuned to the spirit of creation.

19 Achieve Fortune, Victory and Liberation

Attain – Grow – Rise – Become

Actions can be classified as sattwika-rajasika-tamasika karma. The first one is truth-centric action, the second is power-centric action and the third is the action driven by tamas features or ignorance in realistic terms. It is thus the basic actions in life. Whereas God makes no discrimination in life, the factors of a good life should be sattwa-driven or inclined to sattwa.

> *Niyatam sanga rahitam ragah dweshatah kritam.*
> *Auphala prepsu na karma yat tat sattwikam uchyatae.* (G. 18/23)
> The action which is performed without any accomplished desire or the sense of doership or sense of ego in the action, the action which does not have any kind of attachment and without any seeking for the return, that action is called the best action or the sattwika action, the action which is truth-oriented.

Sattwa basically projects goodness of intent, purpose and work. A person is sattwa-driven means she or he is not only inclined to truth in principle or at the level of thoughts but also it's present as an inherent principle in all cases of actions. Thus, when the action of a person is truthful in thoughts, in principle and in action, it is attributed as a sattwa personality. In the context of the world, a sattwa personality is thought of as the essence of the creative contribution by individuals in the world of corporates, industry, business and society. This is of immense importance for a sustainable future.

> *Yat tu kamepsu na karma sah ahamkarena ba punah.*
> *Kriyatae bahula aayasam tad rajasam udahritam.* (G. 18/24)
> That action, however, which involves mass strain and is performed by one who seeks enjoyment and who has got the egoistic control or egoistic impression of the action and its result, who expects the results to satisfy his or her ego, is a rajasic action.

The factor that differentiates the role of a sattwa from that of a rajas personality is actually the creative aspect of organizations of various types in the world. The sattwa person being honest, truthful and with integrity create the fundamental strength of the world. This strength is something that it makes a headway into the perspective of the system in the world. The sattwa person is fully committed to the objective-purpose- mission-vision of any organization. It is thus the universal architectural unit and a building block of good life.

Aunubandham kshayam himsam aunapekshya cha pourusham.
Mohad aarabhyatae karma yat tat tamasam uchyatae. (G. 18/25)
The action which is undertaken through sheer ignorance and with regard to the consequences or loss to oneself, injury to others, the action which causes badness, the action which creates a problem for others or injury to the others is an action which is a tamasika action.

Deviations from the sattwta principle as it is attempted by the factors of life and work deviated from the principle of integrity, honesty, truthfulness, trust, faith, dedication in the context of the work and life. Thus, the loss of potential energy of human being is as such the focus of goodness of the factors of life. It makes the person happy with selfish gains, caring little or nothing for the sense of doing good to the world or actually takes the sense to goodness only.

Mukta sangah na ahambadi dhriti utsaha samanavitah.
Siddhah ausiddhou nirbikarah karta sattwika uchyatae. (G. 18/26)
Free from attachments, un-egotistic, endowed with firmness, zeal and un-swayed by success or failure, such a doer is said to be the swattika doer.

Human attributes, once having got freedom of approaches in the flow of thoughts that identify the right routes in the journey towards excellence. Excellence in works and life demands honesty-integrity. The strength of the vital force as created, maintained at the perspective of the world in a way makes the finer dimensions of life actively revealed in its own way. The dynamism or active energy refers to the fact of principle potential energy is the exercise of it towards fulfilling the organizational goal.

Raagi karmaphala prepsuh lubdhou himshatmakah aushuchih.
Harsha shokannitah karta Rajasah parikirtitah. (G. 18/27)
The doer who is full of attachment, seeks the fruits of action and is greedy after it, have a egoistic control or wants to have a egoistic control over the results of the action, process of action and the entire set of the action is a rajasic action.

Thus the rajas person with her or his power of vitality may play an urgent or extremely important in the flow of work and fulfilling the agenda of life. A sattwa person with all goodness, honesty, truthfulness, integrity may fall short of the required energy and power of functioning to make things happen in the best possible way. Thus it may require the support of the rajas attribute of dynamism to make things happen in the right way and have the right output for life in a long-term scale, organizations and entities would strive for getting a combination of the good and noble intent of having the outlook and cherished objective that entities are all serving the world by way of developing an outlook of sustainable future. For a corporate sustainable future can only be achieved by the giving mind.

Human nature comprises of varied features. Certain tenets of personalities are common to human behaviour and character, however there could be certain other aspects of the personality that could be nonspecific to the nature of the person, whereas there are other dimensions of the personality which are specific to the individual.

Auyukah prakritah sthabadhah shathoh neishkritikah aulasah.
Bishadih dirghasutri cha karta Tamasah uchyatae. (G. 18/28)
The action which reveals that the person does not have any self-control, uncultured, arrogant, deceitful and inclined to such other actions which could be damaging to others, to the world and this loathful and downhearted action and procrastinate doer is an action which is done by tamasika doers.

Whatever be the fundamentals of a person, it is the very basic reality of the entities of the person that makes the scheme of things of life that are basic to the pool of things in the world. The pool of things is drawn from the basic core of the person; however, it can be taken as the presence of the personality through the realm of thoughts and actions. It is in this context that we thought of the concept of personality. At times, we would find that the person acts in this world without any involvement of the personal self. In this context, we thought of the concept of personality. At times, we would find that the person acts in this world without any involvement of the personal self. Personal self is thus kept outside the domain of the person. In this situation, it turns into the scenario of the individual in the context of the world.

Buddhih bhedam dritae cha eva gunah tat tribidhaham shruhuh.
Prochyamanam ausheshanah prithak tvena Dhananjoyoh. (G. 18/29)
Lord says to Arjuna, now hear the threefold division based on the predominance of each guna or the understanding of buddhi and dhriti, the firmness, which I shall explain in detail one after the other.

Impersonal personality is that kind of a person who performs and thinks in a way that does not get inclined to that of individual self, rather gets involved in the forms of personalities who are in the frame of a form but at the same time is a non-form structure of air or sometimes that of void.

It is thus the basis of the form of divinity that makes it workable to the tune of its making of the dimensions that combine different aspects of the produce of good thoughts to cultivate that into good spirit and overall goodness. This kind of person is thus not only non-discriminating but universal in its approach. This context is further understood when similar minds emerge from this.

> *Prabrittih cha nivrittih cha karyae aukaryae bhauyo aubhauya.*
> *Bandham Moksham cha yah bettih buddhih sa partho sattwiti.* (G. 18/30)
> The intellect that correctly determines the path of activity and renunciation, what ought to be done and what should not be done, what is fear and what is fearlessness and what is bondage and what is liberation, that intellect is sattwika intellect.

Behaviour and its factors originate from the fundamentals of human behaviour. This is somewhat coming back to the basics of the person. At the fundamental level, the person neither belongs to the world nor to the spirit of things. He is rather all profound and unified in the approach. The core elements of this personality is thus basic to the life and growth of this individual. Essence of an individual is thus understood in the absence of any kind of coloured feature or the attribute of the personal colour in the basics of the person. It is thus the empirical perceptive of the person that makes and colours the habit of the person and tunes it to the original vibration of the cosmic system to take a call about the world of spirituality as against that in the world of the material transactions.

> *Yaya dharmam audharman cha karya cha aukaryena eva cha.*
> *Auyathabat prajanati buddhih sa partho Rajasih.* (G. 18/31)
> The intellect by which man does not truly perceive what is dharma and what is adharma is an intellect and is done with an assertion of the ego, is an intellect of the rajasika.

Righteous principles in life have the transformational dimension wherein a life has to broaden its purview to discover the factors of goodness and the spirit in life. Righteous principles are based about the inclination of the core personality that makes it sure about something happens on time, current or that on a delayed scale of time. A few important attributes are there where the basics of the person having attained somewhat spiritual and somewhat practical aspect of the maintenance of the creation.

> *Audharmam dharmam iti yah manyatae tamasam aabritah.*
> *Sarba aurthan biparitan cha buddhi saa Parthah Tamasih.* (G. 18/32)
> Stepped in ignorance and the intellect which has got these images the adharma to be dharma and the unrighteousness as righteousness and perceives the bad as good is an intellect of Tamosika person.

When the person is deviated from the path of God, truth turns into an alien matter. It may so happen that the conscious choice of the person becomes the untruth. It may become such that the real untruth is considered by the person as truth. Deluged in the impacts of the factors of untruth, the person talks about the making of a realistic journey in the flow of activities in life. Therefore, in a way, when the mind is influenced by the goodness of the spirit, these factors of delusion are contributing to the making of tamas personality. Tamas person makes his presence in the world as the power of negation or the power becomes autonomous. This makes the person thus makes the presence of the supreme being in an invisible for the period of focus in life.

Character is fundamental in the ways of good realization. A weak character is easily pushed to slip down to the spell of darkness. Darkness is an automatic feature in any person. However, conscious efforts thus helped to get out of darkness.

Dhritya yauyah dharayatae manah pranae indriyah kriyah.
Yogenah aubyabhicharinyah dhritih saa Partho Sattwiki. (G. 18/33)
The unwavering firmness by which a man controls through the yoga of meditation, the function of the mind, the vital airs of the senses, that firmness is Arjuna, no, for it is sattwika firmness.

Restraining a person in life is a step forward to remove the patches of darkness and at the same time to have truth and illumination in place. God in life is the advent of true illumination in life. It is such that the moment life becomes inclined to God, it receives the divine light in flashes. Truth and reality in life then take the right turn and unfold in the appropriate sense. The basic purpose of living life is thus reflected in the consciousness, as Lord Krishna has put it to Arjuna, the goodness of divine illumination cannot be understood by an impure mind or a corrupted character. The mind usually carries a certain type of impurities in most of the mind.

Yayah tu dharma kamarthan dhritya dharayatae Arjunah.
Prasangena phalakamkhi dhrih saa partho Rajasih. (G. 18/34)
The perseverance, however, by which the man seeks reward for his or her actions, clutches with extreme firmness, virtues, early possessions and worldly enjoyments, that perseverance or dhriti is known as a rajasika.

Disciplining mind is fundamental to spiritual attainment. It is natural way of normal human being. Arjuna is destined to perform the disciplined way of accomplishment. It required that mind which is trained as the storehouse of good attributes. Anger-greed-lust-jealousy-envy-covetousness-hatred-sloath etc. are destructive in nature. Once the mind get influenced by any of these or any combination of these the person looses the power to turn the personality to sattwa orietation. In this condition carrying out the Divine urge or fulfilling the Divine wish through the agenda of action becomes impossible.

A mind whicgh is deidcated to God can bring over all these conditions and situations at any point of time provided the dedication is pure and honest. Greed, anger, lust have their roots in the basic forms of desire. Again, desire draws its roots from the basic ego of the person. This means, anger, greed, lust can be controlled only when the person has the reach and control over the basic roots of ego of the person. Internalization happens in life through the meditative form when illumination flourishes within. The fire of aspiration for God is the best way to contain the virtues in life.

> Yayah swapanang bhayam shokam bishadam ma madamah eva cha.
> Na bishnu murtih durmedhah dhritih saa Partho Tamasih.   (G. 18/35)
> The firmness by which an able-minded person does not give up sleep, fear, anxiety, sorrow and vanity and the ego as well as the firmness is lost is a tamasika firmness.

Vices such as anger, jealousy, envy, all these do fundamental balance in the mind. All these are negative aspirations thus may lead to actions passing through which the person may wake up to the call of noble elements. Person may question the purpose reason of certain actions and this is the fire of aspiration of God is a cleanser. it takes the person's conscious understanding to the level of basics – 'who am I? why do I reckon to this kind of action? What could be the better ways of thinking or doing things in life? In whatever ways can I achieve the desired goal of being truthful always?'

> Sukham tu idanim tribidham shrinu mae Bhararshav.
> Aubhyasad ramayatae yatra duhkhah auntah cha
> nigachchhati.   (G. 18/36)
> Lord Krishna says Arjuna, now hear from me the threefold joy too, that in which the sadhaka or the aspirant finds enjoyment through the practice of adoration, meditation and service to God and loves God, whereas he or she reaches the end of sorrow.

In the way of self-questioning, the devotee gradually starts discovering the right dimension of involvement. God and the devotee, a relation is identified where the mind of the devotee gets through the energy and strength in life that she or he gradually gets oriented to discover the true self within. Service to God is the right way to move forward in life. God is not before you in this world. So, how to offer service to God? It's very straight way that we may opt for by serving the humanity.

> Yat tat augrae bisham eva parinama aumritah upamam.
> Tat sukham sattwikam proktam aatmabuddhi prasadajam.   (G. 18/37)
> Such a joy through appearing as poison in the beginning but tastes like nectar at the end, hence the joy born of it in the placidity of mind brought about by meditation on God has been described as sattwika.

Service to human beings does not necessarily mean that you offer service to humanity begins with making a neutral personality. Selfish considerations in life to be shaken off in the process, the person may get inclined to the spirit of God and thus become free from the bondages of personal gains and be oriented to the broader perspective of the world in general and human society in particular.

The usual trend is to earn personal satisfaction in life for now. Personal satisfaction for now may prove to be against the spirit of human emergence and the concerns for true sustainability in the creation. The concern for happiness or satisfaction for the broader humanity for now is something that requires somewhat elevation or transcendence in life, and certainly needs the ways of life to get oriented to God in spirit or God on Earth.

Human organs have a tendency to aspire for satisfaction on no time. Satisfaction of organs also does not stop at a point, even for a revival or relook at what has happened. Rather, this is such that the organs contribute to life, their individual worth and are expensive. Each organ thus has its own perspective. However, the elemental focus on and analysis may reveal reality.

Bishayo indriyah samyogat yat tat aumritoh upamam.
Parinamae Bisham eva tat sukham rajasam smritam. (G. 18/38)
The delight which follows from the conduct, senses, mastery of the sense objects, eventually is poison-like and appears as nectar and is spoken as rajasika.

In the real sense of the term getting constrained by the habits and immediate choice by the organs is a trend which may be called as the 'Rajasic happiness'- or happiness that resembles kingly. Kingly habits are good in terms of attaining personal gains and immediate satisfactions in life, to take example, matters of pleasure for the reproductive organs or the organs of food intake and assimilation, once allowed to go limitless, may lead to results that would prove disastrous in many ways. The tongue secretes saliva to attract food with flavours, taste, look, etc. But the quantum of consumption as well as the quality of consumption may lead to the creation of reactive positions and repulsive conditions within the human system.

Yat augrae cha aunubandhae cha sukham mohana aatmanah.
Nidrah aalashyah promadah uttham tat Tamasam udahritam. (G. 18/39)
[That action which stupefies the self, defeating the enjoyment as well as in the end, derived from the sleep, ignorance, obstinate error and delightful, is a delight which is based on falsehood, is a tamasika.

Rajasic happiness is fleeting; it brings momentary pleasure but ultimately leads to restlessness and, in many cases, self-destruction. Though it may appear attractive at first, its pursuit often undermines long-term well-being and distorts the sense of overall goodness, as it is driven by immediate gratification and external stimulation.

Even more detrimental, however, is tamasika happiness—characterised by inertia, laziness, excessive sleep, and a passive surrender to comfort and complacency. When such tendencies are cultivated or encouraged, they gradually erode human potential. Tamasika happiness, often referred to as 'dark happiness,' acts as a retarding force on life. It dulls the mind, weakens the will, and obstructs the path to meaningful growth and fulfilment.

> *Na tat austih prithibyam ba dibi debaeshu ba punah.*
> *Sattwam prakritihjeih muktam yat evi syat triguneih.* (G. 18/40)
> There is no being on Earth or in the upper atmosphere, even among the gods or anywhere else, who is free from the three gunas born of prakriti or the nature of the supreme.

The usual human pattern on Earth is to get mixed in nature. Humans in their character and behaviour on Earth have usually certain holy dimensions which are full of goodness and at the same time certain other aspects which represent the facts of the world and are worldly in nature. Worldly attributes are usually combinations of good and bad, truth and falsehood, light and darkness. With these aspects, inbuilt in the human character, is thus constrained by the binds of the codes of earthly components.

> *Braahmanah kshtriyah vaishyanam shudranam cha parantapah.*
> *Karmani prabibhaktani swabhaba prabhaboh gunaih.* (G. 18/41)
> The duties of the wise people and the kshatriyas, the vaishyas as well as the shudras have been divided according to their inborn qualities or the inherent intrinsic characteristic properties of them.

As such, no one is there on Earth who is free from the limits of the three different varieties of gunas or the characteristic properties. Social segregations are based on the dominant type of person. In this analysis, the segregations are not made to depict high and low among the professions. Rather, it is the depiction of the person's supreme focus and competence in a particular way of functioning in the context of the world.

> *Shamoh damoh tapoh shoucham kshantih aarjabam eva cha.*
> *Gjnanam vijnanam aastikyam Brahmakarma svabhabajam.* (G. 18/42)
> Subjugation of the mind and senses, enduring hardships and discharge of one's sacred obligations, external and internal purity, forgiving the faults to others, uprightness of life after death etc., study and teaching of the Vedas and other scriptures and realization of truth relating to God and love for God, all these constitute the natural duties of a brahman or a wise man.

Person having the internal control over the propensities and tendencies of the organs in the human body in the context of the world in general. This can be the main approach to determine the sattwa-oriented person. This means a person having adequate control over inner tendencies and, on the other hand, having truthful control over the organs is sattwa oriented. this person shall have definite faith in God and make her or his life smooth. The person has given up desire and greed, does not get attracted to ignorance and falsehood. Simplicity and orientation to God is one of the most remarkable ways to make the best positive orientation in life and activity.

Control over the organs is a primary step towards proceeding forward to achieving good realization. Not only that, one has to have the control over senses and organs with a volition for the movement of the incidents and occurrences, but it should be autonomous in approach.

Shouryam taejoh dhritih daksham yuddhae cha api aupalayanam.
Danam Ishvaram bhabah cha kshatram karma svabhajam. (G. 18/43)
Possession of valour, possession of might and culture of might, culture of fearlessness, firmness, diligence, undaunted dauntlessness in battle and bestowing gifts and lordliness, all these constitute the natural duty of a kshatriya.

The person who can develop control over the mind and senses such that the aspects of realization of the supreme truth and consciousness, the Brahman, becomes a smooth and obvious journey. In the process, the person gets into various types of attractions, allurements and sensitization towards falling behind worldly material gains in various ways. This could be through allowing greed to become more intense and thus to have the craving for material objects and fulfilments in life.

Krishi Gou rakshga banijyam vaishga karma swabhabajam.
Paricharya aatmakam karma sudrashyam api swabhabajam. (G. 18/44)
After rearing up cows on a straight of merchandising, all these constitute the natural duty of a person in the trading class and community, the vaishya, and service to other classes is the natural duty even of a member of the labouring class or a shudra.

Greed as a factor pulls down the person towards the conditions of hell. It is fulfilment for once multiplies the urge for the next. Thereby, it makes a headway towards infusing animosity among people on Earth. Greed does not come alone. It pulls along its companions like desire, ego, jealousy envy, covetousness, indolence and similar things in a personality. Greed is the seeding to black habits of a personality. It brings in the factors that contain the person around selfishness in the extreme sense of the term. Greed is not only a black puller but also destructive.

Sve sve karmanih aubhi ratah samsiddhim labhatae narah.
Svakarma niratah siddhim yatha bindati tat shrinuh. (G. 18/45)
Seekingly devoted to his own natural duty, man attains the highest perfection in the form of God-realization, here the mode of performance whereby the man engrossed in his or her inborn duty reaches the highest consummation or attains that.

Once a person is under the grip of greed, she or he is certain to be covered in the mind and consciousness with the curtains of doubts and filthy things. Aggressive greed can make a person reach the terminal end of the animal instinct and can prompt the person towards doing something that is thoroughly destructive to the goodness and fairness of spirit in life. It is thus the demonic agent in life that acts as the killer of the noble and good potentials of a person on Earth.

Yatah prabritti bhutanam yenah sarvam edam tatam.
Svakarmanah tam abhyachyah siddhim bindati maanavah. (G. 18/46)
Man attains, man or woman attains the highest perfection by worshipping through his or her own natural duties for him or her and from whom the tide of creation has streamed forth and by whom this universe is pervaded.

The factors that are termed as sharah ripuh or six enemies of goodness and holy living in life are subservient to the lead of greed. Greed is the caustic and acidic destroyer of daivi guna or the divine attributes in life. it is thus the fundamental principle to raise the consciousness of a person high, such that it has forgotten the terms with the spirit of things in life ever on Earth.

Shreyan svadharmoh bigunah paradharmyat svanusthi thyat.
Svabhaba niyatam karma kurban aapnoti kilbisham. (G. 18/47)
Better is one's own duty, though devoid of merit, than a duty of another well-performed. For performing the duty ordained by his own nature, man does not incur sin.

Good spirit in life requires things to happen in a way that enables the spirit to foster smoothly forward. Thus, the spirit of goodness needs to be maintained carefully. Negative emotions categorized as the sharah ripu should not only be avoided, but the counteractive of these would be to urge upon good and invocate the supreme divine in life. Thus a person whenever comes in the way of good realization, comes along the focus area of sustained efforts towards having unfulfilled unfoldment of the intrinsies of a person. Unfoldness happens when a dedicated mind focuses on the Spirit of God. On the other hand, a devoted mind can penetrate deep inside the inner core.

The potential attributes dormant in an individual need to be adhered to in life. A person's personal and intrinsic quality is determined through the kind of orientation in life the way the person proceeds further ahead of time. When it comes to the performance, it is oriented to the best attainable one in one of the best possible ways in the ways that adheres to the factors of life.

Sahajam karma Kounteya sadosham api na tyajet.
Sarba aarambhah hi doshenah dhumena augnih iva aabritah. (G. 18/48)
Arjuna, one should not relinquish one's innate duty, even though it may have a measure of evil, for even as fire is recovered with smoke, all understanding and are beset with the smoke-perfection or the other.

Unattached to the benefits of the actions undertaken can no doubt make the work superior to that with attachments in life. However, when the person performs action in lines of the fundamental tenets of the personality, the autonomous approach to the work makes it tuned to the ways that lead to perfection in the work in the given context in life. Thus, the context would induce the person to take the actions in the right manner. At times, the fundamental attribute of the person may remain thoroughly obscured in the context of work in a situation that makes the approaches to work different and difficult in the condition of uneven flow of resistance in the fundamental context of the work.

Aushaktah buddhih sarbatrah jitah aatma bigatasprihah.
Neishkarma siddim paramam sannyasena audhigachchhatih. (G. 18/49)
He whose intellect is not attached anywhere, whose thirst for enjoyment has altogether disappeared and who has subdued his mind, reaches through sankhya-yoga the path of knowledge, the consummation of actionlessness.

A person addicted to work or any context makes it competent to have the objective of the work very different and deviates from the aspects of the situational dynamics for the same. In a given situation the context of each element of work adheres to the flow of the work as a flow or a continuity. It is thus the kind of work that is tuned to the doctrine of goodness and nishkama karma or selfless work contributes immensely to the transformation of human society.

Siddhim praptoh yatha Brahmoh tatha aapnoti nibodhah mae.
Samasenah eva Kounteyah nishtha gjnanasya ya parah. (G. 18/50)
Arjuna, know from me only briefly the process by which man having attained actionlessness, which is the highest consummation of jnana-yoga, the path of knowledge, reaches Brahman.

The elemental formations of the flow of the work in a way makes its appearance in the situation of the flow of the work at a time and condition spelled out in the variations of the spell of the impositions of the context in a way that makes it happen to the person choosing the work in a way that makes the work more fulfilling that happens to the pulling factor to downscale the forms of work and thereby the results for the work of the continued actions make it happen in the right perspective in all situations.

> *Buddyah bishuddyah yuktoh dhriti aatmanam niyamya cha.*
> *Shabdadin bishayanah tyktvah raga dweshou byudasyah cha.* (G. 18/51)
> Endowed with pure intellect and adopting the light, concerned for the God-realization, a sattwika has a regulated life, controlled diet, prefers to live lonely, an undefiled place, having rejected sound, not into noise, not into chaos, the mind is tuned to one, the control of over the senses.

The God-centric person would focus on the call of the inner soul of the person in the right perspective. Work itself is the tool and makes the way to have concentration of mind and develop the right orientation to divinity. In this perspective it is the best orientation for a person to consider work as the tool and medium to acquire good realization. God realization happens when the focus of the mind is not the material aspect of work but the spirit of work.

> *Bibikta sebi laghu aashih yatah baka-kayah-manashah.*
> *Dhyano yogah parah nityam vairagyam sama upashritah.* (G. 18/52)
> Five senses of reasoning, hear, vision, everything, the control and firmness of truthfulness, resolute on the dispassionate and got rid of all attractions, aversions for remaining and devoted to the meditation of God.

Certain degree of variations would be the variations in the spirit of the work. It is thus the performer is in the real state of mind that tunes up to the context of the work. It is like the spell of the oneness of context of each of the elements of the work. Work turns into the good-centric work in a way that makes it eloquently tuned to the spirit of the cosmic situation. Thus the spirit of the performer now tunes up to the eventual context of the work and the performer may be turned as the person with *karma sannyas* or the personality dedicated to the cause of the supreme spirit in the flow of time.

When certain performances of the situations and thus the context of the situation of the person in the ways of the work and the way that makes it happen to the happening of the work in the context of the world and thus the objective of the situation thus makes it oriented to the factors of the makes of the situations in the realm of the flow of work.

> *Ahankaram balam darpam kamam krodham parigraham.*
> *Vimuchyay nirmamah shantoh Brahmabhuyayo kalpatae.* (G. 18/53)
> Person is devoid of egotism, doesn't have any of the six vices, violence, egotism, arrogance, lust, anger, luxuries, avoid the feeling of miyam and

tranquility of heart, such a person becomes qualified for oneness with Brahman who is truth, consciousness and bliss.

It is the fundamentals of the spirit of the performer. Ego-centric approach as the basic factor of the fundamental aspects of the work. Depending upon the orientation of the individual character of the work as also that of the basics of the fundamental aspect of work. Purity and simplicity of mind thus make the person tuned to the fundamentals of the situation. Thus the opening of the gateways to greatness of the functional aspects of the work and performance. The context of work and its flow should match each other in the sense of its purity of purpose and service to the entire constituents of the stakeholder for the work. If the work is dedicated to God the performance and accomplishment turns into the best of its kind in the context of the changing reality and material dynamism of the current and forward period in the human society.

Brahnah bhutah prasannah aatma na shochati na kamkhotih.
Samah sarveshu bhutaeshu mat bhaktim labhatae param. (G. 18/54)
Establishing identity with the Supreme who is truth, consciousness and bliss, the cheerful mind of the consciousness and cheerful mind with consciousness of a yogi or a God connect, no longer grieves nor craves for anything and maintains the same kind of mental frame for all situations and maintains the supreme devotion to God.

Absorbed in the work, the noble soul gets into the fundamentals of situations. Person does the work for the divine. It is the fundamental orientation that makes headway into the context of the work. This situation begets transformative dimensions in a way that makes headway into the basic objective of the work. The performer now develops faith in the output of the work being that of the worship for the divine to make happen the dimensions of the work with perfection. performer now enjoys the situation in such a way that the work as worship proves dedication.

Bhaktyah mam abhijanatih yaban yashah asmi tattvatah.
Tatoh mam tattotoh gjnawata bishatae tat anantaram. (G. 18/55)
Through that supreme devotion, the person comes to know the God in reality and understands the real identity of God and thereby knowing me truly, forthwith merges with my transcendental being.

The performer who does the work with the totality of mind and gets engrossed in the work in a way that contributes to the making of a divine culture in the human world. Even the work of ordinary nature proves to remain as the work of the contextual reality. The divine thus endows the performer with the spirit of devotion and love with these elements of devotion and love. The person may attain ecstasy in the flow of work making it evident that the performer now attains good realization with a view to the spirit of work and devotion.

Sarba karmani api saudah kurbanoh mat eva aashrayah.
Mat prasadat eva aapnotih shashvatam padam abyayam. (G. 18/56)
The karma yogi however who depends on me attains my grace and eternal imperishable stable state through performing all actions.

The performer gets the fact of love and faith in God, while doing the work in the given context. Thus, the objective situation becomes ready to be transformed into the situation of spiritual journey through the process of work which is performed unattached and with dedication. Dedication makes as the spirit of perfection and total involvement into the realm of the work with the context having transformed forthwith.

Chetasa sarva karmani mayee samnyasya matparah.
Buddhi yogam upashrityah mat chittwah satatam bhabah. (G. 18/57)
Mentally resigning all your duties to me and taking recourse in yoga in the form of even-mindedness, be solely devoted to me and constantly fix your mind on me.

Consciousness of the performer now becomes strongly vibrant. It stands up to make the work fulfil the cause of the supreme on Earth in human conditions. The performer attains all good spirit in life and thus begets a situation that spreads the noble attributes for life in any context of the work. Spirit of the inner realm of the performer now happens to function as the guiding principle in life, sharing the dynamics for the future. Thus, the vitality of the performer brightens the human energy, making it truly spiritual in nature and getting into its elements of devotion to God.

Work dedicated up to God invokes the spirit of the divine supreme. Divine is invisible and cosmic in presence. He cannot be traced or sensed by any mind having its inclinations towards something else. Be it concern for self or the quest for the well-being of the self or any other thing in purview.

Mat chittah sarvodurganih mat prasadayat tarishyasi.
Autho chet tvam ahamkarat na shroshyasi binankhyasih. (G. 18/58)
Lord Krishna told Arjuna, with your mind thus fixed and given to me, you shall be by my grace getting over all, you know, overcome all difficulties but if from egotism you do not care to listen to me, you will be lost.

Divine grace turns autonomous when the mind becomes thoroughly engrossed in the functional domain of the transactions of the human scale with basic human concern for own self. It is thus the effect of dedication and the absorbed mind that makes the dedication happen in the right ways.

work dedicated to God has to turn into the human realm to make the person realize the presence of the omnipresence being present at the right point.

Lord Krishna has mentioned to Arjuna that the best way to perform is to have the performer's mind engrossed in the realm and spirit of the divine. A mind fully dedicated to God, gets the endowment of God realization.

> *Yat ahamkaram aashritya na hoh yatsya iti manyasae.*
> *Mithya esha babasayantae prakritih tvam nih yukshyatih.*   (G. 18/59)
> If taking your stand on egotism, you think I will not fight, vain in this resolve of yourself, nature will drive you to do the act.

The process of God realization may turn autonomous that means it may require the divine spirit for the work of the world. Thus the mind may get deluged to the spirit of the divine with complete and attentive devotion to the aspects of the work in the condition that prevails on Earth in a sequential content. Getting fully tuned to God in mind may appear difficult and sometimes impossible, however a graced soul may find it essentially an automated component or an aspect of the making of the person in the context having spread out in the direction of the divine presence.

> *Svabhabanjena kounteya nibaddhah svenah karmana.*
> *Kartum na ichchhasi yat mohat karishyashya abashah api tat.*   (G. 18/60)
> That action too which you are not willing to undertake due to ignorance, you will perforce perform bound by your own duty born of your nature.

Works that are deviated from the fundamentals of person's characteristic expertise, it may create results that are the indicators of wrong doing. In the process of the flow of works that are the essential elements of the world are the culminating dimensions of the world of works. It is the perspective that make the work more agreeable to the segments of the work, if it is tuned to the basics of the work and its context that attempts to have the associated dimensions of the context. It is that aspect of life which makes the dimensions of living effective on Earth. However, any kind of work in any situation, whether good or bad, dedication to God and submission to God in mind by the Leader or the Performer or the both, make the work functionally and perennially conducive to the divine expectations and the profound goodness for human society.

> *Ishvarah sarbabhutanam hrit deshaeh iha Arjunah tishthati.*
> *Bhramayan sarbabhutani yantra aarhudhani mayayah.*   (G. 18/61)
> Lord says, Arjuna, God abides in the heart of beings causing them to resolve according to their karma by his illusive power, the power of maya and through the mounted on a machine in the body.

350   *Rama Prosad Banerjee*

God is omnipresent and omniscient. He is present in every entity. He is present in invisible entity in all individual on Earth. He is present in a minuscule form. However the divine presence in the lives of the human being can get surfaced once the person realizes the spirit of divine in the right context. God remains within the core of the person in an invisible form. The realization of divine makes the person getting tuned to the effective dimension of the living soul. Thus, the efforts of realizing divine spirit is in a way the path opener in the journey towards Brahman spirit.

> *Tvam eva sharanam gachhaah sarba bhabenah Bharata.*
> *Tat prasadayat param shantim sthanam prapyasi shashvatam.* (G. 18/62)
> Take refuge in me alone in the divine entity with all your beings, Arjuna, by the grace of God, the grace you shall attain supreme peace and eternal state.

Thus, the spirit of the realization in the pathways of achievements in terms of achievements in the world. Thus, the effect of such realization makes a direct unfoldment of the spirit of work and life in the right context in the flow of time. It is thus the most effective initiative in the human context. In the process, the divine attributes get induced in the lives of the persons in the manner in it is present in the spiritual realm of the journey of the spiritual seeker. The Lord not only shapes the intrinsic and the extrinsic at the same time. It is thus the fundamental spirit of the person to be induced to the pathways of the essence of divinity.

The unified presence of God in every soul makes his spirit open to the understanding of the reality of God. It is thus the essential spirit of human beings that actually makes and maintains the path smoothly.

> *Iti tae gjnam aakhyatam gulyat guhyataram mayah.*
> *Bimrishyasyae etad bisheshanah yatha ichchhasi tatha kuru.* (G. 18/63)
> Thus has this wisdom more secret and secrecy itself been imparted to you and to me, fully pondering over it, do as you like.

The knowledge that makes a life induced to the spirit of God. Thus, it is that dimension of the passage of ways that makes the lives oriented to the fundamentals of the nature of life in the context of human progression in a propensity to understand the basics of the living in the context of the flow of lives in the situation where the persons may make the inroads into the factors of living in the fundamentals in the same context for the goodness of life in all situations at a time when God-centric living becomes imperatives.

> *Sarba guhyatamam bhuyoh shrinuh mae paramam bachah.*
> *Istoh ausi mae dridam iti tatoh bakshyami tae hitam.*   (G. 18/64)
> Here again my supreme world, the deeply secret of all truths, you are extremely dear to me, therefore I shall give you this salutary advice.

Lord Krishna now comes to the ultimate call given to human being through Arjuna. In the same stretch the person needs to hear the call of God to understand the spirit of things at a time that unfolds the intrinsics of individuals in the varied focus of the cherished pathways of the dimensions of life that has the right perspective of the emergence of the human spirit. In this the varied and the dimensions of the very much in the process and thus the varied perspective of the various dimensions of the different aspects. It is thus the very grounding of the new dimensions in a way that makes life very much the basics of the new dimensions. Lord initiates the year heartful devotion of the divine.

Manmana bhavoh mad bhaktoh mat yaji mam namaskusuh.
Mam eva aei aeshyasi satyam tae pratijanae priyoh ansi mae. (G. 18/65)
God says to Arjuna you always devote your mind to me, be devoted to me, be concentrated on me, worship me and bow to me, doing so you will come to me alone in my transcendental identity and I truly promise you; you are exceptionally dear to me, you shall remain dear to me in all situations.

Lord Krishna makes the point inviting the dedication of mind body and soul of the devotee in a way that makes it happens that the person has the right perspective to have uniquely crested love and devotion to God. The aspirant may have in mind spirit of God and consciousness. God gives the call to have the spirit of the dimension that opens up the aspects of life. Mind and conscious spirit of the person be induced to the divine realm of God and thus maintain the spirit of God within the self and dedicate to God.

Sarba dharman parityajya mam ekam shasanam brajah.
Ahom tvam sarba papebhya moksha ishyami ma shuchah. (G. 18/66)
Resigning all your duties to me and all powerful and all supporting, Lord, take refuge in me alone, I shall absolve you of all sins, worry, you don't have to worry at all.

Lord Krishna makes the call to Arjuna and through Arjuna to all devotees of the world of humans to dedicate unto God in all situations in a way that makes the life vibrant and the focus is on God in all aspects of life and in all ways. Lord says, leaving aside all other dimensions of the world. Lord Krishna offers the assurance to the devotee to take care of the lives of the persons in a way the person is included in the realm of God that offers fundamental unity of divinity to the spirit of things. Thus, the spirit of life gets a broader dimension of being able to understand this.

Idam tae autapaskayah na abhaktayah kadachanah.
Na cha iha aushushrashaebae bachyam nacha mam yah
abhyasuyatae. (G. 18/67)

> The sacred gospel of the *Gita* should never be imparted to a man who lacks in austerity, nor to him who is wanting in devotion, nor even to him who is not willing to hear and no case to him who finds fault in me.

In order to understand the words of Lord as spelled out by him in the *Bhagavad Gita*, it is the fundamental tenet of the principle of life that makes headway into divine spirit. Thus, functions of Lord has its new dimensions always with the flow of time. But unless the person has the dimensions that are tuned to the spirit realizing the divine truth is far from its unique focus in the world. Thus, the basic aspect of life makes its presence in the human process of progress through moving ahead in time.

Sacred duty in life performed by the person needs the orientation in a way to fulfill the conditions of the mind and the attitude of the person. It refers to the mental orientation that makes the person perform the targeted actions. Actions that are oriented to the dedication to God need the basis of mental poise and purity. Mind that is tuned to God and remains focused on work is the best.

> *Yah idam paramam guhjyam mat bhakteshu abhidhayeshati.*
> *Bhaktim mayee param kritva mamae vaishyati sanshayah.*   (G. 18/68)
> He who offers the highest love for me, preaches the most profound gospel of the *Gita* among my devotees, shall come to me alone, there is no doubt about it.

The supreme is thus open to the factors of life that are in a way tuned to the objects of the work, makes the way forward for the best return from the work. God realization happens to be the focus of the work remains on the spirit of divine. Pure mind and purity of intent makes the headway into the fundamentals of the work situation. Thus, person with any kind of turbulence in mind is unfit for the realization of God or the unfoldment of the spirit of God in the context of the world. Similarly, any mental conditions of the mind that is oriented to the object of the work with the subjective focus on the spirit of the divine in a combined approach that begets realization of God with the basic outlines of the factors of realization in a dynamic context that liberates the mind.

> *Na cha tasmat na manusheshu kashschit mae priya krittamah.*
> *Bhabita na cha mae tasmat aunyah priyotaroh bhubih.*   (G. 18/69)
> I have the greatest love for those who have highest respect and adoration for the utterances and conversations as it is mentioned in the *Bhagavad Gita*. However, there could be even better person who is having in mind and consciousness a total dedication to me.

The dynamism of the mental orientation that makes things happen in the manner that makes the life oriented to the world of work and thus the basis of the action becomes that of the flexible dynamism of the flow of work in a situation that allows the seeding of divine spirit. Lord Krishna is the revealed form of the supreme on Earth. He is having an invisible abode, the purely spiritual body. His abode is all indulgence. His divine weapons include discs and the *Brahmastra* – the atomic weapon and the kind of super celestial weapon which is extremely destructive but have controls in the hand of the person. The reality in the paradigm has the dimensions where in the focus forces of goodness or the forces of the supreme reward in the context of the human being on Earth chasing life.

Audheshyatae cha yah imam dharmyam sambadam auboyoh.
Gjna yogjnenah tenaham ishtah shyam iti mae matih. (G. 18/70)
Whosoever studies the sacred dialogue of ours in the form of *Gita*, by whom shall I be worshipped through yajna of knowledge, such is my conviction.

In the entire paradigm of the Bhagavan in the context of the world, in a way that creates a connectivity with the world. Lord Krishna has accepted Arjuna as a friend on Earth to fulfill the agenda of the divine on Earth. Thus, the very fundamental aspect of realization or being with God remains basic to the growth and advancement of the context of the world.

Shraddhavanan na ausuyah cha shrinuyat api yoh narah.
Sohah api mukta shubhan lokan prapnuyat punyakaramanam. (G. 18/71)
The man who listens to the *Gita* with reverence and in all uncaring spirit, liberated from sin, he too shall reach the happy words of the Punyaloka or the place of the Gods.

Lord Krishna had the exceptional quality of concern and love for the hidden flow of spirit into the realm of the situation. It is thus the basis of the righteous war for which Arjuna was made to take part in, the entire option for this. Thus, the flow of actions in the field of the war of Kurukshetra. It is thus the fundamental quest and concern that makes the function acceptable to Lord.

Kahchit shrutam tam partho tvaeika ekagranah chetasa.
Kaschit gjnanah sammohah pranashantae Dhananjayoh. (G. 18/72)
Have you Arjuna heard this gospel of *Gita* attentively, and has your delusion born of ignorance been destroyed? *Narayan Jayam*, you are the conqueror of riches, have you heard that honestly?

Arjuna was not an ascetic nor was he considered a devotee in the right sense of the term, yet he was the person chosen by the Lord as that of spiritual action. From the very beginning of the war of Kurukshetra, it was understood that Arjuna stood as the main and principal force in the entire gamut of things. Design in this context is to have the righteous spirit in the mind and soul of the person.

> *Arjuna ubacha:*
> *Nashtoh mohah smritih labdhah tat prasadat mayee Achuyatah.*
> *Sthitoh asmi gata sandeshah karishae bachanam tavah.* (G. 18/73)
> Arjuna said, Krishna, by your grace, my delusion is gone and I have gained wisdom. I am free of all doubts and I will do your bidding, whatever you say, you tell me to do, I will do that.

Arjuna, being a dedicated soul, can happen to be contained in the design of things. It is thus the fundamental that makes its presence in the related context. From this point of view, it can be said that Arjuna does not deserve to receive any kind of spiritual message. However, Lord Krishna was the best to advise. Lord Krishna had chosen Arjuna as the best among men, indicating the fact that Arjuna, the skill, knowledge, wisdom and the capacity to face anyone in the war and win.

Arjuna had acquired unmatched in proportion, strength and power of war. It was proved that Arjuna alone could destroy the entire set of enemies. In fact, once charging a single weapon, Arjuna would make the entire army of Duryadhana get stunned. Arjuna could immediately kill them but did not do.

> *Sanjay ubacha:*
> *Iti aham Vasudebasya Parthasya cha mahatmanah.*
> *Sambadam imam aushroushyam adbhutam roma harshanam.* (G. 18/74)
> Sanjay said, thus I heard the mysterious and thrilling conversation between Sri Krishna and the high-soul Arjuna, son of Kunti.

Arjuna had the stock of Dibyastra or the divine weapons endowed with by different forms of God in situations that are varied in different ways. Arjuna was not only the greatest warrior but had a perfectly balanced character. He was the doyen of honesty, discipline and dedication and love for God. Thus, a combination of the right spirit of personality who is competent to have the uniqueness of the combinations of power and values. Lord Krishna had chosen Arjuna because of his uniqueness of being the supreme power and perfect character. Lord Krishna thus opened up an entire set of spiritual lessons for him.

> *Byasah prasadayat shrutavanah etad guhjyam aham param.*
> *Yogam yogaesvarayat krishnyat sakshat kathayatah svayam.* (G. 18/75)
> Having seen, blessed with the divine vision by the grace of Sri Vyasa, I heard in person this supremely exculpatory gospel from the Lord of Yoga, Sri Krishna himself, imparting it to Arjuna.

The proof of Arjuna's character was strongly evident during his period of one year remaining in the thick of different abodes of the God, the Supreme.

Commonly known as heaven or the place where the gods in different forms stay and offer blessings to the creation at times of the need for the same. Arjuna had a destiny of one year stay there in the company of different forms of God. The primary idea was to facilitate Arjuna to obtaining the blessed war power and strength of the major forms of gods. Accordingly, Arjuna had obtained blessed war power from Lord Shiva. The war power of Lord Shiva is his best.

Raajan samsmritya samsmritya sambadam imam adbhutam.
Keshabah Arjunayoh punyam hrishyami cha muhuh muhuh. (G. 18/76)
Remembering over and over that secret and mystic conversation between Bhagavan Sri Krishna and Arjuna, O King, I rejoice again and yet again.

The entire creation can be destroyed and reduced to ashes or void with the war power of Lord Shiva. Arjuna endured with that. Similarly, he was endowed with the four powers of Lord Indra, Agni, the Supreme Goddess and all others. In the process of living of human being, the basis of the spirit of individuals is the abode of the thing, the basis of truth as it were, there in the specific form and identity as in the world of humans. Karma sets and aligns with the point of reward for the best possible class of things in the context of the next set of things that makes the basis of things of life in the right perspective. Karma is in most of the cases determined by the nature of the spirit of mind towards doing the karma from the perspective of the world of work by humans.

Tat cha samsmrilya samsmritya rupam iti adbhutam hareih.
Vishmayoh mae mahan rajan hrishyami cha punah punah. (G. 18/77)
Remembering also again and again that most wonderful form of Sri Krishna, great is my wonder, and I rejoice over and over again.

God himself in the human abode had the intent to stand by his friend of eternity in human context to make the forces of righteousness win in that context. It is thus very fundamental to the divine design that writers' works would take a person ahead in the context of the things of works in a way that attempts to have the basis of the principles of fairness and integrity that takes the effect of the work carried forward in its true perspective. The cause and the effect thus make the outcome of the action pertaining to the quality of inputs.

Yatra yogeshvarah krishnah yatra partho dhanurdharah.
Tatra sreeh vijayoh bhurtih dhrubah nitih matih mama. (G. 18/78)
Wherever there is Bhagavan Sri Krishna and the Lord of Yoga, and wherever there is Arjuna, the builder of Gandiva bow, and the devoted, victorious person, devoted, dedicated person to God, glory, victory, prosperity and unfailing righteousness will surely be there, such is my conviction.

The right of an individual human being to choose the right path of work to get constrained to the rightful task in the context of the flow of happening in the world. It is thus fundamental to the work that orientation and objective of the work make the right trajectory for the very basic and fundamentals of the spirit of actions based on the bent of mind and the objectives. Humans have their own objectives and thus they work for fulfilling their own egoistic focus. Arjuna is the exception. Arjuna has finally resolved to do whatever the God wishes him to do. Arjuna is the instrument in the hand of Lord Krishna and does not have any intent separate from that. Arjuna is dedicated to the Lord. He has unquestioned love and devotion for God. Also, Arjuna has been into god's design of work under god's direct command. This is why Sanjoy has finally reached the understanding in mind that wherever Lord Krishna and the devoted warrior Arjuna remain, fortune, victory are certain with God realization.

Afterword: Message of the Bhagavad Gita

Lord Krishna has driven the entire thought process in the span of the *Bhagavat Gita* to drive to the winning over the evils and create a poise in the human society to make the social life conducive to a set of actions centric to the divine principles and policies of making the lives of people be blessed in good thoughts and works. Such principles are best explained in the following elaborations, based on the teachings of the Divine in the abode of Lord Krishna, to the entire human society through the Arjunas of the emerging human society.

The Fundamental Principles of Divine Actions in the World

Dasatmak Karma Charitam (दशात्मककर्मचरितम्)
Purna Prajnayam Nibeditam (पूर्णप्रज्ञायामनिवेदितम्)

1. *Sada Prasannam Karmam* / सदाप्रसन्नंकर्मम्
   Work with love and always smile in real terms. The work that you are endowed with in your life is a blessing of the cosmic spirit. Maintain a pure and positive outlook on life.
2. *Karyam Vishwachetan Sannibeshitam* / कार्यम् विश्वचेतनसंनिवेशितम्
   Your work is continuously contributing to the emergence and enhancement of the spirit of the cosmic system. Your work is thereby an elemental support to the cosmic consciousness. You are serving the cosmic spirit.
3. *Nibeditam Phalam Karmani Sampaditam* / निवेदितम्फलम्कर्मणिसम्पादितम्
   Dedicate your work to the spirit of the entire cosmic system. Do your work in the best possible manner. You should never be a seeker of the result.
4. *Karmam Karmanandena Kritam* / कर्मम्कर्मानन्देनकृतम्
   The joy of doing is drawn from the domain of the work itself. You will have the work done with the spirit of perfection.
5. *Karmani Paribeshitam Pratirupa Phalam* / कर्मणिपरिवेशितम्प्रतिरूपफलम्
   Like cause – like effect. Never indulge in an action with a known nor understood evil element built in. Do good and honest work, reap in the goodness. Bad work returns evil.

6. *Karma Prajnanah Vishwa Kalyana Sada Ahritam* / कर्मप्रज्ञानविश्वकल्याण सदाआहृतम्
   Work begets the wisdom for the growth, sustenance, and well-being of the entire world. Good thoughts beget good actions. Always cultivate good and honest thoughts. Your work serves the universe.
7. *AhritamNiveditaKarmamDivyaKripayam*/आहृतम्निवेदितकर्मम्दिव्यकृपायम्
   Work has the divine grace infused in it. Any challenge in the work can be met with your graceful work and habits in life.
8. *SadaHridayamDharanamShiva-Sanatanam*/सदाहृदयम्धारणम्शिवसनातनम्
   Suddha Nirmala KarmamAbeshitam / शुद्धनिर्मलकर्मम्आवेशितम्
   Whether in thought or in action, one should remain attuned to the spirit of the Divine in mind and heart.
9. *Karmatwak Vishesha Bhakti-Prajna Sancharam* / कर्मत्वक्विशेषभक्ति-प्रज्ञासं°चारम्
   Work in which you are absorbed contributes to your spiritual realization in terms of divine wisdom, devotion and the blessed span of life.
10. *DivyaKarmaniSadaManasaSampaditam*/दिव्यकर्माणिसदामानससंपादितम्
    Swamokshartham Jagat Hitakalpa Sada Prasarana / स्वमोक्षार्थंजगतहित कल्पसदाप्रसरण
    Work dedicated to God offers the blissful context of life. This is the ultimate attainment in and through dedicated work – 'Nishkama Karma'.

[Composed by the author]

Bibliography

Bhagavad Gita. Sanskrit text with English translation (by chapters).
Easwaran, Eknath. *The Upanishads: Kena and Katha.* Tomales, CA: Nilgiri Press, 2010.
Gambhirananda, Swami, trans. *Katha Upanishad.* Kolkata: Advaita Ashrama, Ramakrishna Mission, 17th reprint, 2023.
Gambhirananda, Swami. *Eight Upanishads.* Kolkata: Advaita Ashrama, 2020.
Lokeswarananda, Swami. *Katha Upanishad.* Kolkata: Ramakrishna Mission Institute of Culture, 1993.
Menon, Devdas. *The Awakening of Nachiketa.* Independently Published, 2024.
Nikhilananda, Swami. *The Upanishads. Vol. I.* Kolkata: Advaita Ashrama, 1949.
Nikhilananda, Swami. *The Upanishads: Katha Upanishad (Abridged)*, pp. 65–85. Kolkata: Advaita Ashrama, 2008.
Penrose, Roger. *Fashion, Faith and Fantasy: In the New Physics of the Universe.* Princeton and Oxford: Princeton University Press, 2018, pp. 285–286.
Radhakrishnan, S. *The Principal Upanishads.* New Delhi: HarperCollins, 2006.
Ranganathananda, *Swami. The Message of the Upanishads.* Kolkata: Advaita Ashrama, 2020.
Sarker, Sunil Kumar. *T.S. Eliot.* New Delhi: Atlantic Publishers, 2024, pp. 140–155.
Seal, Brajendranath. *The Positive Sciences of the Ancient Hindus.* Reprint. New Delhi: Motilal Banarsidass Publishers, 1991.
Sen, Atul Chandra, Sitanath Tattvabhushan, and Mahesh Chandra Ghosh. Upanishad (in Bengali), *Katho Upanishad.* Kolkata: Haraf Prakashani, 1994, pp. 61–154.

Glossary

Preface

Atman - The self embodied within humans
Atmano viddhi - You know yourself
Dukha - Sorrow
Karuna - Compassion
Maitreyi - Wife of Yajnavalka
Mudita - A delightful mind about others success
Nirmalaha - Simple and pure
Nirupeksha - Neutral condition
Patanjali - Sage, founder of Yogashastra
Preya - Something desirable and temporary
Samatwaha - Equal in all situations
Samaha - Equal
Samaha Lustwasmo Kanchanaha - A piece of stone and precious metal considered the same
Shreya - Something electable and sustainable
Sukha - Happiness
Swastwaha - Stationed
Tat tvam asi - You are the person who is having the atman in the core of your heart, in the cave of your heart
Upeksha - Indifference
Vishuddha Manaha - Pure mind

Introduction

Anandamaya Kosha - The blissful sheath
Dharma - The righteous principles
Devadideva - The principal form of the Lord
Ekagra - A concentrated state of mind
Jivatman - The human self
Kshipta - A scattered state of mind
Manomaya Kosha - The mental sheath

Mahakaal - Lord Shiva is the Great Cause and passage of time, owning the causes of life to make it happen and allow it to progress over time
Mudha - A dull state of mind
Niruddha - A poised state of mind
Prajnanam Brahma - Wisdom of Brahman is Brahman
Pranamoya kosha - The vital sheath in human life
Vijnanamaya Kosha - The wisdom sheath
Vikshipta - A turbulent state of mind

Chapter – 1

Adharma - Sinful actions
Arjuna - Warrior friend of Lord Krishna
Bahujana hitaio cha bahujano sukhaio cha - For the well-being of many and the happiness of many
Chatur Varga - Four facets of living a total and comprehensive life. These were: dharma – artha – kama – moksha – or, the righteous ways of living
Dharma - Righteousness
Dharmakshetra - The place of righteous war
Dhritarashtra - The blind king
Draupadi - Wife of Pandava Brothers
Duryadhana - Son of Dhritarashtra
Kouravas - Sons of Dhritarashtra
Kurukshetra - The place of the Mahabharata War
Indra - King of the domain of heaven
Dronacharya - The teacher of war preparations
Dharmic - Righteous
Moksha - Supreme Bliss
Raj Dharma - The attributes of state-leadership
Satyam Vadishami, Ritam Vadishyami - Shall speak truth and maintain truth in life
Sanjoy - Dhritarashtras assistant
Ubacha - Says
Visma - The grandfather of Kauravas and Pandavas
Yudhisthira - King of Pandavas

Chapter – 2

Paramatma - The supreme self
Ritam - Truth in action
Satyam - Truth embodied

Chapter – 3

Samskar - Intrinsics of life

Virat - The large

Chapter – 4

Adhyasyh - Self-unfoldment
Brahmagyana - Supra Wisdom
Chatuskal Brahman - Four different ways of realising the truth of creation
Goutama - Sage
Rik, Sam, Yaju and Atharva - Four different Vedas, each with their distinctive ways to earn the knowledge of Brahman
Satyakama - Sage
Swadhyay - Self-learning
Tyaga - Giving up

Chapter – 5

Atmatattwa - The knowledge of self
Gandiva - The unique weapon of Arjuna that was associated with his name and his valour
Karma - Action
Mahat-Tattwa - The Noble Existence, Truth
Purusha - God embodied
Sanatana - Continuation through the scale of time and eternal in its own identity
Shaswata - It is primordial
Yoga - Connection

Chapter – 6

Ananda - Underlying spirit of bliss
Chit - The cosmic consciousness
Gatimayam - Dynamism in the scope for and the objectives of the work for it
Gunannwitam - Quality and quantum of the work per unit of the invested time and resources
Samani Vyaptam - Compatibility of the work with the contextual and factual realities prevailing
Samartham - Effectiveness of the work in the context of the available unit of resources
Sat - Eternal truth
Sharhaprakriti Karmani - Six functional natures of work
Tat ejati sarvashah tat bhi na ejati - The supreme entity, Brahman, is the abode of the Mahakaal
Viswatmakam - Universality in the corporate functional approaches
Visheshattwam - Particularity in the corporate approach to the work chosen for it

Chapter – 7

Brahma Jnana - Wisdom of the Divine
Ghritam - The fuel in clarified butter
Mughals - Invaders of India
Nataraj-Shiva - The Dancing Lord Shiva
Pancha Vayu - Apana, Samana, Vyana, Udana— five different properties of air
Pathans - Invaders of India
Pranayama - The vital sheath
Puja - An offering to God
Varna - Brahman, Kshatriya, Vaishya and Shudra - or the clans created, were only for betterment of the works
Vibaswan - Was the first identity of this empirical sun
Yajna - Sacrificial Action

Chapter – 8

Aarabdha Karma - The divinely bestowed karma
Aasuric Manava - Demonic Man
Brihadaranyaka Upanishad - An Upanishad under Yajur Veda
Da – Dattah - Be a giver, give it up to the extent required and possible. Practice giving in life
Da-Da-Da; Dayaddhamah - Dattah – Damyatah, Da – Dayaddhamah - Hold on, take care, no further sin be committed in life, or else the obvious end would be the destruction
Daivi Manava - Man with Divinely Quality
Jnana - Knowledge
Manabic Manava - Man with humanist view
Ritam Vadishyami, Satyam Vadishyami - Means that a vow is taken to be truthfully oriented in thoughts and actions always
Sadhu - Monk
Sankhya and Yoga - Two streams of meditative practice

Chapter – 9

Aajna Chakra - The sixth plexus
Anahata - The fourth plexus in yoga
Bhagavan ubacha - God speaks
Brahma Randhra - A microscopic orifice at the central point of the skull
Kumbhaka - The containing of air within
Lila - Play of actions
Muladhara - The primordial store of cosmic energy
OM BHUOH - Invoking God
Om Namah Bhagavatae - Offering gratitude to God

Om Namah Shivayo Namah - Offering of gratitude to Lord Shiva
Pranic - Vital
Sakha - The true friend
Samadhi - Oneness with the spiritual identity of creation
Sannyasi cha yogi cha na nih agnih cha - The monk, the meditative person, and the fire

Chapter – 10

Aurtarthi – Meaning, he had a valid and urgent spiritual reason to ask and get answers from
Bhakta - The devotee
Gnyana Yogi - The knowledge-driven intellect
Karma Yogi - Workaholic
Kaurishyae bachanam tavah - "Shall do whatever you tell me to do"
Manmana bhabah, mad bhakta, mad yaj - "Be turned to me in your mind, be my devotee, expect me in your life and thoughts"

Chapter – 11

Aarabdha Karma - Destined work
Kartavya Karma - Dutiful work
Navipadma - Umbilical plexus
Nibedanam - Worship
Om - Root of all mantras: Au, Eu, Mau: this earth, the world of inner space, and the cosmic system
Paramatma - The absolute atman
Sishyah - Disciple

Chapter – 12

Adhyakshma - The head
Lokanam Ishvaram - God of all human beings
Prakriti - Externalities of a person

Chapter – 13

Abyay Sanatan - The immutable cosmic being and the eternal provider of the truth in life
Aditi - Mother form
Aeiteriya Aranyaka - Extension of the Upanishad by Sage Autri
Airavata - King of elephants serving the king of the Vedas, Indra
Aksharah Brahma - Transcendental divinity
Ashitah, Devolah, Vaisah, Naradah - Sages of great wisdom
Aryama - Form of a divine entity

Aukarah - The first syllable
Aukaroi Vai Sarvah Vakah - Words comprise the first syllable
Avyayibhaba - The limitless consciousness
Ayurveda - Science of life
Bahubrihi - Multiple resources
Bharatclan - One of the kingly lineages
Bibhuti - The demonstrative revelations of the presence of God
Brihaspati - Heavenly teacher
Chanda - Rhythm
Danda - Legal impunity
Dhriti - Power of containing
Durga - Mother goddess
Dvandva - Conflict
Ficus Religiosa - It is the fig tree with the scientific identity
Gajendra - The king of elephants serving the world
Gayatri Mantra - Verse of invocation
Kalpa - The pages of human existence through the turns of human races
Kamdhenu - Among the cows, he is the celestial cow
Kandarpah - Man with qualified wisdom
Kirti - Achievement
Kshama - Forgiveness
Kubera - Resourceful
Maharshi - Great sage
Medha - The intellect
Meru Parvatah - The polar mountain
Merue - Pole
Narayana - Form of God
Narayana Sage - Spiritual wisdom in man
Nara Sage - Wise man
Pitri - Parental
Prahlad - A great devotee
Shakti of Pavan - Power of wind
Sam Veda - One of the major Vedas
Samudra Manthan - Churning of the Ocean
Saptarshi Mandal - These seven great sages: Marichi, Angira, Autri, Pulastha, Pulaha, and Vashistha
Smriti - The memory
Sri - Pleasing to the mind
Sri Raam - Divine embodiment
Tatpurusa - Identified divine personality
Udgee - The intrinsic song
Uma Haimavati - Mother goddess
Ushana - A oet famous for his wisdom poems
Ushana - Wisdom poet
Vak - The voice

Vasuki - The king of the serpents
Vccaihshrava - Celestial horse
Vrigu / Bhrigu - The sage who bears the torch of wisdom of the world and spreads the truth of the Vedas among the aspirants of truth in the world
Vishnu - One of the forms of God
Vrishnis - The particular clan of Kshatriyas, the warrior class
Yakshas or Rakshas - Demonic clan
Yama - God of death

Chapter – 14

Adideva - The primordial form of God
Bhishma, Drona, Karna, Asatthama - Great warriors were on the side of the Kauravas
Narada - A sage
Purushottama - The supreme Godhead
Selyachi-Arjuna - Arjuna qualified

Chapter – 15

Aunapeksha - Non-dependent on anything
Bhaba Loka - The world of consciousness
Jagat Prakriti - The nature of the world
Jeeva Prakriti - The nature of human person
Kshetra - The entity
Kshetrajna - Wisdom of entity
Mukta-maun - The open mind
Nirmoha - Unattachment
Param Purusha - The supreme truth
Rasa Loka - The world of spirit
Rupa Loka - The world of forms

Chapter – 16

Akaash - The space
Bhakta - Devotee
Chandi - The mother goddess
Dama - Power of control
Ekasya Prapyam - Lone receiver
Mahadev-Bhagwan - Lord Shiva
Sama - Unity of thought
Sattwika - The truthful being
Shraddha - Intrinsic respect
Sukha - Happiness
Titiksha - The power to get away from

Vairagya - Non-attachment
Viveka - The conscience

Chapter – 17

Aasuric Guna - Demonic attribute
Abhimanyu - Son of Arjuna
Apsara - The personality of divine culture
Sattwa Bhakta - Devotee with the positive and truthful limits in life

Chapter – 18

Ahamkara - High ego
Asat - Untruth
Karmashu Koushalam - The art of work
Om Tat Sat - Is the inclusive idea of all
Patra - The person
Prarabddha Karma - Destined work
Prarabddha Chinta - The endowed thoughts
Sri Hanuman - A great devotee of Lord Rama in the abode of Bakki

Chapter – 19

Brahmastra - The atomic weapon and the kind of super celestial weapon
Dibyastra - The divine weapons